Montreat College

School of Arts and Sciences

Academic Catalog
2016-2017

Montreat College
2016 – 2017 Academic Catalog

Published by Montreat College, Montreat, NC 28757

This catalog provides general information about Montreat College and summarizes important information about the College's policies, requirements for graduation, regulations, and procedures. It is not intended to establish, nor does it establish, a contractual relationship with students. Rather, the catalog is published to acquaint students with information that will be helpful to them during their college careers.

It is necessary in the general administration of the College to establish requirements and regulations governing the granting of degrees. Academic advisors, department chairs, and academic staff members are available to aid students in understanding these requirements and regulations. It is the student's responsibility, however, to meet them. Students are urged to keep this catalog as a reference.

Changes in curricular requirements may occur during catalog publications. Students will be informed of such changes. When this occurs, students may follow the requirements in effect at the time they entered Montreat College, or they may petition to follow the changed requirements. Students must choose to follow one catalog or the other; they may not pick and choose from the various requirements outlined in two or more catalogs. Reasonable substitutions will be made for discontinued and changed courses.

Information in the catalog is considered to be an accurate representation of Montreat College policy as of the date of publication. The College reserves the right to make such changes in educational and financial policy as the College's Faculty, Administration and/or Board of Trustees may deem consonant with sound academic and fiscal practice. The College has made a good faith effort to avoid typographical errors and other errors in the statements of policy and degree requirements as published. In any case, erroneous catalog statements do not take precedence over properly adopted policies. Please see the College website at www.montreat.edu for the most updated version of the catalog.

Montreat College is an independent, self-governing college, related to the Presbyterian Church by history, location, and long-standing relationships with the Mountain Retreat Association and the Association of Presbyterian Colleges and Universities. The College seeks to honor Jesus Christ and our Presbyterian and Reformed heritage while remaining uninvolved in denominational politics and administration and welcoming students without regard to religious affiliation.

As an institution in the Presbyterian and Reformed tradition, the College seeks to treat all persons equally and emphasizes the dignity and worth of the individual. In compliance with Title IX of the Education Amendments of 1972, Sections 503 and 504 of the Rehabilitation Act of 1973 and the Americans with Disabilities Act, Montreat College admits students of any race, color, religion, sex, age, national or ethnic origin to all rights, privileges, programs, and activities generally accorded or made available to students at the school. It does not discriminate on the basis of race, disability, military service, color, religion, sex, age, national and ethnic origin in administration of its educational policies, admissions policies, scholarship and loan programs, and athletic and other school administrative programs.

In accordance with federal and state statutes, Montreat College is committed to maintaining a community that is free from sexual harassment and all forms of sexual intimidation, exploitation, coercion, and violence. Inquiries concerning the College's policies, compliance with applicable laws, statutes, and complaints may be directed to the Academic Affairs Office, Montreat College, P.O. Box 1267, Montreat, NC 28757, (828) 669-8012 (ext. 3621).

Table of Contents

Campus Locations

Montreat College Main Campus
P.O. Box 1267
310 Gaither Circle
Montreat, NC 28757

828-669-8012
800-622-6968
828-669-9554 fax

Black Mountain
Montreat College
191 Vance Avenue
Black Mountain, NC 28711

828-669-8012
800-690-7727
828-669-0500 fax

Charlotte
Montreat College
School of Adult and Graduate Studies
212 South Tryon Street, Ste. 1700
Charlotte, NC 28281

704-357-3390
800-436-2777
704-676-4618 fax

Asheville
Montreat College
School of Adult and Graduate Studies
29 Turtle Creek Drive
Asheville, NC 28803

828-667-5044
800-806-2777
828-667-9079 fax

Morganton
Montreat College
School of Adult and Graduate Studies
PO Box 1389
Morganton, NC 28680-1389

828-475-2431

*Our Online Campus has administrative headquarters at the Montreat, NC location.

Visit us online: www.montreat.edu

About Montreat College

At Montreat College, a student's experience is enhanced by an education of value, grounded in a strong liberal arts core, taught by outstanding Christian faculty, and prized by employers and graduate schools. Students benefit from Montreat College's small classes where their opinions matter and they grow through one-on-one interaction with professors and classmates. Students are challenged to integrate faith and learning while considering subjects in new ways. Hands-on experiences in the majors (internships, field studies, mission programs, community service, and independent research) enable students to gain practical career and life preparation.

Montreat College welcomes students of many denominations and cultural backgrounds, including students from all corners of the world. In a diverse, multicultural environment, students learn how to investigate the unfamiliar, think critically, and communicate and clarify their ideas. In the process, they develop the skills, personal values, and faith to confidently take their place in the world. In the residence halls or over dinner at a professor's house, students find themselves sharing perspectives and exchanging ideas. The distinct spirit of community goes beyond the faculty, staff, and students and extends to visiting Christian conference members, residents of the town of Montreat and neighboring Black Mountain, as well as to the "cottagers" who vacation here throughout the seasons.

Montreat College is a place where students can set themselves apart through an extraordinary range of leadership opportunities on the Montreat Campus. A nationally recognized Discovery Wilderness Program takes advantage of the mountain location and offers a unique twenty-one-day adventure for academic credit. Outdoor recreation opportunities available to students range from hiking to whitewater adventures to snow skiing. Students can also choose from a variety of off-campus volunteer opportunities such as serving at nursing homes, churches, children's homes, and shelters.

Montreat College is a member of the Appalachian Athletic Conference (AAC) of the National Association of Intercollegiate Athletics (NAIA). At Montreat College, men compete in baseball, basketball, cross country, golf, track and field, lacrosse, tennis, and soccer. Women compete in basketball, cross country, golf, track and field, soccer, softball, lacrosse, tennis, and volleyball. Students also enjoy an active intramural program where exciting competition takes place throughout the year.

Montreat College includes the main campus in Montreat and sites in Black Mountain, Asheville, Morganton, and Charlotte. The School of Adult and Graduate Studies seeks to provide adult students a Christ-centered education through evening classes and online.

The School of Adult and Graduate Studies is designed especially for the adult learner who has completed some college work and desires to finish a degree in an accelerated program by attending class one night per week. Through this School, the College offers Associate in Science (AS), Bachelor of Business Administration (BBA), Bachelor of Science in Management (BS), Bachelor of Science in Psychology and Human Services (BS), Bachelor of Science in Bible and Religion (BS), Master of Business Administration (MBA), Master of Science in Environmental Education (MS), Master of Arts in Clinical Mental Health Counseling (MA), and Master of Science in Management and Leadership (MS) degrees.

History

The beauty and tranquility of the Blue Ridge Mountains led Congregationalist minister John C. Collins to form the Mountain Retreat Association in 1897 "for the encouragement of Christian work and living through Christian convention, public worship, missionary work, schools, and libraries." By 1907, J. R. Howerton of Charlotte, NC, conceived and carried out the idea of purchasing Montreat for the Presbyterian Church in the United States. Then, in 1913, Dr. Robert C. Anderson, president of the Mountain Retreat Association, proposed that the grounds and facilities of the Association be used for a school during the academic year. In 1915, the General Assembly decreed "that the property of the Mountain Retreat Association be used for a Normal School and that the establishment of the school be referred to the Synods".

The Synods of Appalachia, Georgia, Alabama, North Carolina, Tennessee, and Virginia elected trustees who met in Montreat on May 2, 1916, and elected Dr. Robert F. Campbell of Asheville, NC, chairman, Mr. W. T. Thompson Jr. of Knoxville, TN, secretary, and Ruling Elder T. S. Morrison of Asheville, NC, treasurer. The Montreat Normal School, a four-year preparatory and two-year college combination, opened its first session in October 1916 with eight students. Montreat Normal School continued to grow over the years. Throughout times of war, economic fluctuations, and rapid social change, the school sought to provide a Christian setting in which to prepare young women to become teachers.

In 1934, during Dr. Robert C. Anderson's tenure as president, Montreat Normal School (College Department) was renamed Montreat College. The College grew as its academic program expanded. It began a four-year degree program in 1945. After 14 years as a four-year women's college, the College was restructured in 1959 as a coeducational junior college and was given a new name, Montreat-Anderson College.

In 1986, the College Board of Trustees, realizing the demands and changing circumstances in higher education, made the decision to become again a baccalaureate institution. The dream of its first president, Dr. Anderson, was for the College to serve as an accredited baccalaureate institution. The College has realized that dream. It returned to the original name of Montreat College in August of 1995, sharing the original vision and identity. The change reflects the Montreat College of today, a four-year college with several growing campuses and a graduate program.

Montreat College's School of Adult and Graduate Studies began as the School of Professional and Adult Studies offering classes on September 19, 1994. The College's Charlotte campus was officially opened on September 11, 1995, and the Asheville campus held its grand opening on October 8, 1996. Montreat College purchased 72 acres of land with 21 buildings in Black Mountain in the summer of

2001, resulting in a total of four Montreat College campuses.

In June 1998, Montreat College was accredited by the Commission on Colleges of the Southern Association of Colleges and Schools as a level three institution to offer the master's degree in business administration. Since then Montreat College has added three more master's degrees to its program offerings: the Master of Science in Management and Leadership, the Master of Science in Environmental Education, and the Master of Arts in Clinical Mental Health Counseling. In January 2013, the College launched its first three fully online degree programs offering its Christ-centered education in the virtual world.

The Presidents of the College have been Dr. Robert Campbell Anderson, 1916–1947; Dr. J. Rupert McGregor, 1947–1957; Dr. Calvin Grier Davis, 1959–1972; Dr. Silas M. Vaughn, 1972–1991; Mr. William W. Hurt, 1991–2002; Dr. John S. Lindberg, 2002–2003; Dr. Dan Struble, 2004–2013; and Dr. Paul J. Maurer, 2014 to the present.

Campus Locations

Montreat College is located in the beautiful Blue Ridge Mountains of western North Carolina. The scenic main campus is nestled into sloping woods just 15 miles east of Asheville, NC, and three miles from I-40. Students enjoy the proximity of Asheville, one of North Carolina's most architecturally and culturally diverse cities. Adjacent to Montreat is the historic town of Black Mountain, with picturesque avenues, stores, and restaurants.

The climate is widely recognized as one of the world's finest, and the region has been a major summer and fall vacation area for years. A number of ski resorts are located within easy travel from the campus, making the area a winter favorite as well.

Montreat College's main campus is set in the mountain valley town of Montreat. The tree-filled campus contains many small streams. Students enjoy living in the beautiful mountain stone residence halls that provide views of the mountains surrounding the campus. Two men's residence halls and two women's residence halls house more than 75 percent of the main campus student body. A complete facilities listing is available in the back of this catalog in the Facilities Directory.

The Black Mountain location is a softly rolling, wooded estate situated three miles from the main campus in the historic town of Black Mountain. This 72-acre property was purchased in 2001, and an additional 17 acres were purchased in 2004. Montreat College has flourished with the addition of these properties. Originally a conference center, the campus is now home to our Manor House.

The Manor House is a 24,400-square-foot facility built in 1920 and is now listed on the National Register of Historic Places. Originally the summer home of electrical industrialist F. S. Terry, the Manor House contains bedrooms, meeting areas, and service facilities—including an indoor pool and gymnasium. The Manor House also provides space for classrooms, a computer lab, and offices.
The 89-acre property includes the Outdoor Education's Team and Leadership Center with the High Teams Course, Challenge Tower, and Group Initiatives. The property is the location of the Rusty Pullman Stadium (encompasses the Howard Fisher Memorial Park turf field), the cross country course, and the Roxy Hines Memorial Softball Park.

Montreat College's School of Adult and Graduate Studies has facilities located in Charlotte, Morganton, and Asheville, NC. The Charlotte location is centrally located in the uptown and is easily accessible from anywhere in the city. The Asheville location is convenient and practical, having been designed with the adult student in mind.

Campus Facilities
Main Campus Buildings

Gaither Hall (1935, later renovated) houses the President's Office, Advancement Office, Alumni Office, Public Information Office, Office of Records and Registration, Finance Office, Admissions Office and Financial Aid Office. Graham Chapel, classrooms, a language and music laboratory, music faculty offices, and the Fellowship Hall are also located in Gaither Hall. Gaither Hall is an AED (automatic defibrillator) station. This building was given to the College by Mrs. R. C. Anderson as a memorial to her parents, Mr. and Mrs. Thomas Hall Gaither.

McGowan Center for Christian Studies (1998) provides classrooms, conference and seminar rooms and offices for the Biblical, Religious and Interdisciplinary Studies Department and Chaplain. It also features the 212-seat Chapel of the Prodigal with a fresco based on the return of the prodigal son by internationally known artist Ben Long.

L. Nelson Bell Library (1972, later renovated) is a centrally located facility containing more than 83,000 bound volumes, access to numerous full-text journals, study rooms, and a computer lab available for student and community use. The Bell Library belongs to a coalition of college libraries, which greatly enhances study and research by making more than 500,000 volumes available from colleges throughout Western North Carolina. The College has a campus wide fiber-optic computer network linking the computer lab with the campus and providing access to the Internet. Lower Nelson Bell Library also houses Student Health and Counseling Services, and this building is an AED (automatic defibrillator) station.

Hamilton Gallery (1997) is located on the mezzanine of the L. Nelson Bell Library and provides space for student art as well as traveling and local exhibitions.

Morgan Science Building (1969, later renovated) provides ample classroom space for science and mathematics classes and well-equipped laboratories. In addition, it includes the offices of the Natural Sciences department, a large lecture hall, and a seminar room.

McAlister Gymnasium (1954, later renovated) provides classroom facilities for health, physical education and outdoor education disciplines. The structure also houses the offices of the Outdoor Education Department, the Physical Education faculty, and the athletic coaches. This building is an AED (automatic defibrillator) station. In addition are locker rooms, an athletic training facility, a weight room, and the gymnasium.

Anderson Hall (1968, renovated 2014), air-conditioned with private baths and an elevator, provides residence for 144 women. The five-story building has a spacious lobby and is carpeted throughout.

McGregor Hall (1942, later renovated), an air-conditioned residence hall for upper-class women, features an extensive lobby dominated by a large stone fireplace.

Davis Hall (1964, later renovated) is an air-conditioned men's residence hall accommodating 102 students. It has a private lounge and reception area and baths on each floor.

Howerton Hall (1979, later renovated), an air-conditioned men's residence hall housing 112 students, has private or adjoining baths for all rooms.

Howerton Dining Hall (1950, later renovated) provides food service for students, faculty and staff, and guests. A small, private room is also available for group meetings. This building is an AED (automatic defibrillator) station.

W. H. Belk Campus Center (1985) is centrally located on campus beside Gaither Hall. This structure includes a large student recreation area with student mail boxes; the campus bookstore; document center; the offices of Academic Affairs, Student Life, Technology, and the Business and Art faculty; classrooms; and cybersecurity lab.

Anderson House (1912), the former residence of founding President Dr. and Mrs. R. C. Anderson, serves as a comfortable setting for special occasions and receptions.

Newell Athletic Field (1982), with a spectacular view of the mountains, contains the collegiate baseball field, which was literally carved out of the mountainside. Physical education classes and intramural sports are also conducted on this field.

Other Facilities in Montreat Used by the College

The Montreat Conference Center provides facilities often used by Montreat College which include:

The Assembly Inn, an attractive conference hotel across Lake Susan from the College campus, accommodates 180 overnight guests. The spacious lobby, dining room, seminar conference rooms, and a convocation hall are available for College use. Parents and friends of students will find comfortable accommodations here. For reservations, write the Assembly Inn, Montreat, NC 28757, or call (828) 669-2911.

Tennis courts are used for College teams, classes, and personal play.

Anderson Auditorium, the year-round assembly hall which seats more than two thousand people, is available for College commencements, concerts, and convocations.

The Barn serves as the Montreat College center for square dances.

VISION

Montreat College seeks to be a leader in Christ-centered higher education regionally, nationally, and globally.

MISSION

Montreat College is an independent, Christ-centered, liberal arts institution that educates students through intellectual inquiry, spiritual formation, and preparation for calling and career, all to impact the world for Jesus Christ.

STATEMENT OF FAITH

Preamble

The trustees and employees of Montreat College constitute an academic community of caring believers committed to the Lordship of Jesus Christ. Students are welcomed to this Christian community regardless of belief.

Statement of Faith

The trustees and employees commit themselves to the following faith statement drawn from the college's Reformed tradition:

1.   We believe in one sovereign God, eternally existing in three persons: God the Father; His only begotten Son, Jesus Christ, our Lord and Savior; and the Holy Spirit, the giver of life. (Daniel 4:25, 35; Mark 12:29; John 1:1, 14, 18; 14:28; 15:26; 16:28; Romans 9:15-23; Revelation 4:11)

2.   We believe the Bible, the sixty-six books of the Old and New Testaments, is the infallible Word of God, completely inspired and authoritative, and is to govern Christians in every aspect of life and conduct. (I Thessalonians 2:13; II Timothy 3:16; II Peter 1:21)

3.   We believe Jesus is the Christ, the Son of the living God, whom the Father sent into the world to atone for the sin of humanity. Jesus was conceived by the Holy Spirit, born of the Virgin Mary, and lived a life without sin. He was crucified and rose victoriously from the dead. Through His gift of grace, we as believers are redeemed for all eternity and are reconciled to the Heavenly Father. (Luke 1:26-37; 2:6, 7; John 3:16; Romans 3:10, 23; Romans 5:12-15; I John 3:8)

4.   We believe the Holy Spirit is a free gift to believers from the Father and the Son to live within us and to empower us to love and obey the Lord and His Word. (John 14:15-17; John 16:5-15; Ephesians 1:13-14)

5.   We believe the Triune God is the sole Creator and Sustainer of the universe. God created all things and declared all He created to be good. After creating Adam and Eve in His own image, in a state of original righteousness, and distinct from all other living creatures, the Lord gave to all humanity the responsibility of caring for His world. (Genesis 1-2; John 1:1-18)

6.   We believe God's good and perfect creation became tainted in every aspect by sin from humanity's rebellion against God. We acknowledge the existence, evil power, and influence of Satan. (Genesis 3; Ephesians 6:12)

7.   We believe the Church is all who believe in and confess Jesus Christ as Savior and Lord and receive God's grace. We are called by God to be His one body of believers, gathered in communities. Empowered by the Holy Spirit, the Church's call is to declare His Good News of salvation to the fallen and lost world, to make disciples, and to serve all who are wounded, broken, and neglected. (Matthew 28:16-20; Mark 16:15-18; Romans 10:9-10; II Corinthians 5:17-21; Ephesians 2:8-9; 4)

8.   We believe all those who profess Jesus as Savior and Lord are to follow in His Way and are to live as those who magnify and glorify Him, the Head of His Church. As forgiven followers, we are called to live holy and blameless lives through the power of the Holy Spirit until that time when Jesus Christ shall return in all His glory. (I Corinthians 1:2; Ephesians 4:22-24; Hebrews 10:14; I John 3:4-9; 4:4; 5:1-5)

Adopted by Board of Trustees May 5, 2016

Foundations

We believe humanity is God's creation in His own image, and therefore persons are thinking, relational, moral, and spiritual beings of dignity and worth. We seek to serve students in all these dimensions. Our aim is to challenge students to become the complete person a loving God intends them to be, and to live in vital relationship with Him. Therefore, we seek to be a faith community as well as an academic community. We see our educational mission as an extension of the great ends of the church. We seek to graduate students who are committed to Christian servant-leadership in the world, promoting personal and social righteousness by God's grace and to His glory.

As a Christian College in the Presbyterian tradition, we are guided in our pursuit of academic excellence by the framework of Reformed beliefs. We confess the living God as the ultimate foundation of our faith and the source of all truth. We believe God is revealed perfectly in Jesus Christ. We affirm our Lord and Savior Jesus Christ as the center of history, restoring purpose, order, and value to the whole of life. We believe Jesus Christ to be the focus and culmination of scripture and that God's written Word is inspired, authoritative, and rightly interpreted by the Holy Spirit, our infallible rule for faith, conduct, and worship. We study and address a world and humanity that were created good, corrupted by the fall, redeemed through faith in Christ, and are moving toward the final consummation of God's purposes through the work of the Holy Spirit.

Educational Objectives

Approaching the integration of faith and learning from an informed, biblical perspective, faculty, staff, and students form a Christian community of learners that seeks to pursue the premise that all truth is God's truth and explore the significance of this in the various academic disciplines. We are committed to a thorough exploration of the complementary relationship between biblical truth and academic inquiry. We openly embrace students of all cultures, races, and faiths in an atmosphere of academic excellence, intellectual inquiry, and Christian love.

The College seeks to provide a broad, rigorous liberal arts curriculum with an emphasis on traditional and selected professional degree programs, including degree programs for adult learners. The educational goals of the College are that students will develop the following:

- An informed, biblical worldview that includes the following:
  - The sovereignty of God over all creation and knowledge.
  - A lifestyle of Christian service to others and the community.
  - The recognition of the intrinsic worth of self and all persons.
  - A genuine critical openness to the ideas and beliefs of others.
  - The formation of values and ethical reasoning.
  - An appreciation for what is beautiful, true, and good in the arts and literature.
  - A respect for and attitude of stewardship toward the whole of creation.
  - An understanding of the past and its interconnectedness with the present and future.
- Effective written and oral communication skills.
- Critical thinking and problem-solving skills.
- Essential computer information systems skills.
- Competency in their academic majors.
- Interpersonal and team skills and an understanding and appreciation of their personal strengths and weaknesses.
- Dispositions toward reflective and responsible citizenship needed to fulfill callings as effective leaders and committed laity.

Accreditation

Montreat College is accredited by the Commission on Colleges of the Southern Association of Colleges and Schools to award the associate, bachelor, and master degrees. Contact the Commission on Colleges at 1866 Southern Lane, Decatur, Georgia 30033-4097 or call 404-679-4500 for questions about the accreditation of Montreat College. The College is approved to prepare students for elementary education teacher licensure by the North Carolina Department of Public Instruction (NC-DPI). The Master of Science in Environmental Education program is accredited by the North American Association for Environmental Education (NAAEE). Outdoor Education programs are accredited by the Wilderness Education Association and the Commission on Outdoor Education and Leadership.

Affiliation

Montreat College is a member of the Council for Christian Colleges and Universities, Appalachian College Association, Council of Independent Colleges, National Association of Independent Colleges and Universities, North Carolina Independent Colleges and Universities, Association of Christian Schools International, and National Association of Intercollegiate Athletics.

Academic Calendar for the School of Arts and Sciences

Fall 2016 Semester

Event	Day	Date
Fall semester payment or payment plan due	Monday	August 8
Student Leadership Workshop	Sunday-Friday	August 14-19
Faculty Workshop	Tues.-Wed.	August 16-17
New Student Check-In (required)	Friday	August 19
New Students move into residence halls	Friday	August 19
Welcome Week	Friday-Monday	August 19-22
New Student Late Arrivals Check-In begins ($50 Penalty)	Monday	August 22
Continuing Student Check-In (required)	Monday	August 22
Continuing Student Late Arrivals Check-In begins($50 penalty)	Tuesday	August 23
Classes begin at 8:00 a.m.	Tuesday	August 23
Opening Convocation at 10:00 a.m.	Wednesday	August 24
Last day to add a course	Tuesday	August 30
Drop a course with a grade of "W" begins	Wednesday	August 31
Labor Day (college closed)	Monday	September 5
Homecoming and Family Weekend	Friday-Saturday	Sept. 30-Oct. 1
Last day to apply for December graduation	Saturday	October 1
Fall break begins after last class (residence halls close at 5:00 p.m.)	Wednesday	October 5
Residence halls reopen at 7:00 p.m.	Sunday	October 9
Classes resume at 8:00 a.m.	Monday	October 10
Advising Week	Monday-Friday	October 10-14
Board of Trustees meeting	Wednesday-Friday	October 12-14
Midterm Week	Monday-Friday	October 17-21
Seniors reserve Spring 2017 classes	Monday-Friday	October 17-21
Continuing Students reserve Spring 2017 classes	Monday-Friday	October 24-28
Midterm grades due, 5:00 p.m.	Wednesday	October 26
Drop a course with a grade of "WF" begins	Friday	October 28
Calling and Career Symposium	Mon.- Wed.	Oct. 31- Nov. 2
Thanksgiving break begins after last class (residence halls close at 5:00 p.m.)	Tuesday	November 22
College offices closed for Thanksgiving holidays	Wednesday-Friday	November 23-25
Residence halls reopen at 7:00 p.m.	Sunday	November 27
Classes resume at 8:00 a.m.	Monday	November 28
Last day of class	Friday	December 9
Final exams begin at 8:00 a.m.	Monday-Thursday	December 12-15
Christmas break begins after last exam (residence halls close at 5:00 p.m.)	Thursday	December 15
December Commencement at 2:00 p.m.	Saturday	December 17
Final grades due, 5:00 p.m.	Monday	December 19
College offices closed for Christmas holidays	Friday-Monday	Dec. 23- Jan. 2
December degree conferral	Saturday	December 31
Fall grades of Incomplete (I) convert to original grade	Friday	January 27

Academic Calendar for the School of Arts and Sciences

Spring/Summer 2017 Semester

Event	Day	Date
Spring semester payment or payment plan due	Monday	January 2
New Student Check-In (required)	Monday	January 9
Faculty Workshop	Mon.- Tuesday	January 9-10
New Student Orientation	Mon.- Tuesday	January 9-10
Continuing Student Check-In (required)	Tuesday	January 10
New Student Late Arrivals Check-in begins ($50 penalty)	Tuesday	January 10
Continuing Student Late Arrivals Check-in begins ($50 penalty)	Wednesday	January 11
Classes begin at 8:00 a.m.	Wednesday	January 11
Opening Convocation at 10:00 a.m.	Wednesday	January 11
Martin Luther King Day (college closed)	Monday	January 16
Last day to add a course	Thursday	January 19
Drop a course with a grade of "W" begins	Friday	January 20
Board of Trustees meeting	Wed.- Friday	January 25-27
Advising Week	Monday-Friday	Feb. 27-Mar.3
Last day to apply for May graduation	Wednesday	March 1
Seniors reserve Summer & Fall 2017 classes	Monday-Friday	March 6-10
Midterm Week	Monday-Friday	March 6-10
Spring break begins after last class (residence halls close at 5:00 p.m.)	Friday	March 10
Residence halls reopen at 7:00 p.m.	Sunday	March 19
Classes resume at 8:00 a.m.	Monday	March 20
Midterm grades due, 5:00 p.m.	Monday	March 20
Continuing students reserve Summer & Fall 2017 classes	Monday-Friday	March 20-24
Drop a course with a grade of "WF" begins	Wednesday	March 22
Current Students may reserve current room for Fall 2017	Monday-Friday	March 27-31
Current students room draw for Fall 2017	Tuesday	April 4
Easter break begins after last class (residence halls close at 5:00 p.m.)	Thursday	April 13
College Offices closed for Easter holidays	Friday-Monday	April 14-17
Residence halls reopen at 7:00 p.m.	Monday	April 17
Classes resume at 8:00 a.m.	Tuesday	April 18
Honors Convocation	Monday	April 24
Board of Trustees meeting	Wed.-Friday	May 3-5
Last Day of Class	Friday	May 5
May Term classes registration/ payment due	Friday	May 5
Final exams begin at 8:00 a.m.	Mon.-Thursday	May 8-11
Spring Commencement at 2:00 p.m.	Saturday	May 13
Final spring grades due, 5:00 p.m.	Monday	May 15
Faculty Academic Assessment Day	Monday	May 15
May/Summer Term begins	Wednesday	May 17
Last day to drop a May Term class	Friday	May 19
Summer classes registration/payment due	Friday	May 19
Memorial Day (college closed)	Monday	May 29
May degree conferral	Wednesday	May 31
Last Day to Apply for August graduation	Thursday	June 1
May Term ends	Wednesday	June 7
Final May Term grades due, 5:00 p.m.	Friday	June 9

Sping grades of Incomplete (I) convert to original grade	Frdiay	June 23
Summer classes end	Tuesday	August 15
Final summer grades due, 5:00 p.m.	Friday	August 18
August degree conferral	Thursday	August 31
Summer grades of Incomplete (I) convert to original grade	Friday	September 29

Academic Calendar for the School of Arts and Sciences

Fall 2017

Event	Day	Date
Fall semester payment or payment plan due	Monday	August 7
Student Leadership Workshop	Sunday-Friday	August 13-18
Faculty Workshop	Tues.-Wed.	August 15-16
New Student Check-In (required)	Friday	August 18
New Students move into residence halls	Friday	August 18
Welcome Week	Friday-Monday	August 18-21
New Student Late Arrivals Check-In begins ($50 Penalty)	Monday	August 21
Continuing Student Check-In (required)	Monday	August 21
Continuing Student Late Arrivals Check-In begins ($50 penalty)	Tuesday	August 22
Classes begin at 8:00 a.m.	Tuesday	August 22
Opening Convocation at 10:00 a.m.	Wednesday	August 23
Last day to add a course	Tuesday	August 29
Drop a course with a grade of "W" begins	Wednesday	August 30
Labor Day (college closed)	Monday	September 4
Last day to apply for December graduation	Sunday	October 1
Homecoming and Family Weekend	Friday-Saturday	October 6-7
Advising Week	Monday-Friday	October 9-13
Board of Trustees meeting	Wednesday-Friday	October 11-13
Midterm Week	Mon.-Wed.	October 16-18
Fall break begins after last class (Residence halls close at 5:00 p.m.)	Wednesday	October 18
Residence halls reopen at 7:00 p.m.	Sunday	October 22
Classes resume at 8:00 a.m.	Monday	October 23
Crossroads: Faith and Culture Project	Monday-Friday	October 23-27
Seniors reserve Spring 2018 classes	Monday-Friday	October 16-20
Continuing Students reserve Spring 2018 classes	Monday-Friday	October 23-27
Midterm grades due, 5:00 p.m.	Wednesday	October 25
Drop a course with a grade of "WF" begins	Friday	October 27
Thanksgiving break begins after last class (Residence halls close at 5:00 p.m.)	Tuesday	November 21
College offices closed for Thanksgiving holidays	Wednesday-Friday	November 22-24
Residence halls reopen at 7:00 p.m.	Sunday	November 26
Classes resume at 8:00 a.m.	Monday	November 27
Last day of class	Friday	December 8
Final exams begin at 8:00 a.m.	Monday-Thursday	December 11-14
Christmas break begins after last exam (Residence halls close at 5:00 p.m.)	Thursday	December 14
December Commencement at 2:00 p.m.	Saturday	December 16
Final grades due, 5:00 p.m.	Monday	December 18
College offices closed for Christmas holidays	Saturday-Monday	Dec. 23-Jan. 1
December diplomas conferred	Sunday	December 31
Fall grades of Incomplete (I) convert to original grade	Friday	January 26

Academic Calendar for the School of Arts and Sciences
Spring/Summer 2018

Event	Day	Date
Spring semester payment or payment plan due	Tuesday	January 2
New Student Check-In (required)	Monday	January 8
Faculty Workshop	Monday-Tuesday	January 8-9
New Student Orientation	Monday-Tuesday	January 8-9
Continuing Student Check-In (required)	Tuesday	January 9
New Student Late Arrivals Check-in begins ($50 penalty)	Tuesday	January 9
Continuing Student Late Arrivals Check-in begins ($50 penalty)	Wednesday	January 10
Classes begin at 8:00 a.m.	Wednesday	January 10
Opening Convocation at 10:00 a.m.	Wednesday	January 10
Martin Luther King Day (college closed)	Monday	January 15
Last day to add a course	Thursday	January 18
Drop a course with a grade of "W" begins	Friday	January 19
Board of Trustees meeting	Wednesday-Friday	January 24-26
Advising Week	Monday – Friday	Feb 26-March 2
Last day to apply for May graduation	Thursday	March 1
Midterm Week	Monday-Friday	March 5-9
Seniors reserve Summer & Fall 2018 classes	Monday–Friday	March 5-9
Spring break begins after last class	Friday	March 9
(Residence halls close at 5:00 p.m.)		
Residence halls reopen at 7:00 p.m.	Sunday	March 18
Classes resume at 8:00 a.m.	Monday	March 19
Midterm grades due, 5:00 p.m.	Monday	March 19
Continuing students reserve Summer & Fall 2018 classes	Monday-Friday	March 19-23
Drop a course with a grade of "WF" begins	Wednesday	March 21
Current Students may reserve current room for Fall 2018	Monday-Thursday	March 26-29
Easter break begins after last class	Thursday	March 29
(Residence halls close at 5:00 p.m.)		
College Offices closed for Easter holidays	Friday-Monday	March 30-April 2
Residence halls reopen at 7:00 p.m.	Monday	April 2
Classes resume at 8:00 a.m.	Tuesday	April 3
Current students room draw for Fall 2018	Thursday	April 5
Honors Convocation	Monday	April 23
Board of Trustees meeting	Wednesday-Friday	May 2-4
Last Day of Class	Friday	May 4
May Term classes registration/ payment due	Friday	May 4
Final exams begin at 8:00 a.m.	Monday-Thursday	May 7-10
Spring Commencement at 2:00 p.m.	Saturday	May 12
Final spring grades due, 5:00 p.m.	Monday	May 14
Faculty Academic Assessment Day	Monday	May 14
May/Summer Term begins	Wednesday	May 16
Last day to drop a May Term class	Friday	May 18
Summer classes registration/payment due	Friday	May 18
Memorial Day (college closed)	Monday	May 28
May diplomas conferred	Thursday	May 31
Last Day to Apply for August graduation	Friday	June 1
May Term ends	Wednesday	June 6
May Term final grades due, 5:00 p.m.	Friday	June 8
Spring grades of Incomplete (I) convert to original grade	Friday	June 22
Summer classes end	Tuesday	August 14
Final summer grades due, 5:00 p.m.	Friday	August 17
August degree conferral	Friday	August 31
Summer grades of Incomplete (I) convert to original grade	Friday	September 28

Admission Information

For information and application materials for the School of Arts and Sciences, please contact the Office of Admissions:

Office of Admissions
Montreat College (MC 865)
P.O. Box 1267
Montreat, NC 28757
800-622-6968
admissions@montreat.edu
www.montreat.edu/admissions

Montreat College is committed to providing a liberal arts education rooted in Christian faith and committed to the integration of faith and learning. Montreat College enrolls students from a variety of ethnic, social, and economic backgrounds who provide a positive addition to the life of the College and who have the potential to have an impact on the world as agents of renewal and reconciliation. Admissions decisions are based on the following:

- Academic achievement and potential as indicated on the transcripts and standardized test scores of the applicant.
- Personal characteristics, motivation, and integrity.
- Leadership ability as demonstrated by participation in school, community, or religious organizations.

General Application Information

Students may enter Montreat College's School of Arts and Sciences at the beginning of either the fall or spring semester. Although the College has a rolling admission policy for each semester, students are strongly encouraged to apply well before the starting date of the semester they wish to enter. Housing and class space are limited, and early acceptances will receive preference.

A campus visit is the single most important step in determining the right college to attend. Montreat College encourages any interested persons to visit, tour the campus, talk to professors and students, and eat in the dining hall. Individual appointments are available. Visit www.montreat.edu/visit, call 1-800-622-6968, or e-mail admissions@montreat.edu for more information.

When all application forms and credentials are received from the applicant, Admissions personnel will review the file and the applicant will be notified of the decision by mail. Each qualification will be considered in relation to all of the applicant's qualifications—no one item will necessarily be the deciding factor in acceptance or rejection. Students who meet the College's criteria will be admitted with Standard or Conditional status. All accepted students are required to pay an advance deposit of $150. Regular deposit deadline is May 1.

Montreat College strongly recommends that students have a computer to enhance their learning experience. The suggested minimum requirements can be found on our website or by contacting the Technology Department.

Before any new student can begin classes or move into a residence hall, a medical examination report and immunization record must be filled out in full and signed by a physician. North Carolina State Law requires all students attending a public or private college or university to submit proof of immunizations prior to enrollment. All records of immunization must be certified either by a physician's signature, a health department stamp, or be a copy of a North Carolina school health record. Dismissal from college is mandatory under the law if these immunization requirements are not met.

Note: Validation of all High School Transcripts

According to federal regulations, high school diplomas must be valid in order for a student to be eligible for Title IV funding (i.e. federal funding).
Beginning July 1, 2011, Federal regulations require all colleges and universities to evaluate the validity of a student's high school diploma if the institution or the Secretary of the Department of Education has reason to believe that the diploma is not valid or was not obtained from an entity that provides secondary school education (Higher Education Act § 668.16(p)).

The Admissions Office will confirm that all students' transcripts arrive from a high school with a CEEB code, as well as the high school seal and/or signature. If a transcript is from a high school that lacks a CEEB code or seal/signature, the Admissions Office will investigate to confirm that the state department of education or home school association recognizes the school. The Admissions Office may request a copy of the student's diploma at any point in the admissions process to verify diploma validity. If a diploma is determined invalid, General Educational Development (GED) tests may be required for admission consideration.

Admission of First-Year Students

Students entering the School of Arts and Sciences as first-year students must submit the following:

- A formal application (apply online).
- A letter of recommendation from a high school counselor or teacher. *This requirement is waived if student's academic index calculation is 2,750 or above**.
- An official transcript of high school credits indicating class rank and grade point average (GPA). The un-weighted GPA is used when making an admissions decision.**

- High school core course requirements should include four years English, three years science, three years social studies, three years math (Algebra I, II, and Geometry), and one year of a foreign language. The transcript should indicate successful completion of requirements for graduation with a diploma, State High School Equivalency Diploma, or record of successful completion of General Educational Development (GED) tests.
- Official Scholastic Aptitude Test (SAT) scores from the College Entrance Examination Board, Princeton, NJ 08540, or American College Testing (ACT) scores from the American College Testing Program, Iowa City, IA 52240, as recorded on an official high school transcript, or sent directly by the test center to Montreat College (Code No. 005423). International students must submit either a Test of English as a Foreign Language (TOEFL), or a Test Report Form (TRF) from the International English Language Testing System (IELTS).

* The academic index can be calculated by using the following formula: (Cumulative High School GPA) x (highest combined Critical Reading and Math scores from SAT). If the student takes the ACT, an SAT equivalency will be determined and used in calculating the academic index.

**Admissions decisions may be made based on unofficial transcript(s). However, all required final, official transcripts must be received by the end of the first semester pursued at Montreat College. If these are not received, students will not be allowed to enroll in subsequent semesters.

Students receiving Veterans Affairs benefits cannot have their courses and fees certified until all official transcripts are received.

First-Year Admission Criteria: Montreat College admissions criteria are based on our commitment to student success and academic excellence.

- Standard Admission requirements include a 2.75 (B-) minimum GPA (un-weighted) and a 1000 SAT (combined Critical Reading and Math sections) or 21 ACT (Composite Score). Recommendation is optional.
- Students who do not meet either of these standards are required to submit a letter of recommendation and will be reviewed on a case-by-case basis. These students will be limited to enrollment in 12-14 semester credit hours for their first semester.

International Admission

International applicants must be graduates of a secondary school system or the equivalent and must have sufficient proficiency in the English language to be able to study at the college level.

International students entering the College of Arts and Sciences must submit or complete the following:

- A formal application (apply online).
- An official, translated transcript of the student's secondary school record, preferably indicating class rank and GPA. Montreat College highly recommends, and in some instances requires, that the applicant use a transcript translation and evaluation service (such as World Education Services, www.wes.org; AACRAO International Education Services, www.aacrao.org; International Education Evaluations, Inc., www.foreigntranscripts.com) in order to determine international academic credentials.
- SAT or ACT scores (for students who speak English as their first language)
- TOEFL, IELTS or ITEP results (for students who speak English as a second language). International applicants may also elect to submit an official Scholastic Aptitude Test (SAT) score or an American College Testing (ACT) score.
- The applicant must score a minimum of 71 on the TOEFL, a 6.5 on the IELTS, or a 3.7 on the iTEP.
- Interview with an admissions representative.

International students wishing to transfer college credit must meet the qualifications listed under "Transfer Admission" with the additional provision that all post-secondary transcripts be translated to the English language. The College requires the use of a transcript translation and evaluation service in order to determine international academic credentials. For service referral, please contact the Office of Admissions.

- **June 15 – International Student Application Deadline**

- **July 1 – Missing Information Deadline** –All transcripts, transcript evaluations, and official exam results must be submitted along with housing form, financial obligation form, medical forms, and payment. Once this is completed an I-20 will be created.

It usually takes 4-5 weeks to obtain a student visa and prepare for arrival in the United States after an I-20 is received.

Home School Admission

Students who complete their secondary education in a home school setting must present an official record of their home school courses and official SAT or ACT scores. A cumulative GPA must also be included. All other qualifications listed under "Admission of First-Year Students" must be met.

Transfer Admission

Montreat College welcomes transfer students. A minimum of 30 semester credit hours of transferable credits with a minimum grade of *C* (2.00 on a 4.00 scale) will permit a student to enter with sophomore status; students with 60 semester credit hours will be granted junior status, and students with 90 semester credit hours will be granted senior status. All students seeking degrees must meet the requirements as outlined under "Degree Requirements" regardless of the total credits accepted in transfer. (See "Conditions of Acceptance of Transfer Credit" in this section for details on the College's transfer policy.) Transfer students must submit the following:

- A formal application (apply online).
- An official transcript from all post-secondary institutions previously attended.*
- Students in their first semester of college must submit an official high school transcript directly to Montreat College.**

A preliminary transcript evaluation may be completed using unofficial transcripts. All transcripts, both official and unofficial, must be submitted directly to the Admissions Office. Transcripts submitted to other departments will not be considered for preliminary evaluation.

*Admissions decisions may be made based on unofficial transcript(s). However, all required final, official transcripts must be received by the end of the first semester pursued at Montreat College. If these are not received, students will not be allowed to enroll in subsequent semesters.

Students receiving **Veterans Affairs (VA) benefits cannot have their courses and fees certified until all official transcripts are received. If these students are transferring less than 24 college semester credits, official high school transcripts must be received by Montreat College prior to full admission. VA students' courses and fees cannot be certified until these are received.

Transfer Admission Criteria: Montreat College admissions criteria are based on our commitment to student success and academic excellence.

- Standard Admission requirements include a 2.0 (C) minimum GPA for college level work. If a student is in their first semester of college, an official high school transcript must be submitted directly to Montreat College.
- Students who do not meet these standards will be reviewed on a case-by-case basis. These students will be limited to enrollment in 12-14 semester credit hours for their first semester.

Students wishing to transfer college credit from institutions outside of the United States must have their transcripts translated to the English language. The College requires the use of a transcript translation and evaluation service in order to determine international academic credentials. For service referral, please contact the Office of Admissions.

Conditions of Acceptance of Transfer Credit

Montreat College strives to ensure the highest quality academic experience for all our students. Therefore, we limit the number and type of transfer credits we accept. We require that credits apply to students' degree programs and limit the number of credits applied via credit-by-examination, from non-regionally accredited institutions, and from documented learning. Similarly, we do not accept transfer credits acquired through groups that lack appropriate approval by the American Council on Education.

- Academic work from a regionally accredited school with a grade of *C* or better (2.00 on a 4.00 scale) will be accepted in transfer. Courses that do not apply to a student's degree program will not be accepted.
- Students may transfer up to 2 physical education activity courses in which they received a *P* (passing credit). These are the only courses where a grade of *P* is acceptable for transfer credit.

- Transferred courses must be at the same level and be equivalent in content to the Montreat College courses. If there is any question of course equivalency, it is the responsibility of the student to provide proof that courses are equivalent (i.e. provide course descriptions, syllabus).
- Montreat College endorses the North Carolina Comprehensive Articulation Agreement, which can be viewed at www.northcarolina.edu. Transfer students who have earned the Associate in Arts or Associate in Science degree from a North Carolina Community College and who meet the minimum requirements for admission to Montreat College will receive transfer credit for all eligible courses

subject to normal transfer credit policy. No more than **66** semester hours may be transferred from two-year schools.

- The maximum number of undergraduate credits that may transfer from other institutions is **90** semester credits.
- The combined total of credits that can be accepted from non-regionally accredited colleges or universities, NCA credit, or Credits by Examination is **30** for a bachelor degree, or **15** for an associate degree.
  - Courses from non-regionally accredited colleges or universities are considered on a course-by-course basis; coursework must have an earned grade of *C* or better; *acceptance of such credits is dependent upon Montreat College's evaluation of the equivalency of coursework and level of instruction.*
    - Academic work presented from a nationally accredited agency recognized by the Council for Higher Education Accreditation may be evaluated for transfer equivalency.
    - Students may request that academic work presented from a non-accredited, faith-related institution be considered for transfer equivalency. Courses will be reviewed with the potential for **6** total credits allowed in transfer.
- For courses from an international institution, the transcript must be translated and evaluated by a credible educational evaluation company.
- The transfer of courses into the undergraduate or graduate core must be approved by the Office of Records and Registration, in consultation with a full-time faculty member in the discipline. Approval of transfer credit for the program core should be finalized prior to enrollment into the degree program.
- Credits from regionally accredited institutions will be considered for courses which Montreat College offers no equivalent course, provided that the transferred course is considered within the general framework of the liberal arts curriculum and is relevant to the degree pursued. Only courses that are academic in nature and purpose will be accepted in transfer.
- Vocational training courses, such as air conditioning technology, electrical circuitry, welding, and typing are **not** accepted. However, some vocational courses that are academic in content may be considered for up to 30 semester credit hours.

- Transferred quarter credit hours will be converted to semester credits using the following formula: **Semester credit = quarter hours x 2/3.**
- A degree-seeking Montreat College student who wishes to enroll in courses offered by another institution must complete the required form and receive approval to do so from the Records and Registration Office. Failure to follow this procedure may result in loss of transfer credit for these courses.
- Students transferring with senior status from another institution must successfully complete at least **18** semester credit hours in their major and a minimum of **32** credits overall at Montreat College.

- A student who is transferring from another institution and who has been placed on academic probation/warning for the previous semester will be automatically placed on academic probation at Montreat College.
- Courses transferred to Montreat College will be assigned the grade of *P* (passing) and will be considered as earned credit but will not affect the grade point average or graduation honors.

Students who are transferring and are participating in athletics must also follow guidelines established by the NAIA in order to be considered eligible. Meeting athletic eligibility requirements does not automatically qualify a student for admission to the College.

Official transcripts are required in order to receive transfer credit from an approved institution. For printed paper copy transcripts to be considered official, they must be received directly from the institution in a sealed envelope. For electronic transcripts to be considered official, they must be received by the College via a recognized online transcript service. The Office of Records and Registration will determine the authenticity of a transcript if there is any uncertainty.

Readmission of Former Students

The Office of Records and Registration oversees the readmit process. Students formerly enrolled at Montreat College who, for any reason, have not attended classes at Montreat for a semester or more must submit the following:

- A formal readmit application (obtained from the Office of Records and Registration or through the Montreat College website).
- A medical examination report and immunization record filled out in full and signed by a physician (See "Admission of First-Year Students"). The Records office will contact Health Services to see if a previous record is still on file.
- Official transcripts from each institution attended since leaving Montreat College.
- Any student readmitting to Montreat College must have a minimum combined GPA of 2.0 on a 4.0 scale for all academic work completed while at Montreat College and at any other institutions during the time since attending Montreat College.
- Students who have left Montreat College on Academic Probation must submit an essay to the Admissions Review Committee explaining why they will now be academically successful.
- Students who have left Montreat College on Academic Suspension and wish to be readmitted may apply after an absence of one semester. They must submit an essay explaining why they will now be academically successful and transcript(s) showing completion of two college-level courses from another institution(s) with grades of "C" or above since leaving Montreat College. These documents will be examined by the Admissions Review Committee which may request an interview or letters of recommendation prior to making an admissions determination.
- Students who have been suspended due to academic dishonesty will not be eligible to reapply to Montreat College for at least two (2) years after dismissal. These students must write letters of appeal for readmission addressed to the Vice President for Academic Affairs and Dean of the College.
- Students must be cleared by Financial Aid, Student Accounts, Student Services, and Athletics, if applicable, prior to readmission.
- Students who do not meet all standards for readmission will be reviewed on a case-by-case basis by the Admissions Review Committee.

The Office of Records and Registration should be consulted for appropriate readmission procedures. If students have been withdrawn for more than five years, they are classified as new students and must go through either the "Admission of First-Year Students" or the "Transfer Admission" process.

Admission of Part-Time Students

Students are considered part-time when they are seeking a degree, have applied and been accepted as a regular student, and are taking fewer than 12* credit hours in a given semester. Students seeking to enroll part-time must follow the application guidelines and meet the admission requirements as outlined under "Admission of First-Year Students" and/or "Transfer Admission."

Admission of Special Students

Students may be admitted to the College to take academic courses for transfer or for their personal edification without pursuing a degree at Montreat College. Special student classifications include the following:

- Visiting = degree-seeking at another institution
- Non-degree = receiving college credit but not seeking a degree
- Audit = attending college course without receiving credit*

*Students planning to audit a course must also receive approval from the instructor of the course; see *auditing courses* under Academic Information.

Students wishing to enter under the "special" classification should submit the following:

- A special student application indicating the desired admission status.
- An official transcript from the most recent institution (students auditing a course do not need to submit transcripts).
- An official transcript showing the completion of pre-requisite or co-requisite courses if planning to enroll in courses for which these are required.
- Immunization and other medical forms (required for all students taking 4 or more hours on campus). All records of immunization must be certified either by a physician's signature, a health department stamp, or be a copy of a North Carolina school health record. Dismissal from school is mandatory by law if these immunization requirements are not met.

Special students are not eligible for financial aid.

Time-Shortened Degree Opportunities

Montreat College accepts and provides numerous programs by which students may accelerate their academic careers, have a wider range of course choices, and reduce the overall length of time spent in completing degree requirements.

Early Admission

This program allows superior students to be admitted following completion of their junior year in high school. To be considered, students must have a *B* average or above for all high school work attempted. The high school must first agree to allow college credits obtained at Montreat College to count towards high school graduation requirements. Students considering early admission must meet the same requirements as those listed under "Admission of First-Year Students." Applicants will be considered on an individual basis. Students who have not completed high school are not eligible for federal financial aid. For additional information, contact the Office of Admissions.

Dual Enrollment

High school students who are juniors or seniors can take up to 12 credits on the Montreat campus at the reduced tuition charge of $100 per credit hour. Course fees, if any, still apply. Additional credits will incur charges based on the current part-time tuition rate (contact the Office of Admissions for details). Students interested in dual enrollment should submit the following:

- A dual enrollment application.
- An official copy of the high school transcript.

Immunizations and other medical forms (required for all students taking 4 or more hours on campus). All records of immunization must be certified either by a physician's signature, a health department stamp, or be a copy of a North Carolina school health record.

Credit by Examination

A student may participate in a variety of credit by examination programs in order to earn credit toward degrees awarded by Montreat College. A maximum of **30** semester credit hours may be awarded through any combination of these programs. Credit earned will be recorded as *P* (passing) on a student's transcript. The student must request official score transcripts from the examination program and have them sent to Montreat College. Credit for Montreat College will not be based upon academic credit awarded by another institution.

Advanced Placement Program (AP): This credit by examination program is sponsored by the College Entrance Examination Board for evidence of completion of college-level courses taken in high school. Scores of 3, 4, or 5 will be accepted, depending on the discipline.

College Level Examination Program (CLEP): The CLEP subject area examination will award credit toward graduation to students who receive a passing score on the exam according to ACE recommendations.

Defense Activity for Nontraditional Education Support (DSST): This credit by examination program uses various subject area examinations. Guidelines developed by the American Council on Education (ACE) for awarding these credits are followed. Tests may not be taken for credit if the student has ever taken a course in the subject area.

ECE: This credit by examination program is similar to other subject area examinations. Guidelines developed by the American Council on Education (ACE) for awarding these credits are followed.

International Baccalaureate (IB): The International Baccalaureate Organization's Diploma Program is a demanding two year, pre-university course of study that leads to examinations. It is designed for highly motivated secondary school students aged 16 to 19. Similar to Advanced Placement (AP) examinations, students enrolled in the International Baccalaureate (IB) Diploma Program earn credit hours or advanced placement in college courses. Scores of 5 or 6 will be accepted, depending on the discipline.

Modern Foreign Languages: Spanish placement exams are given during Welcome Week at the beginning of the fall semester, during New Student Orientation at the beginning of the spring semester, and during Pre-Registration in November and March. Students who place into a course by exam will receive credit for the preceding lower-level course(s) upon successful completion of the course into which they have been placed. A maximum of six credit hours may be earned by placement exam.

The American Council on the Teaching of Foreign Languages (ACTFL) offers proctored proficiency assessments in many world languages for reading and listening comprehension and reading and writing skills. Montreat College awards college level credit based on recommendations by the American Council for Education (ACE) for the different levels of competency demonstrated, whether the student learned the language in a classroom or non-classroom setting.   These assessments must be arranged through the College, by contacting the Academic Affairs office.

Military Credit

Military credit is treated in the same way as general transfer credit. Military credits may count toward specific course requirements beyond general electives. Following the review of military transcripts by the Office of Admissions and the Office of Records and Registration, Department Chairs will be consulted to review courses for major-specific transfer credit.

Montreat College uses the American Council on Education's (ACE) guide to evaluating educational experiences in the armed services for evaluating all military credit. An official Joint Services Transcript (JST) or officially certified DD-214 is carefully evaluated for all details concerning military experiences; credits are awarded at face value. The JST should accompany the student's application for admission. The ACE recommendation for use of military credit(s) must fit within a Montreat College program for transfer credit to be approved. Credits can be applied to the major if they closely match Montreat College courses.

Credits completed at the Community College of the Air Force with a grade of *S* are reviewed as general elective credit. Credits with grades of *A – C* are evaluated just like any other two-year college transcript.

Medical Forms and Concerns

New students are required to complete several medical forms related to medical history and current medical health. These are mandated by North Carolina law and needed for certain courses and student activities. These forms are initially collected by the Office of Admissions at the time of deposit to the College. Student athletes and students participating in certain courses (such as those facilitated by the Outdoor Education/Ministry Department and the Physical Education Program) may be required to submit yearly medical updates. Faculty/instructors will also ask students to advise them about any significant medical conditions or limitations on the students' abilities to participate in courses requiring physical exertion. However, **it is each student's responsibility to inform staff/faculty of any significant medical history or restrictions.**

Financial Aid Information

For financial aid information and application materials for the School of Arts and Sciences, please contact the Office of Financial Aid:

Office of Financial Aid
Montreat College (MC 881)
P.O. Box 1267
Montreat, NC 28757
800-545-4656
financialaid@montreat.edu

The Office of Financial Aid is committed to providing financial resources to students who seek an education at an institution committed to integrating faith and learning. In partnership with college, federal, state, and other organizations, the Office will coordinate the administration of all students' financial assistance awarded to ensure equity and consistency in the delivery of funds to students.

General Information

There are two types of financial assistance at Montreat College – aid based on financial need and aid based on other criteria, such as academic or athletic achievement. Each year, the College administers more than six million dollars in assistance.

The Financial Aid Office is committed to helping students and parents with funding as much as possible. However, the final financial arrangements must be made between the student and the Student Accounts Office.

A student must be classified as a student in good academic standing and meet all federal requirements to receive federal and state funding.

Note: Validation of all High School Diplomas

According to federal regulations, high school diplomas must be valid in order for a student to be eligible for Title IV funding (i.e. federal funding).

Beginning July 1, 2011, federal regulations require all colleges and universities to evaluate the validity of a student's high school diploma if the institution or the Secretary of the Department of Education has reason to believe that the diploma is not valid or was not obtained from an entity that provides secondary school education (Higher Education Act § 668.16(p)).

Application for Financial Aid

Procedure
- Apply for admission to Montreat College.
- Create a FSA ID at fsaid.ed.gov to complete their Free Application for Federal Student Aid (FAFSA). If the student is a dependent, a parent must also have an FSA ID.
- Complete the Free Application for Federal Student Aid (FAFSA) online at fafsa.ed.gov. It is advisable to file tax forms before completing the FAFSA, but it is not required. It is best to have the FAFSA submitted as early as possible.
- Financial aid decisions are made after a student has been offered admission. Students are notified via an official award letter.
- Students receiving a loan for the first time at Montreat College will need to complete the appropriate paperwork, including the Master Promissory Note and the Entrance Counseling Interview for William D. Ford Federal Direct Loans at www.studentloans.gov.
- Students eligible for educational benefits through the Veterans Administration or Vocational Rehabilitation should apply directly to these agencies and inform the Financial Aid Office of pending awards.
- Students must reapply each year for financial aid by completing the FAFSA.
- All outside scholarships (non-Montreat College) must be reported to the Financial Aid Office. Montreat College reserves the right to reduce institutional awards and/or federal loans due to outside resources.

Types of Financial Aid

Financial aid is usually awarded in a package or combination of different types of assistance from various sources. Scholarships, grants, loans, and employment are integral parts of the financial aid program, and some portion of the aid offered may consist of each of these types of financial aid.

Scholarships and grants are non-repayable gifts. These include the Montreat Merit Scholarships, which are based on academics, the Keystone Award, which is based on both academics and need, and awards based on talent, for example musical or athletic achievement. Scholarships from outside the College include state grants (North Carolina Need Based Scholarship), federal grants (Pell, SEOG), and scholarships from other outside entities.

Loans available to Montreat College students include William D. Ford Federal Direct Loans (subsidized and unsubsidized), Perkins Loans, William D. Ford Federal Parents' Loan for Undergraduate Students (PLUS), Grad PLUS and alternative or private educational loans.

Work programs are the Federal College Work Study Program (FCWSP) and the Montreat College Work Program.

Academic Year Definition

To be considered full time, an undergraduate student should be enrolled in a minimum of 30 weeks (15 per semester) of instructional time and a minimum of 24 credit hours (12 per semester) attempted.

Work Study Program

Students who are eligible for work study will be contacted by the Office of Financial Aid with information about the application process. These positions typically allow for 125 hours of work per semester at $7.25 per hour. Students may work only one campus job.

Veterans' Help Desk

The VA certifying official, located in the Office of Records and Registration, works with the Veterans Administration (VA) to assist in administering the education benefit programs to veterans or eligible relatives of veterans. The VA certifying official certifies enrollment, based on number of credits, length of courses, and type of courses (residential or distance learning), and transmits necessary credentials and information to the proper administrative office.

Before a student's enrollment can be certified, the VA certifying official will need the following:

- A copy of the Certificate of Eligibility for the student.
- Signed Memorandum of Understanding detailing the expectations for students using VA educational benefits. The memo has detailed information concerning status for each type of student.

A student must be admitted and actively enrolled in courses at Montreat College before enrollment verification for veterans benefits can begin. Students in the School of Arts and Sciences as well as the School of Adult and Graduate Studies may be eligible for the full monthly allowances, provided they are enrolled full-time as determined by the VA. Students are responsible for reporting any changes in enrollment or attendance to the VA certifying official as soon as possible.

To apply for VA educational benefits, go to https://www.ebenefits.va.gov/ebenefits/vonapp. To check on the status of benefits, contact the Veterans Administration helpdesk at 1-888-442-4551. The VA helpdesk for Montreat College can be reached by email at va@montreat.edu or by calling 1-828-669-8012 x 3732. The *Memorandum of Understanding for Use of Education Benefits for Veteran Students* can be requested from the VA helpdesk.

Statement of Satisfactory Progress for Financial Aid Purposes

It is very important to note that there are two types of Satisfactory Academic Progress (SAP) requirements. The first type is called Academic SAP and applies to **all** enrolled students. It is monitored by the Office of Records and Registration. The second type is called Financial Aid SAP and only applies to students receiving financial aid.

Federal regulations (Sections 668.16, .668.32 and 668.34) require that schools monitor the academic progress of each applicant for federal financial assistance and that the school certify that the applicant is making satisfactory academic progress toward earning their degree.

At Montreat College, this determination of progress is made at the end of each semester, including the summer term, and before the financial aid office disburses any federal aid funds for the subsequent semester. To be eligible to receive Title IV federal funds, Pell Grants, SEOG, Federal College Work Study, Federal Perkins Loans, Federal Direct Loans or state and institutional aid, students must maintain satisfactory progress.

Financial Aid Satisfactory Academic Progress (SAP) has three criteria and students must meet **all** three:

1. A Qualitative measure: All students must maintain a cumulative 2.0 GPA.
2. A Quantitative measure: All students must earn 67% of all credits attempted.
3. A Pace of Progression measure: All students must complete their program in 150% of the credit requirements. For example, a program which requires 120 credit hours for completion must be completed in 180 attempted credit hours (120 x 1.5 = 180). This is also called the Maximum Time Frame (MTF) criteria.

There is one additional SAP criteria that students should be aware of especially if they plan to double major: Automatic Completion. All students who have completed all credit requirements for any of their programs will be considered as having earned a degree for financial aid purposes even if they have not applied for graduation. These students will not qualify for need-based federal grants and state financial aid.

Failure to Meet Satisfactory Academic Progress

Financial Aid Warning: Students who fail to make SAP may continue to receive financial aid for one additional semester. No appeal is necessary for this student at this time.

Financial Aid Suspension: Students who fail to regain SAP at the end of a semester on Warning are not eligible to receive financial aid. A student on Suspension has the option to appeal to have their eligibility reinstated. If the student's appeal is denied, the student remains on Suspension and can only regain eligibility once they meet all three of the SAP criteria.

Financial Aid Probation: Students whose appeals have been approved are placed on Probation. The appeal approval will outline what the student needs to do to keep receiving financial aid. This may range from the student regaining eligibility at the end of the next period of enrollment to the student meeting specific criteria as identified in an Academic Plan.

Effect of Incompletes, Withdrawals, Failures, and Repeats

All incompletes, withdrawals, failures, and repeats are included as **attempts** when determining SAP for financial aid. Depending on when a student withdraws in the semester, their aid may be recalculated. Students should consult a financial aid counselor before making any adjustments to their schedules as it may impact their awards.

Effect of Changing Major/Double Major

A change of academic major or the pursuit of a double major does not extend eligibility for financial aid. Students are still expected to complete their programs within 180 credit hours. A student may appeal if they fail to make SAP for this reason.

Effect of Summer Enrollment/Cooperative Education/Consortium Agreement/Study Abroad

Credit hours attempted during the May Term and summer sessions will be used to determine SAP.

If a student is enrolled via a consortium agreement/study abroad program, a transcript will be obtained from the host school and the credit hours will be included as attempts along with the credit hours earned.

Effect of Credits by Transfer, Examination, Military, and Life Experience

Transfer credits that have been accepted and count towards the student's program of study will be used as attempts and completes and included in determining SAP.

Academic credits received via examination, military, or life experience are counted as attempts and as earned credit.

Effect of a Second Degree

A student who has already been awarded a bachelor's degree may apply for a second degree only if the second degree is different from the first degree. Ordinarily, a second degree at the undergraduate level is discouraged, and a graduate degree is encouraged. Students who have earned a degree are not eligible for need-based federal grants and state aid.

Effect of Auditing Courses

Students do not earn any academic credits for audited courses. They do not count in the calculation of "attempted credit hours."

Reinstatement of Aid

Aid may be reinstated on a probationary status by meeting the requirements for SAP or by an approved appeal. If aid is reinstated, a probationary status will remain in effect. A period of non-enrollment does not reinstate aid eligibility. A student returning after an extended period of non-enrollment must still submit a SAP appeal.

Appeals

Students who wish to appeal the suspension of financial aid eligibility based on mitigating circumstances (i.e., severe illness, death of a close family member, severe injury, or other traumatic experiences) may do so by submitting the SAP appeal form, a letter of appeal, and supporting documentation to the Director of Financial Aid within **ten days** from the date of notification that aid has been canceled.

All appeals must:

1. Include the completed SAP appeal form.
2. Include the student's statement identifying the mitigating circumstances that led to SAP not being maintained. In the first appeal, since SAP is cumulative, the student must address all unearned coursework which appears on the Montreat College transcript.
3. Provide supporting documentation, such as statement from the doctor, death notice, etc.
4. Identify and have approved by the Academic Advisor and/or the Student Success Team, a plan to correct academic deficiencies. This plan must be signed by the student and preparer.
5. Include the student's degree audit, which may be obtained from the Office of Records and Registration.
6. Include the student's Montreat College identification number, or Social Security number, current address, and communication information.
7. Be legible.

All initial and subsequent appeals, supporting documentation, and corrective plans of action must be received within ten days of notice. The Financial Aid Advisory and Appeals Committee will not review incomplete or partial appeals. All documentation is retained by the Financial Aid Office for audit purposes.

The Director of Financial Aid will take the appeal to the Financial Aid Advisory and Appeals Committee and notify the student of the decision to reinstate or deny aid. If approved, conditions may apply. If the conditions are not satisfied, aid may be denied in a subsequent term. As described in federal regulations, **all decisions at this point are final.**

The Student Financial Aid Office will review no more than two appeals from a student during the course of study.

Financial Information

For information or questions about financial information for the School of Arts and Sciences, please contact the Finance Office:

Finance Office
Montreat College (MC 868)
P.O. Box 1267
Montreat, NC 28757
828-669-8012 ext. 3753
financeoffice@montreat.edu

Montreat College endeavors to ensure that the opportunity for Christian higher education be given to all who desire it. By keeping expenses at a minimum and by offering a substantial and comprehensive financial aid program, Montreat College provides an educational opportunity for many students who otherwise might not be financially able to attend college. No qualified student should hesitate to apply because of lack of financial resources.

School of Arts and Sciences Program Fees

Full-Time Tuition, Room, Board, and Fees	Fall or Spring	Academic Year
Full-Time Tuition (12 to 18 credit hours)	$12,370.00	$24,740.00
Student Health Insurance	$1,750.00	$1,750.00
Wellness Center Fee (per semester)	$50.00	$100.00
Technology Fee	$100.00	$100.00
Off Campus Student Charges:	**$14,270.00**	**$26,690.00**
Room – Double Occupancy	$2,098.00	$4,196.00
Board (includes 17 meals per week & $175 Cavalier Cash)	$2,087.00	$4,174.00
Sales Tax on Board	$132.09	$264.18
Residential Student Charges:	**$18,587.09**	**$35,324.18**
Housing Options and Amenities	Fall or Spring	Academic Year
Webbwood Apartments	$3,105.00	$6,210.00
Private Room	$3,310.00	$6,620.00
Campus Laundry and LaundryView™	No Charge	No Charge
High Speed Internet and Email Account	No Charge	No Charge
Local Phone Service and Extended Basic Cable Television	No Charge	No Charge

Off-Campus Commuter Fee	Per Semester	$50.00
Part-Time Tuition (less than 12 credit hours per semester)	Per Credit Hour	$640.00
Tuition Overload (credit hours over 18)	Per Credit Hour	$386.00
CBA/Directed Study Tuition for Winter/Summer Sessions	Per Credit Hour	$386.00
Internship/Practicum for Part-Time or Summer Students	Per Credit Hour	$386.00
Practicum – (all 341 courses, MS 451)	Per Credit Hour	$50.00
Field Internship – (all 441 courses)	Per Credit Hour	$50.00
CBA or Directed Study for Fall/Spring Semesters	Per Credit Hour	$50.00
Audit	Per Course	$100.00
New Student Deposit (nonrefundable, applied to first semester charges		$150.00
Montreat Campus Parking Fee		$100.00
Black Mountain Campus Parking Fee		$25.00
Graduation Fee		$60.00
Late Payment Fee (for balance due after Check-In Day)		$50.00
Delinquent Payment Fee (for balance due after first week of class)		$100.00
Late Check-In Fee (missed Check-In Day without prior approval)		$50.00
Returned Check Fee		$25.00
Student ID Card Replacement/Mailbox Key Replacement		$10.00
Athletic Participation Fee – Annual		$100.00
Transcript Fee		$7.25
Electronic Transcript Fee		$9.00

Special Instructional Fees (in addition to tuition)		
American Ecosystems (ES 305)	Per Course	$1,700.00
Applied Music Lesson Fee	Per Credit	$285.00
Applied Music Group Lesson Fee	Per Credit	$100.00
Art Materials: Drawing/Sculpture (AR 241/341/344)	Per Course	$30.00
Art Materials: Painting (AR 342)	Per Course	$100.00
Beginning Class: Piano (MS 103)	Per Course	$75.00
Biology Lab (BL 101L, 102L, BL 103L, BL 104L)	Per Course	$15.00
Certification Study and Preparation—Course/Testing Fee (CS 380)	Per Course	$ 250.00
CCCU Program – off campus (Various)	Per Course	Variable
Challenge Course Facilitation (OE 210)	Per Course	$150.00
Computer Competency Exam (CS 102E)	Per Course	$100.00
Computer Lab Equipment Fee (CS 207)	Per Course	$250.00

Special Instructional Fees (continued)		
Contemporary Youth Culture and Programming (YM 407)	Per Course	$400.00
Digital Sound Recording & Audio Production Techniques (MS 131/322)	Per Course	$75.00
Discovery (OE 180)	Per Course	$1,250.00
Downhill Skiing (PE 270)	Per Course	$ 300.00
Ensemble Fee (MS 151, 153, 154, 157, 251, 257, 357)	Per Course	$65.00
Environmental Policy and Law (OE 305)	Per Course	$150.00
Exercise Testing & Measurements Equipment (EX 320)	Per Course	$50.00
Field Studies, Cherokee (ES 460)	Per Course	$150.00
Field Studies, Grandfather Mountain (ES 460)	Per Course	$25.00
Field Studies, Smokies (ES 460)	Per Course	$300.00
Field Studies, Wetland Ecosystems (ES 460)	Per Course	$350.00
Gaither 22 Lab Fee	Per Course	$35.00
High Challenge Course Activities Level I and II (OE 480)	Per Course	$364.00
Internship/Practicum/CBA/DS (spring or fall semester)	Per Credit	$50.00
Introduction to Pedagogy (YM 408)	Per Course	$75.00
Low Ropes, Group Initiatives and High Events Level I & II	Per Course	$555.00
Low Ropes, Group Initiatives and Spotted Events Level I & II	Per Course	$364.00
Midi and Sound Synthesis (MS 301)	Per Course	$75.00
Music Arranging Class (MS 319)	Per Course	$75.00
Music Business Junior Nashville Trip	Per Event	$200.00
Music Business Senior Immersion	Per Event	$500.00
Music Studio Recording (MS 221 at Echo Mountain)	Per Course	$300.00
Music Worship Symposium	Per Event	$ 250.00
Outdoor Programming and Leadership Expedition Management Equipment Fee (OE 312)	Per Course	$450.00
Special Interest Courses	Per Course	Variable
Spiritual Formation and Faith Development (YM 401)	Per Course	$75.00
Student Teaching Placement (ED 450)	Per Course	$100.00
Survey of Outdoor Education (OE 103)	Per Course	$50.00

NOTE: Montreat College reserves the right to modify any of these charges at any time.

Full-time, degree-seeking students who are registered for 18 credit hours or more in a semester who still need or want to take music ensemble and applied music courses will be allowed to waive overload fees for these applied music courses. They will still be responsible for paying the applicable course fees for the ensemble and applied music courses.

Payment of Tuition, Fees, Room and Board

Tuition and fees are due after classes have been reserved with the Office of Records and Registration and before the official Check-In date as published in the Academic Calendar. If payment arrangements are not made before the official Check-In date, a late payment penalty of $50.00 will be assessed, and **the student may be subject to delays during the check-in process**. If payment arrangements are not made by the end of the first week of the semester, the penalty will be $100.00. If payment arrangements are not fulfilled, the late penalty will be charged. Bills are mailed to registered students in July and December. "Express" status is given to those who have submitted the required paperwork and made payment arrangements by the payment due date for the semester as listed in the Academic Calendar. "Express" status students will not have to visit the Student Accounts Office during Check-In. **All students are required to attend the official Check-In before the start of each semester**. Students who do not attend Check-In will have their academic schedules dropped. A $50.00 fee will be charged to those who check in late without securing prior approval from the Check-in Committee.

For the convenience of students and their families, an annual payment plan (payable in monthly installments from May through April during the Academic Year) or a semester payment plan (payable in four monthly installments during the semester) is available through College Foundation Installment Payment Plan (CFI). CFI may be reached by phone at (866)-866-CFNC or online at www.CFNC.org. A payment plan is an arrangement made directly between the student and CFI, so in cases where a payment plan arranged is not enough to cover the actual balance due**, the student is responsible to pay the remaining balance directly to Montreat College**. If a payment plan is in default for non-payment, the College will require immediate payment for the balance due. In such cases, payment will be required in full prior to the start of classes and payment plans will not be approved for subsequent semesters.

At the time a student formally registers for classes, either by signing and submitting the appropriate registration forms to the Office of Records and Registration or by registering online through the website, when available, the student agrees to abide by the College's official policies concerning the adding and dropping of classes, or the complete withdrawal from Montreat College. Charges or fees will not be refunded if students withdraw after the add/drop deadline. Students should view their accounts online using Self-Service; link and instructions are available at www.montreat.edu/student-accounts. The student also agrees to assume responsibility for understanding the College's official policy that schedule changes or unsatisfactory academic progress may result in additional charges or the loss of eligibility for certain types of financial aid. Responsibility to understand how these changes can affect his/her financial situation with regard to financial aid eligibility belongs to the student.

If an account must be sent to a collection agency or be litigated due to nonpayment of the outstanding balance, the College reserves the right to demand payment in full for subsequent terms of enrollment, prior to the beginning of each term to ensure enrollment. The College reserves the right to cancel the registration of any student if a balance due from a previous term remains unpaid at the start of a subsequent term.

Student receivable accounts are considered to be educational loans provided for the sole purpose of financing an education at Montreat College, a non-profit institution of higher learning. As such, student receivable accounts are not dischargeable under the provisions of the laws governing either Chapter 7 or Chapter 13 bankruptcy actions.

The College reserves the right to demand payment in the forms of a certified check, money order, cash, or credit cards in the event that one or more checks have been returned unpaid for any reason. Students who have unpaid accounts or other outstanding obligations at the College will not be eligible to reserve classes or return for the next semester. Transcripts, certificates, and diplomas are not issued unless all charges have been paid in full. The College reserves the right to recover all costs involved with the collection and/or litigation of delinquent accounts, as well as levy an interest charge equal to one and one half percent (1.5%) per month, on any account with a balance beyond thirty days past due. Student accounts are assessed fines as incurred for overdue library books, damaged property, parking violations, etc.

The payment of all tuition and fees becomes an obligation upon registration at Montreat College. The Federal Truth-in-Lending Act requires complete disclosure of the terms and conditions controlling payment of the student's obligations. In order to comply with those federal statutes and regulations, the College discloses billing policies in the Academic Catalog and publishes the "Payment and Initial Disclosure Agreement". The Disclosure form is sent to each new student, and is available in the Student Accounts Office or online at www.montreat.edu/student-accounts on the "Forms" page.

Refund/Repayment Policy

Since the College makes arrangements for faculty, staff, services, and supplies based upon enrollment figures at the beginning of each semester, **fees are nonrefundable once classes begin.** If the student withdraws from the College, then the General Institutional Refund Policy below will apply.

A student is considered enrolled for attendance purposes until the last day of attendance or the end of the semester, whichever is first. To withdraw from courses, the student should follow the formal withdrawal process outlined in this catalog. Official withdrawal forms are available in the Office of Records and Registration.

A refund refers to money paid toward college charges that must be returned to financial aid sources and/or the student. A repayment is the amount of cash disbursed to the student that must be repaid to federal, state, or institutional sources.

Requests for refunds are to be directed to the Student Accounts Office. The amount of refund will depend upon whether the student has received Federal Title IV and/or state financial assistance.

Special Interest Courses

All payment arrangements and refund policies for special interest courses are governed by the contract agreement that each individual special interest course maintains. Students should contact the course leader for contract agreement details. In most cases these fees are not refundable.

General Institutional Withdrawal Policy

Normally, if a student withdraws or is administratively withdrawn from the College during the semester, the amount of charges retained by the College depends upon the period of time the student has been enrolled.

IF THE STUDENT WITHDRAWS:	THE COLLEGE RETAINS:
Before the first day of class	0% of total tuition, room and board
Before the end of the first week of class	10% of total tuition, room and board
Before the end of the third week of class	50% of total tuition, room and board
Before the end of the fifth week of class	75% of total tuition, room and board
After the fifth week of class	100% of total tuition, room and board

An administrative fee of $100 will be deducted from any refund of tuition, room, and board. Fees are non-refundable.

Return of Title IV Student Aid

In the event a student withdraws or is administratively withdrawn from the College, the Financial Aid Office is required to process a withdrawal calculation. Such a calculation is based upon the student's last date of documented class attendance. All awards that include Federal Title IV aid will be subject to the Federal Return of Title IV Funds calculation. All State funds will be subject to State requirements to determine award eligibility. All other nonfederal funds are subject to the Montreat College withdrawal calculation. Montreat College has a fair and equitable refund policy, as required under Section 668.22(b)(1) of the federal regulations.

The Federal Return of Title IV Funds calculation determines the percentage of the period of enrollment for which the assistance was awarded. This figure is used to determine the percentage of aid the student earned for the period of enrollment, based on the number of days actually completed. All unearned funds are returned to the proper agencies in the order prescribed by federal and state laws: Unsubsidized Direct Loan; Subsidized Direct Loan, Federal PLUS Loan; Federal Perkins Loan; Federal Pell Grant; Federal Supplemental Educational Opportunity Grant; other state, private, or institutional aid; the student.

Students must pay any charges remaining on their account after funds are returned to the proper agencies.

Appeal Process

A student may request an exception to the normal College withdrawal policy by directing a written appeal to the Vice President of Finance and Administration.

Credit Balances

Students may receive a distribution of a credit balance from their account during the semester, though not prior to the conclusion of the first two weeks of the semester or the **actual receipt of funds**. To receive a check for the credit balance, all requests must be made by submitting a Credit Balance Request form to the Student Accounts Office (SAO). Credit Balance Request forms are available in the Student Accounts Office and online at www.montreat.edu/studentaccounts on the "Forms" page.

Refund requests received in the Student Accounts Office by 4 p.m. Wednesday result in a refund check issued on Friday of the **following** week; or in the case of a delay in the Finance Office, the next available check run. If a student graduates or separates from Montreat College, any remaining credit balance will be refunded by a check mailed to the student's address on file. If a student's current mailing address is different from the address on file, the student must submit a Student Information Change Form to the Office of Records and Registration before the check can be mailed.

If financial aid changes are made or additional charges are added to the account following the issuance of a refund, the student will be responsible for any additional amount due to Montreat College.

Student Life Information

For information or questions concerning student life, please contact the Office of Student Services:

Assistant Dean for Student Life
Montreat College (MC 898)
P.O. Box 1267
Montreat, NC 28757
828-669-8012 ext. 3631
studentlife@montreat.edu

For complete policies and details regarding student life, consult the Student Handbook: http://www.montreat.edu/student-life/student-handbook/

Student Life

Student life outside the classroom is one of the most significant aspects of a full college life. Students grow and develop in their social and spiritual lives just as in the academic area, learning to talk openly, choosing life values, having fun, and discerning those activities that contribute to true joy. Student life is an important area, influencing education with a Christ-centered perspective at Montreat College. The Dean of Students and Student Services staff plan and encourage a wide range of programs to meet the needs and interests of each student, and to fulfill the goals and purpose of the College.

A Christian Community

Montreat College seeks, by the grace of God and the power of the Holy Spirit, to intentionally grow disciples who know Christ and make Him known. Convinced as we are that Christian community is central to this call, we encourage students to regularly involve themselves in small groups that meet for the purposes of friendship, mutual support and encouragement, Bible study, and prayer. In addition, we also seek to challenge students to join their faith with action by serving others with the tangible love of Jesus Christ. Each semester opportunities are provided to minister at a number of locations, including the Black Mountain Home for Children, Manna Food Bank, the Asheville Boys and Girls Club, and area high schools through Young Life. At least once a year, we strive to make an impact in our community through service projects on our campus-wide Community Day.

Worship is crucial to our community development. Every Wednesday at 10 a.m., the Montreat College community gathers in Chapel to worship the living God. Opportunities are also available throughout the week to worship in the evenings through a number of student-led worship services. The College also has two major Christian emphasis weeks called SALT (Servant and Leadership Training) and Crossroads (exploring the intersection of faith and culture).

Montreat College seeks not to be just a collection of students pursuing a degree but a group of disciples who know Jesus Christ and make Him known, not only on this campus, but also in the community and throughout the world.

Expectations and Requirements

It is the desire of the College to create a Christian atmosphere in which all phases of college life will be conducive to the continuous Christian growth of the individual. Bible courses form an essential part of the curriculum. In addition, regular attendance at Chapel is required and local church attendance is encouraged.

The Honor System

Life at Montreat College is based on the belief that the ideal community is made up of honorable individuals. Mutual trust and consideration are essential to such a community, and it is for these that we strive.

Each student and faculty member has a responsibility for himself/herself and for every other member of the College community. The failure of one person to live honorably is in part the failure of all. The movement of one individual toward complete understanding of Christian living is a step toward honorable living for the whole College.

For this reason, the students of Montreat College have accepted the honor system whereby each student agrees to try to discipline his/her own life and to be ready to help others to discipline their lives toward the goal of a community in which each member will merit trust and respect. It is in large part due to the acceptance by faculty and students of the honor system as a way of life, that the spirit of Montreat College is a reality, not only on the campus but also wherever former Montreat students are found.

Standards of Conduct

The trustees, administration, staff, faculty, and students seek to be motivated by Christ's love for us, and we desire to reflect that love for one another; therefore, we are called upon to practice consideration, fair play, and concern in our daily interaction with each other as an expression of our commitment to be a community under the lordship of Jesus Christ. Kindness and consideration demand the deliberate consciousness of other people's feelings and an effort neither to hurt nor offend other members of the community.

Such high aspirations require an understanding of what Christian standards are both in and out of the classroom, and they can be reached only when each one in the Montreat College community makes an honest effort to incorporate them into the pattern of daily living.

An obligation for patience and for the effort toward redemption is inherent in a Christian community. At the same time, the College reserves the authority to ask those members to withdraw who do not accept its delineation of Christian standards, and who are unable to learn to live happily in the framework of its ideals. The College reserves the right to provide information to dependent students' parents or guardians. This information is limited to issues related to student safety and disciplinary or academic decisions that would jeopardize the student's ability to remain enrolled. Expectations for student conduct can be found in the Student Handbook.

Student Participation in Institutional Decision-Making

Students participate in institutional decision-making and policy development through direct access to the President's Cabinet through the Student Government Association.

Chapel/Convocation Attendance Policy

The weekly Chapel services at the College are intended to be a focus of worship for the whole community. They also serve to bring to the College distinguished speakers and groups who address the significance of Christian faith and activity in the world today. Convocation, a time for college community activities, is used for cultural and educational purposes intended to broaden the horizons and enrich the experience of the student body.

All full-time students that have completed fewer than 90 academic credit hours are required to attend a specified number of chapels, convocations, and special gatherings. No student may graduate without meeting the Chapel/Convocation attendance requirement. Specific requirements are distributed at the beginning of each semester. Completion of the Chapel/Convocation attendance requirement is necessary for academic recognition such as the Dean's List and the Distinguished Scholars' List.

All requests for an exemption from the Chapel/Convocation requirement must be made in writing to the Dean of Students prior to registration or no later than one week following the beginning of classes each semester.

Social Opportunities

College social opportunities are extensive. Because the campus is small, students see each other often and there is varied social contact. All persons on campus become known as individuals. Classes and organizations sponsor concerts, banquets, dances, talent shows, plays, hikes, picnics, movies, and intramural competition. There are two semiformal dances each year—Winter Ball and Spring Formal.

Tobacco Use at Montreat College

Smoke and Tobacco Free Campus Policy

Montreat College is committed to providing students, employees, and guests with a safe and healthy environment. Therefore, the College is a smoke and tobacco-free campus.

For purposes of this policy, "smoking" includes, but is not limited to, the burning (or simulating the burning), lighting, or openly carrying of any type of tobacco, tobacco-derived, or vapor products including, but not limited to, traditional and electronic cigarettes, cigars, cigarillos, and pipes, as well as the use of chewing tobacco and snuff.

It is the policy of Montreat College that smoking is not permitted anywhere on College property, whether owned or leased by the College. For purposes of this policy, College property includes any property owned by the College, leased by or in possession and control of the College, and any property owned by the College and leased to other entities for short- or long-term use. It also includes the Montreat Presbyterian Church (EPC) building and property.

Information on smoking cessation classes and educational efforts in the community is available to students and employees of the College. A resource area is located in the Health Center on the lower level of Bell Library.

Enforcing compliance of the Smoke and Tobacco-Free Policy is the responsibility of the campus community at large. College administrators, faculty and staff are asked to remind everyone of the Smoke and Tobacco-Free Policy and report violations to the Dean of Students. Campus police officers will also report policy violations.

The first time a student is observed smoking in violation of this Policy, a written warning of violation of the Smoke and Tobacco-Free Policy will be issued.

The second time a student is observed smoking in violation of this Policy, a $25 fine will be assessed and 10 hours of community service will be assigned.

A third violation will result in a $50 fine, 20 hours of community service and referral to the Dean of Students for consideration of further disciplinary action.

Visitors will be advised of this policy by way of campus signage and announcements prior to all community events such as summer conferences, athletic events, and concerts. Guests who fail to comply will be reminded of the College Smoke and Tobacco-Free Policy with a request that they comply in the future.

Policy violations by employees will be handled through the regular supervisory disciplinary process.

Additional Town of Montreat Restrictions

1. Smoking shall be prohibited in all enclosed public places within the town of Montreat.

2. The disposal and discarding of smoking materials (including but not limited to: cigars, cigarettes, pipes, pipe tobacco, matches, lighters, lighter fluid, containers, wrappers and packaging associated therewith) is prohibited in public areas, undeveloped areas, paths, trails, sidewalks, roads, streets and any trash/garbage receptacles which are located in these areas.

3. Penalties: A fine not to exceed $100 for a first offense, $200 for a second violation within one year, $500 for additional violations within one year. To be enforced by the Town of Montreat.

Residence Life Requirement

The College is committed to developing and providing a strong residential community of servant-leaders, which includes one upper-class women's residence hall (McGregor Hall), one other women's residence hall (Anderson Hall), one women's apartment building (Webbwood Apartments), and two men's residence halls (Howerton Hall and Davis Hall). These residence halls provide a warm, friendly "home away from home" for students. The focus of Residence Life is developing relationships and sharing the love of Christ in a community centered on grace and truth.

Each residence hall is staffed with a professional residence director and student resident assistants who are committed to serving each student as a whole person and who believe that each individual has infinite value to God. As the residence life staff serves the students, the desire is that the residents in turn, will seek to serve others and, by following the example of Christ, will become servant-leaders to each other.

Students are required to live in College-owned or College-controlled housing unless they are at least twenty-one years old, have senior status with good academic standing, are married, have a dependent child, or are living with parents or a legal guardian. Part-time and special students are not included in this requirement. Complete residence life information is published in the Student Handbook.

Student Organizations and Services

Alpha Chi, one of the three most prestigious national honor societies, maintains the North Carolina Tau Chapter at Montreat College. Active membership is based on (1) good reputation and character; (2) rank in the top ten percent of the junior and senior classes; (3) regular student status at Montreat College for no less than one academic year prior to election; (4) approval by the faculty.

The Student Government Association (SGA) is designed to be a mediator between students and the College administration. The SGA serves the students by expressing the overall needs and concerns of the student body. It also serves the administration by informing the student body of matters pertaining to the College.

Student Clubs provide additional ways for Montreat College students to build community, develop leadership, and get involved. All clubs are maintained through SGA (Student Government Association) and must meet the requirements set by SGA in order to become recognized. Every club is required to have a representative that will meet with SGA at least once a semester. Any student interested in starting a club on campus should contact SGA.

Student Publications include a student newspaper (*Whetstone*) and a literary magazine (*Q*). These student-directed publications provide opportunity for students to increase their skills in writing and to voice their concerns for local and world issues.

Student Activities Leadership Team seeks to mobilize student leaders to help shape the campus culture through diverse out-of-the-classroom experiences and by holistically challenging each student to reach full potential in understanding self and giftedness, Biblical stewardship, and living within community. Participation in Student Activities is open to all interested students. Students who are interested in serving in a leadership role should contact the Director of Student Engagement.

Team and Leadership Center (TLC) exists to help groups develop leaders and build stronger community within their context through experience-based learning. The TLC is housed on Montreat College's Black Mountain campus and includes a high team's course, climbing tower, low initiatives course, and meeting pavilion. The TLC serves a variety of groups from churches and schools to international corporations. Students are encouraged to take advantage of leadership opportunities as a part of coursework, campus work positions, internships, and volunteer positions. For more information, email jrogers@montreat.edu. The TLC is an outreach program of the Outdoor Education Department.

Men's and Women's Intramurals are built around a strong intramural program based on participation in various team and individual sports. Intramural sports include flag football, soccer, basketball, volleyball, dodge ball, ultimate Frisbee, pool, Ping-Pong, and other sports depending on student interest.

Montreat College Student Ministry Council (SMC) provides leadership and oversight for ministries connected to Montreat College. Members of the SMC report directly to the Chaplain on a bi-monthly basis for the purpose of coordination, accountability, prayer, and ongoing spiritual support and guidance.

SEEDS is a student led environmental club, believing that Montreat College has a bold responsibility to uphold the biblical mandate to care for God's creation, and work towards a more environmentally sustainable and socially responsible campus. The primary mission of SEEDS is to provide a student voice to assist in these efforts, directly contributing to the fulfillment of the College's greater mission. SEEDS members work toward sustaining the Garden of Eatin' (Black Mountain Campus), reducing the College's energy use and waste, and educating students and administration about current environmental concerns affecting our local, regional, and global communities.

Other Student Opportunities

Sufficient student interest can bring about the formation of other activities such as language clubs, exercise classes, and musical instruction groups.
Montreat College is continually seeking ways to improve and expand its equipment, facilities, and personnel in the area of campus activities. The Director of Student Engagement coordinates the out-of-class activities and co-curricular program.

Supplementing local campus activities, visiting professors, lecturers, and performing artists come to the campus throughout the year. The city of Asheville affords the College community additional cultural and recreational opportunities, such as the Community Concert Series and the Asheville Community Theatre.

Intercollegiate Athletics

Montreat College believes that intercollegiate athletics plays an important role in the overall educational experience of its students. A strong athletic program helps build and sustain a sense of pride, school spirit, excitement, and positive public relations for the College. At the same time, athletes are provided the opportunity to participate at a high level of competition while building important life skills.

All students participating in intercollegiate athletics are expected to maintain satisfactory standards of academic performance. Members of the coaching staff will monitor academic performance and may communicate directly with professors when necessary. Membership on a collegiate athletic team is a privilege afforded to a few and with that privilege comes responsibility. The College sees character development as the most important outcome of intercollegiate athletic participation. Therefore, athletes are held to a high standard of behavior on and off the field of play. The coaching staff adheres to this same high standard. This is reflected in the way in which Montreat College teams approach every competition on the field and in the classroom: being well prepared, playing hard, and playing fair. Athletes and their coaches are expected to model the core values of the National Association of Intercollegiate Athletics' (NAIA) Champions of Character Program, which are respect, responsibility, integrity, sportsmanship, and servant-leadership. They also serve as willing role models to young people in the community. This is reflected by their involvement in ministry and service to the local and extended community and in overseas mission opportunities.

Montreat College is a member of the NAIA and is classified for basketball as Division II. The College competes in the Appalachian Athletic Conference (AAC) composed of 11 colleges in North Carolina, South Carolina, Tennessee, Virginia, Georgia, and Kentucky. Members of the AAC are Bryan College, Columbia College, Milligan College, Montreat College, Point University, Reinhardt University, SCAD Atlanta, St. Andrews University, Tennessee Wesleyan College, Truett-McConnell College, and Union College.

The College offers 17 intercollegiate sports:

Men: baseball, basketball, cross-country, golf, lacrosse, soccer, tennis, and track and field.

Women: basketball, cross-country, golf, lacrosse, soccer, softball, tennis, track and field, and volleyball.

Eligibility

Students are eligible to participate in intercollegiate athletics if they meet NAIA requirements including the following:

- An entering freshman should be a graduate of an accredited high school or be accepted as a regular student in good standing as defined by the College. The GED will be recognized as satisfying the grade point average for home-schooled students. A student graduating from a high school outside of the United States, where the grade point average cannot be determined and the class rank is not available, may be ruled eligible by meeting the College's admission criteria for international students and specific NAIA requirements.
- An entering freshman student must meet two of the three entry-level requirements:
  - A minimum score of 18 on the Enhanced ACT or 860 on the SAT.
  - An overall high school grade point average of 2.0 or higher on a 4.0 scale.
  - Graduate in the upper half of the student's high school graduating class.
- Students considering transferring to Montreat College from a two- or four-year institution who desire to participate in intercollegiate athletics must notify the appropriate coach of their status upon initial contact. The Director of Athletics will request permission of the transferring institution before further contact may occur between the student and coach.
- In order to be eligible for intercollegiate athletics, transfer students must meet all NAIA and AAC requirements with regard to institutional credit hours completed for the number of terms in attendance. Transfer students who were previously identified with an institution within the AAC must meet residency requirements of the conference before becoming eligible for competition.

All entering students are responsible for creating an account at www.playnaia.org. The NAIA will determine a student's initial eligibility for each sport of play through this online account. Students will not be able to participate in any form of collegiate athletics without first being determined eligible through his or her PlayNAIA account as well as being certified by the College.

Guiding Principles

The following vision and mission statements guide the Athletic Department, teacher/coaches, and student/athletes:

Mission Statement

Proclaiming Christ through athletics by passionately:
- Building Community
- Developing Champions of Character
- Pursuing Academic and Athletic Excellence

Vision Statement

Montreat College seeks to become a leading Christ-centered athletic program distinguished by championship teams, strong academic performance and character development, and committed to knowing Christ and making Him known.

Athletic Scholarships

Athletic grant-in-aid (AGIA) scholarships may be awarded for students participating in intercollegiate athletics. A total institutional aid budget is approved yearly by the President's Cabinet and is then assigned to the Director of Athletics, who apportions out an AGIA budget to each Head Coach. AGIA becomes a part of the total financial aid package awarded to each student. The Director of Athletics is responsible to the President for ensuring compliance with current NAIA limits for each sport. Prospective students interested in athletic scholarships should complete an athletic questionnaire and return it to the respective head coach.

Calling and Career Services

The Office of Calling and Career provides vocational and career services including resume and cover letter development, interview preparation, and job and graduate school search planning. All students are encouraged to engage in the process of discovering how God has gifted them and to use their gifts in God-honoring ways. Ephesians 2:10 says, "For we are God's workmanship, created in Christ Jesus to do good works, which God prepared in advance for us to do."

Work Study Program

Students who are eligible for Montreat College and federal work study programs will be contacted by the Office of Financial Aid with information about the application process. These positions typically allow for 125 hours of work per semester at $7.25 per hour.

Counseling Services

College can be a time of great personal growth and change; the Counseling Center at Montreat College provides support for a wide range of issues that may arise for students during this time. Services offered by the Counseling Center include: individual and couples counseling, consultation, referral to community resources, crisis intervention, and educational outreach programs. The College Chaplain, residence directors, Dean of Students, and Student Success Team are also available for personal guidance.

For information specifically about sexual harassment and assault issues, including prevention & response protocols, please consult www.montreat.edu/safecommunity.

Director of Counseling
Office: (828) 669-8012 ext. 3538
counselor@montreat.edu
www.montreat.edu/counseling

Disability Services

The College will provide reasonable accommodations for known disabilities whether visual, hearing, mobility, medical, learning, or for other qualified applicants and students. Eligible students should follow these steps:

- Identify himself/herself to the Student Success Team, specifically the Disability Services Coordinator, (828) 669-8012 x 3538, www.montreat.edu/disability.
- Submit to the Student Success Team current documentation (not older than three years) of his/her disability.
- Be willing to participate in additional evaluation to confirm the disability, if requested.
- Provide clear recommendations for accommodations from a professional care provider.
- Request in writing the specific accommodations needed to enable his/her academic access.

The Student Success Team, in conjunction with other appropriate personnel, will assess a student's documentation and determine the reasonableness of the requested accommodations. The Student Success Team serves as a liaison between students and faculty/staff, working individually with students to develop and implement a plan for academic accessibility. As part of such a plan, the Student Success Team may direct students to the Counseling Center, Health Services, Office of Career and Calling, Writing Center, and/or academic department tutoring. The Student Success Team will communicate with the appropriate faculty and staff regarding the specified accommodations and will work with the student and his/her instructors to ensure that the plans for academic support and success are implemented.

Student Health Services

Students are required to submit immunizations to the College prior to class registration in accordance with North Carolina state law. G.S. 130-A-155 On campus, Student Health Services are located in the lower level of Bell Library. The walk-in illness and injury clinic is staffed by a registered nurse, and emergency medical services are available through urgent care clinics in Asheville and Mission Hospital's emergency room. Students can also be seen in local Black Mountain health clinics. Any transportation needs for medical care can be arranged through residence life staff. See our website for specific service providers: http://www.montreat.edu/student-life/student-services/health-wellness/.

Medical Forms and Concerns

New students are required to complete several medical forms related to medical history and current medical health. Some of these forms are mandated by North Carolina law and others are needed for certain courses and student activities. These forms are initially collected by Admissions at the time of acceptance to the College. Student athletes and students participating in certain courses (such as those facilitated by the Outdoor Education/Ministry Department and Physical Education Program) may be required to submit yearly medical updates. Faculty/instructors will also ask students to advise them about any significant medical conditions or limitations on the students' abilities to participate in courses requiring physical exertion. However, **it is each student's responsibility to inform staff/faculty of any significant medical history or restrictions** since not all staff/faculty have access to student medical information.

Non-Academic Student Grievances

Students are encouraged to submit any complaints or general grievances to Student Government with a copy to the appropriate college department head or administrator. Student Government will designate a member to follow up on the complaint and report back to the student and SGA.

1. A student wishing to appeal a decision by the College, which directly affects the student, should first appeal to the faculty member, student group or administrator making the decision.
2. In a case involving disrespectful treatment, sexual harassment, threatened harm or retaliation by any employee of the College, a formal complaint should be made with the Dean of Students. If the Dean of Students is involved in the complaint, the Dean of Academics will conduct the investigation. The Dean of Students or Dean of Academics will make every effort to investigate the complaint within seven days. The Dean of Students or Dean of Academics may involve other appropriate individuals (counselor, nurse, residence director, administrator, faculty member or staff person) in the investigation, as needed, to offer assistance or to be assigned as an advocate for the student bringing the complaint. Strong consideration will be given to protect the student's identity and to keep the matter as confidential as possible. Final action will be determined by the employee's direct supervisor in consultation with the Dean of Students or Dean of Academics.
3. If not satisfied, the student may appeal in writing within two weeks to the chair (Vice President and Dean of Students) of a general student grievance committee.
4. A written response will be returned within seven days.
5. Final appeal may be made directly to the President of the College in writing within seven days of an action by the committee chaired by the Vice President

for Student Services and Dean of Students. A written response will be returned within two weeks of the appeal.
6. Students seeking redress of their grievances are protected against any retaliation by staff, students or faculty as a result of appeal.
7. The committee includes the appointed chair, the Vice President and Dean of Students, Vice President for Academics, and the chair of the Student Judicial Appeals Court (if not functioning, an appointed member of Student Government).

NOTE: The appeals and due process procedures for disciplinary cases are contained in the Student Government Association Constitution and are printed in the Student Handbook. The Student Services Office should be contacted for assistance.

Campus Store

The Montreat College Campus Store is located in the Belk Campus Center and provides for the purchase of textbooks, supplies, clothing, gift items, and snacks.

Laundry Service

Residential students are required to bring their own linens. Self-service laundry facilities are available in all residence halls at no charge.

Cable Television Service

Free extended basic cable service is available in all campus residence hall rooms. Residents are expected to provide their own cable-ready televisions. Premium services are not available.

Internet Service

Wireless internet access is available in all residence hall rooms and throughout campus.

Outdoor Gear Rental

The Outdoor Education Department offers gear rental to faculty, staff, and students at a nominal fee. Available gear includes backpacks, sleeping bags, tarps, and more! Students who complete boating courses may qualify to rent kayaks or canoes.

Academic Information and Policies

Information contained in this section of the catalog is provided to help students understand Montreat College's School of Arts and Sciences academic policies and procedures. Students should address all questions regarding these academic policies to:

Vice President for Academic Affairs & Dean of the College
Montreat College (MC 850)
P.O. Box 1267
Montreat, North Carolina 28757
828-669-8012 ext. 3621

Only the Vice President for Academic Affairs & Dean of the College may make any exception to the College's academic policies. An exception petition form can be found in the Office of Records and Registration.

Advising and Class Registration

During Advising Week, each student will confer with his or her advisor regarding registration for the following semester. Students are allowed to register for classes online via the course management system during the designated registration periods (see Academic Calendar). Faculty Advisors will then approve or decline the course selections of their advisees. Students will be eligible to register after outstanding obligations to the College have been met. Credit will be awarded only for courses in which a student is officially enrolled.

Eligibility by course ID level: Courses numbered 100 and 200 are open to all students; 300-level are open to sophomores, juniors, and seniors; 400-level are open to juniors and seniors.

Change of schedule: It is the student's responsibility to officially process all course changes in the Office of Records and Registration before the deadline as listed on the Academic Calendar. Appropriate signatures must accompany the schedule change form.

Adding a course: Students may add courses no later than the first week of the semester.

Dropping a course: Students who wish to withdraw from a course, without a notation on their permanent record, may do so during the first week of the semester. After the first week, but before the last day to withdraw without a failing grade, a student may withdraw from a course with a *W* recorded on the transcript. Upon withdrawal after this date, a grade of *WF* will be recorded. If a course grade of *F* has already been incurred, a student may not withdraw from that course.

NOTE: If students attend a course or section for which they are not officially registered, they will not receive credit for the work. If they do not attend a course or section for which they are officially registered and do not officially drop the course through the Office of Records and Registration, they will receive a failing grade for that course.

Medical/Military Withdrawals: If students need to withdraw from one or more courses due to extenuating circumstances after the last date to withdraw with a *W*, a *W* may still be granted. Such circumstances are limited to extreme medical conditions, military duty, or immediate family death/major illness. If this is the case, students should contact the Office of Records and Registration for the appropriate paperwork. They must also submit documentation to verify the reason for the withdrawal. These documents will be sent to the Director of Records and Registration for a final determination.

Repeating courses: A student may repeat a course in which a grade of less than *C* was received by: (1) re-taking the same course at Montreat College or (2) re-taking the course at an appropriate accredited institution. **It is the student's responsibility to notify the Office of Records and Registration of courses to be repeated at another institution and to receive prior approval of the course to be repeated.** Students seeking approval should complete the Pre-Approval of Transfer Credit Request Form and indicate the courses to be repeated. Courses that are repeated at Montreat College for a higher grade will have the better of the two grades included in the academic GPA calculation. Courses that are authorized for repeat at another institution must be successfully completed with a grade of *C* or better. The transferred course will apply as credit only, and will not replace the previous grade in GPA calculations. *Financial aid may not be awarded for courses that are repeated.*

Auditing courses: A student who wishes to take a course for no credit (audit) may do so by receiving approval from the instructor of the course. A specific registration form must be signed by the instructor and student and returned to the Office of Records and Registration for processing. Instructors may set their own requirements for course participants.

Transferring courses: A student who wishes to enroll in courses offered by another institution must complete the required form and receive approval by the Office of Records and Registration. Failure to follow this procedure may result in loss of transfer credit for these courses.

Double counting courses: Students may double count courses between: (1) a major and a minor; (2) a minor and general education requirements; (3) a minor and the 12 specified BA/BS credits; (4) two separate majors. Students may not double count courses between a major and general education requirements. Exceptions to this policy are noted in specific major requirements.

Minimum and Maximum Loads: An average academic load is 16 credit hours per semester. All residential students are required to enroll in a minimum of 12 semester credit hours each term to be considered a full-time student. Students may enroll in up to 18 semester hours. Students who have at least a 3.0 GPA are approved to take one additional course over the 18 credit hour limit. Any other requests to overload must be approved by the Director of the Office of Records and Registration.

Final Examinations: A student absent without excuse from a final examination may receive a failing grade in the course. Excuses from final exams are extremely rare and are granted at the discretion of the Vice President for Academic Affairs & Dean of the College and only in the case of illness or death in the immediate family. **Exams will not be given early in order to meet the travel plans of students. Students are to arrange all transportation well in advance in order to avoid conflict with the exam schedule.**

Definition of the Credit Hour: A credit hour is an amount of work represented in intended learning outcomes and verified by evidence of student achievement that is an institutionally established equivalency that reasonably approximates:

1. Not less than one hour of classroom or direct faculty instruction and a minimum of two hours out of class student work each week for approximately fifteen weeks for one semester or trimester hour of credit, or ten to twelve weeks for one quarter hour of credit, or the equivalent amount of work over a different amount of time, or

2. At least an equivalent amount of work as required outlined in item 1 above for other academic activities as established by the institution including laboratory work, internships, practica, field experiences, studio work, and other academic work leading to the award of credit hours.

Academic Advising

Upon enrollment, students will be assigned a faculty advisor to assist them in clarifying their education objectives, planning programs, utilizing resources, and meeting requirements for graduation. First-time freshmen will be advised by the professor of their IS 102 Foundations of Faith and Learning course. Transfer students will be assigned a faculty advisor in their anticipated major field. When students officially declare a major, they are assigned to an advisor in their major field.

Students and faculty advisors work together with the Office of Records and Registration in arranging an orderly program of study leading toward graduation. The Office of Records and Registration maintains a student's academic program audit, as the close monitoring of students' progress is an important goal of Montreat College. **However, it remains the student's responsibility to become familiar with and to fulfill all degree requirements.**

Camaraderie of Writers

Course descriptions with the Camaraderie of Writers logo are part of the Camaraderie of Writers Program, which uses classroom-based peer tutors to help students improve drafting, writing, and reasoning skills. Writing Center-based scholars are also part of the Camaraderie and are available to assist students in all Montreat College courses.

Course By Arrangement (CBA)

On occasion, students may need a course that is required in their program but is not offered in a given semester or year (for example, a course may not be offered in the semester or year when it is essential for graduation or remediation). While students are expected to plan their programs carefully, there may be times when a required course will need to be taken outside of the normal classroom setting. A course by arrangement is taken with the consent, regular guidance, and periodic evaluation of the instructor. Enrollment in a course by arrangement requires the approval of the instructor, department chair, and the Vice President for Academic Affairs and Dean of the College. CBA registration forms are available in the Office of Records and Registration and through the Montreat College website.

Directed Study and Research

Some academic programs at Montreat College offer qualified students the opportunity to do individualized research and study. A directed study is a customized program of study in a student's major or minor in which the student takes intensive work in an approved subject. Designed in collaboration with a faculty member, the directed study is intended either to be an extension of a previous course or the study of a topic not included in the curriculum. The course is taken with the regular guidance and direction of the faculty member, who will maintain at least 15 contact hours with the student (for a three-credit directed study) during the semester. It may include such options as research, project development, readings, or performance. Prerequisites include junior standing or above, a grade point average of at least 2.5, approval by the faculty supervisor, department chair, and Associate Academic Dean at least three weeks before the start of the semester in which the course will be taken, and completion of all prerequisites stated in each department's directed study course description. Directed Study registration forms are available in the Office of Records and Registration and through the Montreat College website.

Internship and Practicum Courses

Academic departments at Montreat College offer students two kinds of extended opportunities for practical experience in their field of study: internships and practicum courses. Internships and practicum courses enhance students' education with experiential learning in appropriate professional settings through off-campus experiences. Internships and practicum courses allow students to explore the relationship between theory and practice in order to further their spiritual, academic, social, and professional development. These courses are integral to the Montreat College promise to educate students through preparation for calling and career. An Internship/Practicum manual is to be reviewed by the student and his or her advisor. The Internship/Practicum registration form is to be completed with the advisor and provided for registration to the Office of Records and Registration.

Students are required to pass IS 310 (Pre-Practicum/Pre-Internship) prior to an internship or practicum course.

Goals of the Practicum/Internship Program

1. To provide an opportunity for students to integrate theory with practical experience.
2. To assist students in developing a clearer understanding of their chosen occupation.
3. To allow students to test their understanding and theories in a real-life setting.

4. To challenge students to develop a biblical as well as an experiential understanding of the role of work, vocation, and calling as sources of meaning in life.
5. To broaden a student's horizons.

Definition of a Practicum

A practicum is a supervised experiential learning opportunity, generally in an off-campus setting, that provides students with initial exposure to relevant professional activities. Practicum courses may be taken for 1-3 credit hours with a maximum of 3 credit hours to satisfy degree requirements. Each credit hour earned requires 40 hours of on-site involvement during an agreed upon length of time. Prerequisites: IS 310, permission of the student's academic advisor and department chair. Practicums will receive letter grades.

Definition of Internship

Internships are intensive, quality, structured learning opportunities, generally in off-campus settings that immerse students in appropriate professional contexts. Internships require extensive involvement by the students. Supervision is a shared responsibility between the academic department and the on-site supervisor. Most internship experiences earn 3 credit hours and may be repeated once for up to six credit hours toward major requirements (see specific program requirements). The internship course can be repeated once during a separate semester from the original internship. Each credit hour earned requires 60 hours of on-site involvement during an agreed upon length of time. Internship prerequisites: IS 310, junior standing, and approval of the student's academic advisor and department chair. Internships will receive letter grades.

Students who choose to take part in an internship program offered through Montreat College during the summer break must register for those internships during the Summer Session registration.

Summer Coursework

Montreat College offers courses during the summer. A student who wishes to enroll in the summer courses offered by another institution must complete the necessary form and receive approval from the Office of Records and Registration. Failure to follow this procedure may result in loss of transfer credit for these courses.

Online Courses

Online courses are offered to assist undergraduate students in fulfilling degree requirements. These courses also provide opportunities for enrichment to non-degree seeking students and other community members who are engaged in full-time employment. Those seeking to enroll in online courses as a non-degree student must complete the special student application for admission.

Montreat College Honors Program

Mission

The mission of the Montreat College Honors Program is to pursue the intellectual and spiritual formation of students through a series of curricular, co-curricular, and extracurricular activities. This enrichment of the Montreat College experience is designed to cultivate a community of scholars who discern truth, goodness, and beauty through a study of the great works of the Christian, Western and World traditions. The Honors Program offers an enhanced model of the integrated, holistic learning environment of Montreat College and prepares students for lives of reflective and responsible citizenship. The Montreat College Honors Program affirms that human beings reflect the image of God as thinking, relational, moral, and spiritual persons of dignity and worth. Students are challenged to encourage human flourishing and be thoughtful stewards of the creation in their respective vocations.

Model

The Montreat College Honors Program draws inspiration from historical precedents such as the Oxford tutorial model and from outstanding contemporary examples such as Biola University's Torrey Honors Institute. Students engage in intensive reading, formal and informal discussion, writing, and mentorship.

Honors Program participants also engage in co-curricular activities, such as being granted exclusive access to college speakers in a conversational setting, with the intent of exploring ideas more deeply than a general audience venue allows. Students also build community through social outings and service projects. The Honors Program supplements Montreat College's general education core.

Method

The Montreat College Honors curriculum has five main components: great works, discussion, mentoring, writing, and co-curricular opportunities.

Great Books
A rotating set of great works will be used for in the Honors Program. These may include excerpts or entire books that provide a foundational understanding for a liberal arts education. Honors Program classes will emphasize the ongoing relevance of these works to issues and questions that continue to arise in contemporary society.

Formal and Informal Discussion
Classes consist of faculty-led discussions on Great Books readings. This conversational pedagogy is designed to develop student confidence in their critical thinking, ability to engage texts, and to reflect on a range of issues raised by the readings.

Mentoring
Every student is mentored by the Program Director or an assigned faculty member involved in the Honors Program. This relationship encourages students to think more deeply about their courses, to process their questions and concerns, and to have a faculty member encourage them as they think through vocational possibilities.

Writing
Montreat College's campus-wide emphasis on writing across the curriculum is enhanced in the Honors Program by a series of assignments designed to help students be reflective and articulate. These skills serve students well beyond their years at Montreat College.

Co-Curricular and Extracurricular Opportunities
Intentional co-curricular activities will support classroom learning. Students will have exclusive access to select Chapel and Convocation speakers where they can engage in conversations to follow-up content presented and make connections with classroom learning. Other social outings and service projects will allow students to live out the vision of the program and deepen the sense of community between participants.

Four-Year Honors Program Course Schedule

First Year:	Applicable Courses:	Notes:
First Year Experience	IS 102 Honors Track	Foundations of Faith and Learning
English	EN 103 Honors Track	Replaces EN 101 Requirement
English	EN 104 Honors Track	Replaces EN 102 Requirement

Second Year:	Applicable Courses:	Notes:
History	HS 171 Honors Track	Replaces HS 101 Requirement
History	HS 172 Honors Track	Replaces HS 102 Requirement

Third Year:	Applicable Courses:	Notes:
Honors Elective	HN 301 Honors Seminar	Retreat Class, Humanities credit
Honors Elective	HN 302 Honors Seminar	Retreat Class, Humanities credit

Fourth Year:	Applicable Courses:	Notes:
Honors Elective	HN 401 Honors Seminar	Retreat Class, Humanities credit
Senior Year Experience	IS 461 Honors Track	Seminar on Faith and Life

*Honors students also receive waivers into selected upper level elective classes.

Classification of Students

At the beginning of each semester, all students are officially classified by the Office of Records and Registration. Class standing is based on the following:

Student Classification Formula	
Classification	**Semester Credit Hours**
Freshman	One (1) to twenty-nine (29) credit hours
Sophomore	Thirty (30) to fifty-nine (59) credit hours
Junior	Sixty (60) to eighty-nine (89) credit hours
Senior	Ninety (90) or more credit hours

New students at Montreat College are identified as:

- **First-time freshman**: A new student who has no college credits prior to the immediately previous summer sessions, or who has only college credits taken while still a high school student.
- **Transfer**: A student who, after high school graduation and prior to the immediately previous summer session, has been enrolled in another post-secondary institution before enrolling at Montreat College.
- **Readmit**: A student readmitted to the same program level of instruction after an absence of 5 years or less. (If the absence has been more than 5 years, the student is classified as a new student and must go through either the "Admission of First-Year Students" or "Transfer Admission" process.)

Students are classified academically as follows:

- **Full-time**: A student enrolled in 12 or more semester credit hours.
- **Part-time**: A student enrolled in 1-11 semester credit hours.
- **Special**: A student who is not a candidate for a degree and who cannot be classified by academic level, although taking courses in regular classes with other students.
- **Audit**: A student taking course work for no credit.

Declaring a Major/Minor/Concentration

Upon entry into Montreat College, new students are assigned to the major that corresponds to their expressed academic interest. Students should then formally declare a major program of study before the first semester of their junior year (60 credit hours completed) by submitting a Declaration of Major form online via the Office of Records and Registration webpage. Transfer students bringing in 60 credit hours or more should officially declare a major during their first semester at Montreat College.

Students wishing to declare a minor may do so at any time by completing the online Declaration of Major form via the Office of Records and Registration webpage. Students deciding to change their major and/or minor must go through the same procedures used to declare their initial major and/or minor. Please note that some majors require the selection of a concentration and some majors allow for a choice between a Bachelor of Arts and Bachelor of Science degree.

Dual Major

Students may work toward a dual major. Through a comprehensive, concentrated, and diverse education, students with a dual major demonstrate breadth, depth, flexibility, and persistence to potential employers. To complete a dual major, a student must fulfill the general education core requirements and the designated requirements of both majors. When two majors have common course requirements, students may count the required courses towards both majors. Students with dual majors should expect to take overloads, summer classes, and/or attend an extra semester to fulfill the requirements for both majors.

Grading System

Students in the School of Arts and Sciences at Montreat College follow a semester system. The academic proficiency of a student is indicated by the following letter system:

Grade and Associated Quality Points	
Grade	**Quality Points**
A	4.00 quality points awarded per credit hour
A-	3.66 quality points awarded per credit hour
B+	3.33 quality points awarded per credit hour
B	3.00 quality points awarded per credit hour
B-	2.66 quality points awarded per credit hour
C+	2.33 quality points awarded per credit hour
C	2.00 quality points awarded per credit hour
C-	1.66 quality points awarded per credit hour
D+	1.33 quality points awarded per credit hour
D	1.00 quality points awarded per credit hour
D-	0.66 quality points awarded per credit hour
F	0.00 quality points awarded per credit hour
I	Indicates incomplete work and is given when some portion of the work is unfinished. *I* is to be given only when there are circumstances beyond the control of the student, such as serious illness, which prevents the student from taking the final exam or completing a course requirement. An incomplete must be completed within six weeks after the end of the course or the *I* grade will be converted to the grade the student earned before the course extension was granted.
P	*Pass,* equivalent to a minimum letter grade of C, indicates that the credit hours for the course are deducted from the total credit hours needed for graduation with no impact on the grade point average.
W	Indicates withdrawal from a course with permission and within the time limits and according to the procedures established by the Office of Records and Registration.
WF	Indicates withdrawal after the last day to withdraw and receive a grade of *W.* Factors into the grade point average as an *F.*
S	Indicates satisfactory work (used for work that continues over more than one semester), where no credit or competency has been earned. Does not affect GPA or quality points.
NS	Indicates an unsuccessfully attempted course or competency, where no credit or competency has been earned. Does not affect GPA or quality points.
AU	Indicates a course which has been audited and no credit earned.

Incomplete Grades

Incomplete grades are to be given only when there are circumstances beyond the control of the student, such as serious illness, which prevents the student from taking the final exam or completing a course requirement. An incomplete must be completed within six weeks after the end of the course or the *I* grade will be converted to the grade the student earned before the course extension was granted.

Grade Point Average (GPA)

The grade point average each semester is computed by dividing the total number of quality points earned by the total number of credit hours attempted. Courses with a notation of *S* or *NS* will not be counted as credit hours attempted in computing grade point average; grades of *F* and *WF* will be counted as credit hours attempted. No quality points are assigned for grades of *F, WF, W, AU, S, NS, I, or P*. The cumulative grade point average is computed on all courses taken, excluding courses in which a *P* grade has been received.

Midterm Grades

Midterm grades are available to students online via the student information system every semester. Midterm grades are not recorded on the official transcript but serve to notify students of their progress during the first half of the semester. Midterm grade reports are issued prior to the last day to drop a course with a *W*.

Online Transcripts and Grade Reports

Grades are processed by the Office of Records and Registration after the end of each grading period. Students who are in good financial standing may view and print their online transcript and grades by logging into their online account. Students who are unable to view their grades online may request a copy of their current grades from the Office of Records and Registration. Grades are not mailed; however, students may request a certified copy of their grades, if needed. Transcripts will not be released online or in hard copy if the student is financially indebted to the College.

Requesting an Official Academic Transcript

The official record of the academic accomplishment of each student who enrolls is maintained by the Office of Records and Registration. All courses attempted, grades awarded, degrees conferred, and the major program of study, along with identifying personal data, are certified on the transcript. Montreat College is a member of the National Student Clearinghouse. All transcript requests are processed online via the Clearinghouse at http://www.mystudentcenter.org or by contacting them by phone at 703-742-4200. Transcripts will not be released if the student is financially indebted to the College.

Enrollment Verification

Students, for various reasons, may need official written proof that they are currently enrolled. Montreat College is a member of the National Student Clearinghouse, which acts as an agent for all verifications of student enrollment. Please visit the Clearinghouse online at http://www.mystudentcenter.org or contact them by phone at 703-742-4200 to obtain an official enrollment verification certificate at any time.

Degree Verification

Employers or background screening agencies may need proof that a student has earned a degree, but may not require an official transcript. Degree verifications can be obtained through the Clearinghouse online at http://www.mystudentcenter.org

Grade Changes

All grades are final three months after the date of issuance. Grades will be changed due to a computational error within six weeks of the due date for final grade submission. Under no circumstances will a student be allowed to do makeup work to improve a grade once final grades have been submitted. All grade changes must be approved by the Director of Records and Registration.

Petitions for Exception

To petition for an exception to academic policy, students must submit a written petition, stating the grounds for the request and providing any supporting evidence. Petitions for exceptions to academic policies are to be submitted to the Vice President for Academic Affairs & Dean of the College who will render a judgment or will forward the petition to the appropriate College office.

Academic Grievances

An academic grievance must be received no later than 15 business days from the date final grades were issued by the Office of Records and Registration for the course in question. A formal grievance related to a grade may be filed only if at least one of the following conditions apply:

- The student can provide evidence that an assigned grade was based on arbitrary or nonacademic criteria.
- The student can provide evidence that the criteria for evaluating the assignment or course work were not applied or were misapplied, such that the assigned grade does not accurately reflect his or her fulfillment of course requirements and/or course policies as stated in the syllabus (i.e., class attendance, grade standards, penalty for late or incomplete work) and/or the applicable requirements of the College.

Process for Filing an Academic Grievance:

1. A student wishing to appeal an academic decision which directly affects the student should first present the issue in writing to the faculty member or administrator making the decision. Such written grievance shall include statements of the grounds for the grievance, supporting information, and suggested steps to resolve the matter. If a grade inaccuracy is determined, the instructor will submit a grade change request to the Office of Records and Registration.

2. If satisfaction is not reached, the student should appeal in writing to the department chair. If a resolution is not achieved, the student should submit the academic grievance in writing to the Vice President for Academic Affairs & Dean of the College or designee.

3. After careful investigation, the Vice President for Academic Affairs & Dean of the College or designee may summarily dismiss the complaint if, in his or her discretion, the grounds for appeal are frivolous or do not otherwise rise to the level of a legitimate grievance.

4. If the Vice President for Academic Affairs & Dean of the College or designee does not dismiss the grievance, he/she shall, within ten days of meeting (by phone or in person) with the student and faculty member, form a panel of two uninvolved faculty members with whom the Vice President for Academic Affairs & Dean of the College or designee will review all appropriate material and make a determination on the appeal. The faculty panel may a) recommend that the grade be changed; b) recommend that the instructor revise course and/or grading requirements and re-evaluate the grade accordingly; or c) dismiss the case. If the faculty member declines the recommendation (or signifies such through inaction), the student may appeal to the Vice President for Academic Affairs & Dean of the College. The Vice President for Academic Affairs & Dean of the College shall inform the student of the outcome within ten business days after the faculty panel has met and shall also inform the Office of Records and Registration if a change in grade is recommended.

Good Academic Standing and Satisfactory Academic Progress

Degree seeking students must maintain a cumulative GPA of 2.0 in order to maintain Satisfactory Academic Progress (SAP). A student who fails to maintain SAP is subject to academic probation or academic suspension.

Withdrawal from courses with a grade of *W* will not affect good standing or academic progress provided the student meets the SAP criteria of a 2.0 GPA.

Review of SAP will occur at the end of each regular academic term for all degree-seeking students enrolled in that term for any number of credits.

Academic Probation

Students whose cumulative grade point average fails to meet the criteria established for SAP will be placed on academic probation for the next semester. If at the end of that semester the cumulative average is still below the required minimum, students will be placed on final probation for the following semester. Students who leave the College while on academic probation may apply for readmission (see Readmission of Former Students under the section "Admission Information"). If readmitted, students enter on the same probationary status as when they left the College.

Academic Suspension

The administration reserves the right to suspend a student from the College because of poor scholarship. Any student on final academic probation who fails to meet the requirements of probation will face academic suspension without refund of fees.

A student not permitted to continue for academic reasons may appeal the suspension in writing to the Vice President for Academic Affairs & Dean of the College within two weeks of the suspension. A student who is suspended for academic reasons may reapply to the College after one semester (see Readmission of Former Students under the section "Admission Information"). If readmitted, the student will be placed on final academic probation.

Academic Second Chance

An undergraduate student may appeal for an Academic Second Chance (ASC) to request academic forgiveness for Montreat College courses. Forgiveness may apply to a single semester or a continuous consecutive series of semesters within which a student earned grades lower than a C. If approved, those terms would be excluded when calculating the student's grade point average. No courses taken during the period approved for ASC would apply toward requirements for a degree.

A student who wishes to petition for academic forgiveness must meet the following criteria:

- The student must have been separated from all institutions of higher learning for a period of two (2) calendar years.
- The student must have re-entered Montreat College and earned at least 12 credit hours at Montreat College with a minimum GPA of 2.5 on those credit hours. He/she must be currently enrolled at Montreat College.

ASC terms will remain a part of the student's record although the forgiven semesters in their entirety will be excluded when calculating the GPA. The refigured GPA will be the official GPA of the College. A statement to that effect will be placed on the student's record.

Academic Second Chance may be granted only once and applies only to Montreat College credit. It is important to note that ASC may not be recognized by other institutions. A student may submit a letter of appeal including a description of his/her current action plan to achieve academic success to:

Director of Records and Registration
Montreat College
P.O. Box 1267
Montreat, NC 28757
828-669-8012 ext. 3731
registrar@montreat.edu

Attendance

Students are to attend classes regularly. They are responsible for any work discussed or assigned in every class for which they are registered. Faculty members establish their own attendance policies and are responsible to inform students of these in the course syllabus, along with any penalties for absences.

Professors will contact students whenever excessive absences occur. In cases where students do not adhere to the attendance policies established by their professors, and therefore, class performance is in jeopardy, the following procedure will occur:

1. When a student has been absent (unexcused) three times consecutively in a Monday/Wednesday/Friday class, or two times consecutively (unexcused) in a Tuesday/Thursday class, the professor will notify academic success services and the student's academic advisor.
2. Those involved in academic success services will be in contact with the student to determine the cause of the absences. As appropriate, referrals will then be made to other campus personnel (Residence Directors, Counselor, Nurse, Dean of Students, etc.).
3. If the student persists in non-class attendance, the professor will refer the student to the Vice President for Academic Affairs & Dean of the College. The Vice President for Academic Affairs & Dean of the College, or designee, will confer with the student. The student's parents may be notified in accordance with the FERPA policies of the College.
4. If the pattern of non-class attendance continues in a majority of the student's classes, the student may be subject to an administrative withdrawal from the College. Notification of non-class attendance must also be made to the Office of Records and Registration and the Financial Aid Office.

Academic Integrity Policy

Definition of Academic Dishonesty

Academic dishonesty, such as cheating on tests and plagiarizing on essays, violates the fundamental trust underlying all academic work—that the work be the product of the student who submitted it. Montreat College defines academic dishonesty as the representation of another's words, ideas, or images as one's own. It applies equally to intentional and unintentional quotations, paraphrases, visual images, auditory images, and all electronic means of storage and communication. When academic dishonesty occurs, these procedures will be followed.

Discipline of Academic Dishonesty

When an instructor suspects a student of academic dishonesty, the instructor will meet with the student to discuss the incident and determine, to the instructor's satisfaction, whether or not academic dishonesty has occurred. If, in the instructor's judgment, such a violation of academic integrity has occurred, he or she will present the charges, in writing, to the student.

The only possible disciplinary actions are a zero for the assignment or an F for the course. The student may choose to admit her or his guilt of academic dishonesty and waive a hearing. This involves signing the academic dishonesty notice that outlines the disciplinary action. The academic dishonesty notice will be retained in the student's academic record.

A student who does not agree to the instructor's charges must appear before a panel of three faculty members, appointed by the Academic Affairs office or designee, on charges of academic dishonesty. During the intervening period, the student must continue to attend class. The panel will convene a hearing with the student and the instructor at which time the instructor will explain the student's alleged violation. The student may choose to counter with evidence of her or his innocence or may admit responsibility.

Punishment of Academic Dishonesty

If the panel indicates, by simple majority vote, that the student has been dishonest, the panel shall uphold the penalty assessed by the instructor. The Academic Affairs office will notify the student, instructor, academic advisor, and Director of Records and Registration, in writing, of the panel's decision. If the student received a failing grade for the course, the student may remove the impact of the F on her or his grade point average by successfully retaking the course. Two incidents of academic dishonesty will result in a student being dismissed from the College. The student will not be eligible to reapply to Montreat College for at least two years after dismissal. If the panel finds the student not responsible for academic dishonesty, it will notify both the student and the instructor.

If the student wishes to drop the course but has been found guilty of academic dishonesty, the student may withdraw with a grade of W or WF, according to the withdrawal dates on the academic calendar.   The academic dishonesty notice will be kept on file if the student has admitted or been found guilty of academic dishonesty.

Exoneration of Academic Dishonesty

If exonerating information becomes available in the five business days following notification of the panel's decision, the student may appeal to the Vice President for Academic Affairs & Dean of the College. Appeals will be heard only if they meet one of the following conditions: (a) discovery of new information or (b) violation of procedure. A student must remain in the course and work toward its successful completion during the appeal process. The student will be notified, in writing, of the final decision.

A student may be dismissed from the College without refund of tuition or fees after the second incident of academic dishonesty occurs (including, but not limited to, cheating and plagiarism). That student will not be eligible to reapply to the College for at least two years after the dismissal, and any readmission will be subject to review by the Student Success Team in consultation with the Vice President for Academic Affairs & Dean of the College.

Term Withdrawal

Students who wish to withdraw from **all of their courses** during a given semester (which constitutes withdrawal from the College) must obtain a withdrawal form from the Office of Records and Registration and submit the completed form to the Office of Records and Registration within one week of the date of the student's last class attendance. Students will be granted an honorable dismissal and receive a *W* in the registered courses provided the completed withdrawal form is submitted to the Office of Records and Registration within the time limit for dropping courses with a *W*. Students who leave the College after the deadline for dropping courses with a *W* or who leave without completing the withdrawal process will not be granted honorable dismissal and a grade of *WF* or *F* will be assigned for all courses, whichever is appropriate. Students who quit attending class are subject to an **administrative withdrawal** by the College. A grade of *WF* will be assigned for students who have been administratively withdrawn.

For medical reasons or other serious circumstances that prevent the student from completing the withdrawal process, the Vice President for Student Services and Dean of Students will make appropriate arrangements working closely with the Academic Affairs Office.

Course Requirements for Graduation

Montreat College requires each student to enroll in a prescribed program of study and to pursue this curriculum through a carefully planned sequence of courses that will lead to successful completion of the academic program and the awarding of the appropriate degree. Each student must attempt to register for required courses in the General Education Core of courses that the faculty judges to be basic for a liberal arts education before pursuing elective courses. After primary attention has been given to completion of the General Education Core requirements and the General Education Competency requirements, the student and faculty advisor should work collaboratively to select courses appropriate to the student's major program of study, followed by electives. No deviation from the prescribed course of study will be permitted without written permission **prior** to course registration by the faculty advisor and the Office of Records and Registration.

Academic Requirements for Graduation

In order to graduate with a bachelor's degree from Montreat College, students must fulfill the following requirements:

- Earn a minimum of 126 semester credit hours.
- Earn a minimum cumulative grade point average of 2.0, unless the major requires a higher minimum.
- Complete the General Education Core requirements and meet all General Education Competency requirements.
- Successfully complete all requirements in the major field. Normally a major will require that students engage in specialized study in that discipline (and/or closely related ones) with the majority of the course work at the 300- and/or 400-level. A minimum of 36 semester credit hours is required in any major field of study.
- Successfully complete at least 33 semester credit hours in 300-level or above courses.
- Fulfill residency requirement of two semesters and completion of 32 credit hours taken at Montreat College.
- Students transferring in with senior status must successfully complete a minimum of 18 credit hours in the major at Montreat College.
- Students must fulfill all graduation requirements and obligations to the College in order to participate in the Commencement ceremony.
- Attain a minimum 2.0 grade point average and earn a grade of *C* or better, with no more than 2 grades* of *C-*, in courses counted toward the major, the concentration within a major, General Education Core classes required by the major, the minor field, and pre-requisite courses, unless the major requirements are higher.**

*The allowance of 2 grades of *C-* does not apply to General Education Competency requirements.
**Pre-requisite courses that are not part of the major or minor requirements may receive a *C-* unless otherwise stated in the catalog.

Students are subject to the academic requirements stated in the catalog that was current when they first enrolled as students. A student who leaves the College and is later readmitted must meet the requirements current at the time of readmission.

Students whose native language is not English, and whose prior language of instruction was not English, may substitute English for the foreign language requirement for the Bachelor of Arts degree. In addition to the nine credit hours of General Education Core requirements, students may substitute from six to twelve credit hours of approved English courses.

Students who seek to **earn more than one degree** must complete a minimum of 32 credit hours above the 126 that are required for the awarding of the first bachelor's degree. If course work distinctive to a second degree is less than the 32 credit hour minimum, then the balance should be completed in electives related to and complementary to the major of the second degree. If the course work that is distinctive to the second degree is greater than 32 credit hours, then the student must complete the full amount of that work regardless of any other minimums.

Note: In order to complete 126 credit hours in four academic years, you must complete an average of 15.75 credits each semester.

Graduation Participation

Commencement ceremonies are held twice yearly for associate, baccalaureate, and master degree graduates. All students receiving diplomas are encouraged to be present. Graduates may purchase caps and gowns, invitations, and other graduation supplies through the Campus Book Store. Only students who have completed all requirements for graduation and have met all financial obligations to the College will be permitted to participate in the Commencement ceremony.

Application for graduation must be made by:

- October 1 for December graduation
- March 1 for May graduation
- June 1 for August graduation

Students who do not graduate at that time will need to complete a new application for graduation to be considered for the next degree conferral. Students may petition to participate in the Commencement ceremony if the student is within 3 credit hours or one requirement of fulfilling graduation requirements. The petition form must be returned to the Office of Records and Registration in order to be considered.

Graduation and Student Achievement Honors

For graduation with honors from a baccalaureate program, students must earn a minimum of 60 credit hours at Montreat College and meet the following minimum cumulative grade point average requirements:

GPA	HONOR
3.50 – 3.69	*Cum laude*
3.70 – 3.84	*Magna cum laude*
3.85 – 4.00	*Summa cum laude*

Baccalaureate degree honors are recognized by wearing gold cords at Commencement.

Baccalaureate students with 45-59 credit hours at Montreat College and a minimum grade point average of 3.75 or higher may graduate *"with Distinction."*

Associate degree students who graduate with a minimum grade point average of 3.75 or higher and complete at least 45 credit hours at Montreat College may graduate *"with Honors."* Associate degree honors are recognized by wearing gold and white cords at Commencement.

Valedictorian and Salutatorian Honors are recognized among baccalaureate graduates with the two highest cumulative grade point averages having completed a minimum of 60 credit hours at Montreat College. If there is a tie in GPA, the student with the highest number of credit hours earned at Montreat College will break the tie. A valedictorian and salutatorian are chosen twice a year, once at December Commencement chosen from among the combined August and December graduates and once in May from among the May graduates.

Dean's List is made up of those undergraduate degree-seeking students who, during the previous semester, have met the following requirements: (1) received a grade point average of 3.5–3.89 on academic work; (2) earned at least 12 credit hours of academic work; (3) satisfactorily completed the chapel/convocation attendance requirement; (4) received no grade of *I, F, WF*; and (5) maintained a satisfactory citizenship record.

Distinguished Scholars' List is made up of those undergraduate degree-seeking students who, during the previous semester, have met the following requirements: (1) received a grade point average of 3.90 or above on academic work; (2) taken at least 12 hours of academic work; (3) satisfactorily completed the chapel/convocation attendance requirement; (4) received no grade of *I, F, WF*; and (5) maintained a satisfactory citizenship record.

Scholarship Pin is awarded to graduates receiving the bachelor's degree who have fulfilled the requirements for Dean's List (3.50-3.89 GPA) or Distinguished Scholars' (3.90 GPA or above) for six consecutive semesters.

Alpha Chi Honor Society, one of the three most prestigious national honor societies, maintains the North Carolina Tau Chapter at Montreat College. Alpha Chi's purpose is to promote academic excellence and exemplary character among college and university students and to honor those who achieve such distinction. Active membership is based on: (1) good reputation and character (2) rank in the top 10 percent of the junior and senior classes, and (3) regular student status at Montreat College for no less than one academic year prior to election. Potential Alpha Chi members must be approved by the faculty.

Military cords: Montreat College wishes to recognize those who are veterans or active duty members in our U.S. Armed Services. These women and men will be given red, white, and blue honor cords to wear during their graduation commencement ceremonies.

Academic Excellence Awards are made to the freshmen, sophomores, juniors, and non-graduating seniors with the highest cumulative grade point averages. Also, Academic Excellence Certificates are awarded to all students with cumulative grade point averages above 3.85 who have attended at least two semesters as full-time students at Montreat College with the exception of first-year freshmen.

Outstanding Bible and Religion Graduate Award is given to an outstanding graduating Bible and Religion major who has demonstrated academic excellence, theological acuity, Christian maturity, and Kingdom vision.

Outstanding Biology Graduate Award is awarded to a graduating senior in the Biology program who has demonstrated excellence in academics, Christ-like character, and compelling leadership qualities.

Hicks Anderson Outstanding Business Graduate Awards were established in 2001 to recognize graduating Business majors who have best demonstrated outstanding academic performance, selfless service, and exemplary Christian character. This award is presented annually to a School of Arts and Sciences student and a School of Adult and Graduate Studies student.

Outstanding Communication Graduate Award acknowledges a graduating senior within the Communication major, who has displayed academic excellence, Christian character, and a servant's heart.

Outstanding Cybersecurity Graduate Award is presented to a graduating senior in the program who has demonstrated academic excellence, Christ-like character, and servant leadership among students.

Outstanding Environmental Studies Graduate Award is given to a graduating senior within the Environmental Studies major. Award recipients are chosen by department faculty based on academic achievement, Christian commitment, servant leadership, and leadership among students.

Outstanding History Graduate Award may be given at the close of the academic year to a graduating senior deemed especially outstanding as a student of history. The recipient is usually a History major or minor.

Elizabeth H. Maxwell Literature Award is given to a graduating senior who has demonstrated outstanding achievement in literary studies as determined by the English faculty. Requirements include that the student major in English, maintain a GPA of 3.2, take at least one course from each full-time member of the English faculty, and demonstrate creativity and maturity in the field of literary studies.

Outstanding Music Business Graduate Award is presented to a Music Business graduate who has exhibited dedication, innovation, tenacity, the ability to quickly adapt, and a desire to learn – all skills that are necessary for success in the music industry. Above all, the recipient of this award has practiced servant leadership both in the Music Department and in the College community at large.

Outstanding Outdoor Education/Outdoor Ministry Graduate Awards are given to outstanding graduating seniors who are candidates for a Bachelor of Science degree in Outdoor Education/Outdoor Ministry. Requirements include: committed to a career in Outdoor Education or Outdoor Ministry; maintained a 3.0 GPA; pursued certifications; made an outstanding contribution to the Outdoor Education Department; demonstrated creativity, maturity, and excellence in teaching; demonstrated that he/she is a servant leader; and bears evidence of a committed Christian life.

Outstanding Psychology and Human Services Graduate Award recipient is chosen collaboratively by the Psychology and Human Services faculty and graduating seniors within the major. This award is presented to a graduating senior who has demonstrated exceptional scholarship in the major field of Psychology and Human Services, abides by high moral standards, has a clear sense of direction, helps people on and off campus, and shows great promise for using his or her understanding of human behavior to become an agent of transformation, renewal, and/or reconciliation to the glory of God.

Outstanding Worship Arts Graduate Award is presented to the Worship Arts major who exhibits a thorough biblical theology of worship obtained through a passionate pursuit of both the academic and pastoral nature of worship leadership. This graduate has maintained a 3.25 grade point average in all music and worship arts classes. This graduate has demonstrated his/her knowledge and heart for worship planning and leading through active participation in the Montreat College

Chapel program. This graduate grasps both the duty and delight of the calling God has placed on his/her life and is resolved in his/her pursuit of worship renewal in the Church.

Theatrical Excellence Award is available to sophomores, juniors, and seniors who have demonstrated excellence and potential in the field of theatrical arts through exemplary participation in theatre work at Montreat College.

Writing Program Service Award distinguishes a student who combines superior academic writing ability with the talent to inspire fellow students to excel in writing. The recipient is a graduating senior who has served in the writing program for at least two semesters and is graduating with a 3.0 GPA or higher.

Certificate of Excellence in Youth and Family Ministry is awarded by the Youth and Family Ministry Educators' Forum upon the recommendation of the Youth and Family Ministry faculty to a Montreat College student who has demonstrated academic excellence and giftedness in working with young people.

Zondervan Greek Award is presented by Zondervan Publishing House. Upon recommendation of the Biblical, Religious, and Interdisciplinary Studies Department, this award recognizes students for their singular achievement in the study of Biblical Greek.

Faculty Service Award annually recognizes a graduating senior who has made outstanding contributions to Montreat College and who has given evidence of effective Christian citizenship.

Kim Denise Trapnell Servant Leader Award was established in 1994 in honor of Kim Denise Trapnell, an outstanding example of student leadership. It is given annually to the student who best demonstrates a servant's heart in leading others through service, attitude, and relationships.

SGA Staff Person of the Year Award is given annually by the Student Government Association to a staff member who has excelled in all areas of Montreat College.

SGA Excellence Award, established in 1994 by the Legislative Committee, is given annually to the member of the Student Government Association who has shown outstanding dedication and leadership throughout the year.

SEEDS Environmental Stewardship Award is given annually to a student that has exhibited exceptional leadership in helping Montreat College fulfill the Biblical mandate to be wise stewards of creation.

National Association of Intercollegiate Athletics All-American Scholar-Athlete Award recognizes excellence in the classroom and on the field of play. Nominees for this honor must be junior or senior varsity performers who have been enrolled at their nominating institution for a minimum of one full term. They must also have at least a 3.50 cumulative grade point average on a 4.00 scale from their nominating institution.

The Family Educational Rights and Privacy Act (FERPA)

Student: Any person who either attends or has attended Montreat College

Educational Records: Any record (in print, handwriting, microfilm, computer, or other medium) that is maintained by a Montreat College staff or faculty member and is directly related to a student except:

- Sole possession records: Personal records kept by a college official if they are kept in the possession of the individual who made the records, and information contained in the record has never been revealed or made available to any other person except the maker's temporary substitute.
- An employment record of an individual whose employment is not contingent on the fact that he or she is a student, provided the record is used only in relation to the individual's employment.
- Records maintained by the Montreat College security department if the record is maintained solely for law enforcement purposes, is revealed only to law enforcement agencies of the same jurisdiction, and the department does not have access to the educational records maintained by Montreat College.
- Records maintained by the Health Services Office if the records are used only for treatment of a student and made available only to those persons providing the treatment.
- Alumni records that contain information about a student after he or she is no longer in attendance at Montreat College and the records do not relate to the person as a student.

Annual Student Notification

Policy: Students are notified of their FERPA rights and procedures for indicating their FERPA release preferences in the annual Montreat College catalog and via emails sent at the beginning of each term.

Procedure for Student Inspection/Review of Records

Students have the right to inspect and review their educational records upon request to the custodian of the record.

- If a student is requesting to see only one item from their educational record (i.e. an unofficial transcript), no written request or appointment is necessary. Access will be immediate, subject to the availability of the custodian.
- If a student is requesting to see more than one item from their educational record, a written request must be submitted to the records custodian that identifies the record(s) the student wishes to inspect. The custodian will arrange for the access and notify the student of the time and place where the records may be reviewed. By law, access must be provided within 45 days from the receipt of the request. When a record contains information about more than one student, the student may review only the records that relate to him/her.

Montreat College Right to Refuse Access Policy

Montreat College reserves the right to refuse to permit a student to inspect these records:

1. Any financial records of the parent that may be in the student's file.
2. Letters of recommendation for which the student has waived his/her right of access.
3. Admission records if the student's application was denied or the student chose not to attend Montreat College after making application.
4. Records excluded from FERPA's definition of educational records.

Montreat College Right to Refuse Provision of Copies Policy

Montreat College reserves the right to deny copies or transcripts or other records if:

1. The student lives within commuting distance of Montreat College.
2. The student has a delinquent account at Montreat College.
3. There is an unresolved disciplinary action against the student.

Schedule of Fees for Copies

The fee for copies of educational records is .10 per page, plus postage if applicable.

Disclosure of Educational Records Policy

Montreat College will disclose information from a student's educational record only with the written consent of the student, except in the following instances:

1. To school officials who have a legitimate educational interest in the records.
   A school official is:
   - A person employed by the College in an administrative, supervisory, academic, or support staff position.
   - A person elected to the Board of Trustees.
   - A person employed by or under contract to Montreat College to perform a special task, such as an attorney or auditor.

Legitimate educational interest includes:

- Performing a task that is specified in a position description or by a contract agreement.
- Performing a task related to the student's education.
- Performing a task related to the discipline of a student.
- Providing a service or benefit relating to the student or student's family, such as health care, counseling, job placement, or financial aid.

2. To certain officials of the U.S. Department of Education, the Comptroller General, and state and local educational authorities in connection with certain state or federally supported education programs.
3. To the National Student Clearinghouse for enrollment and degree verification purposes.
4. In connection with a student's request for or receipt of financial aid, as necessary to determine the eligibility, amount or conditions of the financial aid, or to enforce the terms and conditions of the financial aid.
5. If required by a state law requiring disclosure that was adopted before November 19, 1974.
6. To organizations conducting certain studies for or on behalf of Montreat College.
7. To accrediting organizations to carry out their functions.
8. To comply with a judicial order or a lawfully issued subpoena (accompanied by a reasonable effort to notify the student).
9. To appropriate parties in a health or safety emergency.
10. Results of a disciplinary hearing to an alleged victim of a crime of violence.
11. Final results of a disciplinary hearing concerning a student who is an alleged perpetrator of a crime of violence and who is found to have committed a violation of the school's rules or policies.
12. Disclosure to the parent of a student under 21 if the institution determines that the student has committed a violation of its drug or alcohol policies.

Directory Information Policy

Montreat College designates the following items as directory information: Student's name, address, telephone number, e-mail address, date and place of birth, participation in officially recognized activities and sports, weight and height of members of athletic teams, dates of attendance, major fields of study, enrollment status, classification, expected graduation date, job title and dates of student work study, degrees and awards received, photographs, and the most recent previous educational institution attended by the student.

Procedure for Students Requesting to Amend Educational Records

Students have the right to request a correction of their educational records under FERPA. If a student believes the educational records relating to the student contain information that is inaccurate, misleading, or in violation of the student's rights of privacy, he/she may ask Montreat College to amend the record. The procedure for requesting a correction of the records is:

1. The student must submit a request to the custodian of the record to amend the record. The request should identify the portion(s) of the record the student wants changed and specify why the student believes that portion of the record to be inaccurate.
2. If Montreat College decides not to comply with the request, the student will be notified of the decision and also advised of his/her right to a hearing to challenge the decision not to amend the record.
3. Upon request, Montreat College will make arrangements for a hearing and notify the student as to the time and place of the hearing.
4. The hearing will be conducted by an individual who does not have a direct interest in the outcome of the hearing. The student will have an opportunity to present evidence relevant to the issues raised in the request to amend the record. The student may be assisted by an attorney of his/her own choice.
5. Montreat College will respond with a written decision within a reasonable period of time after the hearing. The decision will include a summary of the evidence and the reasons for the decision.
6. If Montreat College decides that the information contested is not inaccurate, misleading, or in violation of the student's right to privacy or other rights, it will notify the student, in writing, that they have a right to place a statement in the record commenting on the contested information in the record or stating why he/she disagrees with the outcome of the hearing.
7. That statement will be maintained as part of the student's educational record as long as the contested portion is maintained. If Montreat College discloses the contested portion of the record, it must also disclose the student's statement.
8. If Montreat College decides that the information contested is inaccurate, misleading, or a violation of the student's right to privacy or other rights, it will amend the record accordingly and notify the student, in writing, that the record has been amended.

Official Mail

Students receive mail on campus at their official Montreat College email address or at their designated Montreat College campus mailbox located at the box station on the lower level of Belk Campus Center. Students should check their mailboxes and their email frequently. Official communications will be emailed to students when possible at their official Montreat College email addresses. Confidential information may not be emailed to a non-Montreat College email address. Official communications will also be sent to students at their campus mailbox addresses, so students should check their boxes regularly. Some official College mail will also be sent to the permanent home address listed for the students.

Inclement Weather

During periods of especially inclement weather a decision to close or delay the opening of the College will be made prior to 7:00 am. College closings or delays will be announced on WLOS TV, Fox TV, and Clear Channel Radio stations. Also, a recording will be issued on the College's main telephone greeting (828-669-8011), a message will be posted on the College's main webpage (www.montreat.edu), and an email will be sent to all faculty, staff, and students indicating the status of the institution (closed, two hour delay, etc.). In the event that the College starts with a two-hour delay, the Academic Class Schedule will be as follows:

2-hour Delay Schedule to the Academic Class Schedule

Monday/Wednesday/Friday Classes		
Hour	Normal Class Schedule	2-Hour Delay Class Schedule
1st Hour	8:00-8:50	10:00-10:40
2nd Hour	9:00-9:50	10:50-11:30
Chapel/Convo/Comm	10:00-10:50	11:40-12:20
3rd Hour	11:00-11:50	12:30-1:10
4th Hour	12:00-12:50	1:20-2:00
5th Hour	1:00-1:50	2:10-2:50
6th Hour	2:00-2:50	3:00-3:40
7th Hour	3:00-3:50	3:50-4:30
8th Hour	4:00-4:50	4:40-5:20
	Evening classes continue as scheduled	
Tuesday/Thursday Classes		
Hour	Normal Class Schedule	2-Hour Delay Class Schedule
1st Hour	8:00-9:20	10:00-10:50
2nd Hour	9:30-10:50	11:00-11:50
3rd Hour	11:00-12:20	12:30-1:20
4th Hour	1:00-2:20	1:30-2:20
5th Hour	2:30-3:50	2:30-3:50
6th Hour	4:00-5:20	4:00-5:20
	Evening classes continue as scheduled	

Academic Programs

Academic Program Nomenclature

Major – A coherent program of study that addresses identifiable learning outcomes. A major requires a minimum of 36 semester hours of coursework.

Concentration – An area of specialization under an appropriate major. A major with areas of concentration requires a minimum of 15 semester hours of specialized concentration coursework in addition to other courses in the major.

Minor – A coherent program of study that focuses on breadth, rather than depth, of knowledge in a discipline. A minor requires a minimum of 18 semester hours.

Program of Study Options

Montreat College currently offers thirty-six outcomes-based, learner focused, major programs of study in addition to the student-designed (or customized) Interdisciplinary Studies Major through our main campus. Each program is committed to the integration of faith and learning as it seeks to educate the mind and challenge the spirit. The programs listed below are categorized according to the following codes: AA (Associate of Arts), AS (Associate of Science), BA (Bachelor of Arts), BM (Bachelor of Music), BS (Bachelor of Science), M (Major), MI (Minor), and C (Concentration).

Academic Programs

Program of Study	Degree Option	Category
Adventure-Based Counseling		MI
American Studies	BA, BS	M
Art		MI
Bible and Religion		M, MI
Biblical Scholarship Concentration	BA	C
Cross-Cultural Studies Concentration	BA	C
Preaching and Evangelism Concentration	BA, BS	C
Special Emphasis Concentration	BA	C
Youth and Family Ministries Concentration	BA, BS	C
Biology		M, MI
Applied Biochemical Technology Concentration	BS	C
Environmental Concentration	BS	C
Integrated Preparation for ABSN (Pre-Nursing)	BS	C
Pre-Professional Concentration	BS	C
Special Emphasis Concentration	BS	C
Business Administration		M, MI
Cybersecurity Concentration	BS	C
International Business Concentration	BS	C
Management Concentration	BS	C

Marketing Concentration	BS	C
Special Emphasis Concentration	BS	C
Sports Management Concentration	BS	C
Chemistry		MI
Communication		M, MI
Digital Media Production Concentration	BS	C
General Concentration	BS	C
Journalism Concentration	BS	C
Public Relations Concentration	BS	C
Theatre Concentration	BS	C
Cybersecurity	BS	M, MI
Elementary Education	BS	M
English		M, MI
Creative Writing Concentration	BA	C
Literature Concentration	BA	C
Professional Writing Concentration	BA	C
Special Emphasis Concentration	BA	C
Environmental Studies		M, MI
Conservation Biology and Natural Resource Mgt.	BS	C
Pre-Professional Concentration	BS	C
Special Emphasis Concentration	BS	C
Exercise Science	BS	M
History	BA, BS	M, MI
Interdisciplinary Studies	BA, BS	M, MI
Leadership		MI
Music	BA	M, MI
Music Business	BS	M, MI
Outdoor Education	BS	M, MI
Outdoor Ministry	BS	M, MI
Philosophy and Worldviews		MI
Physical Education		MI
Pre-Law		
Psychology and Human Services		M, MI
Human Services Concentration	BA, BS	C
Psychology Concentration	BA, BS	C
Spanish		MI
Theatre	BA	M, MI
Youth and Family Ministries		MI
Worship Arts	BM	M, MI
Associate of Arts	AA	
Associate of Science	AS	

General Education Core

The General Education Core is the hallmark of a liberal arts education. In this series of courses, students gain the broad base of knowledge that will serve as the foundation for further studies in major areas. In addition, students will develop an appreciation of how the various collegiate disciplines work together to gain a fundamental understanding of the structure and function of world culture from a uniquely Christian perspective.

General Education Core Requirements		
Curricula	**Applicable Courses**	**Hrs**
First Year Experience**	IS 102 (2) or IS 200 (1)	2
Bible*	BB 101 & BB 102	6
Computer	CS 102 or CS 102E	3
Writing*	EN 101 or EN 103 & EN 102 or EN 104	6
Reading/Literature	EN literature 200-level or above (excludes writing courses)	3
History	HS 101 & HS 102 (HS 201 or HS 202 may be substituted for one semester of world history)	6
Humanities and Arts*** (at least two areas must be represented) Applied courses <u>not</u> included (i.e. photography, piano, writing, speech); EN 271, EN 330, and other speech/writing courses <u>not</u> included.	Choose three: AR 101, AR 102 MS 101, MS 113, MS 114, and MS 200-level or above Foreign Language (Including sign language) CM 318, ED 209, HS 371, IS 202, IS 306, TH 110 BB or PH 200-level and above EN 200-level and above except writing courses HN 301, 302, 401 (for Honors students only) WA 101, WA 102 (for non-WA majors)	9
Mathematics	MT 101 or above	3
Natural Science	Choose two from: AT 101, AT 102, BL 101, BL 102, CH 201, CH 202, PC 131, PC 132	8
Oral Expression	CM 220, EN 271, OE 310, PR 310, TH 220, or TH 230	3
Physical Education +	Choose two PE activity courses	2
Social Science	Choose one: 200-level or above in economics, geography, sociology, psychology or history; CM 203, CC 402	3
Seminar on Faith & Life	IS 461	2
	Total General Education Hours:	**56**

* All full-time students **must** be enrolled in BB 101 and EN 101 the first semester of enrollment and BB 102 and EN 102 the second semester of enrollment until they are successfully completed. Refer to "Required Courses Must Be Taken Until Successfully Completed" for more information.

All full-time students **must be enrolled in either IS 102 or IS 200 the first semester of enrollment until successfully completed. IS 102 is for students with less than 12 hours of college credit obtained in a college setting (does not include dual-enrolled classes, AP classes or CLEP credits). IS 200 is for students who have attended another college and are transferring in at least 12 credit hours. Athletes that are forced to miss two or more days of IS 200 will need to drop and re-enroll the next semester.

***Students in the Montreat College Honors Program may count HN 301, HN 302, and HN 401 for six (6) Gen-Ed humanities credits, and are therefore only required to take one of the humanities classes (3 credits) listed above.

+ Athletes may receive 1 credit per semester for full participation in designated college team sports (up to 2 credits total). Verification of participation must be provided by the team coach.

NOTE: Course numbering is specific to Montreat College courses; transfer students will be given consideration based on a course-by-course evaluation of credit.

Required Courses Must be taken until Successfully Completed

Montreat College has chosen to require General Education core courses for several reasons. Instructors strive to integrate Christian faith and worldviews within the context of all subjects and disciplines. Therefore, all students need to have a basic understanding of a Christian worldview and Christian doctrines in order to fully grasp the concepts of further study at Montreat College. BB 101 and 102 provide foundational Biblical knowledge that students may not have received previously. IS 102 and IS 200 expose students to the mission of Montreat College as an academically rigorous community dedicated to seeking God's truth in all its aspects and exploring faith in relation to all studies. EN 101 and 102 ensure that our students possess the writing skills essential to all other college coursework. The General Education core courses also provide a proving ground for the level of scholastic effort required of our students.

All full-time students must be enrolled in the following General Education core courses below (unless they have received transfer, AP, or CLEP credit for them) until they are successfully completed:

First-Year, First Semester Courses: IS 102 Foundations of Faith and Learning (for students new to college or transferring in less than 12 credit hours); IS 200 Seminar on Faith and Learning (for students transferring in 12 credit hours or more); BB 101 Old Testament Survey; and EN 101 English Composition or EN 103 Honors English Composition.

First-Year, Second Semester Courses: BB 102 New Testament Survey and EN 102 English Composition or EN 104 Honors Introduction to Literary Studies.

Students may withdraw from these courses but must re-enroll in them the following semester. Students who do not pass a required course will also be required to re-enroll in the course the following semester. EN 101 or 103 and EN 102 or 104 must be completed with grades of _C_ or better or these courses must be retaken the following semester. Required courses must be taken until successfully completed.

General Education Competencies

In addition to the above core requirements, each student must demonstrate competency in the following areas: mathematical computation, oral expression, reading, writing, and computer literacy. Competency in these areas may be demonstrated as follows:

- **Mathematical Computation Competency:** The study of mathematics at Montreat College prepares students to serve God and neighbor by enhancing their abilities to think logically and solve various kinds of problems by analyzing and interpreting data. Competency may be demonstrated as follows:
  - Minimum grade of C in Math 101 or above or equivalent, **OR**
  - Passing any MT course, 101 or above, and completing the cumulative final exam with a C or better, **OR**
  - Appropriate CLEP or AP scores, or equivalent class from a regionally accredited institution.

- **Oral Expression Competency** is to prepare graduates who can demonstrate skill in oral communication. Specifically, students will give oral presentations that either inform or persuade. Competency will be achieved when students demonstrate in the context of oral presentations clarity of thought, originality of ideas, organizational techniques, appropriate diction, critical thinking, supporting strategies, and effective delivery. Competency may be demonstrated as follows:
  - Minimum grade of C in CM 220, EN 271, OE 310, PR 310, TH 220, TH 230, **OR**
  - Equivalent class from a regionally accredited institution

- **Reading Competency** is to produce graduates who can demonstrate effective reading skills. Competency will be achieved when students evidence college-level reading skills including analytical and critical thinking, comprehension, speed, and vocabulary. Reading competency may be demonstrated as follows:
  - Grade of C or above in an upper-level literature course, **OR**
  - Appropriate CLEP or AP scores, or equivalent class from a regionally accredited institution

- **Writing Competency** may be demonstrated as follows:
  - Grades of *C* or above in both EN 101 or 103 and 102 or 104 or the equivalent, **OR**
  - Appropriate CLEP or AP scores, **OR**
  - Equivalent classes from a regionally accredited institution, **OR**
  - Accepted transfer credit for EN 102 when student tested out of the EN 101 equivalent at previous school (testing out does *not* include progressing to the EN 102 equivalent after making less than a grade of *C* in the EN 101 equivalent)

- **Computer Skills Competency:** All students enrolled at Montreat College must demonstrate computer competency. Competency may be demonstrated by one of the following completed within the last ten (10) years:
  - Completing CS 102 with a grade of *C* or better, **OR**
  - Earning a *C* or better on the computer competency exam (CS 102E). Those who pass the exam will earn three (3) credits recorded as a *P* on the academic transcript, **OR**
  - Equivalent class from a regionally accredited institution.

Computer competency is understood to include the following skills:
  - **Word Processing:** This includes basic formatting and layout skills, including footnotes and endnotes, headers and footers, and integrating pictures and graphs in the text.
  - **Spreadsheet:** This includes organizing data, formatting, basic calculations, and developing charts and graphs.
  - **Presentation:** This includes incorporating text graphs, pictures, and hyperlinks into a presentation.
  - Internet: This includes conducting online research and identifying and evaluating credible web sites.
  - **E-Learning:** This includes accessing an e-learning program, participating in a discussion group, and posting assignments.
  - **E-Mail:** This includes sending and receiving e-mail, sending attachments, and receiving and accessing attachments.

Humanities Definition

The faculty at Montreat College defines the humanities as those academic disciplines that focus on the study of the human experience, including timeless stories, creative works, ideas, and concepts within various cultures through the ages. This study enables students to better understand their life and world and, from this broad perspective, to make better decisions for the good of self and society.

While natural and social sciences describe and explain phenomena in the natural realm and in human societies, the humanities focus on the *interpretation* of human experiences. Thus, the humanities do not include the *creation* of works of art or literature, but rather the critique and appreciation of such works. The disciplines comprising the study of humanities may include: history, philosophy, biblical studies, languages, literature, art, architecture, music, dance, theatre, and film.

Natural Science

Colossians 1 states: "For in Him [Jesus] all things were created…all things have been created through Him and for Him. He is before all things, and in Him all things hold together." The study of life and physical sciences helps to intensify a spirit of inquiry and wonder at God's glory, as revealed in what He has chosen to create, as well as an appreciation of the role of human beings as stewards of that creation.

Montreat College graduates must understand the scientific method and be able to apply scientific principles to interpret, discuss, and create scientific knowledge in ethical and responsible ways that benefit human cultures and natural environments. In order to be responsible workers, citizens, and consumers, students must expand their understanding of the connections among various natural systems and think through sustainability and other current environmental issues.

Bachelor of Arts/Bachelor of Science Degree Requirements

Whereas many of Montreat College's academic programs are built specifically as Bachelor of Arts *or* Bachelor of Science degrees, some majors are designed so that students may choose a BA or BS degree. Where the option is given, students must complete 12 credit hours (or the equivalent) in the requirements specific to their degree below.

Bachelor of Arts

In addition to the General Education Core, students choosing to pursue the Bachelor of Arts degree must demonstrate proficiency in a foreign language through the elementary level (six credit hours), and continue their exploration of culture by completing additional foreign language courses or humanities courses (six credit hours). The BA requirement may be fulfilled via one of the scenarios below:

1. If student passes a foreign language proficiency examination* through the elementary level *or* completes a foreign language sequence through the elementary level:
    - Student earns the equivalent of 6 credit hours in foreign language.
    - Student must complete 6 credit hours in humanities or additional foreign language courses.

2. If student passes a foreign language proficiency examination* through the intermediate level *or* completes a foreign language sequence through the intermediate level:
    - Student earns the equivalent of 12 credit hours in foreign language, and has fulfilled the BA requirement.

3. If student graduated from a high school where all instruction was conducted in a language other than English:
    - Student is considered to have fulfilled the BA requirement and is not required to take additional classes, as the purpose of the BA requirement is to broaden cultural understanding.

*Students who complete a proficiency examination at Montreat College are required to take the next level course in order to receive credit for the lower level(s) passed.

NOTE: American Sign Language is a complex language, spoken by as many as 500,000 Americans. Throughout the state of North Carolina and the United States in general, ASL is often accepted in fulfillment of foreign language requirements. While Montreat College does not offer courses in ASL, students may transfer collegiate-level credits in ASL for use toward Bachelor of Arts, humanities, or elective credit requirements.

Bachelor of Science

Students who choose to pursue the Bachelor of Science degree must complete an additional 12 hours beyond the General Education Core of coursework in mathematics, science, business, or computer studies. This coursework may not be applied to the General Education Core or the major.

Adventure-Based Counseling Minor

The Adventure-Based Counseling Minor

The minor in Adventure-Based Counseling (19-21 hours) combines existing courses from Outdoor Education (OE), Psychology (PY), and Human Services (HU) into a unique program of study. Adventure-Based Counseling and the closely related field of Adventure Therapy are two areas of Outdoor Education that are growing very quickly. This minor will provide a basic understanding of adventure-based counseling for those OE, PY, and HU students interested in pursuing a Master degree in a related area.

Requirements for a Minor in Adventure-Based Counseling (19 credits)

Adventure-Based Counseling Minor Core (12)

OE 300 Introduction to Adventure Based Counseling (3)
OE 211 Challenge Course Facilitation (3)
Choose one:
    PY 201 Psychology Applied to Modern Life (3)
    PY 202 General Psychology (3)
PY 412 Theories and Principles of Counseling (3)

Adventure-Based Counseling Required Minor Electives (7-9)

Choose one of the following: (2)
    PY 341 Practicum (2)
    OE 241 Field Experience (2)
Choose one of the following: (3)
    PY 300 Child and Adolescent Development (3)
    PY 305 Adult Development and Aging (3)
    SC 414 Counseling Adolescents and Families (3)
Choose one of the following (2-4)
    OE 180 Discovery (4)
    OE 182 Wilderness Journey (2-4)
    OE 311 Outdoor Programming and Leadership: Kayaking (4)
    OE 312 Outdoor Programming and Leadership: Expedition Management (4)
    OE 313 Outdoor Programming and Leadership: Rock Climbing (4)
    OE 314 Outdoor Programming and Leadership: Canoeing (4)

American Studies Major

The American Studies interdisciplinary program of study aims to help students develop an appreciation of American culture while making the connection between past political, social, and economic forces and the shaping of our contemporary world. Allied with the history program in many ways, American Studies provides a concentration in the wider areas of study and life in the United States, including American literature, social institutions, economic development, religious life, and other related areas.

The American Studies Discipline

While encompassing primarily the geographical region of the United States from pre-colonial times to today, American Studies recognizes that political, cultural, religious, and economic patterns do not stop at U.S. borders. American Studies seeks to comparatively and critically explore and understand American history, beliefs, and values, concentrating on how these elements inform a perspective on the larger world and taking into account how the many cultures of America have been constantly influenced by movements of people, commerce, and ideas that cross borders.

Why Study American Studies at Montreat College?

American Studies classes at the College are intentionally kept small to ensure that students have a place to voice informed opinions in a safe and collaborative atmosphere. While their primary concern is teaching, professors at Montreat College are engaged in research that they publish and bring into the classroom. Highly personalized faculty advising helps ensure that students develop a plan including professional goals along with the courses they need for graduation. Professors place a high priority on community and collegiality.

After Graduation

The American Studies major will prepare students to enter a wide array of graduate school programs in history, law, ministry, criminology, and other social sciences and for careers that require a well-rounded perspective on American life and cultures. This program of study is designed for students who may be returning to their native land to teach English, American history, or sociology; for those United States citizens who intend to pursue graduate studies in American Studies in other parts of the world, and for international students who are seeking primarily an American course of study apart from the more narrow specialization they have already followed.

Requirements for a Major in American Studies

√ Degree Component

____ Completion of the General Education Core (56 credits)

____   HS 101 & HS 102 required in the Gen-Ed

____ Completion of the General Education Competencies

____ Completion of the American Studies Major Core (21 credits)

____ Completion of the American Studies Major Electives (24 credits)

____ Completion of the Bachelor of Arts or Bachelor of Science courses (12 credits)

____ Completion of required electives to bring total up to 126 credits (~13 credits)

____ Completion of 33 credits at the 300-level or above

____ Completion of the Major Field Test

____ Completion of 126 credit hours with a minimum GPA of 2.0 (two terms and 32 credit hours must be completed at Montreat College)

American Studies Major Core (21 credits)

AS 401   American Studies (3)

BS 101   Introduction to Business (3)

EN 321   Literature of the United States I (3)

EN 322   Literature of the United States II (3)

HS 201   United States History I (3)

HS 202   United States History II (3)

HS 491   Senior Thesis (3)

American Studies Required Major Electives (24 credits)

Choose 15 credits from the following:

HS 331   American Revolution and Republic (3)

HS 333   American Civil War (3)

HS 335   United States History since 1945 (3)

HS 341   American Constitutional History (3)

HS 343   Religious History of America (3)

HS 345   American Cultural and Intellectual History (3)

HS 361   The World at War (3)

HS 481   Directed Study & Research (3)

Choose 9 credits from the following:

BS 203   Macroeconomics (3)

BS 204   Microeconomics (3)

CC 201   Comparative Cultures (3)

IS 202   Modern Secular-Christian Worldviews (3)

IS 441   Internship (3) (Prerequisite: IS 310)

IS 460   Council for Christian Colleges & Universities Seminar (6)

HS 481   Directed Study & Research (3)

SC 204   Introduction to Sociology (3)

SC 205   Marriage and Family (3)

Four Year Plan: Bachelor of Arts or Science in American Studies

Freshman Year

Fall Semester		Spring Semester	
IS 102 Foundations of Faith and Learning	2	CS 102 Computer Applications and Concepts	3
BB 101 Survey of Old Testament	3	BB 102 Survey of New Testament	3
EN 101 English Composition I	3	EN 102 English Composition II	3
HS 101 History of World Civilization I	3	HS 102 History of World Civilization II	3
Bachelor of Arts or Science requirement	3	Bachelor of Arts or Science requirement	3
PE activity course	1	PE activity course	1
	15		16

Sophomore Year

Fall Semester		Spring Semester	
HS 201 United States History I	3	HS 202 United States History II	3
Bachelor of Arts or Science requirement	3	Bachelor of Arts or Science requirement	3
BS 101 Introduction to Business	3	Gen-Ed Literature	3
Gen-Ed Natural Science	4	Gen-Ed Natural Science	4
Gen-Ed Mathematics	3	Major Elective	3
	16		16

Junior Year

Fall Semester		Spring Semester	
EN 321 Literature of the United States I	3	EN 322 Literature of the United States II	3
Gen-Ed Oral Competency	3	Gen-Ed Humanities	3
Gen-Ed Social Science	3	Major Elective	3
Gen-Ed Humanities	3	Major Elective	3
Major Elective	3	Elective	3
	15		15

Completion of the General Education competencies by the end of the junior year.

Senior Year

Fall Semester		Spring Semester	
AS 401 American Studies	3	HS 491 Senior Thesis	3
Major Elective	3	Major Elective	3
Major Elective	3	Major Elective	3
Gen-Ed Humanities	3	Elective	3
IS 461 Seminar on Faith and Life	2	Elective	3
Elective	3	Elective	1
	17		16

Completion of 33 credits at the 300-level or above.
Completion of the Major Field Test by the end of the Senior Year.

		Total hours required for degree:	126

*See General Education for optional course offerings

Art Minor

The Art minor offers a strong foundation in the classical methods of learning visual art-making processes. In each studio course, the elements and principles of visual art are approached through observation, interpretation and response. Although formalism is taught and encouraged, it is woven into the resulting artwork rather than standing alone as "abstract." By this method of learning, the faculty and student have a common source, similarly perceived, which guides the process of decision-making and problem solving when creating works of art.

Requirements for a Minor in Art (18 credits)

The following courses are best taken in numerical sequence.

Art Minor Core

Choose one class:
> AR 101   Survey of Art I (3) **OR**
> AR 102   Survey of Art II (3)

Choose one class:
> AR 241   Drawing I (3) **OR**
> AR 341   Drawing II (3)

Take all of the following four classes:
> AR 349   Graphics & Photojournalism (3)
> AR 342   Painting (3)
> AR 344   Sculpture (3)
> AR 461   Seminar in Art (3)

The Art minor complements other academic majors through strengthening the student's ability to communicate visually.

Bible and Religion Major

The Bible and Religion program of study prepares students to pursue graduate studies in a broad range of fields as well as to prepare them to work with children, youth, and families in a variety of organizations both in the United States and other cross-cultural contexts.

The Bible and Religion Discipline

The Bible and Religion major offers four areas of concentration: Biblical Scholarship, Cross-Cultural Studies, Preaching and Evangelism, and Youth and Family Ministry. Students should select an area of concentration that reflects their specialized interest.

Students who elect to concentrate in Biblical Scholarship or Cross-Cultural Studies will earn a Bachelor of Arts degree. These programs are designed to prepare students to enter theological seminaries or graduate schools of religion. The Biblical Scholarship concentration requires the use of the Greek New Testament by the senior year and a senior thesis. The Cross-Cultural Studies concentration includes an overseas internship experience. These concentrations provide instruction and mentoring in the fields of Biblical and Cross-Cultural studies from a distinctively Reformed perspective.

Students choosing the Preaching and Evangelism or Youth and Family Ministry concentration can earn either a Bachelor of Arts or Bachelor of Science degree. These concentrations seek to provide necessary biblical, theoretical, and practical skills.

Each concentration provides a balance of instruction in biblical studies, educational leadership, worldview studies, counseling, communication, and understanding of people of varying ages within a cultural context that is rooted in a Reformed theology.

Why Study Bible and Religion at Montreat College?

Montreat College provides a unique mentoring environment that facilitates interaction between students and faculty both in and outside the classroom context. The department's commitment to exploring the relationship between faith and learning, alongside the relevance of the Christian faith for all disciplines of study, provides learners with a rich liberal arts experience to prepare them for graduate study or a wide range of occupations. The departmental faculty challenges students academically, assisting them in wrestling with the spiritual and practical implications of the subject matter. The full-time faculty is complemented by part-time and adjunct faculty who share the College's and department's mission, providing specific expertise to enhance the educational experience.

After Graduation

Students who graduate with a degree in Bible and Religion are free to pursue a wide spectrum of career choices. Some students enter the ministry by continuing their education in seminary and /or seeking ordination by their denomination. Others build on the knowledge and skills they acquired from the Bible and Religion major by entering careers in education, law, criminal justice, psychology, and counseling. Regardless of what goals are chosen, a Bible and Religion major prepares one for a career and a lifestyle guided by religious faith.

Requirements for a Major in Bible and Religion

√	Degree Component
___	Completion of the General Education Core, noting concentration-specific requirements (56* credits)
___	Completion of the General Education Competencies
___	Completion of the Bible & Religion Major Core (15 credits)
___	Completion of a Bible & Religion Concentration (24-32 credits)
___	Completion of the Bachelor of Arts or Bachelor of Science courses, noting concentration-specific requirements (12 credits)
___	Completion of required electives to bring total up to 126 credits (~11-19 credits)
___	Completion of 33 credits at the 300-level or above
___	Pass the Biblical, Religious, and Interdisciplinary Studies departmental exam with a score of 75 or better**
___	Completion of 126 credit hours with a minimum GPA of 2.0 (two terms and 32 credit hours must be completed at Montreat College)

*PR 310 in the Preaching and Evangelism concentration can count toward oral expression competency in the Gen-Ed.
**The departmental exam will be given at the beginning of the senior year and offered at the end of each semester.

Bible and Religion Major Core (15 hours)

BB 211   Christian Doctrine (3)
BB 302   Romans (3)
Choose 9 additional hours of BB, CC, PH, PR, WA or YM courses at the 200 level or above; HS 353; or IS 202

Choose from five Bible and Religion Concentrations:

Biblical Scholarship (24 credits)
Cross-Cultural (28 credits)
Preaching and Evangelism (31 credits)
Youth and Family Ministries (31 credits)
Special Emphasis (32 credits)

Biblical Scholarship Concentration (24 hours)

The Biblical Scholarship Concentration (Bachelor of Arts) is composed of the following:

BB 201 Old Testament Theology (3)
BB 202 New Testament Theology (3)
BB 208 Gospels (3)
BB 209 Epistles (3)
BB 303 Prophetic Literature (3)
BB 305 Biblical Interpretation (3)
BB 308 Apocalyptic Literature (3)
BB 491 Senior Thesis (3)

Biblical Scholarship students must take two years of biblical languages to fulfill their BA language requirements:

GR 201 New Testament Greek I (3)
GR 202 New Testament Greek II (3)
    AND
Choose one of the following sequences:
    GR 303 Greek Grammar and Syntax (3)
    GR 304 Greek Exegesis (3)
        OR
    HB 303 Elementary Biblical Hebrew I (4)
    HB 304 Elementary Biblical Hebrew II (4)

Cross-Cultural Concentration (27 hours)

The Cross-Cultural Concentration (Bachelor of Arts) is composed of the following:

BB 306 World Religions (3)
CC 301 Foundations of Cross-Cultural Ministry (3)

CC 402 Cultural Anthropology (3)
CC 403 Cross-Cultural Communication (3)
CC 441 Overseas Internship (3)
HS 353 History of Christianity (3)
IS 202 Modern Secular-Christian Worldviews (3)
IS 310 Pre-Internship (1)
YM 303 Discipleship & Lifestyle Evangelism (3)

Choose one of the following:
    BB 480 Special Topics (3)
    YM 401 Spiritual Formation & Faith Development (3)

Preaching and Evangelism Concentration (30 hours)

The Preaching and Evangelism Concentration (Bachelor of Arts or Science) is composed of the following:

BB 305   Biblical Interpretation (3)
HS 353   History of Christianity (3)
PH 301   Ethics (3)
PR 310   Biblical Preaching and Communication (3)
PR 410   Preparing the Gospel (3)
PR 420   Preaching the Gospel (3)
PR 430   Prayer and the Holy Spirit (3)
PR 491   Seminar on Ministry (1)
YM 303   Discipleship and Lifestyle Evangelism (3)
YM 380   Administrative Ministry and Organization (3)
YM 401   Spiritual Formation and Faith Development (3)

Note: 3 courses in the Preaching and Evangelism concentration are taught online incorporating materials from the Billy Graham Evangelistic Association.

Youth and Family Ministries Concentration (31 hours)

The Youth and Family Ministry Concentration (Bachelor of Arts or Science) is composed of the following:

IS 302   Philosophy of Leadership (3)
IS 310   Pre-Practicum/Pre-Internship (1)
SC 414   Counseling Adolescents and Families (3)
YM 203   Foundations of Youth and Family Ministries (3)
YM 303   Discipleship and Lifestyle Evangelism (3)
YM 360   Ministry to Children (3)
YM 380   Administrative Ministry & Organization (3)
YM 401   Spiritual Formation and Faith Development (3)
YM 407   Contemporary Youth Culture and Programming (3)
YM 408   Introduction to Pedagogy (3)
YM 441   Ministry Internship (3)

Note: Students in Youth and Family Ministries Concentration must take PY 201 Psychology Applied to Modern Life (3) as a General Education Requirement.
Note: Students may replace either a 300 or 400 level course requirement in the concentration with YM 481 Directed Study and Research (3) with approval.

Special Emphasis Concentration (32 hours)

The Special Emphasis Concentration (Bachelor of Arts) allows students to design a program of study focused on an area of interest outside the core curriculum of their particular major. Working with a faculty member in their major, the student selects courses from other institutions or departments at Montreat College that can be integrated into their specific discipline. The Special Emphasis must be approved by the student's academic advisor prior to completing sixty (60) credit hours.

The Special Emphasis proposal must meet all the General Education and Competency requirements published in the Academic Catalog, including the language requirement for the BA degree. The proposal must include the following elements: (1) a rationale for the program, (2) a description of one's career objectives, (3) identification of at least thirty-two (32) credit hours of coursework with supporting rationale from within the student's academic program, and (4) identification of at least eighteen (18) credit hours of additional coursework with supporting rationale, generally outside the student's chosen department, that directly supports the student's career objectives. The proposal, once approved by the academic advisor, will be submitted to the Department for final approval.

Four Year Plan: Bachelor of Arts or Bachelor of Science in Bible and Religion
Concentrations in Biblical Scholarship (BA), Cross-Cultural Studies (BA), Preaching and Evangelism (BA/BS), Youth and Family Ministries (BA/BS)

Freshman Year			
Fall Semester		**Spring Semester**	
IS 102 Foundations of Faith and Learning	2	CS 102 Computer Applications and Concepts	3
BB 101 Survey of Old Testament	3	BB 102 Survey of New Testament	3
EN 101 English Composition	3	EN 102 English Composition II	3
HS 101 History of World Civilization I	3	HS 102 History of World Civilization II	3
Gen-Ed Natural Science	4	Gen-Ed Natural Science	4
	15		**16**

Sophomore Year			
Fall Semester		**Spring Semester**	
BB 211 Christian Doctrine	3	BB 302 Romans	3
BB 200+ level course for major (not part of concentration)	3	Concentration Requirement	3
Gen-Ed Social Science (PY 201 required for Youth & Family Ministries)	3	Gen-Ed Mathematics	3
Gen-Ed Literature	3	Gen-Ed Oral Competency	3
B.A. or B.S. requirement (Biblical Scholarship: GR 201)	3	B.A. or B.S. requirement (Biblical Scholarship: GR 202)	3
PE activity course	1	PE activity course	1
	16		**16**

Junior Year			
Fall Semester		**Spring Semester**	
BB 200+ level course for major (not part of concentration)	3	BB 200+ level course for major (not part of concentration)	3
Concentration Requirement	3	Concentration Requirement	3
Concentration Requirement	3	Concentration Requirement	3
Gen-Ed Humanities	3	Gen-Ed Humanities	3
B.A. or B.S. requirement (Biblical Scholarship: GR 303/HB 303)	3	B.A. or B.S. requirement (Biblical Scholarship: GR 304/HB 304	3
	15		**15**

Completion of the General Education competencies by the end of the junior year.

Senior Year			
Fall Semester		**Spring Semester**	
Gen-Ed Humanities	3	BB 441 Internship or BB 491 Senior Thesis	3
Concentration Requirement	3	Concentration Requirement	3
Concentration Requirement	3	Concentration Requirement or Elective	3
Concentration Requirement or Elective	3	Concentration Requirement or Elective	3
Concentration Requirement or Elective	1	IS 461 Seminar on Faith and Life	2
Elective	3	Elective	3
	16		**17**

Completion of 33 credits at the 300-level or above.
Completion of the Departmental Exam by the end of the Senior Year.

Total hours required for degree:	**126**

*See General Education for optional course offerings

Bible and Religion Minor

Requirements for a Minor in Bible and Religion (18 credits)

> 12 credits from Bible and Religion, Greek and/or Hebrew
> 6 credits from Cross-Cultural Studies and/or Youth and Family Ministries
> At least 12 of the 18 credits must be at the 300- or 400-level

The Bible and Religion minor is designed to assist students to strengthen their understanding of the Bible and explore the relationship between it and their major discipline. It seeks to prepare students to be biblically informed agents of renewal and reconciliation in the world.

Youth and Family Ministries Minor

The Youth and Family Ministries minor is designed specifically for students who wish to explore their gifts in children's, youth, and/or family ministries while earning a separate specialized degree. The program intends to provide learners with broad knowledge and basic skills necessary for serving the needs of the church in these vital areas.

Requirements of a Minor in Youth and Family Ministries (18 credits)

Youth and Family Ministries Core (12 credits)
> YM 203 Foundations of Youth and Family Ministries (3)
> YM 380 Administrative Ministry & Organization (3)
> YM 401 Spiritual Formation and Faith Development (3)
> YM 407 Contemporary Youth Culture and Programming (3)

Youth and Family Ministries Required Electives (6 credits)
> Choose two courses from the following:
> > BB 211 Christian Doctrine (3)
> > BB 302 Romans (3)
> > CC 301 Foundations of Cross-Cultural Ministry (3)
> > YM 303 Discipleship and Lifestyle Evangelism (3)
> > YM 360 Ministry to Children (3)
> > YM 408 Introduction to Pedagogy (3)

Biology Major

The Biology program of study prepares students to understand the fundamental concepts and methodologies of the biological sciences, to engage in scientific research, and to investigate the relationships between biology and other fields of study, including social and environmental sciences. The biology program prepares students for numerous careers in specific areas of applied biology such as medical (including pre-medicine and pre-veterinary), agricultural, and environmental fields. In addition, the program includes components that target a student's preparation for successful graduate studies.

The Biology Discipline

Defined simply, biology is the study of life. The 21st century world will have to find solutions for many biological and environmental issues. Those biologists most capable of devising these solutions will understand the connections between biological knowledge and other scientific disciplines such as chemistry, geology, physics, meteorology, and climatology.

Why Study Biology at Montreat College?

At Montreat College, the biology major is uniquely developed with a Christ-centered approach and small, intimate classes. Within the department, the faculty is highly accessible and genuine in their approach to students. The faculty works directly with students in developing research projects and career opportunities that are congruent with the student's goals, while additionally providing connections with the Au Sable Environmental Institute, the Council for Christian Colleges and Universities, and the Appalachian College Association.

Set in the Southern Appalachian Mountains, adjacent to the Pisgah National Forest, Montreat College is equally adept at immersing the student into the subject matter. Students have the opportunity to learn experientially, whether inside the classroom or in the outdoors. Yet, those trained in biology must have more than a solid understanding of basic principles. They must possess an understanding of the ethical and worldview implications involved in the application of biological knowledge. Montreat College students are challenged to understand these implications through discussions and inquiry.

The biology major allows much room for individualization. Possible academic choices are the Pre-Professional Biology Concentration, which can be augmented by the honors track or professional honors track, the Environmental Biology Concentration, and the Special Emphasis (self-designed) Concentration. These options ensure a well-tailored education for any student.

After Graduation

With a comprehensive education in biology, students are prepared to enter such fields as field biology, ecology, applied research, teaching, environmental biology, and many other possible career paths. The biology program also equips student for graduate school in a variety of disciplines, including physical therapy, veterinary medicine, biology, ecology, and medicine.

Requirements for a Major in Biology

√	Degree Component
___	Completion of the General Education Core (56 credits)
___	BL 101 or 103 and BL 102 or 104 required in the Gen-Ed
___	Completion of the General Education Competencies
___	Completion of the Biology Major Core (42.5 credits)
___	Completion of a Biology Concentration (22-27 credits)
___	Completion of required electives to bring total up to 126 credits (~1-6 credits)
___	Completion of 33 credits at the 300-level or above
___	Completion of the Major Field Test
___	Completion of 126 credit hours with a minimum GPA of 2.0 (two terms and 32 credit hours must be completed at Montreat College)

Biology Major Core (42.5 Credits)

BL 205   Animal Diversity and Ecology (4)
BL 206   Human Anatomy & Physiology I (4)
BL 215   Plant Diversity and Ecology (4)
BL 301   Biometrics (3)
BL 311   Plant Physiology (3)
BL 315   Cell Biology (4)
BL 401   Genetics (3)
CH 201   Environmental Inorganic Chemistry I (4)
CH 202   Environmental Inorganic Chemistry II (4)
ES 206   Ecology (4)
ES 230   Sophomore Science Seminar I (0.5)
ES 445   Senior Science Seminar (1)
MT 191   Applied Calculus I (4)

Choose from five Biology Concentrations:

Pre-Professional (26-27 credits)
Applied Biochemical Technology (25 credits)
Environmental Biology (21-24 credits)
Integrated Preparation for Accelerated Baccalaureate of Science in Nursing (21 credits)
Special Emphasis (22 credits)

Pre-Professional Concentration (26-27 credits)

The Pre-professional concentration offers a wide range of courses designed to prepare students for entrance into *medical school, veterinary school, dental school, physical therapy* programs, and other professional or graduate schools.

Pre-Professional Concentration Courses

    BL/ES 340 Research Methods (3)
    CH 320   Organic Chemistry I (3)
    CH 322   Organic Chemistry Lab- I (2)
    CH 321   Organic Chemistry II (3)
    CH 323   Organic Chemistry Lab- II (1)
    BL 421   Contemporary Biological Investigations (3)
    MT 192   Applied Calculus II (4)
    PC 131   College Physics I (4)
    Plus *one* of the following courses:
        BL 404   Microbiology (3)
        BL 406   Conservation Biology (3)
        ES 315   Freshwater Ecosystems (4)
        BL 415   Biochemistry/Toxicology (4)
        CH 315   Chemistry of the Environment I (3)

Honors Option

Honors recognition will be indicated on the student's transcript. Students pursuing this option must meet the following requirements in addition to those listed above:

- Complete an acceptable research proposal by the end of the fall semester of the junior year.
- Complete six semester hours of independent research (ES/BL 340 and ES/BL 440).
- Orally present research findings prior to graduation.
- Complete an additional nine semester hours of courses specific to the concentration.

Professional Honors Option

This option is designed to challenge students of an advanced academic ability by providing a program of study involving a unique set of courses and distinguished research. Completion of this program will be indicated as "Professional Honors" on the transcript. Those pursuing this option must complete all the requirements for the honors option (including the selection of BL 404, BL 415, CH 316, and PC 132 for the fourth requirement in the honors option) plus submit a publication-quality research manuscript based on their independent research project.

Applied Biochemical Technology Concentration (25 credits)

The Applied Biochemistry Technology track is a customized investigation of technologies in Biology and Chemistry that are designed around the interests of the student. The student develops a research project that will make a significant contribution in addressing an issue in our world.

The unique student research within our Biology program initiates in the sophomore year when the student enters the program and continues as a component of many classes through their senior year. This broad based, extensive research project brings distinction to our biology students. The student directing their interests towards technology can extend this project work into our technology track and develop significant research contributions in responsible Biochemical technologies.

Applied Biochemical Technology Concentration

BL/ES 340 Research Methods (3)
CH 320   Organic Chemistry I (3)
CH 322   Organic Chemistry Lab-I (2)
CH 321   Organic Chemistry II (3)
CH 323   Organic Chemistry Lab-II (1)
BL 421   Contemporary Biological Investigations (3)
PC 131   College Physics I (4)
BL 404   Microbiology (3)
BL 415   Biochemistry / Toxicology (3)
Recommended:
    MT 192 Applied Calculus II (4)
    PC 132 College Physics II (4)
    CH 315 Environmental Chemistry I (3)
    CH 316 Environmental Chemistry II (3)

By the completion of Junior Year and Summer: Official Entrance into the Biology Applied Biochemical Technology Program is earned by completing the following:
1. Biotechnology Research Project is approved and included within a grant that is either successfully funded or monies are available to continue the student's work in the track program.
2. Meet with a faculty member during the sophomore or junior year to journal and develop the following topics: Ethics/Faith, Development/Project Development/Grant Writing/Required Grant Funding
3. Summer Biotechnology Certificate or Specified Training Established

Note: If any component of the junior year requirements is not fulfilled, the student is not allowed to continue and must meet with an advisor and make plans to enter another Biology track program.

Four Year Plan: Bachelor of Science in Biology
Pre-Professional Concentration & Applied Biochemical Technology Concentration

Freshman Year

Fall Semester		Spring Semester	
IS 102 Foundations of Faith and Learning	2	MT 191 Applied Calculus I*	4
BB 101 Survey of Old Testament	3	BB 102 Survey of New Testament	3
EN 101 English Composition	3	EN 102 English Composition II	3
HS 101 History of World Civilization I	3	CS 102 Computer Applications and Concepts	3
BL 103 Advanced Survey of Biological Prin. I	4	BL 104 Advanced Survey of Biological Prin. II	4
	15		17

*MT 121 College Algebra must be taken if student does not have the prerequisite for MT 191 Applied Calculus

Sophomore Year

Fall Semester		Spring Semester	
BL/ES 230 Sophomore Science Seminar	0.5	BL 315 Cell Biology	4
BL 206 Human Anatomy and Physiology I	4	BL 205 Animal Diversity and Ecology	4
CH 201 Environmental Inorganic Chemistry I	4	CH 202 Environmental Inorganic Chemistry II	4
ES 206 Ecology or PC 131 College Physics	4	Gen-Ed Oral Competency	3
MT 192 Applied Calculus II (Pre-Prof) or BL 404 Microbiology (Biochem)	4	Gen-Ed Literature	3
	16		18

Junior Year

Fall Semester		Spring Semester	
BL 215 Plant Diversity and Ecology	4	BL 311 Plant Physiology or BL 301 Biometrics	3
BL 401 Genetics	3	CH 321 Organic Chemistry II	4
CH 320 Organic Chemistry I	4	CH 322 Organic Chemistry I Lab	2
Gen-Ed Social Science	3	Gen-Ed Humanities	3
PE activity	1	HS 102 History of World Civ II	3
		PE activity course	1
	15		16

Completion of the General Education competencies by the end of the junior year.

Junior Summer

Internship or partnership opportunity (required for Biochem; optional for Pre-Prof)

Senior Year

Fall Semester		Spring Semester	
Major elective (Pre-Prof) or BL 415 Biochemistry/Toxicology (Biochem)	3	BL 301 Biometrics or BL 311 Plant Physiology	3
ES 445 Senior Science Seminar I	1	BL 421 Contemporary Biological Investigations	3
Gen-Ed Humanities	3	CH 323 Organic Chemistry Lab II	1
ES/BL 340 Research Methods	3	Gen-Ed Humanities	3
PC 131 College Physics or ES 206 Ecology	4	IS 461 Seminar on Faith and Life	2
BL/CH/ES/MT elective recommended		Elective (PC 132 recommended)	3
	14		15

Completion of 33 credits at the 300-level or above.
Completion of the Major Field Test by the end of the Senior Year.

	Total hours required for degree:	126.5

*See General Education for optional course offerings

Environmental Biology Concentration (21-24 credits)

The Environmental Biology concentration offers a wide range of courses designed to prepare students for entrance into such fields as biology, ecology, field research, and many other possible career paths. The concentration also equips students for graduate school in a variety of disciplines, including biology, ecology, and botany.

Environmental Biology Concentration Courses

CH 320   Organic Chemistry I (3)
CH 322   Organic Chemistry Lab-I (2)
BL/ES 340 Research Methods (3)
PC 131   College Physics I (4)
Plus 9-12 hours selected from courses in Biology, Environmental Studies, Math, Chemistry, and Physics, in consultation with the advisor.

Four Year Plan: Bachelor of Science in Biology			
Environmental Biology Concentration			
Freshman Year			
Fall Semester		**Spring Semester**	
IS 102 Foundations of Faith and Learning	2	MT 191 Applied Calculus I*	4
BB 101 Survey of Old Testament	3	BB 102 Survey of New Testament	3
EN 101 English Composition	3	EN 102 English Composition II	3
HS 101 History of World Civilization I	3	CS 102 Computer Applications and Concepts	3
BL 103 Advanced Survey of Biological Prin. I	4	BL 104 Advanced Survey of Biological Prin. II	4
	15		17
*MT 121 College Algebra must be taken if student does not have the prerequisite for MT 191 Applied Calculus			
Sophomore Year			
Fall Semester		**Spring Semester**	
BL/ES 230 Sophomore Science Seminar	0.5	BL 315 Cell Biology	4
BL 206 Human Anatomy and Physiology I	4	BL 205 Animal Diversity and Ecology	4
CH 201 Environmental Inorganic Chemistry I	4	CH 202 Environmental Inorganic Chemistry II	4
ES 206 Ecology or PC 131 College Physics	4	Gen-Ed Oral Competency	3
Concentration Requirement	3	Gen-Ed Literature	3
	15.5		18
Junior Year			
Fall Semester		**Spring Semester**	
BL 215 Plant Diversity and Ecology	4	BL 311 Plant Physiology or BL 301 Biometrics	3
BL 401 Genetics	3	Concentration Requirement	4
CH 320 Organic Chemistry I	3	CH 322 Organic Chemistry Lab I	2
Gen-Ed Social Science	3	Gen-Ed Humanities	3
PE activity	1	HS 102 History of World Civilization II	3
		PE activity course	1
	14		16
Completion of the General Education competencies by the end of the junior year.			
Junior Summer			
Optional internship or partnership opportunity			
Senior Year			
Fall Semester		**Spring Semester**	
ES 445 Senior Science Seminar I	1	BL 301 Biometrics or BL 311 Plant Physiology	3
Gen-Ed Humanities	3	Concentration Requirement	3
BL/ES 340 Research Methods	3	Concentration Requirement or Elective	3
ES 206 Ecology or PC 131 College Physics	4	Gen-Ed Humanities	3
Elective	3	IS 461 Seminar on Faith and Life	2
		Elective	3
	14		17
Completion of 33 credits at the 300-level or above.			
Completion of the Major Field Test by the end of the Senior Year.			
*See General Education for optional course offerings		Total hours required for degree:	127

IP for ABSN [Integrated Preparation for Accelerated Baccalaureate of Science in Nursing] Concentration (21 credits)

The IP for ABSN [Pre-Nursing] track is a customized to provide entrance to an Accelerated Baccalaureate of Science in Nursing [ASBN] program so that the student interested in Health Sciences can receive a Biology degree that has integrated the prerequisite courses required by most ABSN or second degree programs around the country. The student is allowed to customize their Biology track to suit the admission requirements of the ABSN program with which the student wishes to link their Montreat College Biology degree, as there may be slight variance in prerequisite courses for different ABSN programs. Most ABSN programs require a 12 month period to meet the requirements of this second undergraduate degree. Some of the Pre-Nursing track courses are taken at community colleges or online through other institutions, as approved by a Montreat College faculty advisor and specific to the student's ABSN program selection.

IP for ABSN Concentration

IP/ABSN Core (16)

BL 207 Human Anatomy & Physiology II (4)
BL 404* Microbiology (3)
BL 421* Contemporary Biological Investigations (3)
HL 201 Human Nutrition (3)
PY 202 General Psychology (3)

IP/ABSN Required Electives (5)

Choose at least 5 credit hours from the courses below in consultation with faculty advisor and specific to your ABSN program selection:

CH 321 Organic Chemistry (3)
CH 322 Organic Chemistry Lab (2)
BL 415 Biochemistry (3)
PY 300[†] Child and Adolescent Development (3)
PY 305[†] Adult Development and Aging (3)
Pathophysiology [Fulfilled at another institution with prerequisite qualifications]
Global Health Care Issues [Fulfilled at another institution with prerequisite qualifications]

*BL 404 and BL 421 to be taken concurrently
[†] Students may only take one psychology class to fulfill the concentration elective requirement.

Four Year Plan: Bachelor of Science in Biology
Integrated Preparation for Accelerated Bachelor of Science in Nursing Concentration

Freshman Year				
Fall Semester		**Spring Semester**		
IS 102 Foundations of Faith and Learning	2	MT 191 Applied Calculus I*		4
BB 101 Survey of Old Testament	3	BB 102 Survey of New Testament		3
EN 101 English Composition	3	EN 102 English Composition II		3
HS 101 History of World Civilization I	3	CS 102 Computer Applications and Concepts		3
BL 103 Advanced Survey of Biological Prin. I	4	BL 104 Advanced Survey of Biological Prin. II		4
	15			**17**

*MT 121 College Algebra must be taken if student does not have the prerequisite for MT 191 Applied Calculus

Sophomore Year				
Fall Semester		**Spring Semester**		
BL/ES 230 Sophomore Science Seminar	0.5	BL 315 Cell Biology		4
BL 206 Human Anatomy and Physiology I	4	BL 207 Human Anatomy & Phys. II		4
CH 201 Environmental Inorganic Chemistry I	4	CH 202 Environmental Inorganic Chemistry II		4
ES 206 Ecology or PC 131 College Physics	4	CM 220 Public Speech and Rhetorical Analysis		3
HL 201 Human Nutrition	3	Gen-Ed Literature		3
	15.5			**18**

Junior Year				
Fall Semester		**Spring Semester**		
BL 215 Plant Diversity and Ecology	4	BL 311 Plant Physiology or BL 301 Biometrics		3
BL 401 Genetics	3	BL 205 Animal Diversity & Ecology		4
Concentration Elective	3	Concentration Elective		2
PY 202 General Psychology or PY 201 Psychology Applied to Modern Life	3	Gen-Ed Humanities		3
PE activity	1	HS 102 History of World Civ II		3
		PE activity course		1
	14			**16**

Completion of the General Education competencies by the end of the junior year.

Junior Summer
Optional internship or partnership opportunity

Senior Year				
Fall Semester		**Spring Semester**		
BL 404 Microbiology	3	BL 301 Biometrics or BL 311 Plant Physiology		3
ES 445 Senior Science Seminar I	1	BL 421 Contemporary Biological Investigations		3
Gen-Ed Humanities	3	Gen-Ed Humanities		3
Elective	4	IS 461 Seminar on Faith and Life		2
Elective	3	Elective		3
Elective	3			
	17			**14**

Completion of 33 credits at the 300-level or above.
Completion of the Major Field Test by the end of the Senior Year.

Total hours required for degree:	**127**

*See General Education for optional course offerings

Special Emphasis Concentration (22 credits)

Students may transfer a set of courses from other institutions, study abroad and certification programs (e.g., Au Sable Institute), or complete courses in other departments at Montreat College to fulfill the requirements of this emphasis. Students develop the special emphasis curriculum in consultation with the faculty advisor. The advisor and the Biology Review Committee must approve a formal proposal of emphasis requirements by the end of the student's sophomore year.

Special Emphasis Concentration

Minimum of six (6) courses totaling at least 22 credit hours, selected in consultation with faculty advisor.

In addition to the student developing their own program, below are a few pre-approved Special Emphasis programs:

Pre-Approved Special Emphasis Programs of Study with Au Sable Institute

Au Sable Institute of Environmental Studies' Certificate Program [http://www.ausable.org] is pre-approved as Special Emphasis Concentration plans of study. The student selecting an Au Sable certificate program must adhere to the Au Sable certification guidelines and fulfill all components of the certification program and Special Emphasis requirements. The student must be awarded the certificate by Au Sable. All six courses can be pursued at Au Sable, but if a certification program does not provide the full complement of 6 courses, the additional courses can be pursued at Montreat College or other approved institution. Final plans of how all components of the Special Emphasis are to be fulfilled are prepared with you department advisor and submitted to the department faculty for approval.

Pre-Approved Certification Programs:

Certified Naturalist
Certified Land Resources Analyst
Certified Water Resources Analyst
Certified Environmental Analyst
[Full list of courses offered through Au Sable for Montreat College can be found on the Au Sable website.]

Biology Minor

Requirements for a Minor in Biology (20 credits)

BL 101   Survey of Biological Principles I (4)
BL 102   Survey of Biological Principles II (4)
Choose an additional 4 hours from Biology
Choose an additional 8 hours from Biology, Chemistry, and/or Environmental
Studies.

Business Administration Major

The Bachelor of Science in Business Administration offers concentrations in International Business, Cybersecurity, Management, Marketing, and Sports Management. A Bachelor of Science in Music Business is also offered. See **Music Business (MB)**.

Business and Cybersecurity Department Mission Statement

The mission of the Business and Cybersecurity Department is to equip students with knowledge necessary for them to serve in today's competitive business environment and to cultivate in all students, at all levels, (undergraduate and graduate) an entrepreneurial and ethical spirit in their approaches to business decision making.

Bachelor of Science (BS) in Business Administration Degree Mission Statement

The Montreat College Bachelor of Science in Business Administration program graduates students that possess a sound Christian world-view and are prepared to make an immediate and continuing contribution in a market-driven, free enterprise economy and/or attend graduate school if desired.

BS in Business Administration Program Goals

1. Ability to integrate their Christian world-view and ethics in business decision-making.
2. Proficiency and confidence in applying servant leadership.
3. Technical ability in business functional areas.
4. Effective oral and written skills in business communication.
5. Critical thinking, analytical, and business making skills in business.

The Business Discipline

There is a strong argument that everyone needs to have some business education. Whatever one does in his/her professional life, the chances are that it will involve some 'business.' Scientists, engineers, even artists, will inevitably have to understand at least the basics of business, and probably a lot more. Further, companies of the future will consist of teams, groups of specialists who work together on a specific project and then disband. One of the consequences of this reality is that many more people, whatever their specialty, will need to understand more about the opportunities and constraints of various aspects of business: accounting, management, economics, finance, information systems, and quantitative analysis. The combination of specialist qualification and practical business knowledge is becoming vital.

Why Study Business at Montreat College?

The program builds upon Montreat College's strong liberal arts core with professional training in business administration designed to prepare students for entry-level professional positions in a variety of business organizations. Our unique approach to teaching combines the theoretical with the practical, as all faculty bring extensive business experience to the classroom. Advanced classes are typically small, providing significant personal attention and one-on-one time with professors. Classroom instruction is often augmented with outside business speakers and plant/facility visits. In many courses, student projects involve solving problems and providing services to actual real-world business organizations. Additionally, all students will complete at least one internship in the industry in which they desire to seek employment after graduation.

After Graduation

The Bachelor of Science in Business Administration prepares students for a wide variety of entry-level professional positions in both for-profit and not-for-profit business organizations, depending on the student's area of concentration. For example, students concentrating in Marketing can pursue careers in Advertising, Sales, Market Research, Retailing, Public Relations, and Product Management. Students concentrating in International Business are primed to work for global firms doing business in foreign countries. Students concentrating in Sports Management develop expertise in business management with an orientation toward the world of sports, and thus are equipped to manage sports and recreation programs. Many of these business fields offer strong prospects for continued job growth with excellent earnings potential, and broad opportunities to influence others for Christ.

Requirements for a Major in Business Administration

√	Degree Component
____	Completion of the General Education Core (50* credits)
____	MT 114 is required in the Gen-Ed
____	Completion of the General Education Competencies
____	Completion of the Business Major Core (46 credits)
____	Completion of a Business Concentration (15-32 credits)
____	Completion of required electives to bring total up to 126 credits (~0-12 credits)
____	Completion of 33 credits at the 300-level or above
____	Completion of the Major Field Test
____	Completion of 126 credit hours with a minimum GPA of 2.0 (two terms and 32 credit hours must be completed at Montreat College)

*BS 203 in the major can count toward Gen-Ed social science.
*EN 271 in the major can count toward oral expression competency in the Gen-Ed.

Business Major Core (46 credits)

BS 101   Introduction to Business (3)
BS 201   Principles of Accounting I (3)
BS 202   Principles of Accounting II (3)
BS 203   Macroeconomics (3)
BS 204   Microeconomics (3)
BS 209   Principles of Management (3)
BS 214   Quantitative Methods (3)
BS 230   Principles of Marketing (3)
BS 306   Corporate Finance (3)
BS 309   Business Ethics (3)
BS 312   Business & the Legal Environment (3)
IS 310   Pre-Internship (1)
BS 441   Internship (3)
BS 460   Strategic Management (3)
CS 204   Fundamentals of Information Systems (3)
EN 271   Business Communication (3)

Choose from six Business Concentrations:

Cybersecurity (18 credits)
International Business (30 credits)
Management (15 credits)
Marketing (15 credits)
Sports Management (26 credits)
Special Emphasis (32 credits)

Cybersecurity Concentration (18 hours)

Cybersecurity Courses
    CS 207   Principles of Operating Systems and Comp. Hardware (3)
    CS 215   Introduction to Computer Networking (3)
    CS 335   Computer and Systems Security (3)
    CS 345   Principles of Cybersecurity (3)
    CS 350   Management of Cybersecurity (3)

    Choose 3 hours from the following:
        CS 370   Network Defense and Countermeasures (3)
        CS 375   Linux Operating Systems and Security (3)
        CS 380   Certification Study and Preparation (3)
        CS 441   Cybersecurity Internship (3)

International Business Concentration (30 hours)

International Business Courses
    Choose four (4) courses from the following:
        BS 301   International Finance (3)
        BS 303   Human Resource Management (3)
        BS 320   International Business (3)
        BS 338   Marketing Research (3)
        BS 405   International Marketing (3)

    Plus a minor in a foreign language* (18)

*See Spanish Minor, or if you have taken college courses in a foreign language other than Spanish and wish to continue studies in that language, speak with the Office of Records and Registration about options for additional transfer credit.

Management Concentration (15 hours)

Management Courses
    Choose five (5) courses from the following:
        BS 303   Human Resource Management (3)
        BS 304   Labor-Management Relations (3)
        BS 307   Organizational Behavior (3)
        BS 308   Servant Leadership (3)
        BS 310   Total Quality Management (3)
        BS 313   Production/Operations Management (3)
        BS 402   Management of Not-for-Profit Organizations (3)
        BS 407   Entrepreneurship and Small Business Management (3)

Marketing Concentration (15 hours)

Marketing Courses
 Choose five (5) courses from the following:
  BS 331 Sales Administration (3)
  BS 436 Ecommerce (3)
  BS 335 Retail Management (3)
  BS 336 Principles of Advertising (3)
  BS 338 Marketing Research (3)
  BS 405 International Marketing (3)
  BS 435 Consumer Behavior (3)
  BS 437 Marketing Management (3)
  SM 337 Seminar in Sports Marketing (3)

Sports Management Concentration (26 hours)

Sports Management Courses
Sports Management Core
  PE 302 Methods & Materials of Coaching (2)
  PE 424 Facility Planning for PE Recreation & Athletics (3)
  SM 210 Principles of Sports Management (3)
  SM 337 Seminar in Sport Marketing (3)
Sports Management Required Electives
Choose five (5) courses from the following:
  BS 303 Human Resource Management (3)
  BS 304 Labor-Management Relations (3)
  BS 307 Organizational Behavior (3)
  BS 308 Servant Leadership (3)
  BS 310 Total Quality Management (3)
  BS 313 Production/Operations Management (3)
  BS 402 Management of Not-for-Profit Organizations (3)
  BS 407 Entrepreneurship and Small Business Management (3)

Special Emphasis Concentration (32 hours)

The Special Emphasis concentration allows students to design a program of study focused on an area of interest outside the core curriculum of their particular major. Working with a faculty member in their major, the student selects courses from other institutions or departments at Montreat College that can be integrated into their specific discipline. The Special Emphasis must be approved by the student's academic advisor prior to completing sixty (60) credit hours.

The Special Emphasis proposal must meet all the General Education and Competency requirements published in the Academic Catalog. The proposal must include the following elements: (1) a rationale for the program, (2) a description of one's career objectives, (3) identification of at least thirty-two (32) credit hours of coursework with supporting rationale from within the student's academic program, and (4) identification of at least eighteen (18) credit hours of additional coursework with supporting rationale, generally outside the student's chosen department, that directly supports the student's career objectives. The proposal, once approved by the academic advisor, will be submitted to the Department for final approval.

Four Year Plan: Bachelor of Science in Business Administration
Concentrations in Cybersecurity, Management, Marketing, International Business**, Sports Management, and Special Emphasis

Freshman Year			
Fall Semester		**Spring Semester**	
IS 102 Foundations of Faith and Learning	2	CS 102 Computer Applications and Concepts	3
BB 101 Survey of Old Testament	3	BB 102 Survey of New Testament	3
EN 101 English Composition	3	EN 102 English Composition II	3
BS 101 Introduction to Business	3	Elective (or Oral Competency, if not double-counting EN 271)	3
Gen-Ed Natural Science	4	Gen-Ed Natural Science	4
	15		16

**The International Business concentration requires a foreign language minor; students should plan their course schedules accordingly.

Sophomore Year			
Fall Semester		**Spring Semester**	
BS 201 Principles of Accounting I	3	BS 202 Principles of Accounting II	3
BS 230 Principles of Marketing	3	BS 209 Principles of Management	3
CS 204 Fund. Of Information Systems	3	Gen-Ed Literature	3
HS 101 History of World Civilization I	3	HS 102 History of World Civilization II	3
MT 114 Elementary Probability and Statistics	3	EN 271 Business Communication	3
PE activity course	1	PE activity course	1
	16		16

Junior Year			
Fall Semester		**Spring Semester**	
BS 203 Macroeconomics	3	BS 204 Microeconomics	3
BS 214 Quantitative Methods	3	BS 306 Corporate Finance	3
BS 309 Business Ethics	3	BS 312 Business and Legal Environment	3
Gen-Ed Humanities	3	Gen-Ed Humanities	3
Concentration Requirement	3	IS 310 Pre-Internship	1
		Concentration Requirement	3
	15		16

Completion of the General Education competencies by the end of the junior year.

Junior Summer	
BS 441 Internship	**3**

Senior Year			
Fall Semester		**Spring Semester**	
Gen-Ed Humanities	3	BS 460 Strategic Management	3
Concentration Requirement	3	Concentration Requirement	3
Concentration Requirement	3	Concentration Requirement or Elective	3
Concentration Requirement or Elective	3	Concentration Requirement or Elective	3
Concentration Requirement or Elective	3	IS 461 Seminar on Faith and Life	2
Concentration Requirement, if needed			
	15		14

Completion of 33 credits at the 300-level or above.
Completion of the Major Field Test by the end of the Senior Year

Total hours required for degree:	**126**

*See General Education for optional course offerings

133

Business Administration Minor

Requirements for a Business Administration Minor (18 credits)

BS 101   Introduction to Business (3)
BS 203   Macroeconomics (3)
BS 209   Principles of Management (3)

Choose nine (9) additional hours of BS courses at the 300-400 level

Chemistry Minor

The Chemistry minor is designed to cultivate a broader understanding of scientific knowledge by developing skills involving research, processing data, observation and decision making, analytical skills and performing experiments. Theories are reinforced by observation and analysis in a laboratory setting. The applications of these skills are benefited in other course work where logic and reasoning are required to make student success a reality.

Requirements for a Minor in Chemistry (20 credits)

    CH 201   Environmental Inorganic Chemistry I (4)
    CH 202   Environmental Inorganic Chemistry II (4)
    CH 320   Organic Chemistry I (3)
    CH 322   Organic Chemistry I Lab (2)
    Choose one from the following:
        CH 315   Chemistry of the Environment I (3)
        ES 415   Biochemistry/Toxicology (4)
    Choose one from the following:
        CH 316   Chemistry of the Environment II (3)
        CH 321/CH 323 Organic Chemistry II (3)/Lab (1)

A minor in Chemistry assists in preparing students for numerous careers in specific areas of applied science such as medical (including pre-medical, pre-veterinary, and physical therapy), agricultural, environmental fields, and engineering. In addition, the Chemistry minor includes components that fulfill a student's preparation for many graduate studies programs.

Communication Major

The Communication Major prepares students to use their God-bestowed gifts of language and image use. The grace and power of words provide a foundation for Communication study. Students explore how language and images can be employed to create meaningful messages that can influence, equip, encourage, and teach. Students are challenged to be agents of truth, reflection, transformation and reconciliation in a way that celebrates God's faithfulness and uses all means of media to be instruments of positive change for Christ.

The Communication Discipline

The Communication Major consists of 39-41 hours of core classes beyond the General Education Core. For the General Communication Major, the student takes 30 hours of core classes and then picks 9 hours of Communication electives. The Communication Major also offers a Public Relations Concentration (39 hours) and a Theatre Concentration (41 hours). Classes are designed to give students knowledge of theory and an opportunity to practice it in real-world settings. As a result, short internships or practicums are woven into several of the courses, with a 3-hour professional internship required as an upper classman. Students of other majors can get a Communication Minor by completing 18 hours of coursework in the department.

Why Study Communication at Montreat College?

Every Communication course blends a Biblical worldview with scholarship. Christ composed parables, demonstrated visually with miracles, and preached to communicate truth. The Communication major allows students to examine the disciplines of Public Relations, Mass Media, Public Speaking, and Theatre. Students learn that communicating to other people is a wide knowledge area, incorporating audience analysis, live presentations, mediated messages, and written communication that can change the world for Christ.

Montreat College is set apart, a beautiful piece of God's world. What better place to spend four years, becoming part of a wonderful community, and learning together what it means for you to use communication as a tool to make a difference in the world.

How Can You Get Involved?

- *The Whetstone* (Montreat College's student newspaper) and *Q* (Montreat College's literary magazine) provide student journalists, photographers, poets, and writers a significant voice in campus affairs.
- Students have the opportunity to write, produce and direct original plays and video shorts for Film Production, Playwriting, and Acting for Camera.
- Special Topic courses are regularly offered that provide students with unique opportunities, such as broadcast journalism and webcasting.
- Student filmmaking is becoming an increasing presence on our campus providing opportunities to gain experience in producing, directing, camera, sound, acting, and writing.
- Students in public relations and communication methods have to plan and sometimes conduct PR events and do meaningful quantitative and qualitative research on our campus.
- Students are encouraged to attend regional and national communication conferences and to present their research there.
- Students are required to do a professional internship as upperclassmen, and several short internships before that, that will provide professional employment experience and contacts that make a difference after graduation.

Off-Campus Study Opportunities

Off-campus study opportunities are a great asset to any student. These study programs provide opportunities to obtain professional and life experiences that give polish and maturity to a student. They also provide opportunities to meet and work with professionals that can serve as mentors or job contacts after graduation.

The CCCU provides many such programs (see Off-Campus Study Opportunities further in the catalogue), but four of these may be of particular interest to Communication Majors: the Los Angeles Film Studies Center; the Contemporary Music Center in Nashville, Tennessee; and the American Studies Program in Washington, DC. Courses from an off-campus study program may substitute for certain Communication Major courses where it is deemed appropriate by your advisor and the department chair.

After Graduation

Upon completion of the Communication program at Montreat College, the student has a wide selection of options. One might become an advertising executive, lobbyist, producer, public relations specialist, reporter, speech writer, journalist, editor, video engineer, web designer, broadcast technician, screen writer, publisher, public speaker, photojournalist, marketing researcher, teacher, online marketing specialist, film crew, film director, communication studies researcher….the list goes on and on. After working in the field, students may consider graduate study to further expand their career choices. Government agencies and private companies eagerly look to the present generation to staff their offices as a source of youthful creativity, mature beliefs, and a strong communication background.

At the end of the day, everyone communicates. Being able to effectively communicate through mass media, verbally, or in written form means that you are able to get your ideas across to others. Completing this program also means you are able to research and listen to others well, too. The skills of effective listening and communication insure you will be a vital participant in whatever career field and ministry God prepares for you.

Requirements for a Major in Communication

√	Degree Component
___	Completion of the General Education Core (53* credits)
___	MT 114 and two 300-level English courses are required in the Gen-Ed
___	Completion of the General Education Competencies
___	Completion of the Communication Major Core (18 credits)
___	Completion of a Communication Concentration (24-25 credits)
___	Completion of required electives to bring total up to 126 credits (~30-31 credits)
___	Completion of 33 credits at the 300-level or above
___	Completion of the Departmental Exam
___	Completion of 126 credit hours with a minimum GPA of 2.0 (two terms and 32 credit hours must be completed at Montreat College)

*CM 220 in the major can count toward oral expression competency in the Gen-Ed.

Communication Major Core (18 credits)

CM 220 Rhetoric & Public Speaking (3)
CM 203 Communication & Culture (3)
CM 228 Media Studies (4)
CM 342 Communication Research Methods (4)
IS 310   Pre-Practicum (1)
CM 441 Internship (3)

Choose from five Communication Concentrations:

General Communication (25 credits)
Digital Media Production (25 credits)
Journalism (24 credits)
Public Relations (25 credits)
Theatre (25 credits)

General Communication Concentration (25 credits)

The General Communication Concentration is designed to give students exposure to the Communication field's wide knowledge base. Students receive training in web design, graphic design & photojournalism, news writing, public relations planning, public speaking, and grant writing, while exploring the sociological and cultural implications of communication and media studies. The major strives to balance theoretical exploration with an opportunity to learn practical skills. Students have the freedom to focus the General Communication Major according to their interests by taking 9 additional Communication Electives of their choice.

General Communication Courses

CM 313 Public Relations (3)
CM 344 Nonprofit Organizational Communication (4)
CM 346 Web Studies & Design (3)
CM 349 Graphics & Photojournalism (3)
CM 348 Newswriting (3)
9 hours of Communication electives (see list following concentrations)

Four Year Plan: Bachelor Science in Communication
General Communication Concentration

Freshman Year			
Fall Semester		**Spring Semester**	
IS 102 Foundations of Faith and Learning	2	CS 102 Computer Applications & Concepts	3
BB 101 Survey of Old Testament	3	BB 102 Survey of New Testament	3
EN 101 English Composition	3	EN 102 English Composition II	3
CM 203 Communication and Culture	3	CM 220 Public Speech & Rhetorical Analysis	3
Gen-Ed Natural Science	4	Gen-Ed Natural Science	4
PE activity course	1		
	16		**16**

Sophomore Year			
Fall Semester		**Spring Semester**	
CM 228 Media Studies*	4	CM 313 Public Relations*	3
CM 348 Newswriting*	3	Concentration Elective	3
Gen-Ed Literature	3	Elective	3
MT 114 Elementary Probability and Statistics	3	Gen-Ed Humanities (excluding EN courses)	3
HS 101 History of World Civilization I	3	HS 102 History of World Civilization II	3
		PE activity course	1
	16		**16**

Junior Year			
Fall Semester		**Spring Semester**	
CM 346 Web Studies and Design*	3	CM 349 Graphics and Photojournalism*	3
Gen-Ed Social Science	3	CM 342 Comm. Research Methods*	4
300-level English Literature	3	300-level English Literature	3
Elective	3	IS 310 Pre-Internship	1
Elective	3	Elective	3
	15		**14**

Completion of the General Education competencies by the end of the junior year.

Junior Summer	
CM 441 Internship	**3**

Senior Year			
Fall Semester		**Spring Semester**	
CM 344 Nonprofit Organizational Comm.	4	Concentration Elective	3
Elective	3	Concentration Elective	3
Elective	3	Elective	3
Elective	3	Elective	3
Elective	3	IS 461 Seminar on Faith and Life	2
	16		**13**

Completion of 33 credits at the 300-level or above.
Completion of the ACAT Exam by the end of the Senior Year.

		Total hours required for degree:	**126**

*Offered every other year
**See General Education for optional course offerings

Digital Media Production Concentration (25 credits)

A concentration in digital media production is designed to expose students to the craft of videography, defined as the process of capturing moving images on electronic media. This includes pre-production, visual design, handling a camera, directing actors, scheduling & budgets, lighting, sound capture, digital editing, and distribution considerations. Students can take videography skills into a number of fields, including PR & marketing, youth & camp ministries, ethnographic research, travel & nature documentaries, and narrative filmmaking.

Digital Media Courses

    CM 249 Digital Media Production (3)
    TH 335   Playwriting/Screenwriting (3)
    CM 318 Film History & Theory (4)
    CM/TH 202   Acting for Camera (3)
    CM 329 Film Production (3)
    9 hours of Communication electives
    Los Angeles Film Studies Program*

*Students are expected to apply to the CCCU's LA Film Studies Program (16 credits, including internship). Exceptions can be made for financial hardship. The 16 hours for this semester away would substitute for Montreat College courses. If students do not get into the LA Film Studies Program or legitimately cannot attend due to financial constraints, it is recommended that they do a practicum in addition to the required internship. The optional practicum and required internship should focus on the area of videography in which the student is interested.

Four Year Plan: Bachelor of Science in Communication
Digital Media Production Concentration

Freshman Year

Fall Semester		Spring Semester	
IS 102 Foundations of Faith and Learning	2	CS 102 Computer Applications and Concepts	3
BB 101 Survey of Old Testament	3	BB 102 Survey of New Testament	3
EN 101 English Composition	3	EN 102 English Composition II	3
CM 203 Communication and Culture	3	CM 220 Public Speech and Rhetorical Analysis	3
Gen-Ed Natural Science	4	Gen-Ed Natural Science	4
PE activity course	1		
	16		16

Sophomore Year

Fall Semester		Spring Semester	
CM 228 Media Studies*	4	CM/TH 202 Acting for the Camera	3
CM 249 Digital Media Production	3	Concentration Elective	3
Gen-Ed Literature	3	Elective	3
MT 114 Elementary Probability and Statistics	3	Gen-Ed Humanities (excluding EN courses)	3
HS 101 History of World Civilization I	3	HS 102 History of World Civilization II	3
		PE activity course	1
	16		16

Junior Year

Fall Semester		Spring Semester	
CM 318 Film History and Theory*	4	TH 335 Playwriting/Screenwriting*	3
Gen-Ed Social Science	3	CM 342 Communication Research Methods*	4
300-level English Literature	3	300-level English Literature	3
CM 329 Film Production	3	IS 310 Pre-Internship	1
Elective	3	Elective	3
	16		14

Completion of the General Education competencies by the end of the junior year.

Junior Summer

CM 441 Internship	3

Senior Year

Fall Semester		Spring Semester	
Concentration Elective	3	Concentration Elective	3
Elective	3	Elective	3
Elective	3	Elective	3
Elective	3	Elective	3
Elective	3	IS 461 Seminar on Faith and Life	2
	15		13

Completion of 33 credits at the 300-level or above.
Completion of the ACAT Exam by the end of the Senior Year.

Total hours required for degree:	126

*Offered every other year
**See notes about the LA Film Studies Program
***See General Education for optional course offerings

Journalism Concentration (24 credits)

A concentration in journalism exposes students to the field of journalism in general, proper news data gathering & reporting, news editing considerations, layout & design, convergent journalism, visual rhetoric, internet news considerations, photojournalism, blogging, & digital editing.

Journalism Courses

CM 249 Digital Media Production (3)
CM 347 News Editing (3)
CM 348 News Writing (3)
CM 349 Graphics & Photojournalism (3)
CM 346 Web Studies & Design (3)
9 hours of Communication electives

*Students are recommended to take CM 341 Practicum (3), in addition to CM 441 Internship (3), in order to gain more experience in the journalism industry. The optional practicum and required internship should focus on the area of journalism in which the student is interested.

Four Year Plan: Bachelor of Science in Communication
Journalism Concentration

Freshman Year			
Fall Semester		**Spring Semester**	
IS 102 Foundations of Faith and Learning	2	CS 102 Computer Applications and Concepts	3
BB 101 Survey of Old Testament	3	BB 102 Survey of New Testament	3
EN 101 English Composition	3	EN 102 English Composition II	3
CM 203 Communication and Culture	3	CM 220 Public Speech and Rhetorical Analysis	3
Gen-Ed Natural Science	4	Gen-Ed Natural Science	4
PE activity course	1		
	16		**16**
Sophomore Year			
Fall Semester		**Spring Semester**	
CM 228 Media Studies*	4	CM 347 News Editing*	3
CM 348 News Writing*	3	Concentration Elective	3
Gen-Ed Literature	3	Elective	3
MT 114 Elementary Probability and Statistics	3	Gen-Ed Humanities (excluding EN courses)	3
HS 101 History of World Civilization I	3	HS 102 History of World Civilization II	3
Elective	1	PE activity course	1
	17		**16**
Junior Year			
Fall Semester		**Spring Semester**	
CM 346 Web Studies and Design*	3	CM 349 Graphics and Photojournalism*	3
Gen-Ed Social Science	3	CM 342 Communication Research Methods*	4
300-level English Literature	3	300-level English Literature	3
CM 249 Digital Media Production	3	IS 310 Pre-Internship	1
Elective	3	Elective	3
	15		**14**

Completion of the General Education competencies by the end of the junior year.

Junior Summer	
CM 441 Internship	**3**

Senior Year			
Fall Semester		**Spring Semester**	
Concentration Elective	3	Concentration Elective	3
Elective	3	Elective	3
Elective	3	Elective	3
Elective	3	Elective	3
Elective	3	IS 461 Seminar on Faith and Life	2
	15		**14**

Completion of 33 credits at the 300-level or above.
Completion of the ACAT Exam by the end of the Senior Year

Total hours required for degree:	**126**

*Offered every other year
**See General Education for optional course offerings

Public Relations Concentration (25 credits)

The Public Relations Concentration offers a wide range of courses designed to effectively prepare students for the many skills required by a public relations practitioner. Students will be exposed to web design, graphic design, grant writing, news writing, communication theory, and marketing & communication research methods. Students are also required to complete a 3-hour internship in the public relations sector, providing them with professional experience and contacts.

Public Relations Courses

    CM 313 Public Relations (3)
    CM 344 Nonprofit Organizational Communication (4)
    CM 346 Web Studies & Design (3)
    CM 249 Digital Media Production (3)
    CM 349 Graphics & Photojournalism (3)
    9 hours of Communication electives (Recommended: BS 230 Principles of Marketing (3) and BS 338 Marketing Research (3))

Four Year Plan: Bachelor of Science in Communication
Public Relations Concentration

Freshman Year				
Fall Semester		**Spring Semester**	
IS 102 Foundations of Faith and Learning	2	CS 102 Computer Applications and Concepts	3
BB 101 Survey of Old Testament	3	BB 102 Survey of New Testament	3
EN 101 English Composition	3	EN 102 English Composition II	3
CM 203 Communication and Culture	3	CM 220 Public Speech and Rhetorical Analysis	3
Gen-Ed Natural Science	4	Gen-Ed Natural Science	4
PE activity course	1		
	16		**16**

Sophomore Year				
Fall Semester		**Spring Semester**	
CM 228 Media Studies*	4	CM 313 Public Relations*	3
CM 249 Digital Media Production	3	Elective	3
Gen-Ed Literature	3	Elective	3
MT 114 Elementary Probability and Statistics	3	Gen-Ed Humanities (excluding EN courses)	3
HS 101 History of World Civilization I	3	HS 102 History of World Civilization II	3
		PE activity course	1
	17		**16**

Junior Year				
Fall Semester		**Spring Semester**	
CM 346 Web Studies and Design*	3	CM 349 Graphics and Photojournalism*	3
Gen-Ed Social Science	3	CM 342 Communication Research Methods*	4
300-level English Literature	3	300-level English Literature	3
Concentration Elective (BS 230 recommended)	3	IS 310 Pre-Internship	1
Elective	3	Elective	3
	15		**14**

Completion of the General Education competencies by the end of the junior year.

Junior Summer		
CM 441 Internship		**3**

Senior Year				
Fall Semester		**Spring Semester**	
CM 344 Nonprofit Organizational Comm.	4	Concentration Elective (BS 338 recommended)*	3
Elective	3	Concentration Elective	3
Elective	3	Elective	3
Elective	3	Elective	3
Elective	3	IS 461 Seminar on Faith and Life	2
	16		**13**

Completion of 33 credits at the 300-level or above.
Completion of the ACAT Exam by the end of the Senior Year.

	Total hours required for degree:	**126**

*Offered every other year

**See General Education for optional course offerings

Theatre Concentration (25 credits)

The Theatre Concentration allows students to explore the field of theatre and blend it with a communication curriculum. Students have an opportunity to study stage acting, acting for camera, directing, voice & movement, stagecraft, and writing for stage and screen. Students will also gain experience in grant writing, public relations, web design, public speaking, and communication theory. Students must do a 3-hour internship in the theatre or film field, as an upperclassman. The goal is to effectively prepare students in the writing, directing, creating, and performing of professional theatre whether it is in a ministry setting in a church or in missions, a nonprofit regional theatre, or the pursuit of a career in Los Angeles or New York.

Theatre Courses
    TH 110   Theatre History (3)
    TH 230   Acting (3)
    CM 202 Acting for Camera (3)
    CM 249 Digital Media Production (3)
    TH 317   Directing (4)
    TH 330   Advanced Acting (3)
    6 hours of Communication or Theatre electives

Four Year Plan: Bachelor of Science in Communication
Theatre Concentration

Freshman Year				
Fall Semester			**Spring Semester**	
IS 102 Foundations of Faith and Learning	2		CS 102 Computer Applications and Concepts	3
BB 101 Survey of Old Testament	3		BB 102 Survey of New Testament	3
EN 101 English Composition	3		EN 102 English Composition II	3
CM 203 Communication and Culture	3		CM 220 Public Speech and Rhetorical Analysis	3
Gen-Ed Natural Science	4		Gen-Ed Natural Science	4
PE activity course	1			
	16			16

Sophomore Year				
Fall Semester			**Spring Semester**	
CM 228 Media Studies*	4		TH 110 Theatre History	3
TH 230 Acting	3		CM/TH 202 Acting for the Camera	3
Gen-Ed Literature	3		Elective	3
MT 114 Elementary Probability and Statistics	3		Gen-Ed Humanities (excluding EN courses)	3
HS 101 History of World Civilization I	3		HS 102 History of World Civilization II	3
			PE activity course	1
	16			16

Junior Year				
Fall Semester			**Spring Semester**	
CM 249 Digital Media Production	3		TH 317 Directing	4
Gen-Ed Social Science	3		TH 330 Advanced Acting	3
300-level English Literature	3		CM 342 Communication Research Methods	4
Elective	3		300-level English Literature	3
Elective	3		IS 310 Pre-Internship	1
	15			15

Completion of the General Education competencies by the end of the junior year.

Junior Summer				
CM 441 Internship				3

Senior Year				
Fall Semester			**Spring Semester**	
Concentration Elective	3		Concentration Elective	3
Elective	3		Elective	3
Elective	3		Elective	3
Elective	3		Elective	3
Elective	3		IS 461 Seminar on Faith and Life	2
	15			13

Completion of 33 credits at the 300-level or above.
Completion of the ACAT Exam by the end of the Senior Year.

Total hours required for degree:	**126**

*Offered every other year
**See General Education for optional course offerings

Communication Major Electives (9 Credits)

(If a course below is not required for your concentration, you may use it as a Communication elective)

CM 106	Theatre Production (1)
CM 205-206	Theatre Production (1, 1)
CM/TH 202	Acting for the Camera (3)
CM 249	Digital Media Production (4)
CM 313	Public Relations (3)
CM 318	Film History & Theory (4)
CM 329	Film Production (4)
CM 340	Musical Theatre (3)
CM 341	Practicum (1-3)
CM 344	Nonprofit Organizational Communication (4)
CM 346	Web Studies & Design (3)
CM 347	News Editing (3)
CM 348	News Writing (3)
CM 349	Graphics & Photojournalism (3)
CM 441	Internship (3) (in addition to your required internship)
CM 480	Special Topics in Communication (1-3)
CM 491	Senior Thesis (2)
BS 209	Principles of Management (3)
BS 230	Principles of Marketing (3)
BS 336	Principles of Advertising (3) (BS 230 pre-req. or permission of professor)
BS 435	Consumer Behavior (3) (BS 230 pre-req. or permission from professor)
BS 307	Organizational Behavior (3) (BS 209 pre-req. or permission of professor)
CC 201	Comparative Cultures (3)
CC 403	Cross-Cultural Communication (4)
EN 271	Business Communication (3)
EN 310	The Writing Process: Theory & Practice (3)
EN 311	Creative Nonfiction Writing (3)
EN 313	Poetry Writing (3)
EN 317	Short Story Writing (3)
EN 325	Literary Magazine Editing (1)
EN 326	Writing Children's Literature (3)
EN 329	Outdoor & Nature Writing (3)
EN 404	Spiritual Memoir Writing (3)
MS 131	Introduction to Digital Sound Recording (3)
MS 461-462	Music Business Seminar (1, 1)
OE 306	Leadership and Group Dynamics (3)
PY 320	Social Psychology (3) (PY 202 pre-req. or permission of instructor)
SC 206	Social Problems (SC 204 pre-req. or permission of professor)
TH 230	Beginning Acting (3)
TH/CM 202	Acting for the Camera (3)
TH 220	Voice and Movement (3)
TH 232	Stagecraft (3)
TH 317	Directing (3)
TH 330	Advanced Acting (3)
TH 333	Theatre Ensemble (4)
TH 335	Playwriting (3)
TH 492	Theatre Practicum (3)
WA 301	Technology in the Church (3)

Communication Minor

Communication is an excellent subject to combine with other majors. EVERYONE communicates! And effective communication is required for every career. If you can communicate well, you are much more apt to be successful in your field. Furthermore, the exploration of what it means to communicate, how we create our own culture and a sense of what it means to be a human are topics that are relevant across all disciplines.

Requirements for a Minor in Communication (18 credits)
    CM 220 Public Speech and Rhetorical Analysis (3)
    CM 203 Communication and Culture (3)
    CM 228 Media Studies (4)
    Choose a minimum of eight (8) additional hours from the Communication Core and/or elective courses.

Cybersecurity Major

Bachelor of Science in Cybersecurity Degree Mission Statement

The mission of the Business and Cybersecurity Department is to equip students with knowledge necessary for them to serve in today's competitive business environment and to cultivate in all students, at all levels, (undergraduate and graduate) a data-driven approach and ethical spirit in their approaches to business decision making.

Cybersecurity Program Goals

1. Ability to integrate Christian worldview and ethics in the work environment.
2. Knowledge and experience in information systems technology on business functional areas.
3. Knowledge and experience in Cybersecurity to support organizational mission and goals.
4. Critical thinking, analytical, and problem-solving skills.
5. Effective communications and interpersonal and team skills.

Why Study Cybersecurity at Montreat College?

The program builds upon Montreat College's strong liberal arts core with extensive training and preparation in information technology, cybersecurity, business administration, and quantitative analysis, preparing students for entry-level professional positions in a variety of technology specializations. Our unique approach to teaching combines the theoretical with the practical, as faculty bring extensive real-world technology experience to the classroom. Small classes provide personal attention and one-on-one interaction with professors. Classroom instruction is often augmented with outside technology speakers and information technology facility visits. In many courses, student projects involve solving technology problems and providing information technology services to actual real-world organizations. Additionally, all students complete a cybersecurity internship prior to graduation. These internships can lead to permanent employment opportunities.

After Graduation

The Cybersecurity degree program prepares graduates for a variety of careers in consulting, financial and banking institutions, health care, services and manufacturing industries, government, and not-for-profit organizations. A graduate of the major may look forward to a Cybersecurity career to support information technology fields such as incident response and business continuity analysis, information systems analysis, programming, database administration, web development, network engineering, systems administration, security analysis, vulnerability assessment, penetration testing or enterprise consulting. According to the Bureau of Labor Statistics, these fields are expected to be among the fastest growing occupations through 2020. Employment of cybersecurity professionals are expected to grow much faster than the average for all occupations as organizations continue to adopt and integrate increasingly sophisticated cybersecurity technologies. Average annual salaries in these fields are well above those in many other professional occupations. Further, many information technology occupations offer broad opportunities to influence others for Christ.

Requirements for a Major in Cybersecurity

√	Degree Component
___	Completion of the General Education Core (56 Credits)
___	MT 114 is required in the Gen-Ed
___	Completion of the General Education Competencies
___	Completion of the Cybersecurity Major Core (64 credits)
___	Completion of the Cybersecurity Major Electives (6 credits)
___	Completion of 33 credits at the 300-level or above
___	Completion of 126 credit hours with a minimum GPA of 2.0 (two terms and 32 hours must be completed at Montreat college)

Cybersecurity Major Core (64 credits)

BS 101	Introduction to Business (3)
BS 201	Principles of Accounting I (3)
IS 310	Pre-Internship (1)
CS 204	Fundamentals of Information Systems (3)
CS 207	Principles of O.S. & Computer Hardware (3)
CS 215	Introduction to Computer Networking (3)
CS 221	Introduction to Secure Programming Logic (3)
CS 289	Cyber Defense I (2)
CS 310	Database Programming (3)
CS 335	Computer and Systems Security (3)
CS 341	Internship I (3)
CS 345	Principles of Cybersecurity (3)
CS 350	Management of Cybersecurity (3)
CS 365	The 3 C's: Cybercrime, Cyber Law & Cyber Ethics (3)
CS 370	Network Defense and Countermeasures (3)
CS 375	Linux Operating Systems and Security (3)
CS 389	Cyber Defense II (2)
CS 428	Penetration Testing (3)
CS 438	Network Forensics (3)
CS 441	Internship II (3)
CS 448	Incident Response and Contingency Planning (3)
CS 489	Cyber Defense III (3)
MT 121	College Algebra (3) *or* higher

Required Major Electives (choose 6 hours)

CS 287	Cyber Competition I (2)
CS 380	Certification Study and Preparation (3)
CS 387	Cyber Competition II (2)
CS 475	Cybersecurity Programs and Strategies (3)
CS 480	Special Topics (3) CS 487 Cyber Competition III (2)

Four Year Plan: Bachelor of Science in Cybersecurity

Freshman Year

Fall Semester		Spring Semester	
IS 102 Foundations of Faith and Learning	2	BB 102 Survey of New Testament	3
BB 101 Survey of Old Testament	3	EN 102 English Composition II	3
EN 101 English Composition I	3	CS 204 Fund. Of Information Systems	3
CS 102 Computer Applications and Concepts	3	CS 207 Prin. Of Operating Systems & Comp. Hardware	3
Gen-Ed Natural Science	4	Gen-Ed Natural Science	4
PE activity course	1		
	16		**16**

Sophomore Year

Fall Semester		Spring Semester	
HS 101 History of World Civilization I	3	HS 102 History of World Civilization II	3
CS 215 Intro to Computer Networking	3	MT 114 Elementary Probability and Statistics	3
CS 221 Intro to Secure Programming Logic	3	CS 335 Computer and Systems Security	3
Gen-Ed Literature	3	CS 288 Cyber Defense I	2
MT 121 College Algebra	3	IS 310 Pre-Internship	1
PE activity course	1	Gen-Ed Oral Competency	3
	16		**15**

Sophomore Summer

CS 341 Internship I			3

Junior Year

Fall Semester		Spring Semester	
BS 101 Intro to Business	3	CS 310 Database Programming	3
CS 365 The 3 C's: Cybercrime, Cyberlaw, and Cyberethics	3	CS 350 Management of Cybersecurity	3
CS 345 Principles of Cybersecurity	3	CS 370 Network Defense Countermeasures	3
CS 375 Linux Operating Systems and Security	3	CS 388 Cyber Defense II	2
Gen-Ed Social Science	3	Gen-Ed Humanities	3
	15		**14**

Completion of the General Education competencies by the end of the junior year.

Junior Summer

CS 441 Internship II			3

Senior Year

Fall Semester		Spring Semester	
Gen-Ed Humanities	3	CS 448 Incident Response and Contingency Planning	3
CS 428 Penetration Testing	3	CS 488 Cyber Defense III	2
CS 438 Network Forensics	3	Major Elective	3
BS 201 Principles of Accounting I	3	IS 461 Seminar of Faith and Life	2
Major Elective	3	Gen-Ed Humanities	3
	15		**13**

Completion of 33 credits at the 300-level or above.

Total hours required for degree:	**126**

Cybersecurity Minor

Requirements for a Minor in Cybersecurity (18 credits)

Cybersecurity Minor Core (15 credits)
- CS 207   Principles of O. S. and Comp. Hardware (3)
- CS 215   Introduction to Computer Networking (3)
- CS 335   Computer and Systems Security (3)
- CS 345   Principles of Cybersecurity (3)
- CS 350   Management of Cybersecurity (3)

Cybersecurity Minor Required Electives (3 credits)
Choose 3 hours from the following:
- CS 289   Cyber Defense I (2)
- CS 341   Internship I (3)
- CS 365   The 3 C's: Cybercrime, Cyberlaw, Cyberethics (3)
- CS 370   Network Defense and Countermeasures (3)
- CS 375   Linux Operating Systems and Security (3)
- CS 380   Certification Study and Preparation (3)
- CS 428   Penetration Testing (3)

- CS 448   Incident Response & Contingency Planning (3)
- CS 475   Cybersecurity Program and Strategies (3)
- CS 488   Cyber Defense (4)

Elementary Education Major

The Education Division offers a licensure program (i.e., certification) in Elementary Education. The program of study outlined in this catalog leads to a Bachelor of Science degree in the discipline as well as North Carolina Initial Licensure.

The Education Discipline

The Bachelor of Science in Elementary Education prepares candidates under the knowledge-based model of "Teacher as Leader and Innovator for 21st Century learning in the classroom, school, district, and profession at local, regional, national, and global levels." The Department's mission and conceptual framework are based on the Christian calling to the ministry of education within the framework of 21st Century skills, knowledge, expertise, and literacies required for success in work and life. The department believes that effective teachers are leaders who not only care about their students and their profession, but also possess the qualities of Christian character and citizenship to effectively impact both during their calling and career "in a world where change is constant and learning never stops" (2016, P21 Partnership for 21st Century Learning, p.1).

Upon completion of the undergraduate Elementary Education Program, the candidate should be able to meet six goals:

1. Demonstrate a body of core knowledge and professional skills and a commitment to continual renewal of these through lifelong learning and professional development. (Philippians 3:12 "Not that I have . . . already been made perfect, but I press on.")

2. Demonstrate a disposition inclined to 21st Century leadership both in communicating a subject and in differentiating instruction according to the needs of learners. (North Carolina Professional Teaching Standard 2; II Timothy 2:24, 25 "The Lord's servant . . . be kind to everyone, able to teach, not resentful. Those who oppose him he must gently instruct.")

3. Use a variety of methods and materials to engage students in the processes of critical thinking, problem solving, and collaboration. (North Carolina Professional Teaching Standard 4; I Corinthians 14:20 ". . . in your thinking be adults.")

4. Demonstrate effective communication, using a variety of methods, in interactions with students, parents, and members of the professional community. (North Carolina Professional Teaching Standards 1 & 5; Ephesians 4:29 "what is helpful for building others up according to their needs")

5. Serve proactively and model the tenets of ethical codes in carrying out responsibilities of the profession within the school community. (North

Carolina Professional Teaching Standard 1; Colossians 3:23 "Whatever you do work at it with all your heart, as working for the Lord, not for men.")

6. Demonstrate an appreciation for diversity as an expression of the manifold image of God in humankind, and build on diversity as an asset in the classroom by consistently integrating culturally relevant materials and ideas. (North Carolina Professional Teaching Standards 2 & 4; I Corinthians 9:22 "I have become all things to all men.")

Student Learning Outcomes:

1. The candidate will be able to interpret and employ content curriculum areas specific to elementary education as reflected in the North Carolina Standard Course of Study.

2. The candidate will be able to analyze and demonstrate pedagogy appropriate to research based cognitive, affective, and skill development models of teaching.

3. The candidate will be able to analyze research-based curriculum and integrate it with the academic/developmental needs of the student.

4. The candidate will be able to create lesson plans that demonstrate requisite competencies in applying the North Carolina Standard Course of Study (NCSOS) and 21st Century Skills/Standards.

5. The candidate will be able to demonstrate dispositions characteristic of a teaching candidate committed to sustained, high quality performance (leadership, humility, commitment to excellence, responsibility, punctuality, and cooperation).

6. The candidate will become involved in professional organizations and lifelong learning.

Why Study Education at Montreat College?

Education is a dynamic profession, in which the classroom teacher remains on the front edge of research and methods applied in an ever-changing global environment.

Educational theory is integrated with professional practice and professional service, and is taught through the lens of a Christian worldview. Graduates of Montreat College Teacher Education Program will be prepared through intellectual inquiry, spiritual formation, and an understanding of their calling and career to pursue the ministry of education in both public and private schools at home in the United States or abroad, wherever the calling of God takes them.

After Graduation

The faculty of the Education Department remains available to all graduates whether they are preparing to enter the professional world or are already in it. Graduates from this program should always feel welcome to contact the Education Department should questions or a need of assistance arise.

Entrance Requirements for Education Candidates

Acceptance by Montreat College should not be confused with acceptance into the Montreat Teacher Education Program (TEP). Admission to Montreat TEP is open to all Montreat College students who meet the standards established by Montreat College's Teacher Education Committee (TEC) and the North Carolina State Department for Public Instruction (NC-DPI).

Formal admission to Montreat TEP usually occurs after the junior year. Candidates will meet the following guidelines:

1. Proficiency in oral and written communication through completion of General Education competency requirements and interviews with the Education faculty and representatives of the Montreat TEC.
2. State designated minimum scores:
   (156) on the ETS CORE Reading, (162) on CORE Writing, and (150) on CORE Math, or minimum scores on the SAT of 1100 on the appropriate subtests, or minimum scores of 24 on the ACT on the appropriate subtests.
3. Minimum overall GPA of 2.75 and a 3.0 in all education courses.
4. A recommendation from the Department Chair and one other faculty member regarding the candidate's interest in and suitability for teaching.

Students are required to have a background check, TB test, and current North Carolina Health Form on file with Montreat College in order to participate in all education courses that include Focused Field Experiences.

Requirements for Continuation in the Program after Gateway 1
- Maintain a cumulative GPA of 3.0 in the education core courses.
- Maintain a cumulative GPA of no less than 2.75.
- Demonstrate dispositions identified within the program.
- Complete appropriate Gateways.

Entrance Requirements for the Professional Year / Montreat Teacher Education Program (TEP)
- Maintain a cumulative GPA of 3.0 in the education core courses.
- File an "Application for Student Teaching" form with the Education Department.
- Update all necessary vaccinations and health tests.
- Complete an interview with Education faculty and representatives of the Montreat TEC for the purpose of determining professional competence/dispositions.
- Complete appropriate Gateways.
- Appropriate SAT or ACT scores or passing scores on the ETS CORE tests
- Passing scores on the Pearson Foundations of Reading and General Curriculum tests

Requirements for Licensure in Education

To receive a teaching license, candidates must major in Elementary Education and take the licensure courses in education. In addition, graduates must also pass the Pearson Tests for NC: Foundations of Reading and General Education to be eligible for employment in the North Carolina school system.

Students are required to have a background check, TB test, and current North Carolina Health Form on file with Montreat College in order to participate in all education courses requiring Focused Field Experiences.

Gateway 1: Requirements Check for Continuing in Education Courses

1. 2.75 overall GPA and 3.0 GPA in education courses.
2. Disposition Self-Evaluation (Completed in ED 150).
3. ETS CORE: attempted/or meet state designated minimum scores

Typically, candidates will complete Gateway 1 at the end of the sophomore year. Candidates will not be allowed continued enrollment in education courses without approval of their advisor based on the GPA check by the Department of Education.

Gateway 2: Entrance Requirements for Education Candidates

Acceptance by Montreat College should not be confused with acceptance into the Montreat Teacher Education Program (TEP). Admission to Montreat TEP is open to all Montreat College students who meet the standards established by Montreat College's Teacher Education Committee (TEC) and the North Carolina Department of Public Instruction (NC-DPI).

Formal Admission to Montreat TEP usually occurs after the junior year. Candidates will meet the following guidelines:

1. Minimum overall GPA of 2.75 and a 3.0 in all education courses.
2. Meet State designated minimum scores:
(156) ETS CORE Reading, (162) CORE Writing, and (150) CORE Math, or minimum scores on the SAT of 1100 on the appropriate subtests, or minimum scores of 24 on the ACT on the appropriate subtests.
3. Reference: K-6 Faculty.
4. Reference: Content Faculty.
5. Reference: Education Faculty.
6. Submit Application to Montreat Teacher Education Program.
7. Interview with Montreat Teacher Education Committee representatives.
8. Meet the Montreat College minimum scores on the Pearson Foundations of Reading and General Curriculum tests.
9. Clear background check, TB test, and current North Carolina Health Form on file.

10. . Must submit a completed and signed Code of Ethics for North Carolina Educators.
11. Present evidence of liability insurance by presenting current membership in the Student North Carolina Association of Educators (SNCAE) or another organization that provides comparable insurance.
12. Keep address, phone number, email address and other changeable information up-to-date in the Education Office.
13. Must be admitted by the Teacher Education Committee which has representation from the College and public and private school systems.

Unless candidates have been admitted to the Montreat Teacher Education Program, they will not be permitted to continue with classes in the Education Major if they are seeking NC licensure.

Gateway 3: Entrance Requirements for Student Teaching II

1. Maintain a cumulative GPA of 3.0 in the education core courses.
2. Submit "Application for Student Teaching II" with the Education Department.
3. Evaluation: Student Teaching I – college supervisor.
4. Evaluation: Student Teaching I – cooperating teacher.
5. Evaluation: Student Teaching I – candidate (self-evaluation).
6. Interview with Education faculty and Montreat Teacher Education Committee representatives for the purpose of determining professional competence and dispositions.
7. Formal approval by the Montreat Teacher Education Committee.

Gateway 4: Exit from the Montreat Teacher Education Program

1. Exit interview
2. Completion of Student Teaching II
3. Participation in ED 451 Forum III: Issues in Education
4. Exit Portfolio

Unless a candidate successfully completes her/his student teaching, including portfolio submission and participation in ED 451 Forum III: Issues in Education, s/he will not be approved for licensure in the State of North Carolina.

The Montreat College Director of Teacher Education/licensure officer will also determine if a candidate is suitable for the North Carolina Public School classroom. His/her signature is also required for approval for licensure, and will not be given until the candidate has earned passing scores on the North Carolina Pearson Tests: Foundations of Reading and General Curriculum.

Requirements for Licensure-Only Students

Candidates with a baccalaureate degree can enter the College as a licensure-only, non-degree seeking student. The general policy for licensure-only students is that they must meet similar entry, exit, and course requirements as degree-seeking students.

Candidates already possessing a baccalaureate degree must apply for acceptance into the College. Transcripts will then be forwarded to the education department chair who will determine the equivalence of specialty area courses. Following this evaluation, the department chair will prepare a course of study leading to certification.

To gain full acceptance into a program, the candidate must pass ED 150 and must have a minimum 3.0 grade point average. Licensure-only candidates with a 3.0 grade point average from an accredited college or university will also have to pass the CORE reading, mathematics, and writing tests.

Because licensure-only candidates have already completed a program of general studies, they may not have to take courses in the liberal arts. However, candidates must have had coursework in the arts, communication skills, history, literature, mathematics, philosophy and/or religion, and science. The department chair will require courses in these areas if the student (1) is lacking coursework in one or more of these areas; (2) has low grades in a given area; (3) needs to retake courses to raise the overall grade point average; or (4) has a deficiency in one of these areas as noted on a standardized test or in an interview. All ED courses will be required.

The licensure-only candidate will take all courses and tests in the professional and specialty areas required of degree-seeking candidates (including Student Teaching I and II) and meet all other requirements of degree-seeking candidates. At least 70 % of the courses must be taken through the College. All proposed transfer courses must be pre-approved by both Department Chair and the Registrar.

Requirements for a Major in Elementary Education
<u>V</u> **Degree Component**
<u> </u> Completion of the General Education Core (53 credits*)
      PY 201 or SC 204 is recommended for a Gen-Ed Social Science requirement
      IS 202 is recommended for a Gen-Ed Humanities requirement
<u> </u> Completion of the General Education Competencies
<u> </u> Completion of the Elementary Education major (68 credits)
<u> </u> Completion of 33 credits at the 300-level or above
<u> </u> Maintain a minimum 3.0 grade point average in Education courses
<u> </u> Completion of all Gateways

___ Completion of student teaching experience with a minimum score of 3 or higher
___ Completion of all forms for licensure
___ Completion of the senior exit portfolio
___ Completion of 126 credit hours with a minimum GPA of 2.75 (two terms and 32 credit hours must be completed at Montreat college)
*ED 209 in the major can count toward a Gen-Ed Humanities requirement.

Elementary Education major classes (68 Credits)

ED 150	Foundations of Education (3)
ED 209	Children's Literature (3)
ED 240	Computers for Education (3)
ED 260	Integrating Health & the Arts (3)
ED 270	Diversity in Education (3)
ED 320	Math Methods K-3 (3)
ED 325	Math Methods 4-6 (3)
ED 330	Teaching Reading and Language Arts (3)
ED 350	Teaching Science (3)
ED 350L	Teaching Science Lab (1)
ED 351	Forum I: Education in North Carolina (1)
ED 360	Teaching Social Studies (3)
ED 365	Christian Philosophy of Education (Optional for ACSI Cert.) (3)
ED 370	Language and Literacy (3)
ED 406	Educational Psychology (3)
ED 410	Classroom Management (3)
ED 420	Assessment in Education (3)
ED 421	Forum II: Issues in Education (1)
ED 430	Teaching Exceptionalities (3)
ED 449	Student Teaching I (5)
ED 450	Student Teaching II (12)
ED 451	Forum III: Issues in Education (3)

Bachelor of Science in Elementary Education

Freshman Year

Fall Semester		Spring Semester	
IS 102 Foundations of Faith and Learning	2	Gen-Ed Math	3
BB 101 Survey of Old Testament	3	BB 102 Survey of New Testament	3
EN 101 English Composition	3	EN 102 English Composition II	3
ED 150 Foundations of Education	3	Gen-Ed Humanities	3
CS 102 Computer Applications and Concepts	3	ED 240 Computers for Education	3
PE activity course	1	PE activity course	1
	15		16

Sophomore Year

Fall Semester		Spring Semester	
CM 220 Public Speech and Rhetorical Analysis or TH 230 Acting	3	Gen-Ed Literature	3
HS 101 History of World Civilization I	3	HS 102 History of World Civilization II	3
ED 260 Integrating Health & the Arts	3	Gen-Ed Natural Science	4
Gen-Ed Social Science (PY 201/SC 204 Recommended)	3	ED 209 Children's Literature (counts for Humanities)	3
Gen-Ed Natural Science	4	ED 270 Diversity in Education	3
	16		16

Completion of Gateway 1 at the end of the sophomore year.

Junior Year

Fall Semester		Spring Semester	
ED 320 Math Methods K-3	3	ED 325 Math Methods 4-6	3
ED 330 Teaching Reading Language Arts	3	ED 370 Language and Literacy	3
ED 360 Teaching Social Studies	3	ED 350 Teaching Science	3
Gen-Ed Humanities (IS 202 Recommended)	3	ED 350L Teaching Science Lab	1
Elective	1	ED 351 Forum I: Education in NC	1
ED 365 Christian Philosophy of Education (Optional)	3	IS 461 Seminar on Faith and Learning	2
		Elective	3
	16		16

Completion of Gateway 2 at the end of the junior year.
Completion of the Gateway 3 at the end of Fall Semester of Professional Year

Senior Year

Fall Semester		Spring Semester	
ED 430 Teaching Exceptionalities	3	ED 450 Student Teaching II	12
ED 406 Educational Psychology	3	ED 451 Forum III: Issues in Education	1
ED 410 Classroom Management	3		
ED 420 Assessment in Education	3		
ED 421 Forum II: Issues in Education	1		
ED 449 Student Teaching I	5		
	18		13

Completion of Gateway 4 at the completion of the program.

		Total hours required for degree:	126

*Students are required to have a background check, TB test, and current physical on file with Montreat College in order to enroll in ED 211/ED 211L.

English Major

The English major prepares students to use their God-bestowed gift of language. At the core of English study lies the grace and power of words. Students learn how language has been employed to create literature, persuade audiences, and delight readers.

The English Discipline

Three concentrations are available to the English major: Literature, Creative Writing, and Professional Writing. A concentration in literature provides students with a foundational understanding of the world's greatest written works in courses such as Shakespeare and Literature of the United States. By graduation, students in the literature concentration demonstrate familiarity with the major schools of literary criticism, an understanding of literary genres, practical application of literary techniques and language, and a significant understanding of the links between literature and the cultural milieus that produced it. In communication courses students develop their technical and theoretical knowledge in theatre and journalism. By graduation they show their mastery of communication theory and practice for professional settings. Creative writing courses provide English majors a forum for growth of their own literary craft. By graduation they achieve competence in writing poetry, fiction, and literary nonfiction.

Why Study English at Montreat College?

Every English course merges a Biblical worldview with scholarship. Christ composed parables to communicate truth through story. In this sense he modeled literary, communicative, and creative writing study. Blending literature, creative writing and public information into a unified major is a unique feature of Montreat College. Students focus on a single concentration, yet apply courses from the other two concentrations toward their degree requirements. This cohesive approach toward literature, imaginative writing, and professional writing provides students a grasp of literary masterpieces as well as the practical application of literary craft and technical writing skills. English majors write a Senior Thesis, which caps their coursework in literary interpretation, creative writing, or professional writing.

How Can Students Get Involved?

Practicum, EN 341, gives English students the opportunity for professional employment experience, usually in the field of public information. At the Writing Center, students skillful in writing offer one-on-one consultation to their peers on writing assignments. Q, Montreat College's literary magazine, is an excellent way for students to develop their writing, editing, and design skills while receiving academic credit.

After Graduation

Public information and professional editing comprise a large employment field for graduates in English. Ministry, law, library science, and civil service are also fields open to English graduates. In addition, many students majoring in English at Montreat College will continue their education at the graduate level.

Requirements for a Major in English

√	Degree Component
___	Completion of the General Education Core (53* credits)
___	IS 202 or PH 201 is required in the Gen-Ed
___	Completion of the General Education Competencies
___	Completion of an English Major Concentration (~42 credits)
___	Completion of a foreign language (Spanish, Greek, or other approved language) through the intermediate level (12 credits or equivalent)**
___	Completion of the required electives to bring total up to 126 credits (~19-22 credits)
___	Completion of 33 credits at the 300-level or above
___	Completion of the Major Field Test
___	Completion of 126 credit hours with a minimum GPA of 2.0 (two terms and 32 credit hours must be completed at Montreat College)

*One English literature class from the major can count toward the Gen-Ed reading competency.
*EN 271 in the Professional Writing concentration can count toward the Gen-Ed oral competency.
**The foreign language requirement may not be applied toward the general education core, the major, or the minor requirements.

Choose from four English Concentrations:
    Literature (42 credits)
    Creative Writing (42 credits)
    Professional Writing (42 credits)
    Special Emphasis (32 credits)

Literature Concentration

The Literature Concentration allows students to learn literary interpretation by examining a wide range of literary texts. Students select courses from three broad categories: early British literature, later British literature, and United States literature. Historical, Christian, and formal modes of interpretation are stressed, in order to see the connections between classic imaginative stories and the issues of human meaning found in art, economics, history, and current events.

Requirements for a Literature Concentration (42 credits)

Literature Core (24 credits)

    EN 201   Survey of English Literature I (3)
    EN 202   Survey of English Literature II (3)
    EN 203   World Literature I (3)
    EN 301   Shakespeare (3)
    EN 321   Literature of the United States I (3)
    EN 322   Literature of the United States II (3)
    EN 402   Literary Criticism (3)
    EN 490   Bibliography for Research (1)
    EN 491   Senior Thesis (2)

Literature Required Electives (18 credits)

In addition, students must take the specified number of hours in each of the following literary periods:

    Choose 6 hours from *British Literature through the Eighteenth Century*:

        EN 300   Middle English Literature (3)
        EN 304   Restoration & Eighteenth Cent. British Literature (3)
        EN 305   Milton (3)
        EN 319   Renaissance Literature (3)

    Choose 6 hours from *British Literature since the Eighteenth Century*:

        EN 307   Romantic British Literature (3)
        EN 320   Contemporary Literature (3)
        EN 309   Victorian Literature (3)
        EN 324   Twentieth Century British Writers (3)

    Choose 6 hours from *English at the 300-level or above* (may also include CM 318 and/or 341)

Creative Writing Concentration

The Creative Writing concentration at Montreat College is designed to provide students the opportunity to pursue their passion for imaginative writing of poetry, short fiction, literary non-fiction, and the novella. English Creative- Writing majors work alongside professors and peers in small, intensive workshop-style classes. In addition, Creative Writing majors are provided the opportunity to showcase their work through the College sponsored reading series and submissions to Q, the Montreat College literary magazine. Our future poets, essayists, and novelists—all Montreat College student writers—are encouraged to have their voices heard through participation in area writing festivals, contests, lectures, and public readings.

Requirements for a Creative Writing Concentration (42 credits)

Creative Writing Core (18 credits)

EN 201   Survey of English Literature I (3)
EN 202   Survey of English Literature II (3)
EN 203   World Literature I (3)
EN 301   Shakespeare (3)
EN 402   Literary Criticism (3)
EN 490   Bibliography for Research (1)
EN 491   Senior Thesis (2)

Creative Writing Required Electives (24 credits)

Choose 3 hours from:
    EN 321   Literature of the United States I (3)
    EN 322   Literature of the United States II (3)
Choose 12 hours from:
    EN 311   Creative Nonfiction Writing (3)
    EN 313   Poetry Writing (3)
    EN 317   Short Story Writing (3)
    EN 326   Writing Children's Literature (3)
    EN 329   Outdoor and Nature Writing (3)
    TH 335   Playwriting (3)
Choose 9 additional hours in English at the 300-level or above (may also include Communication 318 and/or 341)

Four Year Plan: Bachelor of Arts in English
Literature and Creative Writing Concentrations

Freshman Year			
Fall Semester		**Spring Semester**	
IS 102 Foundations of Faith and Learning	2	CS 102 Computer Applications and Concepts	3
BB 101 Survey of Old Testament	3	BB 102 Survey of New Testament	3
EN 101 English Composition I	3	EN 102 English Composition II	3
HS 101 History of World Civilization I	3	HS 102 History of World Civilization II	3
Elementary Foreign Language 101	3	Elementary Foreign Language 102	3
PE activity course	1	PE activity course	1
	15		16

Sophomore Year			
Fall Semester		**Spring Semester**	
EN 201 Survey of English Literature I	3	EN 202 Survey of English Literature II	3
Intermediate Foreign Language 201	3	Intermediate Foreign Language 202	3
Gen-Ed Natural Science	4	Gen-Ed Natural Science	4
Gen-Ed Mathematics	3	Gen-Ed Social Science	3
Gen-Ed Oral Competency	3	Major Elective	3
	16		16

Junior Year			
Fall Semester		**Spring Semester**	
EN 203 World Literature I	3	EN 402 Literary Criticism	3
EN 301 Shakespeare	3	Major Elective	3
Major Elective	3	Major Elective	3
Gen-Ed Humanities	3	Gen-Ed Humanities	3
Elective	1	PH 201 Intro to Philosophy or IS 202 Worldviews	3
Elective	3		
	16		15

Completion of the General Education competencies by the end of the junior year.

Senior Year			
Fall Semester		**Spring Semester**	
EN 490 Bibliography for Research	1	EN 491 Senior Thesis	2
Major Elective	3	Major Elective	3
Major Elective	3	Major Elective	3
Elective	3	IS 461 Seminar on Faith and Life	2
Elective	3	Elective	3
Elective	3	Elective	3
	16		16

Completion of 33 credits at the 300-level or above.
Completion of the Major Field Test by the end of the Senior Year.

	Total hours required for degree:	126

*See General Education for optional course offerings

Professional Writing Concentration

The Professional Writing concentration allows English students to explore career tracks in English and related disciplines such as Communication. Students also receive a thorough grounding in literature and analytical/critical thinking skills.

Requirements for a Professional Writing Concentration (42 credits)

EN 271* Business Communication (3)
CM 228 Media Studies (4)
CM 313 Public Relations (3)
EN 325 Literary Magazine Editing (1)
CM 344** Nonprofit Organizational Communication (4)
Choose one:
>CM 347 News Editing (3) **OR**
>CM 348 News Writing (3)
EN 490 Bibliography for Research (1)
EN 491 Senior Thesis (2)

Choose 15 credits in Literature:
>Choose one:
>>EN 201 Survey of English Literature I (3) **OR**
>>EN 202 Survey of English Literature II (3)
>EN 203 World Literature (3)
>EN 301 Shakespeare (3)
>Choose one:
>>EN 321 Literature of the United States (3) **OR**
>>EN 322 Literature of the United States (3)
>Choose one:
>>EN 324 Twentieth-Century British Writers (3) **OR**
>>EN 320 Contemporary Literature (3)

Choose 6 hours from EN and/or CM at the 300-level or above

*BS 101 prerequisite waived
**CM 203 prerequisite waived

Four Year Plan: Bachelor of Arts in English
Professional Writing Concentration

Freshman Year

Fall Semester		Spring Semester	
IS 102 Foundations of Faith and Learning	2	CS 102 Computer Applications and Concepts	3
BB 101 Survey of Old Testament	3	BB 102 Survey of New Testament	3
EN 101 English Composition I	3	EN 102 English Composition II	3
HS 101 History of World Civilization I	3	HS 102 History of World Civilization II	3
Elementary Foreign Language 101	3	Elementary Foreign Language 102	3
PE activity course	1	PE activity course	1
	15		16

Sophomore Year

Fall Semester		Spring Semester	
EN 201 Survey of English Literature I*	3	EN 322 Literature of the United States II*	3
Intermediate Foreign Language 201	3	Intermediate Foreign Language 202	3
Gen-Ed Natural Science	4	Gen-Ed Natural Science	4
Gen-Ed Mathematics	3	Gen-Ed Social Science	3
EN 271 Business Communication	3	Major Elective	3
	16		16

*Students may take EN 202 for English Lit. requirement in spring and EN 321 for U.S. Lit. requirement in Fall; must choose one class in each discipline.

Junior Year

Fall Semester		Spring Semester	
EN 203 World Literature I	3	CM 313 Public Relations	3
EN 301 Shakespeare	3	CM 344 Nonprofit Organizational Communication	4
EN 320 Contemporary Literature or EN 324 Twentieth-Century British Writers	3	Gen-Ed Humanities	3
Gen-Ed Humanities	3	PH 201 Intro to Philosophy or IS 202 Worldviews	3
EN 325 Literary Magazine Editing	1	Elective	3
Elective	3		
	16		16

Completion of the General Education competencies by the end of the junior year.

Senior Year

Fall Semester		Spring Semester	
EN 490 Bibliography for Research	1	EN 491 Senior Thesis	2
CM 228 Media Studies	4	Major Elective	3
CM 348 News Writing or CM 347 News Editing	3	Major Elective	3
Major Elective	3	Elective	3
Elective	3	IS 461 Seminar on Faith and Life	2
Elective	1	Elective	3
	15		16

Completion of 33 credits at the 300-level or above.
Completion of the Major Field Test by the end of the Senior Year.

		Total hours required for degree:	126

*See General Education for optional course offerings

Special Emphasis Concentration

The Special Emphasis Concentration allows students to design a program of study focused on an area of interest outside the core curriculum of their particular major. Working with a faculty member in their major, the student selects courses from other institutions or departments at Montreat College that can be integrated into their specific discipline. The Special Emphasis must be approved by the student's academic advisor prior to completing sixty (60) credit hours.

Requirements for a Special Emphasis Concentration (32 credits)

The Special Emphasis Concentration proposal must meet all the General Education and Competency requirements published in the Academic Catalog, including the language requirement for the BA degree. The proposal must include the following elements: (1) a rationale for the program, (2) a description of one's career objectives, (3) identification of at least thirty-two (32) credit hours of coursework with supporting rationale from within the student's academic program, and (4) identification of at least eighteen (18) credit hours of additional coursework with supporting rationale, generally outside the student's chosen department, that directly supports the student's career objectives. The proposal, once approved by the academic advisor, will be submitted to the Department for final approval.

English Minor

The English minor at Montreat College gives students the opportunity to read, discuss, and write about illuminating works in Western Literature, and to receive instruction and practice in creative and professional writing. Students who minor in English are prepared to work as editors and writers in their major fields. Students will develop understanding of the world's social and cultural conditions and learn to communicate effectively through the written word.

Requirements for a Minor in English (18 credits)
    18 hours in English, from 3-credit hour courses only
    At least 12 credits of the 18 must be at the 300-level or above
    The General Education literature course does not double-count

Environmental Studies Major

The Environmental Studies program prepares students to understand and critically examine environmental issues from an interdisciplinary perspective, to teach in various outdoor settings, and to engage in scientific research. The program utilizes biological, chemical, and ecological course work and field experiences to prepare students for further academic studies or professional training and provides opportunities for career preparation and professional development through independent projects, teacher education, internships, and seminars.

The Environmental Studies Discipline

Environmental Studies specialists are needed in order to understand and help solve the ecological problems posed by the 21st century. While these specialists must be knowledgeable in ecology, environmental science, experimental design, mathematical modeling, and physics, they also must be acquainted with ideas drawn from a wide range of related disciplines, including environmental philosophy, ethics, theology, history, literature, policy, law, and psychology. They must be skilled in research methods, written and oral communication, and conflict resolution.

Why Study Environmental Studies at Montreat College?

The program is unique. Montreat College's program is distinctively different. The program integrates a liberal arts education with a Christ-centered worldview. The student trained in environmental studies will gain more than a solid understanding of basic principles. They will possess an understanding of the ethical and worldview implications involved in the application of environmental knowledge. Small, intimate classes foster discussion and interaction in every course. Students receive personalized attention and this allows for further integration of the Christian perspective into the environmental studies curriculum. The instructors are highly accessible and genuine in their approach to students, serving as professors, mentors, and advisors. Faculty members work closely with each student based on his/her interests and career aspirations. It is our goal to help students transition from passive learner to budding colleague.

Montreat College also has vital connections with the International Au Sable Environmental Institute, the Council for Christian Colleges and Universities, and the Appalachian College Association.

The program is integrative and academically rigorous. We expect much from our students but they receive much in return. By providing a strong foundation in environmental studies, Montreat College's program successfully prepares the student for graduate studies in a wide array of disciplines, including environmental studies, plant and animal ecology, environmental economics, physical geography, environmental education, forest science, wildlife and fishery science, natural resource management, and medical research. It also provides opportunities to establish collaborative relationships with various groups, such as the Forest Service, the National Park Service, environmental organizations, research laboratories, and industry.

The program is situated within the ecologically diverse Southern Appalachian Mountains. Located in one of the most ideal areas for environmental studies in the Eastern United States, Montreat College is in close proximity to four major wilderness areas, several national and state forests, the Great Smoky Mountains National Park, Mt. Mitchell State Park, Grandfather Mountain Biosphere Preserve, and numerous unique and diverse ecosystems. These range from Southern Appalachian cove forests to heath bald communities to high elevation spruce-fir forests. Through immersion in the natural environment, an experiential approach to learning, and a Christian perspective, Montreat College ultimately prepares the student for a lifelong adventure with many chances for success.

The Environmental Studies major allows much room for individualization. Possible academic choices are the Pre-professional Concentration, the Conservation Biology and Natural Resource Management Concentration, and the Special Emphasis (self-designed) Concentration. These options ensure a well-tailored education for any student.

After Graduation

Upon completion of the Environmental Studies program at Montreat College, the student has a wide selection of options, such as ecologist, fish or wildlife biologist, naturalist, environmental economist, environmental educator, or environmental consultant. Additionally, students might wish to receive a North Carolina State Certificate in Environmental Education or attend graduate school, thereby expanding their career choices. Government agencies and private companies eagerly look to the present generation to staff their offices as a source of youthful creativity, mature beliefs, and a strong environmental studies background.

Requirements for a Major in Environmental Studies

√	Degree Component
___	Completion of the General Education Core (56 credits)
	BL 101 or 103 and 102 or 104; MT 114; and IS 202 are required in the Gen-Ed
___	OE 310 is recommended for Gen-Ed oral competency
___	Completion of the General Education Competencies
___	Completion of the Environmental Studies Major Core (30.5 credits)
___	Completion of an Environmental Studies Concentration (18-32 credits)
___	Completion of required electives to bring total up to 126 credits (~8-22 credits)
___	Completion of 33 credits at the 300-level or above.
___	Completion of the Major Field Test
___	Completion of 126 credit hours with a minimum GPA of 2.0 (two terms and 32 credit hours must be completed at Montreat College)

*Students wishing to become a North Carolina Certified Environmental Educator should take OE 220 as an elective.

Environmental Studies Major Courses (30.5 hours)

BL 205   Animal Diversity and Ecology (4)
BL 406   Conservation Biology (3)
CH 201   Environmental Inorganic Chemistry I (4)
CH 202   Environmental Inorganic Chemistry II (4)
ES 200   Introduction to Environmental Studies (3)
ES 206   Ecology (4)
ES 230   Sophomore Science Seminar I (0.5)
ES 301   Physical & Environmental Geography (4)
ES 340   Research Methods (3)
ES 445   Senior Science Seminar (1)

Choose from three Environmental Studies Concentrations:

Pre-Professional (31-32 credits)
Conservation Biology and Natural Resource Management (32 credits)
Special Emphasis (18 credits)

Pre-Professional Concentration (31-32 credits)

The Pre-professional track offers a wide range of courses designed to prepare students for graduate studies in the health and science professions, including diverse fields such as applied technology (environmental consulting), biochemistry, ecological research, genetics, environmental science, medicine/medical research, nursing, ecophysiology, toxicology, and veterinary science.

Pre-Professional Courses

Choose one:

BL 311　Plant Physiology (3) **OR**

BL 206　Human Anatomy & Physiology I (4)

BL 401　Genetics (3)

CH 320　Organic Chemistry I (3)

CH 321　Organic Chemistry II (3)

CH 322　Organic Chemistry Lab I (2)

CH 323　Organic Chemistry Lab II (1)

ES 440　Senior Project or Internship**

MT 191　Applied Calculus I (4)

MT 192　Applied Calculus II (4)

PC 131　College Physics I (4)

PC 132　College Physics II (4)

Recommended electives (not required):

CS 480　Special Studies in Information Systems (3)

BL 415　Biochemistry/Toxicology (4)

**Students in the Pre-Professional concentration are required to enter into a professional experience through a cooperative, employment, internship, or research arrangement. Environmental Studies faculty serve as mentors, and each project must be approved and debriefed with the faculty member for the completion of this requirement. Students must make arrangements to set up the professional experience and make a presentation to the faculty for approval before the experience is initiated. The student does not have to complete this experience for credit. If students simultaneously seek credit for the experience, they must enroll in ES 440 each semester of the professional experience. A regular debriefing is required for all professional experiences. If the student has applied for credit, the debriefing each semester of enrollment will be required for credit and grade designation. The student's experience will be assessed each semester whether or not credit is given.

Four Year Plan: Bachelor of Science in Environmental Studies
Pre-Professional Concentration

Freshman Year				
Fall Semester		**Spring Semester**		
IS 102 Foundations of Faith and Learning	2	MT 114 Elementary Probability-Statistics		3
BB 101 Survey of Old Testament	3	BB 102 Survey of New Testament		3
EN 101 English Composition	3	EN 102 English Composition II		3
HS 101 History of World Civilization I	3	BL 104 Advanced Survey of Biological Principles II		4
BL 103 Advanced Survey of Biological Principles I	4	ES 200 Intro to Environmental Studies		3
PE activity	1			
	16			**16**
Sophomore Year				
Fall Semester		**Spring Semester**		
ES 230 Sophomore Science Seminar	0.5	BL 205 Animal Diversity and Ecology		4
BL 206 Human Anatomy and Physiology I (or elective if taking BL 311)	4	CH 202 Environmental Inorganic Chemistry II		4
CH 201 Environmental Inorganic Chemistry I	4	CS 102 Computer Applications and Concepts		3
ES 206 Ecology	4	MT 191 Applied Calculus I		4
Gen-Ed Literature	3	PE activity		1
	15.5			**16**
Junior Year				
Fall Semester		**Spring Semester**		
IS 202 Modern Secular-Christian Worldviews	3	ES 301 Physical and Environmental Geography		4
Gen-Ed Oral Competency	3	BL 311 Plant Physiology (or elective if taking BL 206)		3
Gen-Ed Social Science	3	Gen-Ed Humanities		3
CH 320 Organic Chemistry I	3	CH 322 Organic Chemistry Lab I		2
MT 192 Applied Calculus II	4	HS 102 History of World Civilization II		3
	16			**15**

Completion of the General Education competencies by the end of the junior year.

Junior Summer				
Optional internship or partnership opportunity				
Senior Year				
Fall Semester		**Spring Semester**		
ES 445 Senior Science Seminar	1	BL 406 Conservation Biology		3
ES 340 Research Methods	3	CH 321 Organic Chemistry II		3
Gen-Ed Humanities	3	CH 323 Organic Chemistry II Lab		1
PC 131 College Physics I (offered every other year)	4	IS 461 Seminar on Faith and Life		2
BL 401 Genetics	3	PC 132 College Physics II (offered every other year)		4
Elective	2	Elective		3
	16			**16**

Completion of 33 credits at the 300-level or above.
Completion of the Major Field Test by the end of the Senior Year.

			Total hours required for degree:	**126.5**

The following required, alternate-year courses should be taken in either the junior or senior year:
BL 401 (3), BL 406 (3), BL 311 (3)
*See General Education for optional course offerings

Conservation Biology and Natural Resource Management Concentration (32 credits)

The Conservation Biology and Natural Resource Management concentration is designed to prepare students for graduate studies or for employment in government, industry, consulting, education, and non-profit organizations. This concentration integrates academic coursework with extensive field experience, and provides students with the unique opportunity to study the biologically diverse Southern Appalachian ecoregion. Students learn how to connect scientific principles with conservation and resource management issues and how to develop practical solutions to contemporary environmental issues from an interdisciplinary perspective.

Conservation Biology and Resource Management Courses
- BL 215   Plant Diversity and Ecology (4)
- ES 210   Environmental Sustainability (3)
- ES 305*   American Ecosystems (4)
- ES 315   Freshwater Ecosystems (4)
- ES 341   Practicum (3)
- ES 360   Introduction to Geographic Information Systems (3)
- ES 401   Natural Resource Management (3)
- ES 460   Field Studies (1-6) (minimum of 4 credit hours)
- IS 310   Pre-Practicum (1)
- OE 305   Environmental Policy and Law (3)

*See Financial Information in the Academic Catalog for information on course fee

Four Year Plan: Bachelor of Science in Environmental Studies
Conservation Biology and Natural Resource Management Concentration

Freshman Year

Fall Semester		Spring Semester	
IS 102 Foundations of Faith and Learning	2	MT 114 Elementary Probability and Statistics	3
BB 101 Survey of Old Testament	3	BB 102 Survey of New Testament	3
EN 101 English Composition	3	EN 102 English Composition II	3
HS 101 History of World Civilization I	3	BL 104 Advanced Survey of Biological Principles II	4
BL 103 Advanced Survey of Biological Principles I	4	ES 200 Intro to Environmental Studies	3
PE activity	1		
	16		16

Sophomore Year

Fall Semester		Spring Semester	
ES 230 Sophomore Science Seminar	0.5	BL 205 Animal Diversity and Ecology	4
BL 215 Plant Diversity and Ecology	4	CH 202 Environmental Inorganic Chemistry II	4
CH 201 Environmental Inorganic Chemistry I	4	CS 102 Computer Applications & Concepts	3
ES 206 Ecology	4	ES 210 Environmental Sustainability	3
Gen-Ed Literature	3	PE activity	1
	15.5		15

Junior Year

Fall Semester		Spring Semester	
IS 202 Modern Secular-Christian Worldviews	3	ES 301 Physical and Environmental Geography	4
OE 310 Environmental Interpretation	3	Gen-Ed Humanities	3
Gen-Ed Social Science	3	IS 310 Pre-Practicum	1
ES 315 Freshwater Ecosystems	4	HS 102 History of World Civilization II	3
ES 360 Intro to Geographic Information Systems	3	Elective	3
	16		14

Completion of the General Education competencies by the end of the junior year.

Sophomore or Junior Summer

ES 305 American Ecosystems			4

Senior Year

Fall Semester		Spring Semester	
ES 445 Senior Science Seminar	1	BL 406 Conservation Biology	3
ES 340 Research Methods	3	OE 305 Environmental Policy and Law	3
ES 341 Practicum	3	ES 460 Field Studies	2
ES 401 Natural Resource Management	3	IS 461 Seminar on Faith and Life	2
Gen-Ed Humanities	3	Elective	3
ES 460 Field Studies	2	Elective	2
	15		15

Completion of 33 credits at the 300-level or above.
Completion of the Major Field Test by the end of the Senior Year.

		Total hours required for degree:	126.5

Alternate Year Courses: BL 406; ES 305; ES 315; ES 460
*See General Education for optional course offerings

Special Emphasis Concentration (18 credits)

The Special Emphasis concentration allows students to design a program of study focused on an area of interest outside the core ES curriculum. Past examples include programs in sustainable agriculture, watershed studies, environmental economics, wildlife and fisheries science, and geology. Working with an ES faculty member, the student selects courses from Montreat College or other institutions that can be integrated into an environmental discipline. Such programs must be approved by the academic advisor and by the Environmental Studies Faculty by the end of the sophomore year. *In addition to the student developing their own program, below are a few pre-approved Special Emphasis programs:*

Special Emphasis Requirements
ES 305* American Ecosystems (4)
4 additional courses with a minimum of 14 credit hours, selected in consultation with the faculty advisor.

*See Financial Information in the Academic Catalog for information on course fee

Pre-Approved Special Emphasis Programs of Study with Au Sable Institute
Au Sable Institute of Environmental Studies' Certificate Program [http://www.ausable.org] is pre-approved as Special Emphasis Concentration plans of study. The student selecting an Au Sable certificate program must adhere to the Au Sable certification guidelines and fulfill all components of the certification program and Special Emphasis requirements. The student must be awarded the certificate by Au Sable. All six courses can be pursued at Au Sable, but if a certification program does not provide the full complement of 6 courses, the additional courses can be pursued at Montreat College or other approved institution. Final plans of how all components of the Special Emphasis are to be fulfilled are prepared with you department advisor and submitted to the department faculty for approval.

Pre-Approved Certification Programs:
Certified Naturalist
Certified Land Resources Analyst
Certified Water Resources Analyst
Certified Environmental Analyst
[Full list of courses offered through Au Sable for Montreat College can be found on the Au Sable web site.]

Environmental Studies Minor

Requirements for a minor in Environmental Studies (20 credits)

- BL 101   Survey of Biological Principles I, II (4)
- BL 102   Survey of Biological Principles II (4)
- ES 200   Introduction to Environmental Studies (3)
- ES 206   Ecology (4)
- A minimum of five (5) additional hours chosen from BL, CH, or ES

Accelerated Master of Science in Environmental Education

Undergraduate Montreat College students receiving a degree in Environmental Studies or in Outdoor Education may apply to the Accelerated Master of Science in Environmental Education program. If accepted, these students will complete their BS degree requirements, except for their last course, in 7 semesters, including taking OE 220 as part of their BS degree. During the spring term of their senior year, students will finish the BS with OE 462 and begin the first term of the MS program with EV 500 and EV 505. These students will obtain their BS degree and then complete the MSEE degree in four more terms.

Exercise Science Major

The Exercise Science program at Montreat College is designed to prepare individuals for careers in fitness and health promotion, strength and conditioning, and wellness programs. Students in the program learn how to assess and evaluate fitness levels for individuals and groups, and, how to design, implement, manage, and evaluate fitness programs. Graduates of the program will find employment opportunities in both public and private health and fitness facilities, and worksite and health care settings. The program also provides appropriate preparation for individuals desiring to pursue graduate study in fitness, health, and exercise science programs.

The Exercise Science Discipline

Exercise science deals with the study of immediate and long-term effects of physical activity on the human body. The field of study of exercise science is very diverse and includes several areas of inquiry. Two areas of inquiry for individuals interested in this field include sports performance and health-related components of physical activity. The health-related components of physical activity have been researched and the need for further research is prominent because of the obesity epidemic and the lack of physical activity of children. Sports performance of children, young adults and older adults involves biomechanical analysis, psycho/social analysis of sports as well as nutrition and physiological analysis. Exercise science is a non-teaching major that has emerged in response to concerns about the lack of physical activity, obesity, and increased risks of developing diseases. The exercise science field provides the opportunity to study the scientific basis of sport performance. The National Association for Sport and Physical Education (NASPE) provides guidelines for basic standard courses for the field. This field of study may also be entitled Movement Science, Fitness, or Kinesiology. Some individuals volunteer in a physical therapy setting as well as work in gyms to obtain experience in this area. It is suggested that students do volunteer work in order to gain experience in the field they are to specialize in.

Career Opportunities

Undergraduate programs in Exercise Science prepare students to attend professional schools in physical therapy, medicine, chiropractic, occupational therapy, and exercise physiology. Exercise Science graduates are prepared for careers in corporate fitness, agency fitness (YMCA, YWCA, etc.), health clubs, managers of fitness facilities, personal trainers, and strength and conditioning coaches. Another career option is to attend graduate school. These positions require certification from organizations such as the American College of Sports Medicine (ACSM), National Strength and Conditioning Association (NSCA) or Aerobic and Fitness Association of America (AFAA). There is a diversity of career options in this field – from medicine to personal trainer.

Why Study Exercise Science at Montreat College?

At Montreat College, the Exercise Science degree is designed to prepare individuals for careers in fitness and health promotion, strength and conditioning, and wellness programs.

The program takes a Christ-centered approach in small, intimate classes. Within the department, the faculty is highly accessible and genuine in their approach to students. Students in the program learn how to assess and evaluate fitness levels for individuals and groups, design, implement, manage, and evaluate fitness programs. All students complete a mandatory internship in a local health/fitness facility.

After Graduation

Students will find employment opportunities in both public and private health and fitness facilities, worksite and health care settings. The program also provides appropriate preparation for individuals desiring to pursue graduate study in fitness, health, and exercise science programs.

Requirements for a Major in Exercise Science

√	Degree Requirements
___	Completion of the General Education Core (56 credits)
	BL 101 or 103 and BL 102 or 104 required in the Gen-Ed
___	MT 121 required in the Gen-Ed
___	Completion of the General Education Competencies
___	Completion of the Exercise Science Major Core (49 credits)
___	Completion of an Exercise Science Concentration (18-23 credits)
___	Completion of required electives to bring total up to 126 credits (~0-3 credits)
___	Completion of 33 credits at the 300-level or above
___	Completion of 126 credit hours with a minimum GPA of 2.0 (two terms and 32 credit hours must be completed at Montreat College)

Required Major Courses (49 hours)

BL 220 Medical Terminology (1)
BL 206 Human Anatomy and Physiology I (4)
BL 207 Human Anatomy and Physiology II (4)
BL 301 Biometrics (3)
EX 201 Introduction to Exercise Science (3)
EX 310 Physiology of Exercise (3)
EX 320 Exercise Testing and Measurements (3)
EX 330 Kinesiology and Biomechanics (4)
EX 340 Exercise Prescription (3)
EX 341 Practicum (3)
EX 490 Senior Seminar (3)
HL 101 Health (3)
HL 102 Advanced First Aid (3)
HL 201 Human Nutrition (3)
IS 310 Pre-internship (1)
PE 201 Concepts of Fitness (2)
PE 424 Facility Planning for PE, Recreation, and Athletics (3)

Choose from two Exercise Science Concentrations:

Pre-Professional (23 credits)
Special Emphasis (18 credits)

Pre-Professional Concentration (23 credits)

The Pre-professional concentration offers a wide range of courses designed to prepare students for careers in physical therapy, medicine, chiropractic, occupational therapy, and exercise physiology, and professional or graduate schools.

Pre-Professional Courses
- BL 315   Cell Biology (4)
- BL 404   Microbiology (3)
- CH 201   Environmental Inorganic Chemistry I (4)
- CH 320   Organic Chemistry I (3)
- CH 322   Organic Chemistry Lab I (2)
- PC 131   College Physics I (4)
- EX 441   Internship I (3)

Special Emphasis Concentration (18 credits)

Students may transfer a set of courses from other institutions or complete courses in other departments at Montreat College to fulfill the requirements of this emphasis. Students develop the special emphasis curriculum in consultation with their academic advisor. The advisor and the Departmental Review Committee must approve a formal proposal of emphasis requirements by the end of the students' sophomore year. For example, students may develop a concentration that incorporates coursework from Communications, Marketing, or Outdoor Education.

Special Emphasis Courses
- 18 credits and 5 course minimum

Four Year Plan: Bachelor of Science in Exercise Science
Pre-Professional Concentration

Freshman Year				
Fall Semester		**Spring Semester**	
IS 102 Foundations of Faith and Learning	2	MT 121 College Algebra	3
BB 101 Survey of Old Testament	3	BB 102 Survey of New Testament	3
EN 101 English Composition	3	EN 102 English Composition II	3
HS 101 History of World Civilization I	3	HS 102 History of World Civilization II	3
BL 103 Advanced Survey of Biological Principles I	4	BL 104 Advanced Survey of Biological Principles II	4
PE activity course	1		
	16		**16**

Sophomore Year				
Fall Semester		**Spring Semester**	
EX 201 Intro to Exercise Science	3	Gen-Ed Oral Competency	3
BL 220 Medical Terminology	1	PE 201 Concepts of Fitness	2
BL 206 Human Anatomy and Physiology I	4	BL 207 Human Anatomy and Physiology II	4
CS 102 Computer Applications and Concepts	3	Gen-Ed Literature	3
HL 101 Health	3	Gen-Ed Social Science	3
PE activity course	1		
	15		**15**

Junior Year				
Fall Semester		**Spring Semester**	
EX 310 Physiology of Exercise	3	BL 301 Biometrics	3
EX 320 Exercise Testing and Measurements	3	EX 341 Practicum	3
HL 102 Advanced First Aid	3	EX 330 Kinesiology and Biomechanics	4
CH 201 Env. Inorganic Chemistry I	4	BL 315 Cell Biology	4
Gen-Ed Humanities	3	Gen-Ed Humanities	3
IS 310 Pre-Internship	1		
	17		**17**

Completion of the General Education competencies by the end of the junior year.

Junior Summer		
EX 441 Internship I		**3**

Senior Year				
Fall Semester		**Spring Semester**	
HL 201 Human Nutrition	3	IS 461 Seminar on Faith and Life	2
EX 340 Exercise Prescription	3	PE 424 Facility Planning for Physical Education, Recreation, and Athletics	3
CH 320 Organic Chemistry I	3	EX 490 Senior Seminar	3
BL 404 Microbiology	4	CH 322 Organic Chemistry Lab I	2
PC 131 College Physics (offered every other year)	3	Gen-Ed Humanities	3
	16		**13**

Completion of 33 credits at the 300-level or above.
Completion of the Major Field Test by the end of the Senior Year

Total hours required for degree:	**128**

*See General Education for optional course offerings

History Major

The History major prepares students for vocation, citizenship, and service. Students are equipped with the skills of critical thinking, analysis, data processing, and communication that transfer to a wide range of vocations. These skills are learned through the practice of historical thinking, which suggests that the study of history is more about cultivating critical reflection on the past rather than rote memorization. Students are prepared for citizenship, from local to global, through an understanding of how the persons, events, forces, and ideals of the past have shaped the present and inform the future. Students learn to be engaged and contributing members of society who pursue careers that offer various forms of public service, private enterprise, and cultural flourishing.

The History Discipline
The study of history focuses on exploration and evaluation of various social, political, economic, military, and religious forces that have shaped and transformed the world. This information not only provides perspective on the past but also establishes a marker for future innovation, helping us avoid mistakes and capitalize on strengths.

Why Study History at Montreat College?
The study of History at Montreat College provides expertise in global, European, and American history while also providing opportunities for topical studies, experiential learning, and internship possibilities. History classes are foundational in understanding other disciplines and thus lay the groundwork for a holistic liberal arts education. Students are encouraged to learn from the memories and stories of others, to exercise their moral imagination, and to engage their world with historical consciousness.

Students at Montreat College also explore how the Christian faith enriches historical understanding. The starting assumption of the History Department is that Christianity values the past as real, meaningful, authoritative, and comprehensible. Our approach honors the historical actors of the past, believing that creation in God's image confers dignity to every human person and story. Students are encouraged to pursue historical truth with the acknowledgement of our limited understanding and to engage the larger questions of God, nature, and human nature that have been prominent features of all civilizations.

After Graduation
A major in History can lead to graduate studies in administration, history, law, political science, and theology; even business and medicine are not to be excluded. A graduate in history may find employment in administrative and government services, libraries, public history activities and interpretation, or one of many areas in education.

Requirements of a Major in History

√	Degree Component
____	Completion of the General Education Core (56 credits)
	HS 101-102 are required in the Gen-Ed
____	BS 203 or BS 204 is recommended for the Gen-Ed social science
____	Completion of the General Education Competencies
____	Completion of the History Major Core (11 credits)
____	Completion of the History Major Electives (21 credits)
____	Completion of the Bachelor of Arts or Bachelor of Science requirements (12 credits)
____	Completion of required electives to bring total up to 126 credits (~26 credits)
____	Completion of 33 credits at the 300-level or above
____	Completion of the Major Field Test
____	Completion of 126 credit hours with a minimum GPA of 2.0 (two terms and 32 credit hours must be completed at Montreat College)

History Major Core (11 credits)

HS 201   United States History I (3)
HS 202   United States History II (3)
HS 210   Historical Methods (2)
HS 491   Senior Thesis (3)

History Major Required Electives (21 credits)

Choose twenty-one (21) hours of additional course work from the following:

European History
HS 311   Ancient Greece and Rome (3)
HS 313   Medieval World (3)
HS 315   Renaissance and Reformation (3)
HS 317   Modern Europe (3)
American History
HS 331   American Revolution and Republic (3)
HS 333   American Civil War (3)
HS 335   United States History Since 1945 (3)
HS 341   American Constitutional History (3)
HS 343   Religious History of America (3)
HS 345   American Cultural and Intellectual History (3)
Global History
HS 353   History of Christianity (3)
HS 355   Modern Middle East (3)
HS 361   The World at War, 1914-1945 (3)
HS 363   Global Cold War (3)
HS 365   Empire and Its Discontents

Topical History
- HS 371 History of Political Philosophy
- HS 373 History of Science and Technology
- HS 381 Environmental History (3)
- HS 383 Public History: Cities Through the Ages (3)
- HS 480 Special Topics (1-3)

Major Field Research & Field Experience
- HS 415 Historical Archival Work (2)
- HS 481 Directed Study & Research (3)

Recommended Elective Classes for History Majors
- BS 203 Macroeconomics (3)
- BS 204 Microeconomics (3)
- PY 202 General Psychology
- SC 204 Introduction to Sociology (3)

Four Year Plan: BA or BS in History

Freshman Year

Fall Semester		Spring Semester	
IS 102 Foundations of Faith and Learning	2	CS 102 Computer Applications and Concepts	3
BB 101 Survey of Old Testament	3	BB 102 Survey of New Testament	3
EN 101 English Composition	3	EN 102 English Composition II	3
HS 101 History of World Civilization I*	3	HS 102 History of World Civilization II*	3
Gen-Ed Natural Science	4	Gen-Ed Natural Science	4
PE activity course	1		
	16		16

*Students in the Honors Program will take the US History sequence, HS 201-HS 202, during their freshman year, and take the Honors World History sequence, HS 171-HS 172, during their sophomore year.

Sophomore Year

Fall Semester		Spring Semester	
HS 201 US History I	3	HS 202 US History II	3
HS 210 Historical Methods	2	Gen-Ed Oral Competency	3
Bachelor of Arts or Science requirement	3	Bachelor of Arts or Science requirement	3
Gen-Ed Literature	3	Gen-Ed Humanities	3
Gen-Ed Social Science	3	Elective	3
Gen-Ed Math	3	PE activity course	1
	17		16

Junior Year

Fall Semester		Spring Semester	
Major Elective	3	Major Elective	3
Major Elective	3	Major Elective	3
Bachelor of Arts or Science requirement	3	Bachelor of Arts or Science requirement	3
Gen-Ed Humanities	3	Gen-Ed Humanities	3
Elective	3	Elective	3
	15		15

Completion of the General Education competencies by the end of the junior year.

Senior Year

Fall Semester		Spring Semester	
Major Elective	3	Major Elective	3
Major Elective	3	HS 491 Senior Thesis	3
IS 461 Seminar on Faith and Life	2	Elective	3
Elective	3	Elective	3
Elective	3	Elective	3
Elective	2		
	16		15

Completion of 33 credits at the 300-level or above.
Completion of the Major Field Test by the end of the Senior Year.

Total hours required for degree:	126

*See General Education for optional course offerings

History Minor

Requirements for a Minor in History (18 credits)

    HS 201-202   United States History I, II (3, 3)
    Choose 12 additional hours of history electives at the 300-400 level.

Due to the breadth and depth of historical investigation, students who minor in history find themselves well prepared for careers that require knowledge of the past, interaction with people at home and around the world, and the ability to write and think analytically. An understanding of historical transitions helps one avoid mistakes of the past and capitalize on its strengths.

Interdisciplinary Studies Major

Students normally pursue one of the regular academic majors offered by the College. However, students also have the option of designing their own major so that they may engage in in-depth study that draws on two or more academic disciplines at the College. These programs, called Interdisciplinary Studies majors, are individualized programs of study developed in consultation with the faculty advisor.

A student wishing to propose an Interdisciplinary Studies major must do so before completing 80 hours of course work. Courses which have already been completed must be indicated on the proposal for the major, and these courses may comprise no more than 75% of the total course credits proposed. The major must consist of at least 48 hours of coursework. To ensure sufficient depth in the major, a minimum of 33 credits must be courses numbered 300 or higher. To ensure that the proposed major differs sufficiently from existing majors, there may be no more than a 75% overlap with an existing major. Major courses should be available at Montreat College; limits on transfer credits and independent studies should be within the normal pattern for other majors.

In constructing and seeking approval for an Interdisciplinary Studies major, students must submit a written proposal in collaboration with the faculty advisor to the Vice President for Academic Affairs & Dean of the College or designee. The proposal should include (1) a rationale for the program, (2) a description of appropriate professional goals, (3) a list of General Education courses completed, (4) a list of General Education courses that need to be completed, (5) a list of courses totaling at least 48 hours that one has taken or plans to take with a clear statement on how each course will contribute to meeting the stated goals, (6) a statement on whether an internship or thesis will be completed, and (7) a means of assessing whether the goals articulated have been met. The program must satisfy all General Education and Competency requirements, including the language requirement for a BA. The Vice President for Academic Affairs & Dean of the College or designee will consult with the department chair(s) in which twelve or more hours are taken for their support of the Interdisciplinary Studies major before granting final approval.

The Interdisciplinary Studies minor at Montreat College is structured to provide students with a broad based exposure to Liberal Arts studies. The intent of the program is to offer a sequence of courses that enable students to satisfy educational objectives which might not otherwise be met by a particular, pre-established degree program. By gaining insight into the humanities, students will be better equipped to ascertain the human condition and the relationship of their own majors to those of other academic disciplines.

Interdisciplinary Studies Minor

Requirements for a Minor in Interdisciplinary Studies (18 credits)

Interdisciplinary Studies Minor Core (9 credits)
    PH 201 Introduction to Philosophy (3)
    PH 301 Ethics (3)
    IS 202   Modern Secular-Christian Worldviews (3)

Interdisciplinary Studies Minor Required Electives (9 credits)
    Choose 9 hours from the following courses:
        EN 402 Literary Criticism (3)
        HS 345 American Cultural and Intellectual History (3)
        HS 353 History of Christianity (3)
        HS 371 History of Political Philosophy (3)
        HS 373 History of Science & Technology (3)

The IS minor is designed to complement a student's major through thorough exposure to a broad range of disciplines, enhancement of critical thinking skills, and engagement of issues from a worldview perspective. It prepares students to discern truth, engage others respectfully, and serve as agents of renewal and reconciliation.

Leadership Minor

The Leadership Minor

The Leadership Minor is an Interdisciplinary Studies (IS) program that is supervised by the Outdoor Education Department. The minor is for students from all majors who are interested in a leadership development program that includes elective courses, as well as experiential and service learning opportunities. Students will be challenged to grow in personal faith, to discern truth prior to taking action, and to effectively lead others in the pursuit of accomplishing tasks and developing relationships. Students will be better prepared to live as Christ-following agents of renewal and reconciliation in their careers and communities. (21 hours)

Requirements for a Leadership Minor (21 credits)

Theoretical and Practical Leadership Courses (15 credits)
Choose one ethics course:
      BS 309   Business Ethics (3) **OR**
      PH 301   Ethics (3)
IS 202   Modern Secular-Christian Worldviews (3)
IS 302   Philosophy of Leadership (3)
IS 421   Leadership Practicum (3)
OE 306   Leadership & Group Dynamics (3)

Leadership Minor Required Electives (6 credits)
Choose at least two courses:
      BB 211   Christian Doctrine (3)
      BS 209   Principles of Management (3)
      BS 303   Human Resources Management (3)
      BS 307   Organizational Behavior (3)
      BS 308   Servant Leadership (3)
EN 271 Business Communication (3)
      Only one wilderness course:
         OE 180   Discovery Wilderness Expedition (4) **OR**
         OE 182   Wilderness Journey (2-4)
      PY 412   Theories & Principles of Counseling (3)
      YM 303   Discipleship & Lifestyle Evangelism (3)
      YM 401   Spiritual Formation & Faith Development (3)

Music Major

Martin Luther said that "Music is a fair and glorious gift of God. . . I am strongly persuaded that, after theology, there is no art that can be placed on a level with music; for besides theology, music is the only art capable of affording peace and joy in the heart." Music has always been considered an important part of a classical education and has an important place in the Christian liberal arts education that students receive at Montreat College.

The Music Discipline

Montreat College offers all students opportunities for musical training and experience. Students are encouraged to develop and share their God-given abilities by learning to sing or play an instrument, participating in musical ensembles, attending recitals and concerts, and taking courses appropriate to their level of study.

Why Study Music at Montreat College?

The curricula for all music programs at Montreat College are based upon a philosophy that balances professionalism and excellence in musicianship with the development of the whole person – mind, spirit, and body – through the General Education Core requirements. Underlying all we do is a commitment to the integration of faith and learning. Because music study inherently requires an intensive level of individualized instruction, the modeling of professional and Christian conduct and character by the Music faculty and their attentive care for their students distinguishes the Montreat College Music program.

Entrance Requirements

In addition to meeting the entrance requirements of the College, prospective Bachelor of Arts in Music students must pass a performance audition. The student will declare a principle instrument or voice. Bachelor of Music in Worship Arts also requires a performance audition. No audition is required for Music Business majors or for Music, Music Business, or Worship Arts minors.

Curriculum

The Music curriculum is designed to introduce non-music majors to the basics of music theory and history and to help them acquire a non-professional level of performance competence through at least four semesters of applied instruction in voice or an instrument and through participation in a musical ensemble.

After Graduation

The Bachelor of Arts in Music Degree equips students to succeed as a professional in the diverse world of music. The degree program contains a great deal of flexibility in allowing the students to focus on different areas of calling. A student may focus on performance aspects of music or combine music with studies in another discipline such as business, religion, psychology, theater or worship arts.

Requirements for a Major in Music

√	Degree Component
____	Completion of the General Education Core (56 credits)
____	MS 305 and MS 306 required for humanities
____	Completion of the General Education Competencies
____	Completion of the Music Major Core (30 credits)
____	Completion of the Music Major Electives (24 credits)
____	Completion of required electives to bring total up to 126 credits (~16 credits)
____	Foreign language recommended
____	Completion of 33 credits at the 300-level or above
____	Additional requirements, as explained in Music Program Handbook
____	Completion of 126 credit hours with a minimum GPA of 2.0 (two terms and 32 credit hours must be completed at Montreat College)

Music Major Courses (30 credits)

Foundation Courses

    MS 100 Performance Seminar (2) (4 semesters)

    MS 113 Music Theory I with Lab (4)

    MS 114 Music Theory II with Lab (4)

    MS 213 Music Theory III with Lab (4)

    MS 214 Music Theory IV with Lab (4)

Ensemble Courses

    Choose 4 credits, all repeatable

        MS 151 College Choir (1)

        MS 153 Guitar Ensemble (1)

        MS 154 Instrumental Chamber Ensemble (1)

        MS 156 Accompanying (1)

        MS 157 Rock Ensemble (1)

        MS 251 Chamber Choir (1)

        MS 257 Songwriting Ensemble (1)

        MS 357 Advanced Rock Ensemble (1)

Applied Courses

    Choose one sequence

        MS 141-142, 241-242 Applied Piano

        MS 133-134, 233-234 Applied Group Lessons

        MS 143-144, 243-244 Applied Voice

        MS 145-146, 245-246 Applied Organ

        MS 147-148, 247-248 Applied Guitar, Woodwinds, Strings, Percussion

Music Skills

    Choose 4 credits:

        MS 103 Beginning Class: Piano (2)

        MS 104 Beginning Class: Voice (2)

        MS 105 Beginning Class: Guitar (2)

Music Major Required Electives (24 credits)

Choose 24 credits, 18 must be at 300-level or above

MS 121 Survey of Music Production, Marketing, and Distribution (3)
MS 122 Survey of Music and Artist Management (3)
MS 131 Introduction to Digital Sound Recording (3)
MS 206 Rhythm Studies (2)
MS 301 Midi and Sound Synthesis (3)
MS 303 Special Topics Seminar (3)
MS 307 History of Congregational Song (3)
MS 319 Arranging (3)
MS 221 Introduction to the Recording Studio (3)
MS 322 Live Sound and Lighting
MS 331 Copyright Law (3)
MS 332 Music Publishing (3)
MS 341-342, 441-442 Applied Piano (1, 1, 1, 1)*
MS 343-344, 443-444 Applied Voice (1, 1, 1, 1)*
MS 345-346, 445-446 Applied Organ (1, 1, 1, 1)*
MS 347-348, 447-448 Applied Guitar, Strings, Woodwinds, Percussion (1, 1, 1, 1)*
MS 401 Choral Conducting (2)
MS 405 Choral Methods (2)
MS 480 Special Topics (1-3)
MS 481 Directed Study and Research (1-3)
MS 480 Special Topics: Advanced Audio Production (3)
TH 340 Music Theater (3)
WA 101 Worship Arts Survey 1 (3)
WA 102 Worship Arts Survey II (3)

*If not used for major applied sequence requirement

Four Year Plan: Bachelor of Arts in Music

Freshman Year				
Fall Semester			**Spring Semester**	
BB 101 Survey of Old Testament	3		BB 102 Survey of New Testament	3
EN 101 English Composition I	3		EN 102 English Composition II	3
IS 102 Foundations of Faith and Learning	2		CS 102 Computer Applications and Concepts	3
MS 133/141/143/145/147 Applied Music I	1		MS 134/142/144/146/148 Applied Music II	1
MS 113 Music Theory I	4		MS 114 Music Theory II	4
MS 100 Performance Seminar	0.5		MS 100 Performance Seminar	0.5
Ensemble Course	1		Ensemble Course	1
	14.5			**15.5**

Sophomore Year				
Fall Semester			**Spring Semester**	
MS 213 Music Theory III	4		MS 214 Music Theory IV	4
MS 233/241/243/245/247 Applied Music III	1		MS 234/242/244/246/248 Applied Music IV	1
MS 100 Performance Seminar	0.5		MS 100 Performance Seminar	0.5
Ensemble Course	1		Ensemble Course	1
HS 101 History of World Civilization I	3		HS 102 History of World Civilization I	3
Gen-Ed Mathematics	3		Gen-Ed Oral Competency	3
Gen-Ed Social Science	3		PE activity course	1
PE activity course	1		Elective	3
	16.5			**16.5**

Junior Year				
Fall Semester			**Spring Semester**	
MS 305 Survey of Musical Styles I	3		MS 306 Survey of Musical Styles II	3
MS 103, 104, or 105 Beginning Instrument (Skills)	2		MS 103, 104, or 105 Beginning Instrument (Skills)	2
Music Elective	3		Music Elective	3
Gen-Ed Literature	3		Music Elective	3
Gen-Ed Natural Science	4		Gen-Ed Natural Science	4
Elective	1			
	16			**15**

Completion of the General Education competencies by the end of the junior year.

Senior Year				
Fall Semester			**Spring Semester**	
IS 461 Seminar on Faith and Life	2		Gen-Ed Humanities	3
Music Elective	3		Music Elective	3
Music Elective	3		Music Elective	3
Music Elective	3		Elective	3
Elective	3		Elective	3
Elective	3			
	17			**15**

Completion of 33 credits at the 300-level or above.

			Total hours required for degree:	**126**

*See General Education for optional course offerings

Music Minor

Requirements for a Music Minor (19 credits)

MS 113 Music Theory I (4)

Applied voice or instrument (4-5):
Choose 4-5 1-hour courses:
MS 141-142, 241-242 Applied Piano
MS 133-134, 233-234 Applied Group Lessons
MS 143-144, 243-244 Applied Voice
MS 145-146, 245-246 Applied Organ
MS 147-148, 247-248 Applied Guitar
MS 147-148, 247-248 Applied Woodwinds
MS 147-148, 247-248 Applied Strings
MS 147-148, 247-248 Applied Percussion

Choose 6 hours from Music and Culture Group:
MS 305 Survey of Musical Styles I (3)
MS 306 Survey of Musical Styles II (3) *(pre-requisite: MS 305)*
MS 307 History of Congregational Song (3)

Choose 4-5 hours Ensemble:
MS 151 College Choir (1)
MS 153 Guitar Ensemble (1)
MS 154 Chamber Orchestra (1)
MS 156 Accompanying (1)
MS 157 Rock Ensemble (1)
MS 251 Chamber Choir (1)
MS 257 Songwriting Ensemble (1)
MS 357 Advanced Rock Ensemble (1)

Music Business Major

Our Music Business major bridges the ever-changing divide between art and commerce. The major prepares students with the skill sets to engage the current music industry with new ideas, to think creatively about monetizing talent and to play an integral part in the performance, production, and management of a career in music.

The Music Business Discipline

Beyond the spotlight and center stage, the business of music is a broad field, offering an impressive diversity of career opportunities. A musical concert, for example, requires a promotion team, an agent, a manager and stage crew, supporting musicians, and a host of technicians before a single note is played. The music industry continues to expand and increase in complexity, and this has created the need for a new type of professional – one who understands not only music, but also the many aspects of business that are associated with its production.

Why Study Music Business at Montreat College?

Montreat College offers a unique degree that equips students to manage the legal, financial, artistic, and ethical issues that face the contemporary music business professional. The Bachelor of Science in Music Business degree is an innovative interdisciplinary program. Montreat College's curriculum offers students an unequalled level of flexibility to craft a combination of courses that will match the student's personal interests. Students in the Music Business program are also provided with abundant opportunities for practical learning and career preparation through hands-on instruction, and on the ground experience with professionals at the top of their game in a professional recording studio, in a major live event, and more.

Entrance Requirements

No audition is required for Music Business majors or for Music, Music Business, or Worship Arts minors. In addition to meeting the entrance requirements of the College, the prospective Bachelor of Arts in Music (see Music) and Bachelor of Music in Worship Arts major (see WA) students must pass a performance audition.

After Graduation

The Bachelor of Science in Music Business Degree equips students to succeed as a professional in the diverse world of the music and entertainment industry. In addition to the opportunity to learn hands on skills such as music production graduates understand the legal, financial, artistic, and ethical issues that confront the contemporary music business professional and have been guided to effectively confront them. A diverse and flexible program, Music Business graduates move into career paths such as: record producer, artist manager, studio manager, record promoter, booking agent, music licensing agent, tour manager, fine arts management, as well as being well equipped to succeed as a professional musician. The Music Business Degree also prepares students for graduate studies in Business, Management, Arts Administration and other areas of advanced study.

Requirements for a Major in Music Business

√	Degree Component
___	Completion of the General Education Core (57* credits)
___	BS 203 or 204 required social science for all Music Business majors
	MS 113 and MS 305 or MS 114 required humanities for General Concentration
	MS 113, MS 305, and PH 301 required humanities for MAPP Concentration
___	Completion of the General Education Competencies
___	Completion of the major requirements for Music Business *or* Music Business with a Concentration in Audio Production (69-71 credits)
___	Completion of 33 credits at the 300-level or above
___	Completion of required electives to bring total up to 126 credits (~0-3 credits)
___	Completion of Music Business Portfolio
___	Additional requirements, as explained in Music Program Handbook
___	Completion of 126 credit hours with a minimum GPA of 2.0 (two terms and 32 credit hours must be completed at Montreat College)

*TH 230 in the major electives for Music Business can count toward the Gen-Ed oral expression competency, thereby reducing the total Gen-Ed credits to 54 for that track.

Choose from two tracks:

Music Business (69 credits)

Music Business with a concentration in Audio Production (71 credits)

Music Business Major (69 credits)

Music Component (35 credits)
    MS 100 Seminar in Music Performance (2) (4 semesters)
    MS 106*Music Business Forum (0)
    MS 121 Survey of Music Production, Marketing, and Distribution (3)
    MS 122 Survey of Music and Artist Management (3)
    MS 261-262 Music and Artist Management Seminar I-II
        (2, 2)
    MS 361-362 Music Production, Marketing, and Distribution Seminar I-II
        (3, 3)
    IS 310   Pre-Practicum/Pre-Internship (1)
    MS 332 Music Publishing (3)
    MS 451 Practicum in Music Business (2)
    MS 461 Music Business Seminar V (2)
    MS 462 Music Business Seminar VI (2)
    MS 485 Senior Studies in Music Business (3)
    Choose 4 hours of ensemble courses: (Repeatable up to 4 times)
        MS 151 College Choir (1)
        MS 153 Guitar Ensemble (1)
        MS 154 Instrumental Chamber Ensemble (1)
        MS 156 Accompanying (1)
        MS 157 Rock Ensemble (1)
        MS 251 Chamber Choir (1)
        MS 257 Songwriting Ensemble (1)
        MS 357 Advanced Rock Ensemble (1)
*Required every semester while enrolled as a full-time student
with the exception of off-campus immersion semester.

Performance Component (4 credits)
    Choose one sequence of courses from the following:
        MS 141-142, 241-242 Applied Piano
        MS 133-134, 233-234 Applied Group Lessons
        MS 143-144, 243-244 Applied Voice
        MS 145-146, 245-246 Applied Organ
        MS 147-148, 247-248 Applied Guitar
        MS 147-148, 247-248 Applied Woodwinds
        MS 147-148, 247-248 Applied Strings
        MS 147-148, 247-248 Applied Percussion

Business Component (21 credits)

    BS 101 Intro to Business (3)
    BS 201 Principles of Accounting I (3)
    BS 202 Principles of Accounting II (3)
    BS 209 Management (3)
    BS 230 Marketing (3)
    BS 309 Business Ethics (3)
    MS 331 Copyright Law (3)

Music Business Electives (9 credits)

Music History and Culture (3 credits)

    Choose one:
        MS 101 Introduction to Music (3)
        MS 202 Social History of Rock and Roll (3)
        MS 305*Survey of Musical Styles I (3)
        MS 306 Survey of Musical Styles II (3)
        WA 306 Music in Worship (3)
            *MS 305 may be taken in Music History and Culture if not taken as humanities.

Practical Skills (6 credits)

    Choose two (3 credits must be 300-level or above):
        AR 241 Drawing I (3)
        AR 245 Principles of Design (3)
        AR 341 Drawing II (3)
        AR 342 Painting (3)
        AR 344 Sculpture (3)
        AR/CM 349 Graphics and Photojournalism (3)
        BS 214 Quantitative Methods (3)
        CM 228 Media Studies (4)
        CM 313 Public Relations (3)
        MS 114 Music Theory II (4)
        MS 131 Introduction to Digital Sound Recording (3)
        MS 206 Rhythm Studies (2)
        MS 221 Introduction to the Studio (3)
        MS 301 Midi and Sound Synthesis (3)
        MS 319 Arranging (3)
        MS 322 Live Sound and Lighting (3)
        TH 230* Acting (3)
        TH 232 Stagecraft (3)
        TH 333 Theatre Ensemble (4)
        TH 317 Directing (3)
        TH 330 Advanced Acting (3)
        WA 461 Worship Arts Seminar I (1)
        WA 462 Worship Arts Seminar II (1)

                *TH 230 may double-count in the Gen-Ed to fulfill oral competency.

Four Year Plan: Bachelor of Science in Music Business

Freshman Year

Fall Semester		Spring Semester	
IS 102 Foundations of Faith and Learning	2	CS 102 Computer Application/Concepts	3
BB 101 Survey of Old Testament	3	BB 102 Survey of New Testament	3
EN 101 English Composition	3	EN 102 English Composition II	3
MS 100 Seminar in Music Performance	0.5	MS 100 Seminar in Music Performance	0.5
MS 106 Music Business Forum	0	MS 106 Music Business Forum	0
MS 121 Survey of Music Prod./Mkt./Dist.	3	MS 122 Survey of Music and Artist Mgt.	3
MS 141/143/145/147 Applied Music I	1	MS 142/144/146/148 Applied Music II	1
Ensemble Course	1	Ensemble Course	1
BS 101 Intro to Business	3	PE Activity Course	1
	16.5		15.5

Sophomore Year

Fall Semester		Spring Semester	
BS 230 Principles of Marketing	3	BS 209 Principles of Management	3
BS 203 Macroecon or Gen-Ed Math*	3	HS 102 History of World Civilization II	3
HS 101 History of World Civilization I	3	BS 204 Microecon or Gen-Ed Math*	3
MS 113 Music Theory I	4	MS 100 Seminar in Music Performance	0.5
MS 100 Seminar in Music Performance	0.5	MS 106 Music Business Forum	0
MS 106 Music Business Forum	0	MS 262 Music & Artist Mgt. Seminar II	2
MS 261 Music & Artist Mgt. Seminar I	2	MS 242/244/246/248 Applied Music IV	1
MS 241/243/245/247 Applied Music III	1	Ensemble Course	1
Ensemble Course	1	Gen-Ed Oral Competency	3
	17.5		16.5

Junior Year

Fall Semester		Spring Semester	
BS 201 Principles of Accounting I	3	BS 202 Principles of Accounting II	3
MS 106 Music Business Forum	0	MS 106 Music Business Forum	0
MS 331 Copyright Law	3	MS 332 Music Publishing	3
MS 361 Music Prod, Mkt, Dist Seminar I	3	MS 362 Music Prod, Mkt, Dist Sem II	3
Gen-Ed Literature	3	MS 114** or Practical Skills Elective	3
Gen-Ed Natural Science	4	Gen-Ed Natural Science	4
PE activity course	1		
	17		16

Completion of the General Education competencies by the end of the junior year.

Senior Year

Fall Semester		Spring Semester	
BS 309 Business Ethics	3	Immersion Semester Option	
MS 106 Music Business Forum	0	MS 106 Music Business Forum	0
MS 305** or Practical Skills Elective	3	MS 451 Practicum in Music Business	2
MS 461 Music Business Seminar	2	Music History and Culture Elective or Practical Skills Elective**	3
Gen-Ed Humanities	3	MS 462 Music Business Seminar	2
IS 310 Pre-Practicum	1	MS 485 Senior Studies- Music Business	3
IS 461 Seminar on Faith and Life	2	Practical Skills Elective	3
	14		13

Completion of 33 credits at the 300-level or above.
Music Business Portfolio must be submitted by the end of the senior year.

		Total hours required for degree:	126

*Students may choose BS 203 or BS 204; mathematics must be taken the alternate semester.
**Students are required to take MS 113 and choose MS 114 or MS 305 for humanities courses; a Music History and Culture elective (one class); and Practical Skills electives (two classes).
***See General Education for optional course offerings

Music Business Major with a Concentration in Audio Production (71 credits)
  Montreat Audio Production Program (MAPP)

Music Business Component (17 credits)
    MS 106*Music Business Forum (0)
    MS 121 Survey of Music Production, Marketing, and Distribution (3)
    MS 122 Survey of Music and Artist Management (3)
    MS 261-262 Music and Artist Management Seminar I-II
        (Battle of the Bands) (2, 2)
    MS 361-362 Music Production, Marketing, and Distribution Seminar I-II
        (Album Project) (3, 3)
    IS 310   Pre-Practicum/Pre-Internship (1)
*Required every semester while enrolled as a full-time student
with the exception of off-campus immersion semester.

Audio Production Component (30 credits)
    MS 131 Introduction to Digital Sound Recording (3)
    MS 221 Introduction to the Recording Studio (3)
    MS 223 Advanced Studio Production (3)
    MS 301 Midi and Sound Synthesis (3)
    MS 322 Live Sound and Lighting (3)
    MS 209 MAPP Recording Studio Management (3)
    MS 232 MAPP Critical Listening (1)
    MS 325 MAPP Digital Sound Processing (3)
    MS 326 MAPP Mastering (3)
    MS 451 Practicum in Music Business (2)
    MS 485 Senior Studies in Music Business (3)

Performance Component (9 credits)
    MS 100 Seminar in Music Performance (.5) (2 semesters)
    Choose any 4 hours of an applied instrument from the following:
        MS 141-142, 241-242 Applied Piano
        MS 133-134, 233-234 Applied Group Lessons
        MS 143-144, 243-244 Applied Voice
        MS 145-146, 245-246 Applied Organ
        MS 147-148, 247-248 Applied Guitar
        MS 147-148, 247-248 Applied Woodwinds
        MS 147-148, 247-248 Applied Strings
        MS 147-148, 247-248 Applied Percussion
        MS 147-148, 247-248 Applied Folk Strings

Choose 4 hours of ensemble courses: (Repeatable up to 4 times)
MS 151 College Choir (1)
MS 153 Guitar Ensemble (1)
MS 154 Instrumental Chamber Ensemble (1)
MS 156 Accompanying (1)
MS 157 Rock Ensemble (1)
MS 251 Chamber Choir (1)
MS 257 Songwriting Ensemble (1)
MS 357 Advanced Rock Ensemble (1)

Business Component (12 credits)
BS 101   Intro to Business (3)
BS 201   Principles of Accounting I (3)
BS 202   Principles of Accounting II (3)
MS 331 Copyright Law (3)

Music History and Culture (3 credits)
Choose one:
MS 202 Social History of Rock and Roll (3)
MS 306 Survey of Musical Styles II (3)
WA 306 Music in Worship (3)

Four Year Plan: Bachelor of Science in Music Business with a Concentration in Audio Production (MAPP)

Freshman Year

Fall Semester		Spring Semester	
IS 102 Foundations of Faith and Learning	2	CS 102 Computer Application/Concepts	3
BB 101 Survey of Old Testament	3	BB 102 Survey of New Testament	3
EN 101 English Composition	3	EN 102 English Composition II	3
MS 100 Seminar in Music Performance	0.5	MS 100 Seminar in Music Performance	0.5
MS 106 Music Business Forum	0	MS 106 Music Business Forum	0
MS 121 Survey of Music Prod/Mkt/Dist	3	MS 122 Survey of Music and Artist Mgt	3
Applied Instrument	1	Applied Instrument	1
Ensemble Course	1	Ensemble Course	1
BS 101 Intro to Business	3	BS 204 Microecon or Gen-Ed Math*	3
	16.5		17.5

Sophomore Year

Fall Semester		Spring Semester	
BS 201 Principles of Accounting I	3	BS 202 Principles of Accounting II	3
BS 203 Macroecon or Gen-Ed Math*	3	HS 102 History of World Civilization II	3
HS 101 History of World Civilization I	3	Gen-Ed Literature	3
MS 113 Music Theory I**	4	Gen-Ed Oral Competency	3
MS 106 Music Business Forum	0	MS 106 Music Business Forum	0
MS 261 Music & Artist Mgt Seminar I	2	MS 262 Music & Artist Mgt Seminar I	2
Applied Instrument	1	Applied Instrument	1
Ensemble Course	1	Ensemble Course	1
		PE Activity Course	1
	17		17

Junior Year

Fall Semester		Spring Semester	
MS 305 Survey of Musical Styles I**	3	Music Hist/Culture Elec**	3
MS 106 Music Business Forum	0	MS 106 Music Business Forum	0
MS 131 Intro to Digital Sound Recording	3	MS 301 Midi and Sound Synthesis	3
MS 221 Introduction to the Studio	3	MS 322 Live Sound and Lighting	3
MS 361 Music Prod, Mkt, Mgt Seminar I	3	MS 362 Music Prod, Mkt, Mgt Sem II	3
Gen-Ed Natural Science	4	Gen-Ed Natural Science	4
PE activity course	1		
	17		16

Completion of the General Education competencies by the end of the junior year.

Senior Year

Fall Semester		Spring Semester: Immersion	
	-	MS 106 Music Business Forum	0
MS 106 Music Business Forum	0	MS 209 MAPP Recording Studio Mgt	3
MS 223 Advanced Studio Production**	3	MS 232 MAPP Critical Listening	1
MS 331 Copyright Law	3	MS 325 MAPP Digital Sound Processing	3
PH 301 Ethics	3	MS 326 MAPP Mastering	3
IS 310 Pre-Practicum	1	MS 451 Practicum in Music Business	2
IS 461 Seminar on Faith and Life	2	MS 485 Senior Studies in Music Business	3
	12		15

Completion of 33 credits at the 300-level or above.
Music Business Portfolio must be submitted by the end of the senior year.

Total hours required for degree:	128

*Students may choose BS 203 or BS 204; mathematics must be taken the alternate semester.
**Students are required to take MS 113, MS 305, and PH 301 as humanities courses; and a Music History and Culture elective (one class).

Music Business Minor

Requirements for a Minor in Music Business (18 credits)

Music Business Minor core (12 credits)
    MS 121 Survey of Music Production, Marketing, and Distribution (3)
    MS 122 Survey of Music and Artist Management (3)
    MS 331 Copyright Law (3)
    MS 332 Music Publishing (3)

Music Business Minor Required Electives (6 credits)
    Choose two classes from the following:
        MS 113 Music Theory I (4)
        MS 114 Music Theory II (4)
        MS 131 Introduction to Digital Sound Recording (3)
        MS 301 Midi and Sound Synthesis (3)
        MS 322 Live Sound and Lighting (3)

Outdoor Education & Outdoor Ministry Majors

The purpose of the Outdoor Education department is to develop Christ-centered Outdoor Educators who are equipped with historical and philosophical foundations, technical skills, and teaching/leadership expertise.   The Outdoor Education Department offers two distinct majors, one in Outdoor Education and one in Outdoor Ministry. Four minors, Adventure-Based Counseling, Leadership, Outdoor Education and Outdoor Ministry, are available. The OE Department also offers a Master of Science in Environmental Education degree (see AGS graduate programs).

The Outdoor Education Major (OE)

The Bachelor of Science with a major in Outdoor Education (OE) combines elements of adventure education and environmental education into one unique program of study. Offering a strong emphasis in outdoor skills, leadership training, and environmental knowledge, students learn to teach adventure activities, team building, and environmental awareness in the context of an outdoor setting and from a biblical worldview. The Outdoor Education curriculum is designed to give students the skills, knowledge, and training necessary to both facilitate personal growth and interpret the natural environment.

The Outdoor Ministry Major (OM)

The Bachelor of Science with a major in Outdoor Ministry (OM) combines courses in Outdoor Education and Outdoor Ministry with Youth and Family Ministries courses. This unique program of study focuses on developing a strong ministry mind-set in students and prepares them to utilize the outdoor environment for evangelism and discipleship. While all are welcome to pursue this major, it is particularly suited to students who have had life-shaping experiences at summer camps, Young Life camps, church retreats, or other programs and want to provide similar experiences for others.

The Adventure-Based Counseling Minor

The minor in Adventure-Based Counseling (19-21 hours) combines existing courses from Outdoor Education (OE), Psychology (PY), and Human Services (HU) into a unique program of study. Adventure-Based Counseling and the closely related field of Adventure Therapy are two areas of Outdoor Education that are growing very quickly. This minor will provide a basic understanding of adventure-based counseling for those OE, PY, and HU students interested in pursuing a Master degree in a related area.

The Leadership Minor

The Leadership Minor is an Interdisciplinary Studies (IS) program that is supervised by the Outdoor Education Department. The minor is for students from all majors who are interested in a leadership development program that includes elective courses, as well as experiential and service learning opportunities. Students will be challenged to grow in personal faith, to discern truth prior to taking action, and to effectively lead others in the pursuit of accomplishing tasks and developing relationships. Students will be better prepared to live as Christ-following agents of renewal and reconciliation in their careers and communities. (21 hours)

Why Study Outdoor Education or Outdoor Ministry at Montreat College?

Theory and practice are integrated in the curriculum. Montreat College's OE & OM programs emphasize developing students to become leaders who are competent in using outdoor environments for education and ministry. Through numerous course studies and field experiences, students are prepared to design, implement, and administer outdoor programs that are safe, challenging, and enjoyable. Supported by a liberal arts foundation, students will use their knowledge of the environment and ministry preparation to point others to Christ.

The campus is located among mountainous wilderness areas. Montreat College is adjacent to Pisgah National Forest, close to the Great Smoky Mountains National Park, and within two hours of numerous climbing locations, four major wilderness areas, and several rivers with whitewater rated up to Class V. Montreat College is also within a 14-mile hike or bike ride of Mt. Mitchell, the highest peak east of the Mississippi River.

The faculty brings a diversity of training and depth of experience. Professors are passionate about engaging their students and challenging them to be professional, well-rounded educators. They prioritize the integration of faith and learning in classroom and the importance of field experiences. Professors bring experience from the National Outdoor Leadership School, Outward Bound, American Mountain Guides Association, the National Park Service, U.S. Forest Service, the North American Association for Environmental Education, Christian Adventure Association, Association for Experiential Education, Christian Camping International, Christian Camp and Conference Association, the American Canoe Association and the Wilderness Education Association, the National Association for Interpretation and remain current through active memberships. Students can expect their Outdoor Education professors to be beside them, guiding them and challenging them to reach their full potential both inside and outside the classroom.

Career opportunities are abundant. Graduates in Outdoor Education and Outdoor Ministry from Montreat College go on to a variety of careers in outdoor, adventure, and environmental education programs; camps and conference centers; mission organizations; national and state parks; churches and church-related youth organizations; expedition programs such as the National Outdoor Leadership School,

Wilderness Education Association, and Outward Bound; environmental organizations; nature centers; outdoor science programs; and environmental interpretation centers. Certification programs are available in several different areas. Many graduates report that whatever their career choice, the interpersonal skills, training in teaching and leading, and discipleship experiences they gained through the OE and OM programs prepared them for all aspects of their lives.

Opportunities for Experience. The Outdoor Education Department provides practical opportunities to equip students with technical skills and teaching/leadership experience. The department houses three outreach programs – the Team and Leadership Center (TLC). TLC utilizes challenge course facilities to develop team-building strategies and to strengthen the concept of community through experience-based learning. TLC is housed on the Black Mountain Campus and includes a high team's course, climbing wall and low initiatives course. Participants often include corporate groups, school and church groups, and private organizations.

Summit Adventure: Immersion Service and Adventure Semester (ISAS)

As an alternative to the OE Immersion Semester, Summit Adventure and Montreat College partner in this challenging 17-credit immersion program. If enrolled, students spend two to three weeks backpacking through California's High Sierra. For six to seven weeks students are housed at Summit Adventure's Basecamp where students delve deeply into a variety of subject areas. In addition, students participate in service and adventure-based learning during five to six weeks in Ecuador, putting into practice internationally all that was learned stateside.

ISAS Courses may include:
- CC 301   Foundations of Cross-Cultural Ministry (3)
- IS 302   Philosophy of Leadership (3)
- OE 191   Outdoor Living Skills I (2)
- OE 192   Outdoor Living Skills II (2)
- OE 306   Leadership and Group Dynamics (3)
- OE 312   Outdoor Programming and Leadership: Expedition Mgt. (4)
- OE 313   Outdoor Programming and Leadership: Rock Climbing (4)
- YM 401   Spiritual Formation and Faith Development (3)

*Prerequisite courses do not apply for students enrolled in the ISAS program.

For more information, visit www.summitadventure.com or contact the Outdoor Education Department.

Outdoor Education Major

Requirements for a Major in Outdoor Education

√ Degree Component

____ Completion of the General Education Core (53* credits)
   BL 101-102 are recommended in the Gen-Ed as prerequisites to ES courses;
   HS 101 & HS 102 are recommended in the Gen-Ed as prerequisites to IS 202;
____ IS 202 and PY 201 or PY 202 are recommended in the Gen-Ed
____ Completion of the General Education Competencies
____ Completion of the Outdoor Education Major Core (52 credits)
   Completion of OE 180 Discovery in the first year in OE major
____ Completion of an outdoor activity PE (210, 220, 230, 240, 260) in the first year in OE major
____ Completion of the Outdoor Education Major Electives (8 credits)
____ Completion of required electives to bring total up to 126 credits (~13)
____ Completion of 33 credits at the 300-level or above
____ Completion of Outdoor Education Dept. Comprehensive Exit Exam (included in OE 491)
____ Completion of 126 credit hours with a minimum GPA of 2.0 (two terms and 32 credit hours must be completed at Montreat College)

*OE 310 in the major can count toward Gen-Ed oral expression competency.
NOTE: Students who wish to add an Environmental Studies minor will complete ES 200 and an additional 2 credits in BL or ES courses.
NOTE: Students who double major in Outdoor Education and Outdoor Ministry can count their field experience (OE/OM 241) and internship (OE/OM 441) credits toward both majors.

Outdoor Education Major Core (52 credits)

ES 201   Field Natural History I, II (2)
ES 202   Field Natural History II (2)
ES 206   Ecology (4)
IS 302   Philosophy of Leadership (3)
IS 310   Pre-Internship (1)
OE 103   Survey of Outdoor Education I (3)
OE 111   Facilitating Outdoor Education Experiences (3)
OE 180   Discovery Wilderness Expedition (4) (1st Year Requirement)
OE 191* Outdoor Living Skills I (2)
OE 192* Outdoor Living Skills II (2)
OE 241   Outdoor Education Field Experience (1/1)
OE 306   Leadership & Group Dynamics (3)
OE 310   Principles of Environmental Interpretation (3)
OE 340   OE Teaching Methods & Curriculum Development (4)
OE 404   Administration & Management of OE (4)
OE 441   Internship in Outdoor Education (3)
OE 462   Current Issues in Outdoor Education (3)
OE 491   Senior Seminar (1)
OM 300 Outdoor and Camp Programming (3) (OM 200 pre-req. waived)

*Transfer students may register for OE 191, OE 192 without the OE 180 pre-requisite

Required Major Electives (8 hours)

Choose 6 or more hours from the following:

OE 182 Wilderness Journey (2)

OM 200 Introduction to Christian Camping & Outdoor Ministry (3)

OE 210 Challenge Course Facilitation (3)

OE 220 Survey of Environmental Education Curricula (3)

OE 225 Conference and Event Planning (1-3)

OE 300 Survey of Adventure-Based Counseling (3)

OE 305 Environmental Policy & Law (3)

OE 311 Outdoor Programming/Leadership: Kayaking (4)

OE 312 Outdoor Programming/Leadership: Expedition Mgmt. (4)

OE 313 Outdoor Programming/Leadership: Rock Climbing (4)

OE 314 Outdoor Programming/Leadership: Canoeing (4)

OE 341 Outdoor Education Practicum (1-3)

OE 480 Special Topics (1-6)

Choose 2 or more hours from the following:

BL 205 Animal Diversity and Ecology (4)

BL 215 Plant Diversity and Ecology (4)

ES 301 Physical & Environmental Geography (4)

ES 305 American Ecosystems (4)

ES 315 Freshwater Ecosystems (4)

ES 460 Field Studies (1-4)

Four Year Plan: Bachelor of Science in Outdoor Education

Freshman Year

Fall Semester		Spring Semester	
IS 102 Foundations of Faith and Learning	2	BB 102 Survey of New Testament	3
BB 101 Survey of Old Testament	3	EN 102 English Composition II	3
EN 101 English Composition	3	OE 111 Facilitating Outdoor Ed Experiences	3
OE 103 Survey of Outdoor Education I	3	BL 102 Survey of Biological Principles II	4
BL 101 Survey of Biological Principles I	4	OE 241 Outdoor Education Field Experience I	1
PE 210, 220, 230, 240, or 260	1	PE 210, 220, 230, 240, or 260	1
		ES 200 Intro to Environmental Studies (optional)	
	16		**15**

Freshman Summer

OE 180 Discovery Wilderness Expedition *(All OE majors must complete OE 180 within first year at Montreat College)*	**4**

Sophomore Year

Fall Semester		Spring Semester	
ES 201 Field Natural History I	2	ES 202 Field Natural History II	2
ES 206 Ecology	4	OE 306 Leadership and Group Dynamics	3
OE 191 Outdoor Living Skills I	2	OE 192 Outdoor Living Skills II	2
OE 340 Teaching Methods for OE	4	Gen-Ed Social Science	3
HS 101 History of World Civilization I	3	HS 102 History of World Civilization II	3
OE 241 Outdoor Education Field Experience	1	CS 102 Computer Applications and Concepts	3
	16		**16**

OE 241 Field Experiences must be completed before the student does his/her internship

Junior Year

Fall Semester		Spring Semester	
OE 310 Principles of Environmental Interpretation	3	Immersion Semester Option[1]	
Major Elective	3	IS 302 Philosophy of Leadership	3
Gen-Ed Mathematics	3	OM 300 Outdoor Camp and Programming	3
Gen-Ed Humanities (IS 202 recommended)	3	Major Elective	3
IS 310 Pre-Internship	1	Gen-Ed Literature	3
Elective	1	Gen-Ed Humanities	3
	14		**15**

Completion of the General Education competencies by the end of the junior year.

Junior Summer

OE 441 Internship	**3**

Senior Year

Fall Semester		Spring Semester	
OE 404 Admin & Management of OE	4	OE 462 Current Issues in OE	3
IS 461 Seminar on Faith and Life	2	OE 491 Senior Seminar	1
Major Elective	2	Elective	3
Gen-Ed Humanities	3	Elective	3
Elective	3	Elective	3
	14		**13**

Completion of 33 credits at the 300-level or above.
Completion of the OE Comprehensive Exit Exam (embedded in OE 491) by the end of the Senior Year.

Total hours required for degree:	**126**

[1] Immersion Semester: Wilderness Leadership Certificate or Summit ISAS Option
*See General Education for optional course offerings

Outdoor Education Minor

Requirements for an Outdoor Education Minor (20 credits)
A minimum of six credits must be at the 300-level or above

Outdoor Education Courses (12 hours)
Choose one course from the following:
>OE 103   Survey of Outdoor Education I (3) **OR**
>OE 111   Facilitating Outdoor Education Experiences

Choose 9 hours from the following:
>IS 302   Philosophy of Leadership (3)
>Only one of these courses:
>>OE 180   Discovery Wilderness Expedition (4) **OR**
>>OE 182   Wilderness Journey (2-4)
>
>OE 111   Facilitating Outdoor Education Experiences (3)
>OE 191   Outdoor Living Skills I (2)
>OE 192   Outdoor Living Skills II (2)
>OM 200 Introduction to Christian Camping & Outdoor Ministry (3)
>OE 210   Challenge Course Facilitation (3)
>OE 220   Survey of Environmental Education Curricula (3)
>OM 300 Outdoor and Camp Programming (3)
>OE 300   Survey of Adventure-Based Counseling (3)
>OE 305   Environmental Policy & Law (3)
>OE 306   Leadership & Group Dynamics (3)
>OE 310   Principles of Environmental Interpretation (3)
>OE 311   Outdoor Programming/Leadership: Kayaking (4)
>OE 312   Outdoor Programming/Leadership: Expedition Mgmt. (4)
>OE 313   Outdoor Programming/Leadership: Rock Climb (4)
>OE 314   Outdoor Programming/Leadership: Canoeing (4)
>OE 340   Teaching Method/Curriculum Development in OE (4)
>OE 341   Outdoor Education Practicum (1-3)
>OE 404   Administration/Management of OE (4)
>OE 441   Internship (3)
>OE 462   Current Issues in Outdoor Education (3)
>OE 480   Special Topics (1-6)

Environmental Studies Courses (8 hours)
>ES 206   Ecology (4)
>Choose 4 hours from the following:
>>BL 205   Animal Diversity and Ecology (4)
>>BL 215   Plant Diversity and Ecology (4)
>>ES 201-202 Field Natural History I, II (2, 2)
>>ES 301   Physical & Environmental Geography (4)
>>ES 305   American Ecosystems (4)
>>ES 315   Freshwater Ecosystems (4)
>>ES 460   Field Studies (1-4)

Outdoor Ministry Major

Requirements for a Major in Outdoor Ministry

√ Degree Component

___ Completion of the General Education Core (53* credits)

      BL 101-102 are recommended in the Gen-Ed as prerequisites to ES courses;

      HS 101 and HS 102 are recommended in the Gen-Ed as prerequisites to IS 202;

___ PY 201 or PY 202 is recommended in the Gen-Ed as prerequisite to PY 300/SC 414

___ Completion of the General Education Competencies

___ Completion of the Integrated Outdoor Education Major Core (32 credits)

___ Completion of the Outdoor Ministry Major Courses (26 credits)

      Completion of OE 180 Discovery in the first year in OM major

___ Completion of an outdoor activity PE (210, 220, 230, 240, 260) in the first year in OM major

___ Completion of required electives to bring total up to 126 credits (~15 credits)

___ Completion of 33 credits at the 300-level or above

___ Completion of Outdoor Education Dept. Comprehensive Exit Exam (included in OE 491)

___ Completion of 126 credit hours with a minimum GPA of 2.0 (two terms and 32 credit hours must be completed at Montreat College)

*OE 310 in the major can count toward the Gen-Ed oral expression competency.

NOTE: Students who double major in Outdoor Education and Outdoor Ministry can count their field experience (OE/OM 241) and internship (OE/OM 441) credits toward both majors.

Integrated Outdoor Education Major Core Courses (32 hours)

ES 201   Field Natural History I (2)

IS 310   Pre-Internship (1)

IS 302   Philosophy of Leadership (3)

OE 103   Survey of Outdoor Education (3)

OE 111   Facilitating Outdoor Experiences (3)

OE 180   Discovery Wilderness Expedition (4) (1st Year Requirement)

OE 191* Outdoor Living Skills I (2)

OE 192* Outdoor Living Skills II (2)

OE 306   Leadership & Group Dynamics (3)

OE 310   Principles of Environmental Interpretation (3)

OE 404   Administration & Management of OE (4)

OE 491   Senior Seminar (1)

*Transfer students may register for OE 191, OE 192 without the OE 180 pre-requisite

Outdoor Ministry Major Courses (26 hours)

YM 303 Discipleship & Lifestyle Evangelism (3)

YM 401 Spiritual Formation and Faith Development (3)

Choose one:

YM 407 Contemporary Youth Culture (3) (YM 203 pre-req. waived) **OR**

CC 301   Foundations of Cross-Cultural Ministry (3)

IS 202   Modern Secular-Christian Worldviews (3)

OM 200 Introduction to Christian Camping & Outdoor Ministry (3)

OM 241 Outdoor Ministry Field Experience (1/1)

OM 300 Outdoor & Camp Programming (3)

OM 441 Internship in Outdoor Ministry (3)

Choose one:

PY 300   Child & Adolescent Development (3) **OR**

SC 414   Counseling Adolescents & Families (3)

Four Year Plan: Bachelor of Science in Outdoor Ministry

Freshman Year

Fall Semester		Spring Semester	
IS 102 Foundations of Faith and Learning	2	BB 102 Survey of New Testament	3
BB 101 Survey of Old Testament	3	EN 102 English Composition II	3
EN 101 English Composition	3	OE 111 Facilitating Outdoor Ed Experiences	3
OE 103 Survey of Outdoor Education I	3	BL 102 Survey of Biological Principles II	4
OM 200 Intro to Christian Camping and OM	3	CS 102 Computer Applications and Concepts	3
PE 210, 220, 230, 240, or 260	1		
	15		16

Freshman Summer

OE 180 Discovery Wilderness Expedition *(All OM majors must complete OE 180 within their first year at Montreat College)*	4

Sophomore Year

Fall Semester		Spring Semester	
ES 201 Field Natural History I	2	IS 202 Modern Secular-Christian Worldviews	3
BL 101 Survey of Biological Principles I	4	OE 192 Outdoor Living Skills II	2
OE 191 Outdoor Living Skills I	2	Gen-Ed Literature	3
HS 101 History of World Civilization I	3	HS 102 History of World Civilization II	3
Gen-Ed Mathematics	3	PY 201 or PY 202 General Psychology	3
PE 210, 220, 230, 240, or 260	1	Elective	1
	15		15

OE 241 Field Experiences must be completed before the student does his/her internship

Junior Year

Fall Semester		Spring Semester	
OE 310 Principles of Environmental Interpretation	3	IS 302 Philosophy of Leadership	3
Major Elective	3	OM 300 Outdoor Camp & Programming	3
YM 303 Discipleship and Evangelism	3	OE 306 Leadership and Group Dynamics	3
IS 310 Pre-Internship	1	Gen-Ed Humanities	3
OM 241 Outdoor Ministry Field Experience	1	OM 241 Outdoor Ministry Field Experience	1
Gen-Ed Humanities	3	Elective	3
	14		16

OM 241 Field Experiences must be completed during the junior school year, prior to the internship.
Completion of the General Education competencies by the end of the junior year.

Junior Summer

OM 441 Internship	3

Senior Year

Fall Semester		Spring Semester	
OE 404 Admin & Management of OE	4	YM 401 Spiritual Formation	3
Major Elective	3	OE 491 Senior Seminar	1
Gen-Ed Humanities	3	IS 461 Seminar on Faith and Life	2
Elective	3	Elective	3
Elective	3	Elective	3
	16		12

Completion of 33 credits at the 300-level or above.
Completion of the OE Comprehensive Exit Exam (embedded in OE 491) by the end of the Senior Year.

Total hours required for degree:	126

*See General Education for optional course offerings

Outdoor Ministry Minor

The Outdoor Ministry minor will enhance most majors at Montreat College. With a strong emphasis in group process, discipleship and leadership, all students involved in the minor will grow as well as develop skills that can be used in working with adults and youth in group settings.

Requirements for a Minor in Outdoor Ministry (21 credits)

Required Courses:
ES 201 Field Natural History 1 (2) (Prerequisites: BL 101 & 102)
OE 306 Leadership & Group Dynamics (3)
OM 200 Intro to Christian Camping & Outdoor Ministry (3) OR
    YM 203 Foundations of Youth and Family Ministries (3)
OM 300 Outdoor and Camp Programming (3)

One or two OE courses below for 4 credits total:
    OE 180 Discovery Wilderness Expedition (4)
    OE 182 Wilderness Journey (2-4)
    OE 190 (2) & 192 (2) Outdoor Living Skills (Fall & Spring)

Two YM course options below for 6 credits total:
YM 303 Discipleship & Lifestyle Evangelism (3)
YM 401 Spiritual Formation & Faith Development (3)
YM 407 Contemporary Youth Culture & Programming (3)

Adventure-Based Counseling Minor

Requirements for a Minor in Adventure-Based Counseling (19 credits)

Adventure-Based Counseling Minor Core (12)

OE 300   Introduction to Adventure Based Counseling (3)
OE 211   Challenge Course Facilitation (3)
PY 202   General Psychology (3)
PY 412   Theories and Principles of Counseling (3)

Adventure-Based Counseling Required Minor Electives (7-9)

Choose one of the following: (2)
    PY 341   Practicum (2)
    OE 241   Field Studies (2)

Choose one of the following: (3)
    PY 300   Child and Adolescent Development (3)
    PY 305   Adult Development and Aging (3)
    SC 414   Counseling Adolescents and Families (3)

Choose one of the following (2-4)
    OE 180   Discovery (4)
    OE 182   Wilderness Journey (2-4)
    OE 311   Outdoor Programming and Leadership: Kayaking (4)
    OE 312   Outdoor Programming and Leadership: Expedition Management (4)
    OE 313   Outdoor Programming and Leadership: Rock Climbing (4)
    OE 314   Outdoor Programming and Leadership: Canoeing (4)

Leadership Minor

This minor will enhance most majors at Montreat College. This is a leadership development program that includes many elective courses, as well as experiential and service learning opportunities. (21 hours total)

Requirements for a Leadership Minor (21 credits)

Theoretical and Practical Leadership Courses (15 credits)
Choose one ethics course:

BS 309	Business Ethics (3) **OR**	
PH 301	Ethics (3)	
IS 202	Modern Secular-Christian Worldviews (3)	
IS 302	Philosophy of Leadership (3)	
IS 421	Leadership Practicum (3)	
OE 306	Leadership & Group Dynamics (3)	

Leadership Minor Required Electives (6 credits)
Choose at least two courses:

BB 211	Christian Doctrine (3)
BS 209	Principles of Management (3)
BS 303	Human Resources Management (3)
BS 307	Organizational Behavior (3)
BS 308	Servant Leadership (3)
EN 271	Business Communication (3)

Only one wilderness course:

OE 180	Discovery Wilderness Expedition (4) **OR**
OE 182	Wilderness Journey (2-4)
PY 412	Theories & Principles of Counseling (3)
YM 303	Discipleship & Lifestyle Evangelism (3)
YM 401	Spiritual Formation & Faith Development (3)

Accelerated Master of Science in Environmental Education (MSEE)

Undergraduate Montreat College students receiving a degree in Environmental Studies or in Outdoor Education may apply to the Accelerated Master of Science in Environmental Education program. If accepted, these students will complete their BS degree requirements, except for their last two courses, in 7 semesters, including taking OE 220 as part of their BS degree. During the spring term of their senior year, students will finish the BS with OE 462 and OE 491 and begin the first term of the MS program with EV 500 and EV 505. These students will obtain their BS degree and then complete the MSEE degree in four more terms.

Philosophy & Worldviews Minor

The Philosophy and Worldviews program of study prepares students to pursue graduate studies in a broad range of fields such as Philosophy, Ministerial Studies and many other graduate programs. Students from this major regularly find themselves studying Law or Medicine among other things.

The Philosophy and Worldviews Discipline
The Philosophy and Worldviews Major is housed within the Bible and Religion Department and offers either a Bachelor of Science or a Bachelor of Arts depending on the interests and direction of the student. This program is designed to prepare students to enter theological seminaries or graduate schools in multiple fields of study. This major requires a senior thesis and provides a balance of instruction in Biblical studies, philosophy, and worldview studies from the perspective of a *Reformational* worldview.

Why Study Philosophy and Worldviews at Montreat College?
Montreat College provides a unique mentoring environment that facilitates interaction between students and faculty both in and outside the classroom context. The department's commitment to exploring the relationship between faith and learning, and the relevance of the Christian faith for all disciplines of study, provides the student with a rich liberal arts experience and a solid foundation for graduate study or a wide range of occupations. The departmental faculty challenges students academically, assisting them in wrestling with the spiritual and practical implications of the subject matter. The full-time faculty is complemented by part-time and adjunct faculty who share the College's and department's mission, providing specific expertise to enhance the educational experience.

Requirements for a Minor in Philosophy and Worldviews (18 credits)

Required Minor Courses
    PH 201   Introduction to Philosophy (3)
    PH 210   Logic (3)
    PH 301   Ethics (3)
    IS 202   Modern Secular/Christian Worldviews (3)

Required Minor Electives
    Choose 6 additional hours from the following:
        PH 321   Contemporary Theologies (3)
        PH 403   Philosophy of Religions (3)
        HS 371   History of Political Philosophy (3)

Physical Education Minor

The Physical Education minor is designed to prepare individuals interested in teaching physical education or in coaching various sports. More than just a collection of activities, the concentration includes specialized theory courses that prepare a student to identify and assess the needs of individuals in the domain of fitness and wellness.

Requirements for a Minor in Physical Education (19 credits)

Physical Education Minor Core (14 credits)
    HL 101   Health (3)
    HL 102   Advanced First Aid (3)
    PE 111   Introduction to Physical Education (3)
    PE 201   Concepts of Fitness (2)
    PE 302   Methods & Materials of Coaching (2)
    IS 310   Pre-Practicum (1)

Physical Education Minor Electives (5 credits)
    Choose one:
        PE 341   Practicum (3) **OR**
        OE class at 300 or above (3)
    Choose two PE activity courses (2)

The study and application of Physical Education as a minor is used to provide an understanding of the physiological growth and development of the human body. It also develops skills and techniques for teaching physical education, and explores creative ways in which to implement a physical education curriculum. These combined skills provide an essential role in the pedagogical training of teachers and coaches.

Pre-Law Program

The American Bar Association, the national organization that oversees legal education in the U.S., does not recommend any undergraduate majors or group of courses to prepare for a legal education. Students are admitted to law school from almost every academic discipline. You may choose to major in subjects that are considered to be traditional preparation for law school, such as American studies, history, English, philosophy, political science, economics or business, or you may focus your undergraduate studies in areas as diverse as art, music, science and mathematics, computer science, engineering, nursing, or education. Whatever major you select, you are encouraged to pursue an area of study that interests and challenges you, while taking advantage of opportunities to enrich your ability to read and think critically, and develop your research, writing, and oral communication skills. Taking a broad range of difficult courses from demanding instructors is excellent preparation for legal education. A sound legal education will build upon and further refine the skills, values, and knowledge that you already possess.

If you wish to take some elective courses to introduce yourself to policy and law in one or more fields of your interest, the College offers such courses as Business Ethics; Business and the Legal Environment; Labor-Management Relations; Public Relations; Cybercrime, Cyberlaw, and Cyberethics; Copyright Law; Environmental Policy and Law; History of Political Philosophy; and U.S. Constitutional History.

Pre-Law Advisor
Undergraduate institutions often assign a person to act as an advisor to current and former students who are interested in pursuing a legal education. Montreat College's Pre-Law Advisor, Dr. Ben Smith, J.D. and Assistant Professor of Music Business, can help you find ways to gain exposure to the law and the legal profession and assist you with the law school application process.

Psychology and Human Services Major

The Psychology and Human Services program of study prepares students for the world of work and for graduate school. Upon graduation, students are equipped with the knowledge, skills, and experience they need for working in social agencies, churches, and other settings. In addition, students are prepared to enter graduate programs in areas such as psychology, counseling, and social work.

The Psychology and Human Services Discipline

The Psychology and Human Services major offers two areas of concentration: Psychology and Human Services. Students should select an area of concentration that reflects their specialized interest.

Students choosing the Psychology concentration will engage in a course of study that focuses on psychological theories and research about human behavior and psychological processes. The goals of psychology are to describe, explain, and predict these behaviors and processes.

Students choosing the Human Services concentration will engage in a course of study that integrates the disciplines of psychology, counseling, and social work. Emphasis will be placed on developing and implementing skills for helping individuals and families facing the challenges of our present society. These students will participate in two courses during their sophomore or junior years that provide them with hands-on experience.

Students choosing either concentration can earn either a Bachelor of Arts or Bachelor of Science degree. Both concentrations require the completion of an intensive off-campus internship during the summer after their junior year.

Why Study Psychology and Human Services at Montreat College?

Professors in the Psychology & Human Services major at Montreat College are interested in more than the mastery of theoretical content alone. They are committed to helping students explore the relationship between faith and learning. Students participate in classroom discussions that help them evaluate secular theories from a Christian perspective. Department faculty members encourage students to develop greater self-awareness and help students develop the personal characteristics that are needed in order to succeed in Psychology and Human Services. A 180-hour summer internship at community agencies further reinforce textbook learning and provide networking opportunities for our students. Classes are small and are extremely interactive, ensuring a more personalized learning environment. Students are invited to voice their views in a safe environment that welcomes free inquiry and the exchange of diverse ideas. The major provides students with a rich liberal arts experience and a solid foundation for graduate study or a wide range of occupations.

After Graduation

Graduates with degrees in Psychology and Human Services will find a large number of options available to them whether they want to begin working immediately or desire to attend graduate school. Psychology and Human Services graduates are prepared to pursue further study in a variety of graduate areas such as psychology, counseling, and social work. It is not uncommon for Psychology and Human Services majors to pursue further studies in other fields such as education, seminary, business, and law. Those with undergraduate degrees in Psychology and Human Services are qualified for positions in the workforce that may include a case worker, a counselor aide, or a residential staff member. Graduates with degrees in Psychology and Human Services are qualified to work in a variety of areas, including mental health, children's homes, community health centers, group homes, non-profit public organizations, law enforcement agencies, victims programs, employee assistance programs, religious organizations, and social service agencies.

Requirements of a Major in Psychology and Human Services

√	Degree Component
___	Completion of the General Education Core (53* credits)
___	MT 114 is required in the Gen-Ed
___	Completion of the General Education Competencies
___	Completion of the Psychology and Human Services Major Core (19 credits)
___	Completion of a Concentration (18 credits)
___	Completion of the Bachelor of Arts or Bachelor of Science requirement (12 credits)
___	Completion of required electives to bring total up to 126 credits (~24 credits)
___	Completion of 33 credits at the 300-level or above
___	Completion of ACAT Exam
___	Completion of 126 credit hours with a minimum GPA of 2.0 (two terms and 32 credit hours must be completed at Montreat College)

*One psychology or sociology course from the major can count toward the Gen-Ed social science requirement.

Psychology and Human Services Major Core (19 credits)

Choose one:

PY 201   Psychology Applied to Modern Life (3) **OR**
PY 202   General Psychology (3)

PY/HU 300   Child and Adolescent Development (3)
PY/HU 305   Adult Development and Aging (3)
PY/HU 315   Abnormal Psychology (3)
PY/HU 412   Theories and Principles of Counseling (3)
PY/HU 490   Senior Seminar (3)
IS 310   Pre-Internship (1)

Choose from two Psychology and Human Services Concentrations:

Human Services (18 credits)
Psychology (18 credits)

Human Services Concentration (18 credits)

SC 204   Introduction to Sociology (3)
SC 205   Marriage and Family (3)
SC 311   Social Welfare and Social Services (3)
SC 414   Counseling Adolescents and Families (3)
HU 101   Introduction to Human Services (1)
HU 241   Field Experience (1)
HU 241   Field Experience (1)
HU 441   Internship (3)

Psychology Concentration (18 credits)

PY 310   Research Methods (3)
PY 314   Personality (3)
PY 320   Social Psychology (3)
PY 420   Physiological Psychology (3)
PY 416   Learning and Memory (3)
PY 441   Internship (3)

Four Year Plan: BA or BS in Psychology and Human Services
Concentration in Human Services

Freshman Year				
Fall Semester		**Spring Semester**		
IS 102 Foundations of Faith and Learning	2	MT 114 Elementary Probability-Statistics	3	
BB 101 Survey of Old Testament	3	BB 102 Survey of New Testament	3	
EN 101 English Composition	3	EN 102 English Composition II	3	
HS 101 History of World Civilization I	3	HS 102 History of World Civilization II	3	
Gen-Ed Natural Science	4	Gen-Ed Natural Science	4	
PE activity course	1			
	16		16	

Sophomore Year				
Fall Semester		**Spring Semester**		
PY 201 or PY 202 General Psychology	3	CM 220 Public Speech & Rhetorical Analysis	3	
Bachelor of Arts or Science requirement	3	Bachelor of Arts or Science requirement	3	
CS 102 Computer Applications & Concepts	3	HU 101 Introduction to Human Services	1	
Gen-Ed Literature	3	HU 241 Field Experience	1	
Elective	3	Gen-Ed Humanities	3	
PE activity course	1	Elective	3	
	16		14	

Junior Year				
Fall Semester		**Spring Semester**		
PY 300 Child & Adolescent Development	3	PY 305 Adult Development and Aging	3	
SC 204 Introduction to Sociology	3	SC 205 Marriage and Family	3	
Bachelor of Arts or Science requirement	3	Bachelor of Arts or Science requirement	3	
Gen-Ed Humanities	3	Gen-Ed Humanities	3	
IS 310 Pre-Internship	1	Elective	3	
Elective	3	HU 241 Field Experience	1	
	16		16	

Completion of the General Education competencies by the end of the junior year.

Junior Summer				
HU 441 Internship			3	

Senior Year				
Fall Semester		**Spring Semester**		
PY 315 Abnormal Psychology	3	PY 412 Theories and Prin. of Counseling	3	
PY 490 Senior Seminar	3	SC 311 Social Welfare and Social Services	3	
IS 461 Seminar on Faith and Life	2	SC 414 Counseling Adolescents & Families	3	
Elective	3	Elective	3	
Elective	3	Elective	3	
	14		15	

Completion of 33 credits at the 300-level or above; Completion of the ACAT Test by the end of the Senior Year.

*See General Education for optional course offerings	Total hours required for degree:	**126**

Four Year Plan: BA or BS in Psychology and Human Services
Concentration in Psychology

Freshman Year

Fall Semester		Spring Semester	
IS 102 Foundations of Faith and Learning	2	MT 114 Elementary Probability-Statistics	3
BB 101 Survey of Old Testament	3	BB 102 Survey of New Testament	3
EN 101 English Composition	3	EN 102 English Composition II	3
HS 101 History of World Civilization I	3	HS 102 History of World Civilization II	3
Gen-Ed Natural Science	4	Gen-Ed Natural Science	4
PE activity course	1		
	16		16

Sophomore Year

Fall Semester		Spring Semester	
PY 201 or PY 202 General Psychology	3	CM 220 Public Speech & Rhetorical Analysis	3
Bachelor of Arts or Science requirement	3	Bachelor of Arts or Science requirement	3
CS 102 Computer Applications and Concepts	3	PY 310 Research Methods	3
Gen-Ed Literature	3	Gen-Ed Humanities	3
Elective	3	Elective	3
PE activity course	1		
	16		15

Junior Year

Fall Semester		Spring Semester	
PY 300 Child & Adolescent Development	3	PY 305 Adult Development and Aging	3
PY 314 Personality	3	PY 320 Social Psychology	3
Bachelor of Arts or Science requirement	3	Bachelor of Arts or Science requirement	3
Gen-Ed Humanities	3	Gen-Ed Humanities	3
IS 310 Pre-Internship	1	Elective	3
Elective	3		
	16		15

Completion of the General Education competencies by the end of the junior year.

Junior Summer

PY 441 Internship	3

Senior Year

Fall Semester		Spring Semester	
PY 315 Abnormal Psychology	3	IS 461 Seminar on Faith and Life	2
PY 416 Learning and Memory	3	PY 412 Theories and Prin. of Counseling	3
PY 490 Senior Seminar	3	PY 420 Physiological Psychology	3
Elective	3	Elective	3
Elective	3	Elective	3
	15		14

Completion of 33 credits at the 300-level or above; Completion of the ACAT Test by the end of the Senior Year.

*See General Education for optional course offerings	Total hours required for degree:	126

Psychology and Human Services Minor

Montreat College offers a minor in Psychology & Human Services that requires a minimum of 18 semester hours including:

Requirements of a Psychology and Human Services Minor (18 credits)
Choose one:
  PY 202 General Psychology (3) **OR**
  PY 201 Psychology Applied to Modern Life (3)
Choose 3 credits from the PYHU major core (excluding PY 490 Senior Seminar):
  PY/HU 300   Child and Adolescent Development (3)
  PY/HU 305   Adult Development and Aging (3)
  PY/HU 315   Abnormal Psychology (3)
  PY/HU 412   Theories and Principles of Counseling (3)
Choose 12 credits from the PYHU concentrations:
  SC 204   Introduction to Sociology (3)
  SC 205   Marriage and Family (3)
  SC 311   Social Welfare and Social Services (3)
  SC 414   Counseling Adolescents and Families (3)
  HU 101   Introduction to Human Services (1)
  HU 241   Field Experience (1)
  HU 441   Internship (3) (Prerequisite: IS 310)
  PY 310   Research Methods (3)
  PY 314   Personality (3)
  PY 320   Social Psychology (3)
  PY 420   Physiological Psychology (3)
  PY 416   Learning and Memory (3)
  PY 441   Internship (3) (Prerequisite: IS 310)

Adventure-Based Counseling Minor

The Adventure-Based Counseling Minor
The minor in Adventure-Based Counseling (19-21 hours) combines existing courses from Outdoor Education (OE), Psychology (PY), and Human Services (HU) into a unique program of study. Adventure-Based Counseling and the closely related field of Adventure Therapy are two areas of Outdoor Education that are growing very quickly. This minor will provide a basic understanding of adventure-based counseling for those OE, PY, and HU students interested in pursuing a Master degree in a related area.

Requirements for a Minor in Adventure-Based Counseling (19 credits)

Adventure-Based Counseling Minor Core (12)
OE 300   Introduction to Adventure Based Counseling (3)
OE 211   Challenge Course Facilitation (3)
PY 202   General Psychology (3)
PY 412   Theories and Principles of Counseling (3)

Adventure-Based Counseling Required Minor Electives (7-9)
Choose one of the following: (2)
PY 341   Practicum (2)
OE 241   Field Studies (2)

Choose one of the following: (3)
PY 300   Child and Adolescent Development (3)
PY 305   Adult Development and Aging (3)
SC 414   Counseling Adolescents and Families (3)

Choose one of the following (2-4)
OE 180   Discovery (4)
OE 182   Wilderness Journey (2-4)
OE 311   Outdoor Programming and Leadership: Kayaking (4)
OE 312   Outdoor Programming and Leadership: Expedition Management (4)
OE 313   Outdoor Programming and Leadership: Rock Climbing (4)
OE 314   Outdoor Programming and Leadership: Canoeing (4)

Spanish Minor

Spanish has become the fourth most widely spoken language in the world and the second most frequently used language in the United States. Many American companies are looking for Spanish language personnel since the new international trade agreement was made with Latin America in 2005.

The Spanish minor prepares students to understand, speak, read, and write Spanish proficiently. The Spanish minor familiarizes students with the history, literature, culture, and civilization of the Spanish-speaking nations in order to share the Christian message in a global community.

Requirements for a Minor in Spanish (18 credits)

Minor Core (6 credits)
- SP 201   Intermediate Spanish I (3)
- SP 202   Intermediate Spanish II (3)

Minor Electives (12 credits)

Choose an additional 12 credits at the 300 level.
- SP 303   Advanced Conversation and Composition I (3)
- SP 304   Advanced Conversation and Composition II (3)
- SP 305   Selected Readings in Spanish Literature (3)
- SP 306   Selected Readings in Latin American Literature (3)
- SP 480   Special Topics (1-3)
- SP 481   Directed Study and Research (1-3)

Montreat College provides students with several avenues for foreign study. Students may apply for the Council of Christian Colleges and Universities' Latin American Studies Program in Costa Rica for a semester abroad.

This generation offers widening opportunities for students to join institutions that want to employ Spanish-speaking team members. Employment is available in education, the military, law, public health, journalism, radio, TV, missions, business, translation, civil service, and social service. Other students may decide to proceed with their graduate study in Spanish.

Theatre Major

Theatre carries a very relevant place in the world of Christian Education and practice. It is an interdisciplinary weaving of all God's many gifts. Excellent theatre, seen through the lens of a Christian Worldview, is an art form that can magnify the failings and aspirations of man for the purpose of enjoyment and revelation of failure and potential. As Christians we get to examine and direct the telling of "everyman's" story. Even if a play is blatantly non-redemptive and might disturb some believers, it can image a piece of hope on stage. The goal of the Theatre Program is to provide students with an enriched curriculum and solid foundation of all the facets of the art and craft of theatre by a dedicated faculty providing future professionals with the confidence and skill set needed for entering the professional field, higher education, ministry, sales, public relations, and any number of possible careers. Montreat College's Theatre Program will foster integrity, and help students to gain appropriate knowledge of the artistic, business, and humanitarian side of their pursuits while attentively integrating a Christian worldview.

When I was a child, I talked like a child, I thought like a child, I reasoned like a child. When I became a man, I put the ways of childhood behind me. For now we see only a reflection as in a mirror; then we shall see face to face. Now I know in part; then I shall know fully, even as I am fully known. And now these three remain: faith, hope and love. But the greatest of these is love.

Corinthians 13: 11-13

The Theatre Discipline

The Theatre Major consists of 54 hours of core classes beyond the General Education Core. Classes are designed to give students knowledge of theory and an opportunity to practice it in real-world settings. A 3-credit professional internship required as an upper classman. Students of other majors can get a Theatre Minor by completing 18 hours of coursework in the department.

Why Study Theatre at Montreat College?

The faculty brings a diversity of training and depth of experience. Professors are professionals in their discipline who have worked on stage, and in film and television. They are passionate about engaging their students and challenging them to be reflective, well-rounded artists and communicators.

Every Theatre course blends a Biblical worldview with scholarship. Christ told stories to reveal truth and the Theatre major allows students to examine the discipline as a means of purposing that truth.

Abundant opportunities for personal and artistic discovery and growth. As a new major at Montreat College, the program will offer many possibilities for the student to discover their strengths and have abundant "hands-on" opportunities to create, develop, and practice their own projects. It will be an adventurous endeavor to "grow" the program and put your personal stamp on it.

Voted one of the 50 Most Beautiful Christian Colleges in the World. Montreat College is set apart, a beautiful piece of God's world. What better place to spend four years, becoming part of a wonderful community, and learning together what it means for you to use theatre as a tool to make a difference in the world. Montreat College is adjacent to Pisgah National Forest, close to the Great Smoky Mountains National Park, and is also within a 14-mile hike or bike ride of Mt. Mitchell, the highest peak east of the Mississippi River.

How Can You Get Involved?
- Annual Theatre Production
- Students have the opportunity to write, produce and direct original plays and video shorts for Film Production, Playwriting, and Acting for Camera.
- Special Topic courses are regularly offered that provide students with unique opportunities, such directing, design, acting.
- Join with the Communication students working on films in front of and behind the camera. Filmmaking is becoming an increasing presence on our campus providing opportunities to gain experience in producing, directing, camera, sound, acting, and writing.
- Students will get to evolve their own studio productions and staged readings.
- Students are encouraged to attend regional and national theatre conferences and to present their talents there.
- Students are required to do a professional internship as upperclassmen that will provide professional employment experience and contacts that make a difference after graduation.
- Students are urged to audition for URTA/SETA.
- Develop a Theatre Club.
- Do a Devise Theatre piece for the local community.
- Participate in Theatre Ministry through Theatre Ensemble.

Off-Campus Study Opportunities
Off-campus study opportunities are a great asset to any student. Summer Theatre opportunities, internship opportunities, etc., provide opportunities to obtain professional and life experiences that give polish and maturity to a student. They also provide a means to meet and work with professionals that can serve as mentors or job contacts after graduation.

After Graduation

Upon completion of the Theatre program at Montreat College, the student has a wide selection of options. One might find a calling as a professional actor, director, producer, playwright, stage manager, critic, dramaturgy, artistic director, managing director, Spokesperson, Voiceover artist, crew member in the field of Stage, Film, and Television, ministry leader, teacher, broadcast technician, screen writer, public speaker, marketing researcher, sales representative, workshop leader, administrator....the list goes on and on. After working in the field, students may consider graduate study to further expand their career choices.

The theatre skills of observation, effective interpersonal communication, empathy, group-solving abilities, organizational skills, creative thinking and doing, and self-esteem are all concrete tools for any career field. Learning to Improvise teaches focus and adaptation; Staging a Production helps with team management, accomplishing a job on time and on budget; working creatively with a limited budget is a desired characteristic in any field; knowing how to communicate with people at any level because you are observant, sensitive, and empathetic lends itself well to business, law, sales, and everything you do.

Requirements for a Major in Theatre

√	Degree Component
____	Completion of the General Education Core (53* credits)
____	PY 201 is recommended in the Gen-Ed
____	Completion of the General Education Competencies
____	Completion of the Theatre Major Courses (42 credits)
____	Completion of the Theatre Major Electives (12 credits)
____	Completion of the Bachelor of Arts requirement (12 credits)
____	Completion of required electives to bring total up to 126 credits (~7 credits)
____	Completion of 33 credits at the 300-level or above
____	Completion of 126 credit hours with a minimum GPA of 2.0 (two terms and 32 credit hours must be completed at Montreat College)

*TH 220 or TH 230 in the major can count toward the Gen-Ed oral expression competency.

Theatre Major Core (42 credits)

Interdisciplinary Courses (7 hours)

BS 101   Introduction to Business (3)

CM 346   Web Studies and Design (3)

IS 310   Pre-Practicum/Pre-Internship (1)

Theatre Courses (35 hours)

TH 110   Theatre History (3)

TH 230   Acting I (3)

TH 220   Voice and Movement (3)

TH 232   Stagecraft (3)

TH 317   Directing (4)

TH 333   Theatre Ensemble (4)

TH/CM 335   Playwriting/Screenwriting (3)

TH 441   Internship (3)

TH 491   Senior Thesis (2)

Theatre Production* (7)

     TH 106; 205-206; 305-306; 405-406 (1 credit each = 7 credits)

*Students may be permitted to take two theatre production classes in the same semester.

Theatre Major Required Electives (12 credits)

Choose 12 credits below based on specific area of interest

TH 202   Acting for the Camera (3)

TH 330   Advanced Acting (3)

TH 381   Theatre Workshop: Special Topics (1-3)

TH 340   Musical Theatre (3)

TH 481   Directed Study & Research (2-3)

TH 492   Practicum (2-4) (Prerequisite: IS 310)

CM 249   Digital Media (4)

CM329   Film Production (4)

AR 241   Drawing (3)

AR 245   Visual Design (3)

MS 143-144; 243-244; 343-344; 443-444 Applied Voice (1 credit each, take up to 12)

MS 131   Introduction to Digital Sound Recording (3)

BB 306   World Religions (3)

YM 203   Foundations of Youth & Family Ministry (3)

CM 203   Communication & Culture (3)

CM 220   Public Speaking and Rhetoric Analysis (3)

CM228   Media Studies (4)

BS 407   Entrepreneurship and Small Business Management (3)

PY 314   Personality (3)

PY 320   Social Psychology (3)

Four Year Plan: Bachelor of Arts in Theatre

Freshman Year

Fall Semester		Spring Semester	
IS 102 Foundations of Faith and Learning	2	TH 106 Theatre Production	1
BB 101 Survey of Old Testament	3	BB 102 Survey of New Testament	3
EN 101 English Composition	3	EN 102 English Composition II	3
TH 110 Theatre History	3	CS 102 Computer Applications & Concepts	3
Gen-Ed Natural Science	4	Gen-Ed Natural Science	4
PE activity course	1	PE activity course	1
	16		15

Sophomore Year

Fall Semester		Spring Semester	
TH 230 Acting I	3	TH 220 Voice and Movement	3
TH 232 Stagecraft	3	TH/CM 335 Playwriting/Screenwriting	3
TH 205 Theatre Production	1	TH 206 Theatre Production	1
Elementary Foreign Language 101	3	Elementary Foreign Language 102	3
HS 101 History of World Civilization I	3	HS 102 History of World Civilization II	3
Gen-Ed Mathematics	3	Gen-Ed Literature	3
	16		16

Junior Year

Fall Semester		Spring Semester	
TH 317 Directing	4	Major Elective	3
TH 305 Theatre Production	1	TH 306 Theatre Production	1
Major Elective	3	Bachelor of Arts Humanities	3
Bachelor of Arts Humanities	3	Gen-Ed Humanities	3
BS 101 Introduction to Business	3	Elective	3
PY 201 or PY 202 General Psychology	3	IS 310 Pre-Internship	1
	17		14

Completion of the General Education competencies by the end of the junior year.

Junior Summer

TH 441 Internship			3

Senior Year

Fall Semester		Spring Semester	
CM 346 Web Studies and Design	3	TH 333 Theatre Ensemble	4
TH 405 Theatre Production	1	TH 406 Theatre Production	1
Major Elective	3	TH 491 Senior Thesis	2
Major Elective	3	Gen-Ed Humanities	3
IS 461 Seminar on Faith and Life	2	Elective	4
Gen-Ed Humanities	3		
	15		14

Completion of 33 credits at the 300-level or above.

	Total hours required for degree:	126

*See General Education for optional course offerings

Theatre Minor

A minor in Theatre is an excellent supplement for students planning careers in education, music, business, law, public relations, counseling, ministry, and other fields which demand the ability to work exceptionally well with other people.

Requirements of a Minor in Theatre (18 credits)

Theatre Minor Core (9 credits)
>   CM 220   Public Speech & Rhetorical Analysis (3)
>   TH 110   Theatre History (3)
>   TH 230   Acting I (3)

Theatre Minor Electives (9 credits)
>   Choose 9 hours from the following:
>>   TH 106   Theatre Production (1)
>>   TH 205   Theatre Production (1)
>>   TH 206   Theatre Production (1)
>>   TH 220   Voice and Movement (3)
>>   TH 202   Acting for the Camera (3)
>>   TH 317   Directing (4)
>>   TH 330   Advanced Acting (3)
>>   TH 333   Theatre Ensemble (4)
>>   TH 335   Playwriting (3)
>>   TH 340   Musical Theatre (3)
>>   CM 341 Practicum (3)

Worship Arts Major

The Bachelor of Music in Worship Arts major at Montreat College is committed to preparing a new generation of pastoral musicians, passionate and devoted to the renewal of Christian worship; grounded in the biblical-theological-historical foundation of Christian worship; and informed, skillful, and disciplined regarding the use of music and the non-musical arts in Christian worship.

Why Study Worship Arts at Montreat College?

A graduate of the Worship Arts program will have received a unique grounding in the biblical, theological and historical foundations of Christian worship and excellent and thorough training in music and an introduction to other non-musical arts. Each course in the curriculum is taught from the Christ-centered focus that is a hallmark of Montreat College and will assist in preparing the student for ministry as a worship planner and leader. Small class sizes and personal attention from professors with high levels of academic and practical expertise provide the mentoring needed to prepare students for their future role as pastoral musicians and agents of worship renewal.

Entrance Requirements

In addition to meeting the entrance requirements of the College, the prospective Bachelor of Music in Worship Arts major must pass a performance audition. Bachelor of Arts in Music also requires a performance audition. No audition is required for Music Business majors or for Music, Music Business, or Worship Arts minors.

After Graduation

A Bachelor of Music degree in Worship Arts can lead to graduate studies in music or worship. A graduate of the Worship Arts program may find employment as a worship planner and leader, pastoral music and/or arts director at a church, or an independent artist and/or teacher.

Requirements for a Major in Worship Arts

√	Degree Component
___	Completion of the General Education Core (55* credits)
	MS 113 and MS 114 are required humanities in the Gen-Ed
	HS 353 is a required social science in the Gen-Ed
	TH 220 or TH 230 is recommended for oral expression competency in the Gen-Ed
___	Completion of the General Education Competencies
___	Completion of the Worship Arts Major Courses (71 credits)
___	Completion of sophomore evaluation for major
___	Completion of 33 credits at the 300-level or above
___	Completion of Instrumental Proficiency Examination(s)** (recommended to complete before junior year)
___	Additional requirements, as explained in Music Program Handbook
___	Completion of 126 credit hours with a minimum GPA of 2.0 (two terms and 32 credit hours must be completed at Montreat College)

*TH 220 or TH 230 in the major can count toward the Gen-Ed oral expression competency; if the student elects to take a different class to meet oral competency, an additional 3 credits will be added to the Gen-Ed.

**All Worship Arts majors must pass the four levels of the piano proficiency exam in order to graduate. Students may not participate in the commencement ceremony unless all four levels of piano proficiency have been completed, regardless of catalog year (students may not petition to walk in commencement if any component of the piano proficiency is left outstanding). It is highly recommended that students complete this requirement before entering their junior year.

Required Major Courses (71 credits)

Music Courses (40 credits):

    MS 213 Music Theory III (4)
    MS 214 Music Theory IV (4)
    MS 305 Survey of Musical Styles I (3)
    MS 306 Survey of Musical Styles II (3)
    MS 401 Choral Conducting I (2)
    MS 405 Choral Methods (2)
    MS 100 Seminar in Music Performance for major instrument: 8 semesters (4)
    Applied lessons in major instrument: 8 semesters (See list below) (8)
    Applied lessons in secondary instrument: 2 semesters (See list below) (2)
        MS 141-142, 241-242, 341-342, 441-442 Applied Piano
        MS 133-134, 233-234, 333-334, 433-434 Applied Group Lessons
        MS 143-144, 243-244, 343-344, 443-444 Applied Voice
        MS 145-146, 245-246, 345-346, 445-446 Applied Organ
        MS 147-148, 247-248, 347-348, 447-448 Applied Guitar
        MS 147-148, 247-248, 347-348, 447-448 Applied Woodwinds
        MS 147-148, 247-248, 347-348, 447-448 Applied Strings
        MS 147-148, 247-248, 347-348, 447-448 Applied Percussion

Ensemble: 8 semesters (Repeatable up to 8 times) (8)
>   MS 151 College Choir (1)
>   MS 153 Guitar Ensemble (1)
>   MS 154 Instrumental Chamber Ensemble (1)
>   MS 156 Accompanying (1)
>   MS 251 Chamber Choir (1)

Worship Arts Courses (19 credits):
>   WA 101 Worship Arts Survey I (3)
>   WA 102 Worship Arts Survey II (3)
>   WA 302 Worship Arts Resources (3)
>   MS 307 History of Congregational Song (3)
>   IS 310   Pre-Practicum/Pre-Internship (1)
>   WA 341 Worship Arts Practicum I (2)
>   WA 342 Worship Arts Practicum II (2)
>   WA 461 Worship Arts Seminar I (1)
>   WA 462 Worship Arts Seminar II (1)

Fine Arts Courses (6 credits):
>   Choose one in visual art and one in theatre:
>   AR 241/AR 341   Drawing I/II (3)
>   AR 342   Painting (3)
>   AR/CM 349   Graphics and Photojournalism (3)
>   TH 220* Voice & Movement (3)
>   TH 230* Acting (3)
>   TH 333   Theatre Ensemble (4)

*TH 220 or TH 230 may double-count to fulfill the Gen-Ed oral competency.

Music Electives (6 credits):
>   Choose two from the following:
>   MS 206 Rhythm Studies (3)
>   MS 301 Midi and Sound Synthesis (3)
>   MS 131 Introduction to Digital Sound Recording (3)
>   MS 322 Live Sound and Lighting (3)
>   MS 331 Copyright Law (3)
>   MS 332 Music Publishing (3)

Four Year Plan: Bachelor of Music in Worship Arts

Freshman Year

Fall Semester		Spring Semester	
BB 101 Survey of Old Testament	3	BB 102 Survey of New Testament	3
EN 101 English Composition I	3	EN 102 English Composition II	3
IS 102 Foundations of Faith and Learning	2	WA 102 Worship Arts Survey II	3
WA 101 Worship Arts Survey I	3	MS 142/144/146/148 Applied Music II (major instrument)	1
MS 141/143/145/147 Applied Music I (major instrument)	1	MS 114 Music Theory II	4
MS 113 Music Theory I	4	MS 100 Performance Seminar	0.5
MS 100 Performance Seminar	0.5	Ensemble Course	1
Ensemble Course	1		
	17.5		**15.5**

Sophomore Year

Fall Semester		Spring Semester	
MS 213 Music Theory III	4	MS 214 Music Theory IV	4
MS 305 Survey of Musical Styles I	3	MS 306 Survey of Musical Styles II	3
CS 102 Computer Applications & Concepts	3	WA 302 Worship Arts Resources	3
HS 101 History of World Civilization I	3	Fine Arts (Theatre) Elective (TH 220 or TH 230 recommended)	3
MS 241/243/245/247 Applied Music III (major instrument)	1	MS 242/244/246/248 Applied Music IV (major instrument)	1
MS 141/143/145/147 Applied Music I (secondary instrument)	1	MS 142/144/146/148 Applied Music II (secondary instrument)	1
MS 100 Performance Seminar	0.5	MS 100 Performance Seminar	0.5
Ensemble Course	1	Ensemble Course	1
PE activity course	1	PE activity course	1
	17.5		**17.5**

All Worship Arts majors must pass a sophomore evaluation.

Junior Year

Fall Semester		Spring Semester	
MS 307 History of Congressional Song	3	Gen-Ed Literature	3
Gen-Ed Mathematics	3	HS 353 History of Christianity	3
Gen-Ed Natural Science	4	Gen-Ed Natural Science	4
MS 401 Choral Conducting	2	MS 405 Choral Methods	2
MS 341/343/345/347 Applied Music V (major instrument)	1	MS 342/344/346/348 Applied Music VI (major instrument)	1
MS 100 Performance Seminar	0.5	MS 100 Performance Seminar	0.5
Ensemble Course	1	Ensemble Course	1
WA 461 Worship Arts Seminar I	1	WA 462 Worship Arts Seminar II	1
IS 310 Pre-Practicum	1		
	16.5		**15.5**

Completion of Piano Proficiency by the end of the junior year.
Completion of the General Education competencies by the end of the junior year.

Senior Year

Fall Semester		Spring Semester	
Gen-Ed Humanities	3	IS 461 Seminar on Faith and Life	2
Fine Arts (Visual Art) Elective	3	Music Elective	3
MS 441/443/445/447 Applied Music VII (major instrument)	1	MS 442/444/446/448 Applied Music VIII (major instrument)	1
MS 100 Performance Seminar	0.5	MS 100 Performance Seminar	0.5
Ensemble Course	1	Ensemble Course	1
WA 341 Worship Arts Practicum I	2	WA 342 Worship Arts Practicum II	2
Music Elective	3	HS 102 History of World Civilization II	3
	13.5		**12.5**

Completion of 33 credits at the 300-level or above.

*See General Education for optional course offerings	Total hours required for degree:	**126**

Worship Arts Minor

Requirements for a Worship Arts Minor (20 credits)

Worship Arts Minor Core (14 credits)
- WA 101 Worship Arts Survey I (3)
- WA 102 Worship Arts Survey II (3)
- WA 302 Worship Arts Resources (3)
- MS 307 History of Congregational Song (3)
- WA 461 Worship Arts Seminar I (1)
- WA 462 Worship Arts Seminar II (1)

Worship Arts Minor Electives (6 credits)
Choose one in visual art and one in theatre:
- AR 241/AR 341   Drawing I/II (3)
- AR/CM 349 Graphics and Photojournalism (3)
- AR 342 Painting (3)
- TH 220 Voice & Movement (3)
- TH 230 Acting (3)
- TH 333 Theatre Ensemble (4)

Youth and Family Ministries Minor

The Youth and Family Ministries minor is designed specifically for students who wish to explore their gifts in children's, youth, and/or family ministries while earning a separate specialized degree. The program intends to provide learners with broad knowledge and basic skills necessary for serving the needs of the church in these vital areas.

Requirements of a Minor in Youth and Family Ministries (18 credits)

Youth and Family Ministries Core (12 credits)
    YM 203 Foundations of Youth and Family Ministries (3)
    YM 380 Administrative Ministry & Organization (3)
    YM 401 Spiritual Formation and Faith Development (3)
    YM 407 Contemporary Youth Culture and Programming (3)

Youth and Family Ministries Required Electives (6 credits)
    Choose two courses from the following:
        BB 211 Christian Doctrine (3)
        BB 302 Romans (3)
        CC 301 Foundations of Cross-Cultural Ministry (3)
        YM 303 Discipleship and Lifestyle Evangelism (3)
        YM 360 Ministry to Children (3)
        YM 408 Introduction to Pedagogy (3)

Dual Major

Students may work toward a dual major. Through a comprehensive, concentrated, and diverse education, students with a dual major demonstrate breadth, depth, flexibility, and persistence to potential employers. To complete a dual major, a student must fulfill the general education core requirements and the designated requirements of both majors. When two majors have common course requirements, students may count the required courses towards both majors. Students with dual majors should expect to take overloads, summer classes, and/or attend an extra semester to fulfill the requirements for both majors.

Associate Degrees

The requirements for associate degrees at Montreat College are designed to provide breadth in the liberal arts general education. Students earning an associate degree from Montreat College will be equipped with foundational skills to integrate into professional careers, and prepared to pursue junior and senior level study toward a bachelor degree.

- Earn a minimum of 60 academic hours of credit.
- Successfully complete all courses listed as basic degree requirements.
- Present a grade of *C* or better on transfer hours accepted and a cumulative grade point average of 2.0 on all work attempted for a degree at Montreat College.
- Earn a minimum of 24 semester hours at Montreat College.
- Complete an "Application for Graduation" form during the registration period for the semester immediately prior to the date the degree is to be granted.
- Successfully fulfill General Education competency requirements (mathematical computation, oral expression, reading, writing, and computer literacy).

Students are normally subject to the academic requirements stated in the Catalog that was current when they matriculated. A student who leaves the College and is later readmitted must meet the requirements current at the time of readmission. It is each student's responsibility to be sure all degree requirements are met.

Students wishing to complete an associate degree while pursuing a bachelor degree must have the two-year degree conferred at least one academic year prior to earning the four-year degree.

Associate of Arts (AA) or Science (AS) Degree

Requirements for an Associate of Arts or Associate of Science Degree

√ Degree Component

___ Completion of the AA or AS Degree Requirements (60 credits)

___ Completion of the General Education Competencies*

___ Completion of 60 credit hours with a minimum GPA of 2.0 (a minimum of 24 credit hours must be completed at Montreat College)

*See the bachelor degree General Education section for explanation of competencies and other Gen-Ed components.

Associate Degree Requirements		
Curricula	**Applicable Courses**	**Hrs**
First Year Experience**	IS 102 (2) or IS 200 (1)	2
Bible*	BB 101 & BB 102	6
Computer	CS 102 or CS 102E	3
English Writing*	EN 101 or EN 103 & EN 102 or EN 104	6
English Literature	EN literature 200-level or above (excludes writing)	3
History	HS 101 & HS 102 (HS 201 or HS 202 may be substituted for one semester of world history)	6
Humanities and Arts (two areas must be represented). Applied courses not included (i.e. photography, piano, writing, speech).	Choose two: AR 101, AR 102 MS 101, MS 113, MS 114, and 200-level or above MS courses, not including applied courses Foreign Language (Including sign language) IS 202, IS 306, HS 371, CM 318, TH 110 BB or PH above 100-level EN 200-level and above except writing courses WA 101, 102	6
Mathematics	MT 101 or above	3
Natural Science	Choose two from: AT 101, AT 102, BL 101, BL 102, CH 201, CH 202, PC 131, PC 132	8
Oral Expression	CM 220, EN 271, OE 310, PR 310, TH 220, or TH 230	3
Social Science	Choose one class: 200–level or above in economics, geography, sociology, psychology or history; CM 203, CC 402	3
Physical Education +	Choose two PE activity courses	2
AA or AS requirement	AA students must select an additional humanities course AS students must select an additional mathematics course	3
Electives	Choose ~6 credits of electives to bring total credits to 60	6
Total Associate Degree General Education & Elective Hours:		**60**

* All full-time students **must** be enrolled in BB 101 and EN 101 the first semester of enrollment and BB 102 and EN 102 the second semester of enrollment until they are successfully completed. Refer to "Required Courses Must Be Taken Until Successfully Completed" for more information.

All full-time students **must be enrolled in either IS 102 or IS 200 the first semester of enrollment until successfully completed. IS 102 is for students with less than 12 hours of college credit obtained in a college setting (does not include AP classes or CLEP credits). IS 200 is for students who have attended another college and are transferring in at least 12 credit hours. Athletes that are forced to miss two or more days of IS 200 will need to drop and re-enroll the next semester.

NOTE: Course numbering is specific to Montreat College courses; transfer students will be given consideration based on a course-by-course evaluation of credit.

This chart is reflective of the entire associate program and maximum credits for the entire degree. A minimum of 60 credits is required for the associate degree.

A minimum of 24 credit hours must be completed at Montreat College. Students who leave Montreat College with less than 60 hours or less than a 2.0 grade point average may enroll in another institution and transfer back a maximum of 12 semester hours toward an associate degree at Montreat College.

Students wishing to complete an associate degree while pursuing a bachelor degree must have the two-year degree conferred at least one academic year prior to earning the four-year degree.

If students take a full-load each term, they should complete this program in two years.

Special Programs

Field-Based Wilderness courses

Montreat College offers unique wilderness courses, Discovery Wilderness Expedition and Wilderness Journey, which are open to any student. Course components may include backpacking, whitewater canoeing, rock climbing, route-finding, and a solo experience. Traveling in small groups, students experience the beauty and challenge of the wilderness while developing camping skills and learning backcountry navigation. Through these experiences, students are encouraged to work together, develop an attitude of service, and gain an appreciation for the natural environment. Emphasis is placed on spiritual growth and Christian fellowship. These courses are offered at various times during summer and winter breaks.

McCALL

Montreat College's Center for Adult Lifelong Learning (McCALL) is a community-directed effort to promote noncredit educational experiences on campus. Members of McCALL determine fees, curriculum, and course leaders. Course offerings occur during the College's academic semesters, and classes meet in available classrooms. In addition to educational opportunities, McCALL provides social activities for members, including teas, lecture series, and other cultural events. Lifelong learning, regardless of the format, is the central focus of the McCALL program.

Travel Seminars

As an academic community, Montreat College seeks to provide students with a total educational experience that is international in scope and multicultural in perspective. In this regard, travels both at home and abroad, for credit and noncredit, are made available. Tours of a historical, biblical, and general interest nature are offered during semester breaks and the summer. These travel seminars are led by experienced faculty members and professional tour guides. Travel experiences are arranged in conjunction with the Office of Academic Affairs.

Study Abroad and Off-Campus Study Opportunities

Opportunities in the Council for Christian Colleges and Universities (CCCU)

Because Montreat College is a member of a council of more than 95 private liberal arts Christian colleges and universities, a number of off-campus learning opportunities exist through the programs offered by the CCCU. For further information, contact the Assistant Director of the Office of Records for Database Audits and Advising at Montreat College; the Council for Christian Colleges and Universities, 329 Eighth Street NE, Washington, D.C. 20002, Phone: 202-546-8713, Fax: 202-546-8913; or consult the CCCU website (www.bestsemester.com).

- Participation in the off-campus studies programs requires the approval of the Academic Affairs office.
- Students are encouraged to participate prior to their last semester, and the program is typically limited to juniors and seniors who show serious Christian commitment and a strong academic record.
- Continuing Montreat College degree seeking students should file a FAFSA to be eligible for federal and state awards and loans if applicable. However, no Montreat College funds/scholarships will be awarded. Students will not be eligible for College work-study or any aid that ordinarily requires on-campus participation and effort.
- Students will pay the College, which in turn will be billed by the Council for Christian Colleges and Universities. The College is responsible for ensuring payment of fees, with the exception of the $100 application fee, which is paid directly to the Council by the student. The College will charge a $100 administrative fee in addition to the CCCU charges.
- All academic credit will be issued from Montreat College. Whether credit may be applied toward a major will be a decision made by the academic department of the major. Students will be considered enrolled at the College at an extension campus.
- Students will act at all times as representatives of Montreat College and will comply with the behavioral code of the program.

American Studies Program (ASP)

Founded in 1976, the American Studies Program has served hundreds of students from Council member institutions as a "Washington, D.C., campus." ASP uses Washington as a stimulating educational laboratory where students gain hands-on experience with an internship in their chosen field and explore pressing national and international issues in public policy seminars which are issue-oriented, interdisciplinary, and led by ASP faculty and Washington professionals. Internships are tailored to fit talents and aspirations and are available in a wide range of fields. ASP bridges classroom and marketplace, combining biblical reflection, policy analysis, and real-world experience via on-the-job learning that helps students build for their future and gain perspective on God's call for their lives. Students choose between a global development or public policy track and earn 15-16 semester hours of credit.

Australian Studies Centre (ASC)

Students attend Wesley Institute, a dynamic evangelical Christian community or people from a variety of vocations, locations, churches, languages and cultures. Enrolling in a course of study involves a commitment to personal development through study and fellowship with others who share a common goal: being equipped to undertake ministry opportunities in all aspects of life. All students enrolled in the Australian Studies Program take a course in Australian religion, politics, and economics and a course focusing on Australian indigenous cultures and choose two additional courses from a variety of other areas including Christian Studies, Business, Ministries, Social Science, Education, History, English, or Drama. Students earn 16 semester hours of credit.

Contemporary Music Center (CMC)

The Contemporary Music Center is based in Nashville, Tennessee, and offers students the opportunity to spend a semester studying, living, and working with faculty, music industry experts, and other students who share an interest in making and marketing contemporary music. The program is designed especially for students considering a career as a musician, songwriter, producer, engineer, artist manager, booking agent, A and R director, marketing executive, music publisher, concert promoter, or entertainment industry entrepreneur. In addition to core courses investigating the music industry and the intersection of faith and culture, students can choose between the artist track, business track, and technical track. Students who elect to take the artist track will use their time outside of the formal classroom setting to create a portfolio of original songs, make demo recordings, and develop a compelling live concert presentation. Business track students will work with the artists in career direction and management; recording contract negotiations; planning, budgeting, and producing artist demo sessions; and creating and executing a record marketing and sales plan. Students on the technical track will develop advanced audio engineering and recording skills. All students will participate in a culminating concert tour practicum. Students will earn 16 semester hours of credit.

Latin American Studies Program (LASP)

Students of Council member colleges have the opportunity to live and learn in Costa Rica through the Latin American Studies Program. The program introduces students to as wide a range of Latin American experiences as possible through the study of the language, literature, culture, politics, history, economics, ecology, and religion of the region. Living with a Costa Rican family, students experience and become a part of the day-to-day lives of typical Latin Americans. Students also participate in a service opportunity and travel to Nicaragua for another two-week homestay. Students participate in one of four concentrations: Latin American Studies (offered both fall and spring semesters); Advanced Language and Literature (limited to Spanish majors and offered both fall and spring terms); International Business and Management (offered only in the fall semester); and Environmental Science (offered only in the spring semester). Students in all concentrations earn 16-18 semester hours of credit.

Los Angeles Film Studies Center (LAFSC)

The Los Angeles Film Studies Center is designed to train students of Council member institutions to serve in various aspects of the film industry with both professional skill and Christian integrity. Students live, learn and work in the Los Angeles area near major studios. The curriculum consists of two required seminars focusing on the role of film in culture and the relationship of faith to work in this very important industry. In addition, students choose two elective courses from several offerings in film studies. Internships in various segments of the film industry provide students with hands-on experience. The combination of the internship and seminars allow students to explore the film industry within a Christian context and from a liberal arts perspective. Students earn 16 semester hours of credit.

Middle East Studies Program (MESP)

The Middle East Studies Program, based in Jerusalem, allows Council students to explore and interact with the complex and strategic world of the modern Middle East. The interdisciplinary seminars give students the opportunity to explore the diverse religious, social, cultural and political traditions of Middle Eastern people. In addition to seminars, students study the Arabic language, experience a week-long homestay, and work as volunteers with various organizations in Jerusalem. Through travel to Egypt, Palestine, Jordan, Tunisia and Turkey, students are exposed to the diversity and dynamism of the region. The MESP encourages and equips students to relate to the Muslim world in an informed, constructive, and Christ-centered manner at a time of tension and change. Students earn 16 semester hours of credit.

Oxford Summer Programme (OSP)

This five-week program, taken for six credits, allows students to do intensive scholarship in areas that interest them, while exploring the relationship between Christianity and the development of the British Isles. Each student participates in two seminars with tutorials, under expert Oxford academics, and a lecture series involving field trips to sites of historical interest that are related to the work undertaken in the seminars.

The Scholars' Semester at Wycliffe Hall, Oxford University

The Scholars' Semester takes students to Oxford, England, the academic home of such notables as John Wycliffe, Erasmus, John Donne, John and Charles Wesley, C. S. Lewis, and J. R. R. Tolkien. The program centers on a CCCU-organized British Studies core course and an integrative seminar in which students meet together to discuss and debate critical and timely issues. In addition, they enroll in two tutorials—the unique learning system of Oxford University, with sessions in their selected areas of interest led by Oxford scholars. The CCCU's partnership with Wycliffe Hall, Oxford provides special benefits to students. Participants are granted visiting student status and are fully matriculated members of Oxford University. As members of the university, students are able to join a collegiate athletic team; be a part of drama, music, or fencing clubs; participate in the Junior Common Room; attend university lectures; and take in debates at the world-famous Oxford Union. Students live in an environment emphasizing integrity and community. Pastoral care and student development are overseen by experienced CCCU staff. Students in this program can earn up to 17 semester hours of credit. This program is for upper class students with a grade point average of 3.5 or higher.

Uganda Studies Program (USP)

The Uganda Studies Program offers an invaluable opportunity for students to understand and participate in Ugandan culture. Students may live with a Ugandan family or a residence hall at Uganda Christian University and can choose from courses in African literature, history, religion, and politics. Electives allow participants to study an African language or engage in a cross-cultural ministry practicum. Students will take weekend trips throughout Uganda and a 10-day excursion to Rwanda and will earn 13-16 credits for the semester.

Other Off-Campus Study Opportunities

Montreat College students have the opportunity to participate in the following approved study abroad or off-campus study programs sponsored by other institutions. See the guidelines for all off-campus study programs for more information.

Au Sable Institute

As part of a partnership with CCCU institutions, Montreat College students can take a number of 4-credit Biology or Environmental Studies courses at Au Sable Institute for credit at Montreat College. Courses, dates, and locations include:
- "Ecology of the Indian Tropics" during the late December-early January term in India
- "Tropical Agriculture and Missions" during May Term in Costa Rica
- "Field Biology in Spring" during May Term on the shores of the Great Lakes in Michigan
- Courses in aquatic biology, conservation biology, field botany, animal ecology, land resources, molecular tools for field biologists, and research methods during the Summer I term in Michigan
- Courses in water resources, restoration ecology, environmental chemistry, watershed stewardship, wildlife ecology, and research methods II during Summer II term in Michigan.
- Courses in environmental health, ecological agriculture, marine biology, international development and sustainability, marine mammals, and alpine ecology during Summer II term on the Puget Sound in Washington State.

The Institute provides generous financial aid and room and board at all instructional sites. For more information, visit www.ausable.org.

EduVenture

EduVenture is a cross-cultural educational program that challenges Christian college students to grow in active faith through discipleship, academics, adventure, and community. EduVenture employs an educational philosophy that emphasizes guided experiential learning, yet combines both traditional and non-traditional approaches. Five core courses (15 credit hours) may be taken at either one of two sites, one in Fiji and one in Indonesia: Spiritual Formation, PE /Outdoor Education, Community Development, Cross-Cultural Communications, and Applied Missions. An additional 3 credit hours may be earned through an optional independent or guided study in Cultural Anthropology, with a concentration on Ethnography. For more information, visit www.eduventure.net.

Hannam University Programs

Through a partnership with Hannam University in South Korea, Montreat College students may earn credits at the University for discounted and sometimes free tuition. During the summer semester, students may earn 3 humanities or elective credits in the three-week Korea Studies Summer Program while learning about Korean culture (music, art, film, cuisine, fashion, architecture, and religion), history, language, martial arts, and technology and seeing the sights of South Korea. During the academic year, Montreat College students may study at Hannam for one semester or a full year and earn academic credit for a wide variety of courses. For more information, contact the Associate Academic Dean or email the Center for International Relations at Hannam University at cir@hannam.ac.kr.

Leadership and Discipleship in the Wilderness (LDW)

LDW is a wilderness leadership course offered by the Outdoor Leadership Team of the Coalition for Christian Outreach for learners who desire to grow in the areas of leadership development and discipleship to college students using wilderness as the context for ministry. The program uses the Leave No Trace outdoor ethics curriculum and the Wilderness Education Association (WEA) curriculum, which is designed to develop hard skills, judgment and decision-making and situational leadership principles. LDW is a unique leadership development experience rooted in six areas of discovery for the participants: spiritual disciplines, community, leadership, knowing, servant hood/Christ-likeness and outdoor living skills.

Rome With Purpose

Students taking part in this program can earn 16 credits in a fall or spring semester while experiencing Italy in Christian community. Participants live on one floor of a convent in Rome and take classes from qualified professors from a Christian worldview, including Italian language and culture and excursions in Rome, Florence, & Ostia. Students will experience the sites of ancient Rome as well as the current influences of Italian politics, religion, and customs that make Italy the complex culture that it is today. Opportunities to volunteer with local Christian ministries or to experience weekend homestays are available. Students may engage in independent travel or stay in Rome over three one-week breaks between classes. No visa is required for the 90-day program, and scholarships are available. For more information, visit RomeWithPurpose.com, Facebook.com/romewithpurpose, or @romewithpurpose.

Summit Adventure: Immersion Service and Adventure Semester (ISAS)

Summit Adventure and Montreat College partner in this challenging 17-credit immersion program. If enrolled, students spend two to three weeks backpacking through California's High Sierra. For six to seven weeks students are housed at Summit Adventure's Basecamp where students delve deeply into a variety of subject areas. In addition, students participate in service and adventure-based learning during five to six weeks in Ecuador, putting into practice internationally all that was learned stateside. ISAS Courses may include IS 302, OE 306, CC301, CE401 OE 191, OE 192, OE 312 and OE 313. For more information, visit www.summitadventure.com or contact the Outdoor Education Department.

Study Program In Contemporary Europe (SPICE)

Through the College's partnership with Dordt College, students have the opportunity to earn 16 credits in a spring semester for study in one of four tracks: International Business, Western European Culture, Nursing, or Education. Students live with families in Zwolle, Netherlands, and have many opportunities to interact with Dutch and Romanian students and explore how their faith affects their relationships with persons from other countries. For more information contact the Associate Academic Dean or visit www.dordt.edu/spice.

Studies Program in Nicaragua (SPIN)

SPIN is a fall semester academic and cultural opportunity offered through the College's partnership with Dordt College. Students will live with host families in Leon and have opportunities to interact with other Nicaraguans as they earn 16 credits studying the Spanish language, Nicaraguan/Central American worldviews, culture, history, and contemporary society, and engage in service learning. Electives include options for specialized study in Spanish language, Nicaraguan Studies, or Agriculture in the Developing World. For more information contact the Associate Academic Dean or visit www.dordt.edu/spin.

Irish-American Scholars Program

Through Montreat College's participation in the Association of Presbyterian Colleges and Universities Business Education Initiative, the College may send up to three students per year to study for one semester or a full year in Northern Ireland. Programs of study include business, computing, performing arts, communication, and teacher education. Application deadline: February 1 for the following year. For more information, contact the Associate Academic Dean.

Veritas

Students who study on a Veritas program will have opportunities to work with local missionaries in Argentina, Brazil, Chile, Peru, Costa Rica, Dominican Republic, Spain, South Korea, London, Paris, or Rome, while they earn college credit toward their degree. Serving others in the host culture for a semester or summer program will enhance the immersion experience and give students a broader understanding of the joys and challenges of cross-cultural missions beyond the experience of a short-term mission trip. Veritas Christian Study Abroad is an affiliate company of International Studies Abroad (ISA), which for 25 years has been providing high quality academic programs. Veritas utilizes the experience and infrastructure of ISA to create study abroad programs for students interested in integrating faith and learning. Students take one Veritas course and then choose from a wide selection of courses taught at the host university in each city, either in English or in the language of the host country. The program is offered in fall, spring and summer semesters. For more information visit www.veritasabroad.com.

Academic Support Services

Academic Assistance for Students with Special Learning Needs

Students with special learning needs are urged to contact the Disability Services Coordinator as soon as they arrive on campus. Academic support services personnel can assist these students in identifying any needed accommodations, in acquiring a tutor, or in gaining smooth access to other support services. Under the Americans with Disabilities Act (ADA), the student must take the initiative to request any special accommodations and must do so in writing. The Disability Services Coordinator is available to talk with students and parents about reasonable accommodations as well as resources available at the College for students with special learning needs. Academic support services remain a resource for these students throughout their time at Montreat College.

Tutoring

The tutoring program is organized to assist students of all scholastic levels in reaching their academic goals and is coordinated by the Associate Dean of Calling and Career. The services offered by the program include assistance in locating a private tutor, if needed; accountability conferences to assist students in planning for academic improvement; and study skills counseling and resources which include note-taking, time management, and test-taking strategies.

Writing Center

Students are encouraged to take advantage of the resources provided by the Writing Center, located on the first floor of Bell Library and also available on the Web (www.montreat.edu/writing). Student writing consultants are trained to assist students in developing strategies for specific college papers and in shaping strong written arguments. They also aid students in mastering grammar and punctuation, understanding research techniques, and in tackling related writing tasks. Writing consultants are available throughout the academic year; electronic and phone consultations are also available (see the website for more information).

L. Nelson Bell Library

The library is an integral part of the College's academic program. The librarians, collection, resources and services support the educational program and research needs of the faculty and students at all campuses. The library serves faculty and students in the School of Arts and Sciences and the School of Adult and Graduate Studies.

Services include access to numerous databases and e-book collections, research assistance, library instruction, and interlibrary loan. Librarians work closely with faculty to offer multimodal instruction to individual classes. Librarians are available for research consultations, to assist students in locating information from a wide variety of formats for research purposes and in the use of electronic resources. Faculty and students can access the library's databases from any location and search an extensive range of scholarly journals. The Appalachian College Association Bowen Central Library and NC LIVE provide Montreat College with access to thousands of ebooks, streaming videos, and online resources to support all degree programs.

The building is equipped with wireless access and study and research areas for individual and group work, as well as an active learning classroom equipped with technological learning tools. The library facility also houses a computer lab, Writing Center, college archives, art gallery, and classroom.

Special collections include the memorabilia of Dr. L. Nelson Bell, the Crosby Adams Music Collection, Montreat College historical materials, and Terry Estate papers.

Course Descriptions for the School of Arts and Sciences
Undergraduate

Course Numbering System and Abbreviations

The first digit of the course number generally indicates the level of the course, i.e. 100 = freshman, 200 = sophomore, 300 = junior, 400 = senior. The number in parentheses after the course title provides the credit in semester hours.

Courses numbered 100 and 200 are open to all students; 300-level courses are normally open to sophomores, juniors, and seniors; 400-level courses are open to juniors and seniors.

The following list of abbreviations is used for academic subjects:

AR	Art	**HU**	Human Services
AS	American Studies	**IS**	Interdisciplinary Studies
AT	Astronomy	**MT**	Mathematics
BB	Bible and Religion	**MS**	Music
BL	Biology	**OE**	Outdoor Education
BS	Business Administration	**OM**	Outdoor Ministry
CH	Chemistry	**PH**	Philosophy
CM	Communication	**PE**	Physical Education
CS	Computer Studies	**PC**	Physics
CC	Cross-Cultural Studies and Missions	**PR**	Preaching
		PY	Psychology
EN	English	**SC**	Sociology
ES	Environmental Studies	**SP**	Spanish
EX	Exercise Science	**SM**	Sport Management
GG	Geography	**TH**	Theatre
GR	Greek	**WA**	Worship Art
HL	Health	**YM**	Youth and Family Ministries
HB	Hebrew		
HS	History		

Not every course listed in the Catalog will be offered each year. The College publishes a listing of courses to be offered each semester.

AMERICAN STUDIES (AS)

AS 401   American Studies (3)
This seminar is designed to help students to see America through the eyes of the global community, providing insights into and an analysis of the way America is viewed throughout the world.

ART (AR)

AR 101   Survey of Art I (3)
A survey of painting, sculpture, architecture, and the minor arts of Western and non-Western cultures from ancient times to the thirteenth century.

AR 102   Survey of Art II (3)
A survey of painting, sculpture, architecture, and the minor arts of Western and non-Western cultures from the thirteenth century to the present.

AR 241   Drawing I (3)
A studio course emphasizing the fundamentals of drawing and composition through a variety of tools, materials, and techniques.

AR 245   Principles of Design (3)
A foundation course presenting the elements and organizational principles of visual design applied to pictorial composition and graphic arts.

AR 341   Drawing II (3)
An advanced studio drawing course emphasizing understanding and illustration of the human form.

AR 342   Painting (3)
A studio course for observing and interpreting the natural world and/or still-life to create works of art through painting, both on location and within the studio.

AR 344   Sculpture (3)
A studio course developing three-dimensional forms through earthenware clay sculpture techniques.

AR/CM 349   Graphics & Photojournalism (3)
This course explores the theoretical and practical aspects of choosing, creating, & composing photographic images for graphic arts and journalism. Students will explore an historical overview of photography to critically evaluate the visual rhetoric of images in popular culture and journalism. Students will create effective images for a series of graphic arts and journalism projects. Cross listed with CM 349.

AR 404   Exhibition (3)
An independent studio course, supervised by the art department, through which the student must prepare and document a final exhibition of personal artwork/research. *Pre-requisites: Art 101 or 102, 241, 244, 245, 246, or permission of professor.*

AR 461   Seminar in Studio Art (3)
An advanced visual art studio course of study, varied by medium, objective, and faculty, to present unique techniques and aesthetic philosophies. May be repeated once as content varies. Up to three hours can be applied to an Art minor studio course (drawing, photography, sculpture), and up to six hours toward overall graduation requirements.

AR 481   Directed Study and Research (1-3)
Students may choose to participate in a directed study of their own choice contingent on faculty availability. Credit varies from 1-3 hours although a student can repeat for up to six hours of credit. *Prerequisite: Junior status or above. A cumulative GPA of 2.5 and approval of the department chair is required.*

ASTRONOMY (AT)

AT 101   The Solar System (4)
This course will explore the historical foundations of astronomy, the laws of Newton and Kepler, the planets and their moons, and the smaller objects in the solar system. Three hours of lecture and two hours of lab per week.
AT 102   Stars and Galaxies (4)
This course will explore the means by which we learn about stars and galaxies. Stellar and galactic life cycles and the origin and structure of the universe will be considered. Three hours of lecture and two hours of lab per week.

BIBLE AND RELIGION (BB)

BB 101   Survey of the Old Testament (3)
This course introduces the student to the tools and background necessary for understanding, interpreting, and applying the Old Testament to contemporary life. Furthermore, the course prepares the student to discuss intelligently the factual material in the Old Testament and to make clear, critical judgments regarding the validity of various interpretations of the Old Testament. Required of all full-time, first year students in the fall semester.
BB 102   Survey of the New Testament (3)
An introduction to the tools and background necessary for understanding, interpreting, and applying the New Testament to contemporary life, designed to prepare students to intelligently discuss the factual material in the New Testament and to make clear, critical judgments regarding the validity of various interpretations of the New Testament. Required of all full-time, first year students in the spring semester.
BB 201   Old Testament Theology (3)
An in-depth study of Old Testament themes with a view to their relevance for Christian theology, worship, and ethics. These include God's self-revelation, creation, covenant/kingdom, fall, law, worship, prophecy, and hope. The course will include an introduction to proper exegetical, hermeneutical, and theological method. This course may be taken in lieu of BB 101 with the permission of the department chair. *(Offered every fall.)*
BB 202   New Testament Theology (3)
An introduction to the major themes of New Testament theology and their specific relevance for Christian theology, worship, and ethics. These include: the Kingdom of God, justification, sanctification, and Pauline theology. This course may be taken in lieu of BB 102 with permission of the department chair. *(Offered every spring.)*
BB 208   Gospels (3)
A study of the broad outlines of the life of Jesus and the Gospel literature of the New Testament. The course will examine the distinguishing theological interests of the gospel accounts, drawing particular attention to the similarities and differences between the Synoptic Gospels and the Gospel of John. *(Offered fall semesters, odd-numbered years.)*

BB 209   Epistles (3)
A study of the broad outlines of the epistolary literature of the New Testament. The course will examine the distinguishing theological interests of the Epistles, especially the dominant motifs conveyed in the apostolic epistolary addressed to the earliest churches. *(Offered fall semesters, even-numbered years.)*

BB 211   Christian Doctrine (3)
A basic study of the major doctrines of the Christian faith and their application to contemporary thought and life. Includes studies in revelation, authority, the existence and nature of God, the person and work of Christ, the Holy Spirit, the Church, man, and Christian ethics. *(Offered every spring)*

BB 280   Special Topics in Bible and Religion (Lower Level) (1-3)
This course will provide students and faculty the opportunity to examine current issues or specialized topics within the discipline at a lower-level of study (appropriate for freshmen or sophomore academic experience). Topics will be determined by the department. Class will meet 15 hours for each hour of credit offered. Repeatable for different topics. *(Offered by department discretion.)*

BB 302   Romans (3)
An intensive study of the letter and its setting in Paul's ministry. The course also treats the biblical theology developed in the letter. *(Offered every spring)*

BB 303   Prophetic Literature of the Old Testament (3)
A comprehensive study of the Hebrew prophets interpreted in light of their context. *(Offered fall semesters, odd-numbered years.)*

BB 305   Biblical Interpretation (3)
A study of the history, problems, and methods of biblical interpretation, including a study of biblical-theological themes of the Old and New Testaments. *(Offered every fall)*

BB 306   World Religions (3)
This class will offer a survey of contemporary world religions and attempt to compare the worldview of these religious systems with a biblical worldview. Students will be equipped to converse with followers of these religions and to make clear comparisons between their beliefs and a biblical worldview. *(Offered every fall.)*

BB 307   English Bible (1-3)
Demonstration of inductive Bible study methods and treatment of a particular book or books of the Old and New Testaments based on the English text. Additional work will be required for those seeking upper division credit. May be repeated for credit as the book(s) under consideration change. *(Offered spring semesters as requested and approved.)*

BB 308   Apocalyptic Literature (3)
A survey of the history, development, and interpretation of biblical apocalyptic literature with special emphasis on Daniel and the Revelation of John. *(Offered fall semesters, even-numbered years.)*

BB 351   Biblical Studies Abroad (1-6)
Selected biblical topics or books - authors, historical developments, theological themes, and missionary movements - with emphasis on their geographical and cultural settings associated with the biblical literature. Residence abroad. *(Offered spring semesters, odd-numbered years.)*

BB 480   Special Topics in Bible and Religion (Upper Level) (1-3)
This course will provide students and faculty the opportunity to examine current issues or specialized topics within the discipline at an upper-level of study (appropriate for junior or senior academic experience). Topics will be determined by the department. Class will meet 15 hours for each hour of credit offered. Repeatable for different topics. (*Offered by department discretion.*)

BB 481   Directed Study and Research (1-3)
Students may choose to participate in a directed study of their own choice contingent on faculty availability. Credit varies from 1-3 hours although a student can repeat for up to six hours of credit. *Prerequisite: Junior status or above. A cumulative GPA of 2.5 and approval of the department chair is required. (Offered by department discretion)*

BB 491   Senior Thesis (3)
Students will develop an extensive paper under the direction of a faculty member that demonstrates their ability to do senior-level research and writing on a specialized topic in biblical studies or theology. A committee consisting of the course professor, another member of the division, and one member chosen by the student will evaluate and grade the thesis. (*Offered every semester as needed.*)

BIOLOGY (BL)

BL 101,102   Survey of Biological Principles I, II (4, 4)
General introductory study stressing principles common to all living organisms: their structure, function, basic chemical and physical properties, inheritance, evolution, and ecology. Three hours of lecture and two hours of lab per week.

BL 103,104   Advanced Survey of Biological Principles I, II (4, 4)
General introductory study stressing principles common to all living organisms: their structure, function, basic chemical and physical properties, inheritance, evolution, and ecology. Three hours of lecture and two hours of lab per week. The advanced biology course will have more in-depth coverage of all topics in lecture, and more challenging inquiry-based laboratory activities.

BL 204   Animal Physiology (3)
Physiology of animals with an emphasis upon systems integration and related environmental, biological, and toxicological issues and concerns. Three lecture hours. *Pre-requisites: BL 101, BL 102 or permission of professor.*

BL 205   Animal Diversity & Ecology (4)
Lectures deal with taxonomy, morphology, ecology, and relationships of principal vertebrate groups. Laboratories treat ecology, population biology identification and morphology, with emphasis on local forms. Three hours of lecture and three hours of lab per week. *Pre-requisites: BL 101, BL 102.*

BL 206   Human Anatomy and Physiology I (4)
An introduction to basic concepts of biology and the in-depth anatomy and physiology of the skeletal and muscular systems with additional overviews of human respiratory, cardiovascular and nervous system anatomy and physiology for health sciences students. The laboratory portion emphasizes the scientific method, involving observation, experimentation, data analysis and critical thinking, as applied in the study of human anatomy and physiology. *Pre-requisites: BL 101, BL 102.*

BL 207   Human Anatomy and Physiology II (4)
An introduction to the anatomy and physiology of the nervous, digestive, respiratory, cardiovascular, immune, renal, reproductive, and endocrine systems for health sciences students. The laboratory portion emphasizes the scientific method, involving observation, experimentation, data analysis and critical thinking, as applied in the study of human anatomy and physiology. *Pre-requisite: BL 206.*

BL 215   Plant Diversity & Ecology (4)
Taxonomy and ecology of indigenous flora with concentration upon vascular plants. An introduction to plant structure, function, and systems will be included. The development of a collection and the use of a herbarium will be integrated into this program's effort to survey the natural surroundings of the College. One and one-half hours lecture, one and one-half hours lab per week. *Pre-requisites: BL 101, BL 102 or permission of professor.*

BL 220   Medical Terminology (1)
This on-line course is designed to introduce students to medical terminology commonly used in a variety of health care fields. Emphasis is placed on prefixes, suffixes, and building and analyzing medical terms.

BL/ES 230   Sophomore Science Seminar (0.5)
Science training in academic and professional skills. These courses will complement students' development at progressive levels of their program training.

BL 280   Special Topics in Biology (Lower Level) (1-3)
This course will provide students and faculty the opportunity to examine current issues or specialized topics within the discipline at a lower-level of study (appropriate for freshmen or sophomore academic experience). Topics will be determined by the department. Class will meet 15 hours for each hour of credit offered. Repeatable for different topics. *(Offered by department discretion.)*

BL 301   Biometrics (3)
The application of statistical methods in the biological sciences. Topics include experimental design, sampling techniques, and data analysis techniques including regression analysis and analysis of variance and covariance.

BL 311   Plant Physiology (3)
Focusing on the mechanisms regulating the growth and development of higher plants, topics include photosynthesis, mineral nutrition, water relations, stress physiology, and growth regulators. *Pre-requisites: BL 101, BL 102 and ES 206, or permission of professor.*

BL 315   Cell Biology (4)
Structure and physiology of cells with an emphasis on the homeostasis of molecular processes and how cellular functions are integrated in multicellular organisms. Three hours lecture and 4 hours laboratory. *Pre-requisites: BL 103 and BL 104, CH 201 (or co-requisite) or permission of professor. (Offered every spring)*

BL/ES 340   Research Methods (3)
Participation in faculty-supervised independent research project. Involves a literature review, data collection and analysis, the completion of a written research paper, and an oral presentation. *Pre-requisite: MT 114 or BL 301; Junior standing or permission of professor.*

BL 401   Genetics (3)
Molecular, Mendelian, and population principles will be developed with the inclusion of an introduction to modern experimental techniques. The course will also explore the application of Christian values to ethical issues related to genetics. *Pre-requisites: BL 103, BL 104, CH 321, or permission of professor. (Offered every spring)*

BL 404   Microbiology (3)
Fundamental concepts, biochemistry, and applied aspects of microbiology with a review of current analysis techniques emerging from the field of microbiology. Topics include microbial structure, physiology, genetics, growth, control, and reproduction integrated with selected topics of applied microbiology within the medical (including immunological response), environmental, and industrial fields. Three hours lecture. *Pre-requisites: BL 315, BL 204, or BL 206 and BL 207, CH 320 or permission of professor. (Offered every fall).*

BL 406   Conservation Biology (3)
This course studies an emerging discipline that encompasses the study and conservation of the earth's biodiversity. Topics include population biology, ecology, and conservation of the diversity of species that cohabit the living world. It also examines how theories are used in habitat management practices. Current issues and case studies are used as examples. *Pre-requisites: BL 101, BL 102 and ES 301.*

BL 415   Biochemistry/Toxicology (3)
Application and integration of biochemical processes to the functioning of whole organisms. Toxicological emphasis will be related to medical and environmental concerns. *Pre-requisites: BL 315, CH 201, CH 202 and recommend CH 320 and CH 321 or permission of professor.*

BL 421   Contemporary Biological Investigations (3)
Exploration of contemporary topics through applied research in Animal Physiology, Microbiology, Genetics, and Biochemistry culminating in a senior biology research project. Three hours and an occasional additional hour for senior project development. *Prerequisites: BL 315, CH 201, CH 202, CH 320, recommend CH 321, and a recommended background in Genetics, Biochemistry, and some experience in biological research techniques and investigation, or permission of professor.*

BL/ES 440   Senior Project or Internship (honors option) (3)
Students are responsible for a project/internship design and proposal. Employment is pursued through a student job search. This project is typically developed during the junior year, employment is during the summer, and the final project presented during the senior year. A research-based project may be considered for honors recognition. All proposals and evaluation of projects will be approved through the Environmental Studies Review Committee.

BL/ES 445   Senior Science Seminar (1)
Science training in academic and professional skills. These courses will complement students' development at progressive levels of their program training. *Pre-requisite: ES 230 or permission of professor.*

BL 480   Special Topics in Biology (Upper-Level) (1-3)
This course will provide students and faculty the opportunity to examine current issues or specialized topics within the discipline at an upper-level of study (appropriate for junior or senior academic experience). Topics will be determined by the department. Class will meet 15 hours for each hour of credit offered. Repeatable for different topics. *Prerequisite: Permission of department chair. Offered by department discretion.*

BL 481   Directed Study and Research (1-3)
Students may choose to participate in a directed study of their own choice contingent on faculty availability. Credit varies from 1-3 hours although a student can repeat for up to six hours of credit. *Prerequisite: Junior status or above. A cumulative GPA of 2.5 and approval of the department chair is required.*

BUSINESS ADMINISTRATION (BS)

BS 101   Introduction to Business (3)
A survey course that introduces students to the fundamentals of business with particular attention given to the historical and economic foundations of our capitalistic system; the global marketplace; social and legal environments; human resources; marketing; management information systems; and financial management. *(Offered every semester.)*

BS 201   Principles of Accounting I (3)
Proprietary-based treatment of the accounting cycle, financial statements, merchandising, cash receivables, payables, inventories, plant property and equipment, payroll, accepted accounting principles and partnerships. *Pre- or Co-requisite: BS 101. (Offered every fall.)*

BS 202   Principles of Accounting II (3)
Treatment of corporations, investment, consolidated statements, tax impact on decision, statement analysis, changes in financial position, responsibility account, manufacturing, cost process job order, and standard. *Pre- or Co-requisite: BS 201. (Offered every spring.)*

BS 203   Macroeconomics (3)
A study of modern explanations of national income and employment. The course will give special emphasis to the American economy, its production, inter-relationships of households, business, and government, nature and function of money, monetary and fiscal policy, and public finance. *Pre- or Co-requisite: BS 101. (Offered every fall.)*

BS 204   Microeconomics (3)
A study of price theory and the interplay of supply and demand in competitive markets as a multitude of individual prices, wage rates, profit margins, and rental changes are created. *Pre- or Co-requisite: BS 101. (Offered every spring.)*

BS 209   Principles of Management (3)
An introductory course to management structured around the basic management functions of planning, organizing, leading, and controlling. The course explores the functions of the management process in for-profit and not-for-profit organizations, large and small. Special topics include: globalization, quality, competitiveness, teamwork, ethics, and entrepreneurship. *Pre- or Co-requisite: BS 101. (Offered every spring.)*

BS 214   Quantitative Methods (3)
Models for decision-making for marketing, finance, accounting, production and operations management, parametric and nonparametric statistics. An introduction to simple regression models, constrained and unconstrained optimization, and other techniques. *Pre-requisite: MT 114. (Offered every fall.)*

BS 230   Principles of Marketing (3)
An introductory study of the marketing process with a background in the elements of the marketing mix, product distribution structure, price system, and promotional activities. The importance of customer orientation is stressed. *Pre- or Co-requisite: BS 101. (Offered every fall.)*

BS 280   Special Topics in Business (Lower-Level) (1-3)
This course will provide students and faculty the opportunity to examine current issues or specialized topics within the discipline at a lower-level of study (appropriate for freshmen or sophomore academic experience). Topics will be determined by the department. Class will meet 15 hours for each hour of credit offered. Repeatable for different topics. *(Offered by department discretion).*

BS 301   International Finance (3)

This course exposes the student to the techniques of financial management unique to a multinational enterprise. Students also learn the basics of the macroeconomic and financial environments within which the multinational firm must function. Foreign exchange management is emphasized. Specific topics include—the International Monetary System and the Balance of Payments, International Bond, Equity and Money markets, Futures & Options on Foreign Exchange, Currency Swaps, Exposure Management, International Capital Structure, Capital Budgeting and Short-term financial management. *Pre-requisite: BS 203, 204 and MT 114 (Offered fall semesters, odd years)*

BS 303   Human Resource Management (3)

A course exploring the management of human resources to help companies meet competitive challenges. Included are discussions of global, quality, social and technological challenges facing United States businesses and the role of human resource management? Current practices and research on motivating, training, and supporting people will be examined. *Pre- or Co-requisite: BS 209. (Offered spring semester, even years.)*

BS 304   Labor-Management Relations (3)

A study of the history and development of labor relations, structure of union organizations, and process of collective bargaining negotiations and contract administration. With declining union membership over the last ten years, special emphasis is placed on employee relations in nonunion organizations. Contemporary issues include public sector and international labor relations. *Pre- or Co-requisite: BS 209 or permission of professor. (Offered fall semesters, even years.)*

BS 306   Corporate Finance (3)

Study of financial functions of a business enterprise conducted from the standpoint of the financial manager. Emphasis on analysis, planning and control, working capital management, capital budgeting, long-term financing, financial structure and valuation, and required rate of return. *Pre-requisite: MT 114; pre- or Co-requisite: BS 202. (Offered every spring.)*

BS 307   Organizational Behavior (3)

This course examines the development and maintenance of organizational effectiveness in terms of environmental effects, improving motivation, behavior modification, systems aspects, communications, structure, and the dynamics of problem solving, goal setting, team building, conflict resolution, and leadership. *Pre- or Co-requisite: BS 209. (Offered fall semesters, odd years.)*

BS 308   Servant Leadership (3)

A study of the concept of servant leadership and its applicability to today's business environment. Students will examine leadership characteristics and strategies of the Great Teacher, Jesus Christ, and compare them to historical and current models for leadership including Nehemiah, Gandhi, Greenleaf, Deming, Covey, and others. *Pre-requisite: BS 101; pre- or Co-requisite: BS 209; or permission of professor. (Offered fall semesters, odd years.)*

BS 309   Business Ethics (3)

This course includes an analysis of business policies and practices with respect to their social and moral impact. It raises basic questions on moral reasoning and the morality of economic systems, both nationally and internationally. It also examines the impact of governmental regulations on corporate behavior, and the ethical relationships between the corporation and the public. *Pre-requisite: BS 101. (Offered every fall.)*

BS 310   Total Quality Management (3)
An overview of the philosophy and tools of total quality management beginning with a study of W. Edwards Deming's Theory of Profound Knowledge. Students will be actively involved in team-building exercises employing statistical tools and techniques for innovation while solving real-world productivity problems. *Pre- or Co-requisite: MT 114 and BS 209 or permission of professor. (Offered fall semesters, even years.)*

BS 312   Business and the Legal Environment (3)
An introduction to the fundamentals of law in which managers manage and entrepreneurs conduct business. A basic understanding of court procedures, legal contracts and related components, contractual capacity issues, and the application of this information to the business environment will be provided through interactive class discussion. Students will also be exposed to issues relating to sales, warranties, agency, employee rights, and the legal forms of business ownership in order to strengthen their decision-making skills. *Pre- or Co-requisite: BS 101. (Offered every spring.)*

BS 313   Production/Operations Management (3)
A study of the management of the production functions of a manufacturing business to include world-class production theory. The course will include the study of forecasting, location analysis, allocating resources, designing products and services, scheduling activities, and assuring quality of outputs. *Pre-requisite: MT 114; pre- or co-requisite: BS 214. (Offered spring semesters, even years.)*

BS 320   International Business (3)
A study of the approach to doing business in other nations and cultures. The influences of political systems, competition, economic systems, social, legal, and technology environments on the main business functions (marketing, production, finance) and business effectiveness will be examined. *Pre- or Co-requisite: BS 101. (Offered fall semesters, odd years.)*

BS 331   Sales Administration (3)
A course on the professional, ethical, needs-based, non-manipulative, low-pressure, consultative approach to sales. Theories of selling, communicating, time management, and the relationship of sales to marketing and promotion are covered. Ethical business issues are examined in simulated selling situations. *Pre- or Co-requisite: BS 230. (Offered spring semesters, even years.)*

BS 335   Retailing Management (3)
This course employs a balance between a descriptive and conceptual approach for understanding the retailing industry and the decisions made by retailers. Types of retailers, trends in retailing, needs of customers, and factors affecting store and merchandising choices will be examined. Extensive case analysis and actual retailer comparisons will complement the classroom discussion. *Pre- or Co-requisites:*
BS 230. *(Offered fall semesters, even years.)*

BS 336   Principles of Advertising (3)
An overview of the non-selling methods of promotion, including advertising, sales promotion, and public relations. Primary emphasis on the field of advertising includes a review of the history and economics of advertising, research, copy, layout, production, budgeting, and advertising organization. *Pre- or Co-requisite: BS 230. (Offered fall semesters, even years.)*

BS 338   Marketing Research (3)
A study of the role of research in marketing decisions. Special emphasis on data gathering, compilation, analysis, and interpretation including the writing and analysis of surveys. Students will work on business problems with actual companies or evaluate new product concepts. *Pre- or Co-requisite: BS 230. (Offered spring semesters, even years.)*

BS 402   Management of Not-for-Profit Organizations (3)
A practical course designed to familiarize students with the unique management challenges of not-for-profits to include accounting and financial controls, bylaws, boards of directors, program planning, fund-raising, staffing, and community relations. Case studies of mission organizations, church administration, para-church organizations, and other nonprofits are examined. *Pre-requisite: BS 209; pre- or Co-requisite: BS 202. (Offered spring semesters, odd years.)*

BS 405   International Marketing (3)
An in-depth study of the operational and cross-cultural aspects of international marketing, including the nature of competition, developmental structures and channels, price and credit policies, promotional challenges, research, product trade barriers, and other international arrangements. The international competitive position of the United States is discussed and evaluated. *Pre- or Co-requisite: BS 230. (Offered spring semesters, odd years.)*

BS 407   Entrepreneurship and Small Business Management (3)
A practical course designed to familiarize students with the application of managerial responsibilities that are uniquely critical to small businesses including entrepreneurship, location analysis, forms of ownership, financing alternatives, accounting practices, marketing and advertising techniques, and inventory control. *Pre-requisites: BS 209, 230. (Offered spring semesters, odd years.)*

BS 435   Consumer Behavior (3)
This course stresses the understanding of consumer behavior in developing marketing strategy. Opportunities are provided for the analysis of advertising's objective, target audience, and the underlying behavioral assumptions. Students will apply consumer behavior knowledge to social and regulatory issues as well as to business and personal issues. *Pre- or Co-requisite BS 230. (Offered fall semesters, odd years.)*

BS 436   Ecommerce (3)
This course provides insights into the applications of rapidly evolving electronic commerce to determine and satisfy the needs of customers via the internet. Issues and practices that deal with concepts, theories, tactics, and strategies of information technologies and changes in marketing functions to meet the organization's objectives while delivering customer satisfaction and value are analyzed.
Pre- or Co-requisite: BS 230, CS 204. (Offered spring semesters, odd years.)

BS 437   Marketing Management (3)
An integrated course in marketing systematically oriented with emphasis on the marketing mix, formulation of competitive strategies, and special attention to control function, market analysis, marketing information, and sales forecasting. Case analysis and simulation is stressed. *Pre- or Co-requisite: BS 230. (Offered fall semesters, odd years.)*

BS 441   Internship (3)
Supervised internship provides students with the opportunity to integrate classroom instruction with on-the-job learning in an area associated with their concentration. A maximum of six hours may be counted toward the degree. *Pre-requisite: Twelve hours of BS course work and IS 310. (Offered every semester.)*

BS 460   Strategic Management (3)
This course is designed to provide students with an overview of the strategic management process. Emphasis is placed on developing a vision, setting objectives, and crafting strategy to achieve desired results. The course stresses the importance of analyzing external competitive conditions and the organization's internal capabilities, resources, strengths, and weaknesses in order to gain and sustain a competitive advantage. Approaches to organizational structure, policy, support systems, and leadership required to effectively execute strategy are all examined. *Pre-requisite: Senior standing in BS. (Offered every semester.)*

BS 480   Special Topics in Business (Upper-Level) (1-3)
This course will provide students and faculty the opportunity to examine current issues or specialized topics within the discipline at an upper-level of study (appropriate for junior or senior academic experience). Topics will be determined by the department. Class will meet 15 hours for each hour of credit offered. Repeatable for different topics. *Prerequisite: Permission of department chair. (Offered by department discretion.)*

BS 481   Directed Study/Research (1-3)
Students may choose to participate in a directed study of their own choice contingent on faculty availability. Credit varies from 1-3 hours although a student can repeat for up to six hours of credit. *Prerequisite: Junior status or above. A cumulative GPA of 2.5 and approval of the department chair is required.*

CHEMISTRY (CH)

CH 201   Environmental Inorganic Chemistry I (4)
CH 201 is one of two semester courses that together provide an introduction to chemistry for the science major. Topics considered include atomic and molecular structure, nomenclature, chemical bonding, stoichiometry, properties of gases, oxidation-reduction, and electrochemistry with biological and environmental applications. The laboratories will concentrate on chemical experimentation with qualitative and quantitative inorganic analysis. Three hours of lecture and three hours of laboratory per week. *Pre-requisite: Two years of high school algebra or permission of professor.*

CH 202   Environmental Inorganic Chemistry II (4)
CH 202 is one of two semester courses that together provide an introduction to chemistry for the science major. This course provides a further development of introductory inorganic chemistry with topics in molecular forces, physical chemical properties, kinetics, chemical equilibria, thermodynamics, and an introduction to nuclear and organic chemistry with biological and environmental applications. The laboratories will concentrate on chemical experimentation with qualitative and quantitative inorganic analysis. Three hours of lecture and three hours of laboratory per week. *Pre-requisites: CH 201, two years of high school algebra or permission of professor.*

CH 315   Chemistry of the Environment I (3)
CH 315 is one of two semester courses that together provide both Environmental Studies and Biology students the background to understand the environmental interface of inorganic and organic principles and systems. Topics will launch an understanding of these principles within various environmental processes, including topics centering on contemporary environmental chemistry. Additionally, the course will investigate student interests with application of these concepts to the field. *Pre-requisites: CH 201, CH 202 and ES 206.*

CH 316   Chemistry of the Environment II (3)
CH 316 is one of two semester courses that together with CH 315 will build on introductory principles and develop strong foundations in topics of environmental chemical systems integrated specifically to the academic focus of the students enrolled in the class. The course will also provide an opportunity to customize individual research projects integrated with course topics of interest. *Pre-requisites: CH 201-202, CH 315, and ES 206.*

CH 320   Organic Chemistry I (3)
CH 320 is one of two semester courses that together provide foundational organic chemistry training for the biology and health career major. The structure, nomenclature, stereochemistry, energy relations, and reaction mechanisms of major classes of organic compounds are studied in application to biological, toxicological, and environmental topics.

The course will deal with the introductory mechanisms and instrumentation techniques of structural investigations. Three hours lecture per week. *Pre-requisites: CH 201, CH 202, or permission of professor.*

CH 321   Organic Chemistry II (3)

CH 321 is one of two semester courses that builds upon the foundational principles of CH 320 with studies in further reaction mechanisms starting with delocalized Pi systems and Benzene. Mechanisms of additional classes of organic compounds will focus on carboxylic acid derivatives and develop mechanism application with compounds in industry, nature, biological, environmental, and medical systems. *Pre-requisites: CH 201, CH 202, CH 320, CH 322 or permission of professor.*

CH 322   Organic Chemistry Lab I (2)

Experimental techniques of synthesis, isolation, and identification of compounds using classical and contemporary instrumentation are utilized to establish a foundation of organic chemistry processes, an understanding of reaction mechanisms, and a basic background in investigation techniques. The course will include the use of analytical instrumentation that are typically integrated into contemporary investigations in Chemistry and Biochemistry. *Prerequisites: CH 201, CH 202, CH 320 (co-requisite), or permission of professor. [2 credit hours, 4 hour class hours per week]*

CH 323   Organic Chemistry Laboratory II (1)

Building upon the foundational components of previous Organic Chemistry training, students will engage in Organic Chemistry research and use advanced analytical instrumentation. Students will develop independent investigations in applied Organic Chemistry and Biochemistry. *Prerequisites: CH 201, CH 202, CH 320, CH 321 (co-requisite), CH 322, or permission of professor. [1 credit hour, 4 hour class hours]*

COMMUNICATION (CM)

CM 181   Summer Fine Arts Intensive (3)

Students will sign up for a theatre, music, or production track, but will be required to do work in the other tracks as well. The goal is to explore how various art forms can be utilized to explore and expound upon a theme. The integration of the Christian faith into the arts will be explored as well through discussion, observing performances of established Christian artists, and talk-backs with these artists. The week-long intensive will culminate in a juried final performance that brings together what has been taught. Journals, reflection papers, and a research paper are part of the assessment process.

CM/TH 202   Acting for the Camera (3)

This course aims to inform the student to learn how to present himself on camera in a variety of genres. It will provide instruction and experience in the basics of acting for both television and film. It will also examine informational and news journalism. Cross listed as TH 202. Prerequisite: permission of instructor.

CM 203   Communication and Culture (3)

How do you as an individual create meaningful communication? Who do you become in a group or organization, and how does that influence your communication? How are you, along with millions of others, creating popular culture? These questions and many more will be explored in an overview of communication's vital role in society. Discussions will focus on the interaction of individuals, groups, organizations, media, and popular culture as viewed through the fascinating lens of communication theory.

CM 220   Public Speech and Rhetorical Analysis (3)
How do you become an excellent communicator? In this class we will examine excellent public communication from throughout history from a practical and theoretical perspective. At the same time, students will prepare and deliver their own speeches in a variety of formats. Emphasis will be placed on historical context, speaker ethos, and rhetorical analysis, with special attention paid to modern and post-modern rhetorical theory.

CM 228   Media Studies (4)
This course examines the history of mass media in terms of its relationship with our culture and sense of identity. All mass media will be discussed, but particular focus will be given to the internal structure of electronic media production in terms of process and job roles. This course will include a student project or a 12 to 15 hour/week student internship.

CM 249   Digital Media Production (4)
This course covers the steps to create a short film/documentary. Students will explore the techniques, aesthetics, and theory that inform lighting, cameras, editing, crew organization, work flow, and production requirements. Students will complete short film projects in journalism, advertising/PR and a final short narrative or documentary piece. This course will make demands of students' time in that project. *Pre-requisites: EN 101-102*

CM 280   Special Topics in Communication (Lower-Level) (1-3)
This course will provide students and faculty the opportunity to examine current issues or specialized topics within the discipline at a lower-level of study (appropriate for freshmen or sophomore academic experience). Topics will be determined by the department. Class will meet 15 hours for each hour of credit offered. Repeatable for different topics. *(Offered by department discretion.)*

CM 313   Public Relations (3)
A course emphasizing the practical application of communication theory to the tasks of public relations and professional written communication. Course assignments include writing news releases, researching organizational communication strategies, and applying legal and ethical issues to the public relations practice. *Pre-requisites: English 101-102 with a minimum grade of C-.*

CM 318   Film History and Theory (4)
This course looks at cinema history through the lens of film theory. We will trace the development of film as an art form and communication tool in the US and Europe from the silent era through today. Two major goals will be 1) to understand the influence of culture, philosophy, and world events upon film, and 2) to understand film as an expression of these realities. To this end, films that have made significant contributions to world culture will be viewed and discussed on a weekly basis. Finally, film theory will be discussed as it arises within the context of history and may include techniques, narrativity, diegesis, cinematic codes, "the image", genre, subjectivity, and authorship. Genres studied may include comedy, westerns, action/adventure, drama, war, crime/gangster, musicals, and science fiction.

CM 329   Film Production (4)
This course will explore what is required to create a collaborative film. Students will explore the techniques, aesthetics, and theory that informs the good use of lighting, cameras, editing, crew organization, and the production process. Students will have short projects in which they learn various filmmaking techniques and a final project in which they create a short film. Students will use class members and friends as their cast and crew. *Pre-requisites: EN 102, CM 249, CM 335, and/or permission of the instructor.*

CM/TH 335   Playwriting/Screenwriting (3)
This course covers the foundational elements of stage and/or film script writing: structure, character development, plot development and use of image. It will also develop the use of the imagination and address how to utilize that effectively with the discipline of writing well. Semester will conclude with staged readings of the students' final scenes.

CM 341   Practicum (1-3)
Supervised practical experience provides students with opportunity to integrate classroom instruction with on-the-job learning in various areas of communication-related fields. *Prerequisite: IS 310, Permission of professor.*

CM 342   Communication Methods (4)
This field course introduces students to examples and practice of research in communication including critical, quantitative and qualitative methods of investigation. Students will write research questions, select methodology, collect data, analyze data, and present results. Prerequisite: MT 114 Elementary Probability and Statistics.

CM 344   Nonprofit Organizational Communication (4)
This course will focus in communicating the mission and vision of nonprofit organizations—including Christian organizations--with passion and sophistication. A primary focus of the course will be in the development, preparation, and stewardship of grant proposals. Students will also be introduced to nonprofit communication and management theory and participation in a practicum. Prerequisites: English 101 and 102 or 104, with C or better and CM 203.

CM 346   Web Studies and Design (3)
From a theoretical viewpoint, this course will examine ways the internet influences how we create identity, community, and particular cultures. From a practical viewpoint, this course will teach basic web design and aesthetics. A goal of this course is to equip students for entry level positions in webpage design.

CM 347   News Editing (3)
A practical examination of design principles, copy editing and feature writing for print media. Design elements cover software applications for text, photo and graphics. Copy editing covers AP Stylebook rules, including headline and cutline composition. Writing topics include basic reporting, story structure and feature content. *(Offered spring semesters, even years).*

CM 348   News Writing (3)
A practical examination of investigative reporting in print media. Topics include: developing the news story, exploring leads, interviewing sources, and understanding the reporter/editor relationship. Related issues address the ethical, legal, and social responsibilities of the journalist. Students will sharpen their reporting skills through the researching, writing, and editing of several publishable-quality news stories. *Prerequisite: Completion of EN 101-102 with a grade of C- or higher.*

CM/AR 349   Graphics & Photojournalism (3)
This course explores the theoretical and practical aspects of choosing, creating, & composing photographic images for graphic arts and journalism.
Students will explore an historical overview of photography to critically evaluate the visual rhetoric of images in popular culture and journalism.
Students will also learn how to use digital and single-lens cameras to create effective images for a series of graphic arts and journalism projects. Cross listed with AR 349.

CM 441   Internship (3)
An intensive, quality, structured learning opportunity that immerses students in appropriate professional contexts. Supervision of the internship is a shared responsibility between the faculty advisor and on-site supervisor. *Pre-requisite: IS 310*

CM 480   Special Topics in Communication (Upper-Level) (1-3)
This course will provide students and faculty the opportunity to examine current issues or specialized topics within the discipline at an upper-level of study (appropriate for junior or senior academic experience). Topics will be determined by the department. Class will meet 15 hours for each hour of credit offered. Repeatable for different topics. *(Offered by department discretion.)*

CM 491   Senior Thesis (2)
Students will develop an extensive capstone project. A departmental committee will specify the thesis parameters, approve the topic, and grade the final product.

COMPUTER STUDIES (CS)

CS 102   Computer Applications and Concepts (3)
This course will enable students to improve their skills as knowledge workers with an emphasis on personal productivity concepts through using functions and features in computer software such as word processing, spreadsheets, presentation graphics, communications and scheduling, and online learning systems. This course provides an overview of microcomputer applications including a brief introduction to computer concepts, Microsoft Windows 7, Outlook 2013, Word 2013, Excel 2013, PowerPoint 2013 and Moodle, an online learning management system. (8 weeks)

CS 102E   Computer Competency Exam (3)
An examination to fulfill the computer competency requirement. Credits given if student passes exam with the equivalent of a *C* grade or better.

CS 204   Fundamentals of Information Systems (3)
Providing an introduction to systems and development concepts, information technology, and application software, this course explains how information is used in organizations and how information technology enables improvement in quality, timeliness, and competitive advantage in organizations. Topics include systems concepts, system components and relationships, cost/value and quality of information, competitive advantage and information, specification, design and reengineering of information systems, application versus system software, and package software solutions. *Pre-requisite: CS 102 or permission of professor.* (8 weeks)

CS 207   Principles of Operating Systems and Computer Hardware (3)
An in-depth study of operating systems and computer hardware covering the domains of the A+ Certification. Focus is on identification, installation, configuration, and troubleshooting of field replaceable components. Topics include microprocessors, memory, BIOS and CMOS, expansion bus, motherboards, power supplies, floppy drives, hard drives, removable media, video, audio, portable PCs, printers, networks, the Internet, computer security, and Windows operating systems. *Pre-requisites CS 204.*

CS 215   Introduction to Computer Networking (3)
An in-depth study of computer networking theories and concepts covering the domains of the Network+ Certification. Focus is on the configuration, maintenance, and troubleshooting of network devices using appropriate network tools and understanding of the features and purpose of network technologies. *Pre-requisite: CS 207.*

CS 221   Introduction to Secure Programming Logic (3)
This is an introductory course in structured programming logic. Students will learn to analyze problems; define data using simple data types and arrays; and create algorithmic solutions using basic control structures (sequence, selections, and loops) and functions. Students learn to systematically break down a problem into manageable parts; plan and design logical

solutions; and write effective, structured, and well-documented instructions. Emphasis will be on problem-solving approaches (algorithms) and the fundamental concepts and programming techniques common to modern computer languages including variable assignment, expressions, input/output statements, loops, if-then-else and case constructs, functions, arrays, etc. The concepts learned in this course are applicable to multiple modern programming languages. *Pre-requisite: CS 204 or permission of professor.*

CS 280   Special Topics in Computer Studies (Lower-Level) (1-3)

This course will provide students and faculty the opportunity to examine current issues or specialized topics within the discipline at a lower-level of study (appropriate for freshmen or sophomore academic experience). Topics will be determined by the department. Class will meet 15 hours for each hour of credit offered. Repeatable for different topics. *(Offered by department discretion.)*

CS 287   Cyber Competition I (2)

This course, open to freshmen and sophomores, prepares students to be part of a cyber competition such as the National Cyber League (NCL) or similar. Said competitions can be 'offensive' in nature (Capture the Flag etc.). *Pre-requisite: permission of professor.*

CS 289   Cyber Defense I (2)

This course, open to freshmen, sophomores and juniors, prepares students to be part of a Cyber Defense competition such as the Southeast Collegiate Cyber Defense Competition, SECCDC. *Pre-requisite: Permission of professor.*

CS 310   Database Programming (3)

A course introducing the student to the logic, design, implementation, and accessing of organizational databases as contrasted to older conventional data file techniques introduced in COBOL programming. Particular emphasis is placed on relational database management that focuses on the logical nature of databases. Popular microcomputer-based database programs will be utilized. *Pre-requisite: CS 302 or permission of professor. (Offered every spring)*

CS 335   Computer and Systems Security (3)

An in-depth study of computer and systems security covering the domains of the Security+ Certification. Focus is on the knowledge and skills required to
identify risk and participate in risk mitigation activities, provide infrastructure, application, operational and information security, apply security controls to maintain confidentiality, integrity and availability, identify appropriate technologies and products, and operate with an awareness of applicable policies, laws and regulations. *Pre-requisite: CS 215.*

CS 341   Internship I (3)

Supervised internship provides students with the opportunity to integrate classroom instruction with on-the-job training in an area associated with information systems, information technology, information security or cybersecurity. *Pre-requisite: IS 310, sophomore standing or permission of professor. (Offered by department discretion)*

CS 345   Principles of Cybersecurity (3)

Examination of current standards of due care and best business practices in Cybersecurity. Includes examination of security technologies, methodologies and practices. Focus is on the evaluation and selection of optimal security posture.
Topics include evaluation of security models, risk assessment, threat analysis, organizational technology evaluation, security implementation, disaster recovery planning and security policy formulation and implementation. *Pre-requisite: CS 335.*

CS 350   Management of Cybersecurity (3)

Detailed examinations of a systems-wide perspective of Cybersecurity, beginning with a strategic planning process for security. Includes an examination of the policies, procedures and staffing functions necessary to organize and administrate ongoing security functions in the organization. Topics include security practices, security architecture and models, continuity planning and disaster recovery planning. *Pre-requisite: CS 345.*

CS 365   The 3 C's: Cybercrime, Cyberlaw and Cyberethics (3)

A study of the impact of cybercrimes affecting various entities and organizations engaged in cyberspace transactions and activities including the government, military, financial institutions, retailers and private citizens. The course covers broad areas of law pertaining to cyberspace, including Intellectual Property (Copyright, Patent, Trademark, and Trade Secret), Contract, and the U.S. Constitution. The study of Cyberethics addresses a definition of ethics, provides a framework for making ethical decisions undergirded by a biblical worldview, and analyzes in detail several areas of ethical issues that computer professionals are likely to encounter in cyberspace and in business.

CS 370   Network Defense and Countermeasures (3)

Detailed examination of the tools and technologies used in the technical securing of information assets. This course is designed to provide in-depth information on the software and hardware components of Cybersecurity. Topic covered include: firewall configurations, hardening Linux and Windows servers, Web and distributed systems security, and specific implementation of security models and architectures. *Pre-requisite: CS 345.*

CS 375   Linux Operating Systems and Security (3)

An in-depth study of Linux operating system covering the domains of the Linux+ Certification Focus is on implementing GNU and UNIX commands from the command line, installing and configuring Linux, and maintaining securing the Linux system. *Pre-requisite: CS 215.*

CS 380   Certification Study and Preparation (3)

The Cybersecurity concentration is optimally designed to equip our graduates with the necessary skills and knowledge to enter the IT workforce. This course will assist students who plan to study and prepare for IT certifications in A+ or Network+ or Security+ or Linux. *Pre-requisites: CS 207 or CS 215 or CS 335 or CS 375.*

CS 387   Cyber Competition II (2)

This course prepares sophomore or junior status students who are returning participants to compete in a cyber-competition such as the National Cyber League (NCL). Said competitions can be 'offensive' in nature (Capture the Flag etc.). *Pre-requisite: CS 287 or permission of professor.*

CS 389   Cyber Defense II (2)

This course prepares sophomore or junior status students who are returning participants to compete in a cyber-defense competition such as the Southeast Collegiate Cyber Defense Competition (SECCDC) or similar. To promote teamwork and leadership, students may serve as sub-team (Windows, Linux, Firewall and Incident Response etc.) leads. *Pre-requisite: CS 288 or permission of professor.*

CS 428   Penetration Testing (3)

A detailed examination of real world cybersecurity knowledge, enabling recognition of vulnerabilities, exploitation of system weaknesses, and safeguards against threats. Students will learn the art of penetration testing through hands-on exercises and a final project. Students who complete this course will be equipped with the knowledge necessary to analyze and evaluate systems security. *Prerequisite: CS 370 or permission of professor.*

CS 438   Network Forensics (3)

In this course, students will learn to identify network security events, incidents, intrusions and sources of digital evidence in a lab environment. The students will develop a comprehensive understanding of network forensic analysis principles including identifying and categorizing incidents, responding to incidents, log analysis, network traffic analysis, and using various tools to integrate network forensic technologies. Student will demonstrate the ability to accurately document network forensic processes and analysis. *May be taken concurrently with CS 428 or permission of professor.*

CS 441   Internship II (3)

Supervised internship provides students with the opportunity to integrate classroom instruction with on-the-job training in an area associated with cybersecurity. *Pre-requisites: IS 310, CS 341, junior standing, permission of department. (Offered by department discretion)*

CS 448   Incident Response and Contingency Planning (3)

An examination of the detailed aspects of incident response and contingency planning consisting of incident response planning, disaster recovery planning, and business continuity planning. Developing and executing plans to deal with incidents in the organization is a critical function in information security. This course focuses on the planning processes for all three areas of contingency planning – incident response, disaster recovery and business continuity, as well as the execution of response to human and non-human incidents in compliance with these policies. *Prerequisite: CS 370 or permission of professor.*

CS 475   Cybersecurity Programs and Strategies (3)

This course integrates learning from all prior CS courses, encourages the student to develop skills in synthesis and communication both written and oral, and teaches new material about the role of the CISO and the strategic and tactical planning and operation of the cybersecurity department in a variety of organizations. A research paper will be prepared and presented in the course. Outside speakers will supplement the course and provide the student additional, outside perspectives on the cybersecurity industry. *Prerequisite: CS 448 or permission of professor.*

CS 480   Special Topics in Computer Studies (Upper-Level) (1-3)

This course will provide students and faculty the opportunity to examine current issues or specialized topics within the discipline at an upper-level of study (appropriate for junior or senior academic experience). Topics will be determined by the department. Class will meet 15 hours for each hour of credit offered. Repeatable for different topics. *Prerequisites: CS 102, CS 204. (Offered by department discretion.)*

CS 487   Cyber Competition III (2)

This course prepares junior or senior status students who are returning participants to compete in a Cyber competition such as the National Cyber League (NCL) or similar. Said competitions can be 'offensive' in nature (Capture the Flag etc.). To promote leadership and teamwork, students may serve as vice-team captain or team captain of the competition. *Prerequisites: CS 387 or permission of professor.*

CS 489   Cyber Defense III (2)

This advanced cyber defense preparation course prepares junior or senior status students who are returning participants to compete in a cyber-defense competition such as the Southeast Collegiate Cyber Defense Competition (SECCDC) or similar. To promote leadership and teamwork, students may serve as sub-team lead, vice-team captain or team captain of the competition. *Prerequisites: CS 388 or permission of professor.*

CROSS-CULTURAL STUDIES AND MISSIONS (CC)

CC 201   Comparative Cultures (3)

Designed to help the student gain a basic knowledge of the concepts and methods needed to compare and understand different cultures and/or subcultures. Instructional methods include on-site participant observation, interviews, case studies, and readings. This course is recommended for those who are not in the cross-cultural studies concentration. *(Offered spring semesters, odd years.)*

CC 280   Special Topics in Cross-Cultural Studies (Lower-Level) (1-3)
This course will provide students and faculty the opportunity to examine current issues or specialized topics within the discipline at a lower-level of study (appropriate for freshmen or sophomore academic experience). Topics will be determined by the department. Class will meet 15 hours for each hour of credit offered. Repeatable for different topics. *(Offered by department discretion.)*

CC 301   Foundations of Cross-Cultural Ministry (3)
An introduction to the study of cross-cultural ministry, this course will examine the biblical theology of cross-cultural ministry, historical perspectives on the expansion of the Christian movement, modern movements in missions, and the strategy and components of cross-cultural work being employed today. *(Offered fall semesters, odd years.)*

CC 302   Journey in Missions: Becoming a Missionary (3)
A practical guide to help students determine their place in the task of global evangelization and ministries of mercy in the name of Christ. This course will include investigation into particular geographical areas of the world and types of missionary activity (medical, educational, evangelistic, and tent-making ministries). It will also deal with deciding whether or not one is called to be a missionary in the international arena; choosing a sending agency and preparing for international missions while still engaged in college life. *(Offered fall semesters, even years.)*

CC 341   Practicum (1-3)
A supervised learning experience in a cross-cultural setting that provides one with initial exposure to relevant professional activities. Supervision of the practicum is a shared responsibility between the faculty advisor and on-site supervisor. This course may be repeated; a maximum of three (3) hours may be used to satisfy degree requirements. *Prerequisite: IS 310, permission of the student's advisor and department chair or designee. (Offered by department discretion.)*

CC 402   Cultural Anthropology (3)
Using selected national cultures, this course teaches methods of analysis and understanding of any culture for the purpose of equipping students to make an effective presentation of the Christian Gospel. *(Offered spring semesters, odd years.)*

CC 403   Cross-Cultural Communication (3)
A technical study of communication across lines of cultural and language differences. *(Offered spring semesters, even years.)*

CC 441   Internship (3)
An intensive, quality, structured learning opportunity that immerses students in appropriate professional contexts. Supervision of the internship is a shared responsibility between the faculty advisor and on-site supervisor. This course may be repeated; a maximum of six (6) hours may be used to satisfy degree requirements. *Pre-requisite: IS 310, permission of the student's advisor and department chair or designee, junior standing. (Offered by department discretion.)*

CC 480   Special Topics in Cross-Cultural Studies (Upper-Level) (1-3)
This course will provide students and faculty the opportunity to examine current issues or specialized topics within the discipline at an upper-level of study (appropriate for junior or senior academic experience). Topics will be determined by the department. Class will meet 15 hours for each hour of credit offered. Repeatable for different topics. *(Offered by department discretion.)*

CC 481   Directed Study and Research (1-3)
Students may choose to participate in a directed study of their own choice contingent on faculty availability. Credit varies from 1-3 hours although a student can repeat for up to six

hours of credit. *Prerequisite: Junior status or above. A cumulative GPA of 2.5 and approval of the department chair is required. (Offered by department discretion.)*

ELEMENTARY EDUCATION (ED)

ED 150   **Foundations of Education (3)**
This course is designed to study the profession of teaching, its' history and foundations, goals, trends, issues, philosophies, and the diversity of our modern school population. Research related to content knowledge necessary to Elementary Education preparation is emphasized. Also, the legal aspects of teaching are introduced and discussed. Introduction to licensure requirements is begun. Students will complete background checks and NC Health Forms to be kept on file for students to complete Focused Field Experiences in remaining Education courses. *(Offered every fall.)*

ED 209   **Children's Literature (3)**
This course emphasizes the practical application of traditional and contemporary writing for children, including picture books, folk literature, modern fantasy, poetry, modern fiction, trauma-specific genres, historical fiction, and multicultural literature. Emphasis on techniques of storytelling, interpretation, and selection according to literary elements and child development needs. *Pre-requisite EN 101 & EN 102 with a minimum grade of B-.).* Course requires 6 hours Focused Field Experiences. *Completed satisfactory background checks and NC Health Forms must be on file for students to complete Focused Field Experiences. (Offered every spring.)*

ED 240   **Computers for Education (3)**
General and content-area applications of computers for elementary education students including databases, spreadsheets, word-processing, Mimeo technology, and multimedia are emphasized. Computer terminology, wikis, social media, ethical issues, and integration into instruction will be included. Course requires 6 hours Focused Field Experiences. *Completed satisfactory background checks and NC Health Forms must be on file for students to complete Focused Field Experiences. (Offered every spring.)*

ED 260   **Integrating Health and the Arts (3)**
Students will study health concepts, art, music, creativity, drama, and physical movement to promote the physical, emotional, social, and cognitive development of young children. Concepts and activities suitable for use with K-6 students will be presented as an integrated approach to use in the elementary curriculum. Course requires 6 hours Focused Field Experiences. *Completed satisfactory background checks and NC Health Forms must be on file for students to complete Focused Field Experiences. (Offered every fall.)*

ED 270   **Diversity in Education (3)**
This course focuses on gaining an understanding of the influence of race, ethnicity, gender, religions, and other aspects of culture on a student's development and school performance. Differentiated instructional strategies, collaboration with specialists, inclusion and other models of effective practice that engage students and ensure their needs are met will be explored. Course requires 6 hours Focused Field Experiences. *Completed satisfactory background checks and NC Health Forms must be on file for students to complete Focused Field Experiences. (Offered every spring.)*

ED 280   **Special Topics in Education (Lower-Level) (1-3)**
This course will provide students and faculty the opportunity to examine current issues or specialized topics within the discipline at a lower-level of study (appropriate for freshmen or sophomore academic experience). Topics will be determined by the department. Class will

meet 15 hours for each hour of credit offered. Repeatable for different topics. (*Offered by department discretion.*)

ED 320   Math Methods K-3 (3)

This laboratory-centered course focuses on implementation strategies of instruction in computation, and the concepts of numbers, geometry, and measurement in grades K-3. Experiences with instructional materials, technology tools, curriculums, and current research are provided. Course requires 6 hours Focused Field Experiences. *Completed satisfactory background checks and NC Health Forms must be on file for students to complete Focused Field Experiences. (Offered every fall.)*

ED 325   Math Methods 4-6 (3)

This course is designed as a laboratory-centered course for implementing strategies of instruction in computation and the concepts of numbers, algebra, geometry, ratios, and measurement in grades 4-6. Experiences with instructional materials, technology tools, curriculums, and current research are provided. Course requires 6 hours Focused Field Experiences. *Completed satisfactory background checks and NC Health Forms must be on file for students to complete Focused Field Experiences. (Offered every spring.)*

ED 330   Teaching Reading and Language Arts (3)

A laboratory-centered course planned for the mastering of skills necessary to implement the principles, procedures, organization, and current practices in the elementary phonics-based reading and language arts program. Materials and Methods of instructional research –based practice are provided and utilized by students. Course requires 6 hours Focused Field Experiences. *Completed satisfactory background checks and NC Health Forms must be on file for students to complete Focused Field Experiences. (Offered every fall.)*

ED 350   Teaching Science (3)

The organization of instruction in elementary school science will be taught through the use of research-based methods, evaluation, materials, strategies, and current curriculums and practices. Hands-on and inquiry-based learning along with 21st Century instructional skills will be emphasized. Course requires 6 hours Focused Field Experiences. *Completed satisfactory background checks and NC Health Forms must be on file for students to complete Focused Field Experiences. (Offered every spring.)*

ED 350L   Teaching Science Lab (1)

Students will learn to teach appropriate lab procedures and lab safety practices, use science labs to expand student knowledge, satisfy curiosity, and integrate 21st century skill and content. Students will become proficient in the following: knowledge of subject matter, use a variety of instructional strategies, wise use of resources in planning, the organization of supplies and equipment, proper arrangement of the room environment, and the acceptance of procedures and rules. *This course must be taken concurrently with ED 350 Teaching Science.*

ED 351   Forum I: Education in NC (1)

This course will provide an overview of education in the state of North Carolina and an overview of Montreat College's Teacher Education Program. (Must be taken the semester before admission to the Montreat College Teacher Education Program (TEP).) Course requires 6 hours Focused Field Experiences. *Completed satisfactory background checks and NC Health Forms must be on file for students to complete Focused Field Experiences. Pre- or co-requisites: All other EDU 200-300 level education courses (Offered every spring.)*

ED 360   Teaching Social Studies (3)

Students will study instructional programs in social science materials, techniques of instruction and student involvement, current research, and their application in the classroom. The use of technology to access current social science data and to communicate with other classrooms in the community, state, and the world will be emphasized. Course requires 6 hours Focused Field Experiences. *Completed satisfactory background checks and NC Health Forms must be on file for students to complete Focused Field Experiences. (Offered every fall.)*

ED 365   Christian Philosophy of Education (3)

This course will examine different philosophies of education and how they relate to the Christian worldview. Candidates will complete readings, focused field experiences in P-6 Christian education, and write a paper describing and defending their own Christian philosophy of education. *This optional course is designed for students seeking ACSI teacher certification and meets the ACSI Christian Philosophy requirement. (Offered by department discretion.)*

ED 370   Language and Literacy (3)

This course is designed to introduce students to a young child's reading and writing foundation and emerging communication capacities. Students will study emerging literacy, phonemic awareness, and apply knowledge of emerging reading/writing literacy in an actual school setting. Students will learn appropriate questioning techniques, problem-solving skills, and how to use literature as a springboard to the writing process, integrate literature into other content areas, and how to use appropriate assessment tools Course requires 6 hours Focused Field Experiences. *Completed satisfactory background checks and NC Health Forms must be on file for students to complete Focused Field Experiences. (Offered every spring.)*

ED 406   Educational Psychology (3)

This course is designed to study the psychological principles and theories that underlie effective educational practices. Attention is given to developmental processes, individual differences and motivation, learning theory, measurement and evaluation, understanding student behavior motivators, and teacher behavior, including the formulation of developmentally appropriate objectives. *Pre-requisite: satisfactory completion of required 200-300 level courses or Permission of Instructor. (Offered every fall.)*

ED 410   Classroom Management (3)

This course is designed to study teaching behaviors and strategies for classroom management that results in sound instructional planning that minimizes behavior problems. Included are effective measurement and evaluation principles, strategies, characteristics of good behavior management, typical educational problems and appropriate solutions, and appropriate educational programs for children who have difficulty managing their own behaviors. *Pre-requisite: satisfactory completion of required 200-300 level courses or Permission of Instructor. (Offered every fall.)*

ED 420   Assessment in Education (3)

This course will examine the assessment, evaluation, and uses of educational assessment and evaluation instruments in elementary (K-6) classrooms. Students will become familiar with using multiple measures, including formative and summative assessment, student self-assessment, and the use of feedback to evaluate student progress and growth to eliminate achievement gaps. *Pre-requisite: satisfactory completion of required 200-300 level courses or Permission of Instructor. (Offered every fall.)*

ED 421   Forum II: Issues in Education (1)

This course explores issues in education, combining principles with practice during the Student Teaching I. In this seminar teacher candidates will reflect on experiences in Student Teaching I and develop a unit to be implemented in Student Teaching II. *Co-requisite: Student Teaching I. (Offered every fall.)*

ED 430   Teaching Children with Exceptionalities (3)

This course is designed to explore alternative ways of viewing, understanding, and teaching the exceptional child. Students will be introduced to the cognitive, behavioral, physical, and emotional characteristics of children who are classified as exceptional learners. Focus will be placed on planning appropriate, differentiated instruction, using a variety of instructional strategies, and collaborating with educational partners and guardians. *Pre-requisite: satisfactory completion of required 200-300 level courses or Permission of Instructor. (Offered every fall.)*

ED 449   Student Teaching I (5)

This course follows a co-teaching model and completes the first half of the professional year. Students will be assigned to classrooms in local schools for the purpose of working every morning, Monday through Friday, with their cooperating teacher, students in that teacher's classroom, and their supervising professor to impact student learning in the elementary (K-6) classroom. Students will prepare bulletin boards, centers, and perform instructional and non-instructional duties as assigned by the cooperating teacher and supervising professor. This class must be taken in the fall of the professional year. *Co-requisite: ED 421 Forum II: Issues in Education. (Offered every fall.)*

ED 450   Student Teaching II (12)

This course follows a co-teaching model and is a specifically planned 15-week student teaching experience. Students will be placed in their respective schools fulltime during this semester. The primary objective of this experience is to provide the opportunity for the acquisition and demonstration of instructional competence as a beginning teacher. This course completes the second half of the Professional Year. *Prerequisite: Successful completion of ED 449 Student Teaching I. (Offered every spring.)*

ED 451   Forum III: Issues in Education (1)

This course further explores issues in education, combining additional principles with practice during the student teaching semester. In this seminar, all students are active participants and have intellectual responsibilities to each other, as each student advances both their new understanding and fellow students' understanding. Current educational practices will be discussed. Students will review job application expectations, development of interviewing skills, and completion of paperwork for licensure. *Pre-requisite: ED 421 Forum II. Co-requisite: ED 450 Student Teaching II. (Offered every spring.)*

ED 480   Special Topics in Education (Upper-Level) (1-3)

This course will provide students and faculty the opportunity to examine current issues or specialized topics within the discipline at an upper-level of study (appropriate for junior or senior academic experience). Topics will be determined by the department. Class will meet 15 hours for each hour of credit offered. Repeatable for different topics. *(Offered by department discretion.)*

ED 481   Directed Study and Research (1-3)

Students may choose to participate in a directed study of their own choice contingent on faculty availability. Credit varies from 1-3 hours although a student can repeat for up to six hours of credit. *Prerequisite: Permission of the Department Chair.*

ENGLISH (EN)

Completion of EN 101 or 103 and 102 or 104 with a minimum grade of C is required for graduation from the College.

EN 101   English Composition I (3)

A course in the composing process emphasizing prewriting, writing, and revision and closely supervised practice in reading and writing expository essays. Students are taught that writing is a way of learning as well as a communication skill. Required of all full-time students in the first semester. *(Offered every semester.)*

EN 102   **English Composition II (3)**

Research techniques and the writing of a research paper are included, in addition to continued practice in expository writing. English 102 or 104 is required of all students in the second semester. *Pre-requisite: EN 101 or EN 103. (Offered every semester.)* Students achieve writing competency by: Earning grades of C or above in both EN 101 (or 103) and EN 102 (or 104) or the equivalent.

EN 103   **Honors English Composition (3)**

An advanced course in the composing process emphasizing prewriting, writing, and revision and closely supervised practice in reading and writing expository essays. Students are taught that writing is a way of learning as well as a communication skill. *Pre-requisite: Acceptance into Honors program. (Offered every fall.)*

EN 104   **Honors Introduction to Literary Studies (3)**

A course in literary studies, including the writing of formal literary research papers and an introduction to literary genres. Strongly recommended for students intending to major in either the literature or the creative writing concentration of the English major, and for other students who desire intense literary exposure. May substitute for English 102. English 102 or 104 is required of all students in the second semester. *Pre-requisite: EN 101 or EN 103, permission of professor. (Offered every spring.)*

EN 201   **Survey of English Literature I (3)**

A survey of English literature before the Romantic Period with a major emphasis on the masterpieces. *Pre-requisites: EN 101, EN 102. (Offered every fall.)*

EN 202   **Survey of English Literature II (3)**

A survey of English literature from the Romantic Period to the present. *Pre-requisites: EN 101, EN 102. (Offered every spring.)*

EN 203   **World Literature I (3)**

An examination of thematic concepts reflected in the literature of Western heritage. Includes Homer and Sophocles. *Pre-requisites: EN 101, EN 102. (Offered by department discretion.)*

EN 223   **Writing Tutor (1)**

The Writing Tutor course is designed for students who are or want to be Writing Center tutors. The course will expose the tutors to writing center theory as well as develop their abilities to assess and address the needs presented in a peer's paper. Tutors will be active participants in course development and create a personalized learning contract for their semester's work. Because of varied topics and individualized learning, the course can be repeated up to three times (designated by addition of letters to the course id to indicate different semesters of enrollment) *Pre-requisite: Instructor Permission. (Offered by department discretion.)*

EN 271   **Business Communication (3)**

A study of communication concepts as they apply to business, including written communication (email, memos, letters, reports, proposals), interpersonal communication, and oral presentation. *Pre-requisites: BS 101 (pre- or co-requisite), EN 101, EN 102, Sophomore status strongly recommended. (Offered every spring.)*

EN 280   **Special Topics in English (Lower-Level) (1-3)**

This course will provide students and faculty the opportunity to examine current issues or specialized topics within the discipline at a lower-level of study (appropriate for freshmen or sophomore academic experience). Topics will be determined by the department. Class will meet 15 hours for each hour of credit offered. Repeatable for different topics. *(Offered by department discretion.)*

EN 300   **Middle English Literature (3)**

A study of Middle English literature with an emphasis on Chaucer's Canterbury Tales. *Pre-requisites: EN 101, EN 102. (Offered by department discretion).*

EN 301   Shakespeare (3)
A study of the major plays of Shakespeare with special emphasis on the tragedies and comedies. May be repeated up to six hours as content varies.
Pre-requisites: EN 101, EN 102. (Offered fall semesters, odd years.)

EN 304   Restoration and Eighteenth Century British Literature (3)
A course in Restoration and Eighteenth Century literature with an emphasis on John Dryden, John Bunyan, Johnathan Swift, Alexander Pope, and Samuel Johnson. *Pre-requisites: EN 101, EN 102. (Offered by department discretion.)*

EN 305   Milton (3)
An intensive study of Milton's poetry with an emphasis on Comus, Samson, Agonistes, and Paradise Lost. *Pre-requisites: EN 101, EN 102. (Offered spring semesters, even years.)*

EN 307   Romantic British Literature (3)
A study of the major Romantic writers, including William Blake, William Wordsworth, Samuel Taylor Coleridge, George Gordon, Lord Byron, Percy Bysshe Shelley, and John Keats. *Pre-requisites: EN 101, EN 102. (Offered fall semesters, even years.)*

EN 309   Victorian Literature (3)
A study of the major Victorian writers, including Alfred Lord Tennyson, Robert Browning, and Matthew Arnold. *Pre-requisites: EN 101, EN 102. (Offered spring semesters, even years.)*

EN 311   Creative Nonfiction Writing (3)
An intensive course in writing with an emphasis on clear, direct prose. Particular consideration is placed on developing voice development, documenting personal experience, and writing as exploration of self and faith. *Pre-requisites: EN 101, EN 102. (Offered fall semesters, odd years.)*

EN 313   Poetry Writing (3)
A workshop course in which students explore principles and techniques of poetry writing through reading and discussion of traditional and contemporary published poets and apply those principles to their own poetry. Includes critical evaluation of students' original works by the instructor as well as the class. *Pre-requisites: EN 101, EN 102. (Offered fall semesters, even years.)*

EN 317   Short Story Writing (3)
The techniques and process of writing fiction with emphasis on the short story. Readings in published short stories and essays on the art of fiction. Students will write fiction and related forms (journals, autobiography). *Pre-requisites: EN 101, EN 102. (Offered spring semesters, odd years.)*

EN 319   Renaissance Literature (3)
A course in sixteenth and seventeenth British literature with an emphasis upon writers of the Elizabethan and Metaphysical periods, including Phillip Sidney, Edmund Spenser, William Shakespeare (non-dramatic works), Ben Jonson, John Donne, and George Herbert. *Pre-requisites: EN 101, EN 102. (Offered by department discretion.)*

EN 320   Contemporary Literature (3)
Focus on literature written during the postmodern era (approximately 1970-present). The course will include American and British writers, as well as authors reflecting a variety of national and cultural perspectives. *Pre-requisites: EN 101, EN 102. (Offered fall semesters, even years.)*

EN 321   Literature of the United States I (3)
Beginnings to 1865. Representative authors include Anne Bradstreet, Edgar Allan Poe, Nathaniel Hawthorne, Walt Whitman, and Emily Dickinson. *Pre-requisites: EN 101, EN 102. (Offered fall semesters, odd years.)*

EN 322   Literature of the United States II (3)
1865 to 1945. Representative authors include Mark Twain, Kate Chopin, Robert Frost, and William Faulkner. *Pre-requisites: EN 101, EN 102. (Offered spring semesters, even years.)*

EN 324   Twentieth Century British Writers (3)
Writers from England and Ireland from World War I to the present, concentrating on William Butler Yeats, T. S. Eliot, D. H. Lawrence, Virginia Woolf, and Seamus Heaney. *Pre-requisites: EN 101, EN 102. (Offered spring semesters, odd years.)*

EN 325   Literary Magazine Editing (1)
An experiential course in editing of the literary magazine Q. Topics include evaluating manuscripts, magazine layout, copyediting, and printing arrangements. *Pre-requisites: EN 101, EN 102 and permission of professor. May be repeated for credit. (Offered every semester.)*

EN 326   Writing Children's Literature (3)
An in-depth study of creative writing technique specific to children's literature. Participants will become familiar with current trends in children's literature, imitate a favorite author's work, read and discuss major children's novels, and draft/workshop/compose twenty pages of original children's literature. *Pre-requisites: EN 101, EN 102. (Offered spring semesters, even years.)*

EN 329   Outdoor and Nature Writing (3)
A writing workshop focused on the study of models and technique specific to writing about experiences in the outdoors in various genres. Models include Thoreau, Muir, and Dillard.   Emphasis is on description, personal expression, and voice. Out-of-classroom field trips and small fees may be required. *Pre-requisites: EN 101, EN 102. (Offered by department discretion.)*

EN 330   The Writing Process: Theory and Practice (3)
A course designed for students who are Writing Scholars in the Camaraderie of Writers Program. Participation is by invitation only. The course will expose the Writing Scholars to composition theory and advanced revision strategies. It will also develop their abilities to assess and address the needs presented in a peer's paper through written feedback and conferencing. Writing Scholars will be active and reflective participants in the course. *(Offered every fall.)*

EN 341   Practicum (1-3)
Supervised practical experience provides students with an opportunity to integrate classroom instruction with on-the-job learning in various areas of English-related fields. *Pre-requisites: EN 101, EN 102, IS 310, and permission of professor. (Offered by department discretion.)*

EN 402   Literary Criticism (3)
A course in the history and development of important critical literary theories from Plato to the present. Special emphasis will be given to a Christian approach to literature. *Prerequisite: EN 201, 202, 203, or 204. (Offered fall semesters, even years.)*

EN 405   The Imagination and Apologetics of C.S. Lewis (3)
This course will offer a comprehensive view of the works of C.S. Lewis with a focus upon how his imagination helped to shape his apologetics. In addition to reading selections from his letters, journals, poems, fiction, non-fiction, and apologetics, students will view and discuss important new video productions of Lewis' life in order to gain a perspective on the ideas, thoughts, and opinions of the most popular Christian author of the twentieth century. Because Lewis has powerfully influenced so many people, this course will explore his approach to making Christianity intellectually reasonable, theologically winsome, and spiritually compelling. While open to all students who have completed a sophomore level literature course, this course is designed in particular for students majoring in English and Bible and Religion. *Pre-requisite: EN 201, 202, 203, or permission of professor. (Offered spring semesters, odd years.)*

EN 480   Special Topic in English (Upper-Level) (1-3)
This course will provide students and faculty the opportunity to participate in examining current issues or specialized topics within the discipline. Topics will be determined by the department. Class will meet 15 hours for each hour of credit offered. A student can repeat for up to six hours of credit. (*Offered by department discretion.*)

EN 490   Bibliography for Research (1)
Recommended to be taken the semester before the senior thesis is due, this course guides students in identifying a topic and selecting appropriate sources in preparation for the senior thesis. Particular attention is given to advanced searching of print and online resources, critical evaluation of Internet information, ethical use of resources in scholarship, and exploring information context and purpose. This course is taught by a librarian in collaboration with the thesis advisor. (*Offered every semester.*)

EN 491   Senior Thesis (2)
Students will develop an extensive presentation or paper, according to their English major concentration—literature or creative writing. A committee which consists of the course professor, the concentration main professor, and one member chosen by the student will specify the thesis parameters, approve the topic at the beginning of the semester, and grade the final paper. (*Offered every semester.*)

ENVIRONMENTAL STUDIES (ES)

ES 200   Introduction to Environmental Studies (3)
This course provides a broad foundational understanding of the field of environmental studies while using the environment as the integrating concept. Topics include environmental philosophy and theology, nature literature, environmental science and related issues, and environmental history, policy, and law.

ES 201-202   Field Natural History I, II (2, 2)
This field-based course covers a broad range of topics useful for environmental educators, naturalists, and environmental biologists, including landscape ecology, taxonomy, geomorphology, winter ecology, and field meteorology. Although science-based, the course integrates discussion of seminal natural history literature into the class structure. Various methods for teaching natural history in the field will be demonstrated. Students develop a nature journal that chronicles seasonal changes in the natural world.

ES 206   Ecology (4)
A course stressing the relationship of organisms to their environment including both living and nonliving factors. Topics include population dynamics, community interactions, energy flow, biogeochemical cycling, winter adaptation, and soil dynamics. Three hours lecture and three hours lab per week. *Pre-requisite: BL 101-102, or permission of professor.*

ES 210   Environmental Sustainability (3)
This course explores the concepts of environmental, social, and economic sustainability as they relate to decision making in the field of natural resource management. Students critically examine real-world environmental problems and develop possible solutions using a systems-based approach. Topics covered include: the nature of ecosystems, sustainable resource management, sustainable community development, environmental stewardship, green building, and sustainable energy. *Pre-requisite: ES 206.*

ES/BL 230   Sophomore Science Seminar (0.5)
Science training in academic and professional skills. These courses will complement students' development at progressive levels of their program training.

ES 280   Special Topics in Environmental Studies (Lower-Level) (1-3)
This course will provide students and faculty the opportunity to examine current issues or specialized topics within the discipline at a lower-level of study (appropriate for freshmen or sophomore academic experience). Topics will be determined by the department. Class will meet 15 hours for each hour of credit offered. Repeatable for different topics. *(Offered by department discretion.)*

ES 301   Physical and Environmental Geography (4)
This course will take an in-depth look at the geographic regions of the world known as biomes. The geological, topographical, and climatic dynamics of each area will be related to ecological integrations. The study of each biome will emphasize representative plant and animal species, as well as rates of successional change. Three hours lecture and three hours lab per week. *Pre-requisite: ES 206 or permission of professor.*

ES 305   American Ecosystems (4)
Ecological analysis of field study sites and public education facilities in selected biomes and life zones. Ecosystem comparisons will be developed with particular attention given to the survey of flora and fauna. This course will also study land management and public utilization of ecological regions. Special emphasis will be placed on environmental education programs that educate the public about each biome or life zone. Course location will vary with each offering. Fee. *Pre-requisite: ES 206 or permission of professor. (Offered on occasion, summers only.)*

ES 315   Freshwater Ecosystems (4)
Chemical, physical, and ecological features of biotic and aquatic systems in the mountains of Western North Carolina. Included are the use and development of chemical and biotic monitoring of freshwater ecosystems and population dynamics associated with nutrient level disruption. Three hours lecture and three hours lab per week. *Pre-requisite: BL 101-102; CH 201-202 or permission of professor. (Offered fall semesters, even years.)*

ES/BL 340   Research Methods (3)
Participation in faculty-supervised independent research project. Involves a literature review, data collection and analysis, the completion of a written research paper, and an oral presentation. *Pre-requisite: Senior standing or permission of professor.*

ES 341   Practicum (1-3)
Supervised practical experience provides students with the opportunity to integrate classroom instruction with on-the-job learning in areas of environmental studies-related fields. *Pre-requisite: IS 310.*

ES 360   Introduction to Geographic Information Systems (3)
This course introduces students to the fundamental concepts of Geographic Information Systems (GIS) with an emphasis on natural resource management applications. Topics covered include: GIS hardware and software components, data capture methods, analysis of spatial information, and map creation and analysis. *Pre-requisite: ES 206.*

ES 401   Natural Resource Management (3)
This course will utilize a systems approach to environmental analysis and management. Topics include positive and negative feedback, nutrient cycling, environmental fate and transport, and ecosystem management. Special emphasis will be placed on contemporary environmental management issues in the Southern Appalachians. *Pre-requisite ES 301 or permission of professor.*

ES/BL 440   Senior Project or Internship (honors option) (3)
Students are responsible for a project/internship design and proposal. Employment is pursued through a student job search. This project is typically developed during the junior year, employment is during the summer, and the final project presented during the senior year. A research-based project may be considered for honors recognition. All proposals and

evaluation of projects will be approved through the Environmental Studies Review Committee.

ES/BL 445   Senior Science Seminar (1)
Science training in academic and professional skills. These courses will complement students' development at progressive levels of their program training. *Pre-requisite: ES 230 or permission of professor.*

ES 460   Field Studies (1-6)
This variable topic course offers an immersion experience for the purpose of studying specific environments. Course is usually offered during the semester, but during brief, concentrated periods, such as weekends or academic breaks. On occasion, the course is offered during the summer. After attending one or more mandatory pre-trip meetings, students will participate in a study trip to the site. Fee, varies by topic.

ES 480   Special Topics in Environmental Studies (Upper-Level) (1-3)
This course will provide students and faculty the opportunity to examine current issues or specialized topics within the discipline at an upper-level of study (appropriate for junior or senior academic experience). Topics will be determined by the department. Class will meet 15 hours for each hour of credit offered. Repeatable for different topics. *Pre-requisite: Permission of department chair. Offered by department discretion.*

ES 481   Directed Study and Research (1-3)
Students may choose to participate in a directed study of their own choice contingent on faculty availability. Credit varies from 1-3 hours although a student can repeat for up to six hours of credit. *Prerequisite: Junior status or above. A cumulative GPA of 2.5 and approval of the department chair is required.*

EXERCISE SCIENCE (EX)

EX 201   Introduction to Exercise Science (3)
Introduces the various workplace settings as well as the various certification and licenses available in the health and fitness industry. All the core disciplines of exercise science are covered, including biomechanics, exercise physiology, sports psychology, motor control and learning, nutrition, and sports injury.

EX 310   Physiology of Exercise (3)
Study of the physiological response of the cardiovascular, respiratory, endocrine, neural, and muscular systems in the human body during exercise. Students will describe, explain and explore how the body performs and responds to physical activity. *Prerequisites: BL 101, BL 102, BL 206, BL 207; Co-requisite: EX 320.*

EX 320   Exercise Testing & Measurements (3)
A study of the theory and application of graded exercise testing and measurement in the evaluation of physical activity. *Co-requisites: EX 310.*

EX 330   Kinesiology and Biomechanics (4)
The study of human movement, this course investigates the musculoskeletal, neuromuscular and mechanical basis for human movement. The laboratory portion of the course will concentrate on the mathematical concepts and problem solving associated with human movement. *Pre-requisites: BL 206, BL 207.*

EX 340   Exercise Prescription (3)
A study of the application of exercise prescription for individuals varying in age, physique, and initial fitness levels. *Pre-requisites: EX 310, EX 320.*

EX 341   Practicum (3)
A supervised learning experience that provides the student with initial exposure to relevant professional activities. *Pre-requisite: IS 310 and permission of department chair.*

EX 350   Prevention and Treatment of Athletic Injuries (3)
A course designed to provide entry level knowledge in the field of sport related injuries. This course includes units dealing with the history of athletic training, basic anatomy of common injuries, evaluation techniques, preventive measures to reduce the incidences of injuries, and a knowledge of basic treatment procedures to be used after injuries occur. Legal and ethical issues will also be discussed.

EX 441   Internship I (3)
A supervised internship that provides the student with the opportunity to integrate classroom instruction with practical on-the-job learning in various areas of exercise science-related fields. *Pre-requisite: IS 310 and permission of the department chair.*

EX 442   Internship II (3)
A supervised internship experience that is designed to serve as a culminating, hands-on experience for students majoring in exercise science. *Pre-requisite: EX 441 and permission of the department chair.*

EX 450   Rehabilitation and Modalities in Sports Medicine (3)
Methods and techniques in the application of therapeutic modalities and their use in the treatment of athletic injuries while under the guidance of a certified athletic trainer.

EX 490   Senior Seminar (3)
Senior Seminar is a capstone course in the Exercise Science program, connecting classroom experience with professional preparedness and/or professional certification. Students are required to develop a resume and professional portfolio. *Pre-requisite: Senior standing.*

GEOGRAPHY (GG)

GG 313   World Cultural Geography (3)
A study of the geographic features, national and international boundaries, geographical basis of economic production, and cultures of the world.

GREEK (GR)

GR 201   New Testament Greek I (3)
Fundamentals of New Testament Greek emphasizing grammar, reading skills, and translation of simple passages. Course not open to freshmen. *(Offered fall semesters, odd-numbered years.)*

GR 202   New Testament Greek II (3)
Fundamentals of New Testament Greek II builds upon GR 201. This course focuses on expanding vocabulary, learning non-indicative verbal forms, and exposure to participles and infinitives. *(Offered spring semesters, even-numbered years.)*

GR 303   Greek Grammar and Syntax (3)
An intensive review of vocabulary, grammar, and syntax that provides an introduction to the principles of exegesis. *Pre-requisites: Greek 201-202. (Offered fall semesters, even years.)*

GR 304   Greek Exegesis (3)
A study of the Greek text of a New Testament epistle in its historical setting with attention given to sentence structure, doctrines, and patterns for Christian living. *Pre-requisite: Greek 303. (Offered spring semesters, odd years.)*

GR 481   Directed Study and Research (1-3)
Students may choose to participate in a directed study of their own choice contingent on faculty availability. Credit varies from 1-3 hours although a student can repeat for up to six hours of credit. *Prerequisite: Junior status or above. A cumulative GPA of 2.5 and approval of the department chair is required. (Offered by department discretion.)*

HEALTH (HL)

HL 101   Health (3)
Includes functions and structures of the human body; nature of disease and care of the body; local, state, national and international health agencies, and services available; and processes and objectives of healthful living.

HL 102   Advanced First Aid (3)
This course follows the guidelines of the American Red Cross for Cardiopulmonary Resuscitation and other nationally recognized certifying agency's guidelines for the administration of basic first aid. The student will learn and become proficient in providing first aid and CPR in emergent situations. Successful completion of this course will lead to certification in CPR, FA, and AED for Adults. *(Offered spring semesters, odd years.)*

HL 201   Human Nutrition (3)
A study of nutrients, including sources, composition, function, and metabolism in the human body. The human life cycle is considered in planning appropriate diets.

HEBREW (HB)

HB 303   Elementary Biblical Hebrew I (4)
An introduction to the basic elements of biblical Hebrew vocabulary and grammar, introduced through workbook translations and exercises. Includes a conversational Hebrew lab. *(Offered fall semesters, even years.)*

HB 304   Elementary Biblical Hebrew II (4)
An introduction to the basic elements of biblical Hebrew vocabulary and grammar, introduced through workbook translations and exercises. Includes a conversational Hebrew lab. This course focuses on expanding vocabulary, learning non-indicative verbal forms, and exposure to participles and infinitives. *(Offered spring semesters, odd years.)*

HISTORY (HS)

HS 101   World Civilizations I (3)
An interdisciplinary survey course providing a survey of civilizations during the ancient, classical, medieval, and Renaissance eras. The religious, political, economic, and social forces that shaped both Western and non-Western cultures are explored. Historical developments are related to how they shape the contemporary world.

HS 102   World Civilizations II (3)
An interdisciplinary survey course providing a survey of civilizations from the Reformation to the present day. The religious, political, economic, and social forces that shaped both Western and non-Western cultures are explored. Historical developments are related to how they shape the contemporary world.

HS 171   Honors World Civilizations I (3)
An Honors Program history course that explores the history of world civilizations from the ancient to the medieval era through the study of Great Books and primary sources. Interdisciplinary course designed to challenge highly motivated students to a deeper reading in history. Enrollment by invitation only. Fulfills requirement of HS 101.

HS 172   Honors World Civilizations II (3)
An Honors Program history course that explores the history of world civilizations from the Renaissance to the modern era through the study of Great Books and primary sources. Interdisciplinary course designed to challenge highly motivated students to a deeper reading in history. Enrollment by invitation only. Fulfills requirements of HS 102.

HS 201   United States History I (3)
A survey of significant, themes, events, and people in United States history from the pre-Columbian past to the Civil War. Emphasis will be given to the important religious, political, economic, and social forces that shaped the culture and constitution of an emerging nation. North Carolina's role in American history will be highlighted.

HS 202   United States History II (3)
A survey of significant, themes, events, and people in United States history from the Civil War to the present day. Emphasis will be given to the important religious, political, economic, and social forces that shaped the culture and constitution of a modern nation. North Carolina's role in American history will be highlighted.

HS 210   Historical Methods (2)
An introduction to the practice of history including techniques, procedures, and skills of the working historian. The course will concentrate on research methodology, analytical and synthetic thinking skills, and the ability to organize and report research findings in both written and oral form. This course is specifically designed for sophomore History majors and minors. *Pre-requisites: HS 101, 102 (or Co-requisite: HS 171 for Honors students).*

HS 280   Special Topics in History (Lower-Level) (1-3)
This course will provide students and faculty the opportunity to examine current issues or specialized topics within the discipline at a lower-level of study (appropriate for freshmen or sophomore academic experience). Topics will be determined by the department. Class will meet 15 hours for each hour of credit offered. Repeatable for different topics. *(Offered by department discretion.)*

HS 311   Ancient Greece and Rome (3)
A study of the ancient civilizations of Greece and Rome that includes the following topics: the formation of the Greek people, the rise of the Greek city-states, the Persian and Peloponnesian wars, the Macedonian conquests of Philip II and Alexander, the rise of the Roman Republic, the Punic Wars and transition to empire, the Pax Romana, the spread of Christianity, and the decline and fall of Rome. The cultural legacy and historical impact of Greece and Rome on the modern world will be highlighted. *Pre-requisites: HS 101, 102 (or 171-172).*

HS 313   Medieval World (3)
A study of medieval civilizations from the fall of Rome to the eve of the Renaissance with a particular focus on Roman, Germanic, Byzantine, and Arab influences across the European, Mediterranean, and Islamic worlds. Themes include the development of Christianity in matters of church and state; feudalism, urbanism, and society in the Middle Ages; the interaction of world civilizations; and the cultural legacy and historical impact of the medieval world. *Pre-requisites: HS 101, 102 (or 171-172).*

HS 315   Renaissance and Reformation (3)
A cultural history of Europe from the fourteenth through the seventeenth centuries probing the origins of the modern West. Themes include the political, social, cultural, and religious developments that created modern Europe and shaped cross-cultural encounters with the continents of Africa, Asia, South America, and North America. Attention is given to the cultural legacy of the Renaissance and to the widespread impact of the rise of Protestantism. *Pre-requisites: HS 101, 102 (or 171-172).*

HS 317   Modern Europe (3)
The history of Europe from the French Revolution to the fall of the Berlin Wall. Special attention is paid to political, social, cultural, and religious developments including the rise of industrial society, ideologies and protest movements, nation-building, mass politics, materialism, interaction with the non-Western world, and the state of Christianity in modern Europe. *Pre-requisites: HS 101, 102 (or 171-172).*

HS 331   American Revolution and Republic (3)
A study of the causes, ideals, and events of the American Revolution and its aftermath. Themes include the disruption of British North America, the Revolutionary War, the formation of a new Constitution, the establishment of a republic, the rise of Jeffersonian Democracy, and the role and influence of religion in the late colonial and early national period. *Pre-requisites: HS 101, 102 (or 171-172).*

HS 333   American Civil War (3)
An examination of the causes, nature, and consequences of the American Civil War with a particular focus on the military and social dynamics of the war. Other topics include the nature of slavery, the rise of abolitionism, secession and disunion, and the effort to reconstruct American society and government. Special reliance will be placed upon the use of primary source documents. *Pre-requisites: HS 101, 102 (or 171-172).*

HS 335   United States History Since 1945 (3)
A study of post-World War II America from the end of the Second World War to the present. Themes explored include the Cold War at home and abroad, the nature of the modern presidency, liberalism and conservatism as dominant political ideologies, consumerism, popular culture, the social movements and cultural revolutions of the Sixties, foreign policy and domestic debates in the post-9/11 world, and the place of religion in American life. *Pre-requisites: HS 101, 102 (or 171-172).*

HS 341   American Constitutional History (3)
A study of the history of constitutional thought from English common law to contemporary Supreme Court decisions. The influences and precursors to the United States Constitution will be explored as will the proceedings of the Constitutional Convention and ensuing ratification debates. The text, amendments, and history of interpretation will be discussed along with issues such as federal-state relations, civil liberties, and civil rights. *Pre-requisites: HS 101, 102 (or 171-172).*

HS 343   Religious History of America (3)
A survey of the variety of religious expressions in the United States from the colonial era to the present day. The role that religion in general and Christianity in particular have played in American social, cultural, and political life will be emphasized. *Pre-requisites: HS 101, 102 (or 171-172).*

HS 345   American Cultural and Intellectual History (3)
A study of American culture and the role intellectual movements play in shaping it. Special emphasis on the development and global impact of American popular culture as well as how ideas related to religion, race, gender, class, and politics help define the American experience. *Pre-requisites: HS 101, 102 (or 171-172).*

HS 353   History of Christianity (3)
A survey of the Christian movement in history, its beliefs, institutions, and worldwide expansion. Attention will be given to doctrinal and ecclesial development, spirituality and devotional practices, historical expressions of service and ministry, and the dynamic between the church and global societies from the ancient world to the present day. *Pre-requisites: HS 101, 102 (or 171-172).*

HS 355   Modern Middle East (3)
This interdisciplinary course provides an opportunity to move beyond the news headlines in order to explore the emergence of the Modern Middle East from the 18th century to "The Arab Spring". Students will examine Middle Eastern languages, religions and cultures; the impact of imperialism, nationalism, secularism, and militant Islam on the region; and ponder the possibility of peace between Israelis and Palestinians. *Pre-requisites: HS 101, 102 (or 171-172).*

HS 361   The World at War, 1914-1945 (3)
A military, political, social, and cultural overview of First and Second World Wars with special emphasis on the interrelatedness of these conflicts. Extensive use will be made of primary source documents in a variety of mediums. *Pre-requisites: HS 101, 102 (or 171-172).*

HS 363   Global Cold War (3)
This course examines world politics from 1941 to the 1990s. Students will examine the origins of the Cold War, the development of the United States as a superpower on the global stage, and the ways in which the American Cold War rivalry with the Soviet Union played out in Europe, the Middle East, and the Majority World. *Pre-requisites: HS 101, 102 (or 171-172).*

HS 365   Empire and Its Discontents
This course examines the social, cultural, and political implications of European colonialism, imperialism and decolonization from 1492 to the present. Focus is placed on the European conquests of the Americas, the global British Empire, and the preponderance of American influence in the recent past. Themes include colonial and post-colonial identity, religious contact and conflict, and orientalism. *Pre-requisites: HS 101, 102 (or 171-172).*

HS 371   History of Political Philosophy
A survey of political thought from the Greek city-states to the political philosophers of the twentieth century. Topics of study include the foundations of authority, the responsibilities of the state, the nature of justice, understandings and critiques of democracy, and historical understandings of the relation of church and state. Primary sources will be emphasized. *Pre-requisites: HS 101, 102 (or 171-172).*

HS 373   History of Science and Technology
A historical examination from a global perspective of how science and technology have transformed societies and exerted cultural influence in a variety of civilizations. A particular focus will be on how scientific inquiry and technological innovation engender "paradigm shifts" of understanding the world, shape our notions of progress, and are themselves shaped by societal, cultural, and religious assumptions. *Pre-requisites: HS 101, 102 (or 171-172).*

HS 381   Environmental History (3)
This interdisciplinary, experiential learning course will explore how human interaction with nature influences historical outcomes. Special attention is paid to the way nature shapes human history, settlement, and conflict; the ways in which humans have understood, utilized, and transformed the natural world; and how religious, cultural, scientific, and political attitudes toward nature have changed over time. *Pre-requisites: HS 101, 102 (or 171-172).*

HS 383   Public History: Cities Through the Ages (3)
This interdisciplinary, experiential learning course traces a particular city's history and its understanding of its own past. Students will travel to cities such as Charleston SC, Savannah, GA, New Orleans LA, or Washington DC to explore a place's historic identity and the internal

debates between preservation and restoration at national parks, historic homes, public spaces, and religious sites. *Pre-requisites: HS 101, 102 (or 171-172).*

HS 415   Historical Archive Fieldwork (3)

Students will participate in exhibit and archival work at a local historical center. Students will be immersed in this professional context, receive supervision from a professor and on-site supervisor, and write an intensive paper on themes related to public history. *Pre-requisites: This course is for History majors only.*

HS 480   Special Topics in History (Upper-Level) (1-3)

This course will provide students and faculty the opportunity to examine current issues or specialized topics within the discipline at an upper-level of study (appropriate for junior or senior academic experience). Topics will be determined by the department. Class will meet 15 hours for each hour of credit offered. Repeatable for different topics. *(Offered by department discretion.)*

HS 481   Directed Study and Research (1-3)

Students may choose to participate in a directed study of their own choice contingent on faculty availability. Credit varies from 1-3 hours although a student can repeat for up to six hours of credit. *Prerequisite: Junior status or above. A cumulative GPA of 2.5 and approval of the department chair is required.*

HS 491   Senior Thesis (3)

After a survey of the study of history, the student will engage in a personal research project from a Christian perspective. *Pre-requisites: HS 101,102 (or 171-172). (Required of all history majors in the senior year.)*

HONORS (HN)

HN 301   Honors Seminar (2)

This course will begin a three-semester, intensive examination of a single 'Great Book,' Dante's Divine Comedy. These three courses will be divided up along the lines of the tripartite division of Dante's work: Inferno, Purgatorio, and Paradiso. HN 301 will focus on the Inferno and consist of weekly discussion meetings and a class retreat toward the end of the semester, after which students will complete an extensive term paper. *Pre-requisite: Junior standing, acceptance in Honors Program.*

HN 302   Honors Seminar II (2)

This is the second class in a three-semester cycle that involves an intensive examination of a single 'Great Book,' or a series of related Great Books. Examples of likely assigned works include Dante's Divine Comedy, Augustine's City of God or Homer's Iliad and Odyssey along with Virgil's Aeneid. The class will include weekly meeting culminating in a retreat toward the end of the semester. *Pre-requisite: HN 301.*

HN 401   Honors Seminar III (2)

This is the third class in a three-semester cycle that involves an intensive examination of a single 'Great Book,' or a series of related Great Books. Examples of likely assigned works include Dante's Divine Comedy, Augustine's City of God or Homer's Iliad and Odyssey along with Virgil's Aeneid. The class will include weekly meeting culminating in a retreat toward the end of the semester.
Pre-requisite: HN 302.

HUMAN SERVICES (HU)

HU 101   Introduction to Human Services (1)
A survey of the many aspects of human services, including history, current events, future trends, theoretical approaches, counseling skills, professional identity, and the world of work.

HU 241   Field Experience (1)
A Human Services major must fulfill the specified requirements of this course once by the end of the junior year before the internship experience. Field experience consists of hands-on opportunities in various human service-related events or organizations. The student's advisor makes available specific requirements and opportunities as determined by the Human Services department. *Restricted to Psychology and Human Services majors.*

HU 280   Special Topics in Human Services (Lower-Level) (1-3)
This course will provide students and faculty the opportunity to examine current issues or specialized topics within the discipline at a lower-level of study (appropriate for freshmen or sophomore academic experience). Topics will be determined by the department. Class will meet 15 hours for each hour of credit offered. Repeatable for different topics. *(Offered by department discretion.)*

HU/PY 300   Child and Adolescent Development (3)
An overview of the physiological, cognitive, psychosocial, and spiritual aspects of development from conception through age 18. *Prerequisite: PY201 or PY 202 and a minimum of sophomore standing.*

HU/PY 305   Adult Development and Aging (3)
An overview of the physical, cognitive, social, spiritual, and emotional aspects of adult development. *Pre-requisites: PY 201 or PY 202 and a minimum of sophomore standing.*

HU/PY 315   Abnormal Psychology (3)
A survey of the current categories of abnormal behavior emphasizing symptoms, major theories of causality, and current treatment methods. *Pre-requisite: PY 201 or PY 202.*

HU 341   Practicum (1-3)
Supervised field education provides the student with practical on-the-job training in various areas of human service-related fields. Each field education experience is administered by the field education advisor and the supervising facility. Field education may be taken more than once. *Pre-requisite: IS 310. (Offered by department discretion.)*

HU/PY 412   Theories and Principles of Counseling (3)
An examination of several of the major theories of counseling in working with individuals, families, and small groups. Included are principles and techniques utilized in assessment, crisis intervention, contracts, and development of the therapeutic relationship. A skills component is also included. *Pre-requisite: PY 201 or PY 202.*

HU 490   Senior Seminar (3)
Examines the curricular themes of epistemology, human nature, and application of psychological theory in order to answer major Christian worldview questions (what is success in life, how do I become more Christ like, etc.). *Pre-requisites: junior standing or above.*

HU 441   Internship (3)
Supervised internship provides the student with the opportunity to integrate classroom instruction with practical on-the-job learning in various areas of human services related fields. This course is normally taken in the summer after the junior year. *Pre-requisites: IS 310, 12 hours of course work completed at the 300 level or above in the major.*

HU 480   Special Topics in Human Services (Upper-Level) (1-3)
This course will provide students and faculty the opportunity to examine current issues or specialized topics within the discipline at an upper-level of study (appropriate for junior or senior academic experience). Topics will be determined by the department. Class will meet 15 hours for each hour of credit offered. Repeatable for different topics. *(Offered by department discretion.)*

HU 481   Directed Study and Research (1-3)
Students may choose to participate in a directed study of their own choice contingent on faculty availability. Credit varies from 1-3 hours although a student can repeat for up to six hours of credit. *Prerequisite: Junior status or above. A cumulative GPA of 2.5 and approval of the department chair is required.*

INTERDISCIPLINARY STUDIES (IS)

IS 102   Foundations of Faith and Learning (2)
This course is designed to facilitate the transition to college by introducing and examining the relationship between faith and learning in light of the College's mission. Topics include the value and role of Christian education, the nature and purpose of an academic community, academic skills and planning, learning styles, advising, and how faith informs and expresses itself in life. The course will include content selected from the instructor's academic discipline to be explored from a Christian perspective and to serve as a basis to demonstrate academic competence. This course is required of all students entering college as first-time freshman as well as transfer students with less than 12 hours of academic credit. *(Offered every semester.)*

IS 200   Seminar on Faith and Learning (1)
This seminar style course is designed to assist new transfer students with their transition to Montreat College. The course will help to support transfer students through an exploration of individual and group learning strategies. Topics include: the value and role of Christian higher education, basic biblical worldview concepts, the purpose and distinctiveness of the Montreat College academic community, and how faith informs and expresses itself in life. This course is required in the first semester enrolled at Montreat College for all transfer students entering the College with more than 12 college transfer credits *(Offered every semester.)*

IS 202   Modern Secular-Christian Worldviews (3)
An interdisciplinary course examining the worldviews, trends, and problems of twentieth-century Western humankind. A Christian worldview and secular thought will be contrasted in several areas, including science and modern literature. *Prerequisite: HS 101-102. (Offered fall semesters, odd years.)*

IS 251   Academic Studies Abroad (1-6)
Selected academic topics—biblical, business, historical, linguistics, literary, mathematics, and science—with emphasis on their relationship to physical and cultural settings. Residence abroad. Normally offered during breaks and summer sessions. *(Offered by department discretion.)*

IS 280   Special Topics (Lower-Level) (1-3)
This course will provide students and faculty the opportunity to examine current issues or specialized topics within the discipline at a lower-level of study (appropriate for freshmen or sophomore academic experience). Topics will be determined by the department. Class will meet 15 hours for each hour of credit offered. Repeatable for different topics. *(Offered by department discretion.)*

IS 302   Philosophy of Leadership (3)
This is an interdisciplinary course designed to stimulate thinking about leadership qualifications, styles, principles, and practices. Emphasis will be placed on developing a personal philosophy of leadership that draws from life experiences, various historical theories, and the Biblical model of Jesus. *Junior standing is strongly recommended. (Offered every spring.)*

IS 306   Science and Theology of Origins (3)
This interdisciplinary course will explore various approaches to the issues surrounding the origins debate. Current theories of origins will be presented and then explored from a variety of world views with special attention to Christian theism. Methods of biblical interpretation will also be explored as they relate to understanding origins as expressed in the Bible. The students will have the opportunity to consider several ways that Christians approach the origins issue and then write a paper expressing their current thoughts on the matter. *(Offered spring semesters, odd years.)*

IS 310   Pre-Practicum/Pre-Internship (1)
The purpose of this course is to prepare students for the practicum/internship experience. Topics included are internship selection, making the most of the internship, resume building, and facing internship challenges. *(Offered every spring.)*

IS 341   Practicum (1-3)
A supervised learning experience that provides one with initial exposure to relevant professional activities. Supervision of the practicum is a shared responsibility between the faculty advisor and on-site supervisor. This course may be repeated; a maximum of three hours may be used to satisfy degree requirements. *Pre-requisite: IS 310, permission of the student's advisor and the BRIS department chair or designee. (Offered by department discretion.)*

IS 421   Leadership Practicum (3)
This course allows leadership minor students to apply the theories learned during specified leadership courses in an active leadership role. Students may serve in a variety of leadership positions in college-approved organizations (such as SGA, SCA, or FCA) as resident assistants, or as captains of varsity athletic teams. The position is for a minimum of one year. Each student must recruit a voluntary advisor within his or her discipline who will serve as counselor and evaluator of the student's leadership performance. Students are required to keep a journal of activities during the term, including lessons learned. Each student prepares, with the approval of the advisor, an evaluation form to include a mission statement, objectives and goals, performance measures, corrective actions, and outcomes. *Prerequisite: IS 310, twelve hours of coursework in the theoretical and applied leadership minor. (Offered by department discretion.)*

IS 441   Internship (3-6)
An intensive, quality, structured learning opportunity that immerses students in appropriate professional contexts. Supervision of the internship is a shared responsibility between the faculty advisor and on-site supervisor. This course may be repeated; a maximum of six hours may be used to satisfy degree requirements. *Pre-requisite: IS 310, junior status, permission of the student's advisor and department chair or designee. (Offered by department discretion.)*

IS 451   Council for Christian Colleges and Universities Internships (1-6)
In cooperation with the council, students may participate in internships through approved CCCU study programs in the U.S. and abroad. Students will be placed in appropriate studies-related work situations. *Pre-requisite: Permission of the Academic Affairs office. See "Special Programs" for more information. (Offered by department discretion.)*

IS 460   Council for Christian Colleges and Universities Seminars (6-8)
In cooperation with the council, students examine selected topics relevant to the approved CCCU study programs in the U.S. and abroad. *Pre-requisite: Permission of the Vice President for Academic Affairs & Dean of the College. See "Special Programs" for more information. (Offered by department discretion.)*

IS 461   Seminar on Faith and Life (2)
A course designed to help students define their personal Christian philosophy of life by integrating faith and learning. Students are challenged to explore their Christian calling and to consider ways in which they can exert Christian influence in the world today. *Pre-requisite: Senior standing or permission of professor. (Offered every semester.)*

IS 480   Special Topics (Upper-Level) (1-3)
This course will provide students and faculty the opportunity to examine current issues or specialized topics within the discipline at an upper-level of study (appropriate for junior or senior academic experience). Topics will be determined by the department. Class will meet 15 hours for each hour of credit offered. Repeatable for different topics. *(Offered by department discretion.)*

IS 481   Directed Study and Research (1-3)
Students may choose to participate in a directed study of their own choice contingent on faculty availability. Credit varies from 1-3 hours although a student can repeat for up to six hours of credit. *Prerequisite: Junior status or above. A cumulative GPA of 2.5 and approval of the department chair is required. (Offered by department discretion.)*

IS 491   Senior Thesis (3)
Students develop an extensive paper under the direction of a faculty member that demonstrates their ability to do senior-level research and writing on a specialized topic in theology, philosophy, or cross-cultural studies. A committee comprised of the course professor, another member of the division, and a member chosen by the student evaluates and grade the thesis. *(Offered by department discretion.)*

MATHEMATICS (MT)

MT 101   Introduction to Mathematics (3)
A survey of mathematics including a sampling of topics from the history of mathematics, logic, set theory, algebra, geometry, number theory, business math, and other topics.

MT 114   Elementary Probability and Statistics (3)
A non-calculus course designed to introduce elementary concepts in descriptive statistics, probability, sampling distributions, linear regression, correlation, estimation, and hypothesis testing. Applications taken from a variety of disciplines including social sciences and business. Analyses of observed data are performed manually, by calculator, and by computer. *(Offered every semester.)*

MT 121   College Algebra (3)
A course that explores fundamental concepts of algebra including properties of real numbers, equations and inequalities, polynomial and other algebraic functions and their graphs. Additional topics may include solving systems of equations and inequalities, matrices and determinants, conic sections, etc. *Prerequisite: Grade of B or above in high school algebra II or the equivalent.*

MT 122   College Trigonometry (3)
A course that explores exponential and logarithmic functions as well as fundamental concepts of trigonometry. Topics covered will include triangle trigonometry, the trigonometric functions, their inverses, and their graphs. Trigonometric equations and trigonometric

identities will be explored as trigonometry is applied to various situations. *Prerequisite: Grade of B or above in high school Algebra II or the equivalent.*

MT 191   Applied Calculus I (4)

Differential and integral calculus of the polynomial, logarithmic, and exponential functions, including limits and continuity; rules of differentiation and integration; applications in the life sciences and business, including maximum/minimum problems and related rates; and the fundamental theorem of calculus. *Prerequisite: Grade of C or above in MT 121 or a grade of B or above in high school algebra II or equivalent.*

MT 192   Applied Calculus II (4)

A continuation of Calculus I that includes trigonometric functions, techniques of integration, functions of two and three variables, differential equations, sequences and series, and probability. Applications will continue to be emphasized. *Prerequisite: MT 191 and 122 or high school equivalent.*

MUSIC (MS)

MS 100   Seminar in Music Performance (.5)

Required weekly attendance for all music majors enrolled in applied music. An important venue for weekly performances, it includes attendance at local area music productions. Successful completion required each semester of enrollment.

MS 101   Introduction to Music (3)

An introduction to materials and properties of music, musical media, and categories of musical literature with a concentration in music of the Baroque, Classical, Romantic, and Modern eras.

MS 103   Beginning Class: Piano (2)

Intended for students who have not previously studied piano. In addition to mastering note reading and playing simple pieces, students develop the ability to play chord progressions, harmonize simple melodies, and explore other keyboard capabilities.

MS 104   Beginning Class: Voice (2)

Intended for students who have not previously studied voice. Students learn basic concepts of producing good sound including proper breath management, good diction, and developing the full range of voice. Opportunity to sing for and listen to colleagues is an important aspect of this course.

MS 105   Beginning Class: Guitar (2)

Intended for students who have not previously studied guitar. Students learn to play notes and chords, read music notation, play simple music from several styles, and do a variety of other guitar-related activities.

MS 106   Music Business Forum (0)

This course will consist of a mixture of guest speakers from the Music and Entertainment Industries, group discussion of current news and special topics in the Music Industry, and songwriting showcase with student feedback.

MS 113   Music Theory I (4)

Music Theory I is a comprehensive study of music fundamentals, including notation, key signatures, scales, intervals, diatonic harmony and non-harmonic tones, in preparation for the study of four-part harmony in MS 213. Aural skills include sight-singing and rhythm exercises; melodic, harmonic, and rhythmic dictation; and the basic keyboard skills required for comprehension of the concepts taught in this course. (*Offered fall semesters, even years.*)

MS 114   Music Theory II (4)
Music Theory II builds upon the fundamental concepts and skills presented in MS 113.
Emphasis is on harmony and voice leading practices in traditional four-part chorale style;
chordal progressions and resolution tendencies; dominant and non-dominant seventh chords;
and modulation to related keys. Continued development of aural skills includes progressive
sight-singing, rhythm, and keyboard exercises; melodic, rhythmic, and harmonic dictation.
(*Offered spring semesters, odd years.*)

MS 121   Survey of Music Production, Marketing, and Distribution (3)
This course provides core knowledge of current business, legal and marketing practices
unique to the music industry. Topics include music publishing, recording, marketing and
distribution.

MS 122   Survey of Music and Artist Management (3)
This course provides core knowledge of current business, legal and marketing practices
unique to the music industry. Topics include artist management, concert promotion, and arts
administration.

MS 131   Introduction to Digital Sound Recording (3)
Introduction to the equipment of the recording studio and its use, audio session procedures,
and guided experiences in recording. Emphasis on independent recording projects using
multi-track recording, sequencing, signal processing, and MIDI technologies. Includes an
overview of acoustics and sound in church and/or performance settings.

MS 133-134, 233-234   Applied Group Lessons (1, 1, 1, 1)
A study of musical performance techniques and literature open to students of all levels of
proficiency. Students apply their studies in a group setting with individual attention given to
each student. Opportunity to play for and listen to music colleagues is an important aspect of
this course. Some studio class and concert attendance requirements are included. *Fee.*

MS 141-142, 241-242   Applied Piano (1, 1, 1, 1)
Students are accepted at various levels of proficiency, and their ability to play the piano in a
musical way is further developed. Piano literature selected is suited to the capacity of the
student and consists of art music pieces from the Baroque era to the present. Some popular
music of the student's choosing may be included. Some studio class and concert attendance
requirements included. *Fee $95.*

MS 143-144, 243-244   Applied Voice (1, 1, 1, 1)
Emphasis is placed on the use of the voice as a natural instrument. The ultimate goal is an
artistic style of singing that includes beautiful tone and dependable technique. As the voice is
developed, literature suited to the capacity of the student and drawn from the best works of
great masters is studied. Some popular music of the student's choosing may be included.
Some studio class and concert attendance requirements included. *Fee.*

MS 145-146, 245-246   Applied Organ (1, 1, 1, 1)
The course includes a thorough grounding in registration, means of expression necessary to
minimize the highly mechanical nature of the instrument, and pedal technique. The choice of
music is determined by the capacity of the student and the instrument being played. *Fee. Pre-
requisites: Moderate level of piano proficiency and permission of professor.*

MS 147-148, 247-248   Applied Music (1, 1, 1, 1)
Instrumental: Guitar, Clarinet, Flute, Saxophone, Violin, Viola, Cello, Percussion, Folk Strings. A
study of technique and literature open to students of all levels of proficiency. Some studio
class and concert attendance requirements included. *Fee.*

MS 151   College Choir (1)
A select choral group of mixed voices that explores all historical and stylistic music that brings
praise to the Lord. The choir presents public concerts, regional tours, and participates in

chapel and church services, convocations, and other events. Purchase of formal wear is required. *May be repeated for credit.*

MS 153   Guitar Ensemble (1)

Intended for students with some experience in reading music and playing classical guitar. Students will develop skills that enable them to perform classical music on a challenging level in an ensemble setting. The ensemble will be expected to perform at events on and off campus. *Prerequisites: Music 105, 147, or permission of instructor. Materials: Classical guitar, footstool, and music as needed. May be repeated for credit.*

MS 154   Instrumental Chamber Ensemble (1)

An ensemble for students with some prior study and ensemble experience on a string or woodwind instrument. The ensemble meets twice per week, and may be expected to perform occasionally on or off-campus. *Pre-requisite: 2 years of study on the instrument, or permission of professor. May be repeated for credit.*

MS 156   Accompanying (1)

A repeatable course designed primarily to fulfill ensemble requirements for Piano majors. Emphasis on development of sight reading, listening, and ensemble skills needed for effective accompaniment. Includes supervised collaboration with student soloists and ensembles, and some performances. *Pre-requisite: permission of professor.*

MS 157   Rock Ensemble (1)

This course provides an introduction to the technique, musical expressiveness, and stylistic performance practices appropriate for rock, pop, country, R&B, and other modern music styles. Students are required to attend rehearsals 3-4 hours per week and to perform live on or off campus. Includes two non-performing opportunities in audio engineering and management. *Audition/ Interview Required.*

MS 202   A Social History of Rock and Roll (3)

This course explores the development of the rock-and-roll phenomenon from its roots in rhythm and blues, jazz and swing and country western music to its maturity and popularity in the latter part of the twentieth century. Carious genres that have been viewed as sub categories or rock-and-roll are defined and examined. A study of influential and popular rock-and-roll musicians, their lives, and their music are included. The course also examines the social and political forces that spawned and nourished this influential genre of music, and also analyzed the effect that rock-and-roll has had on society. Christian principles in relation to participation in rock-and-roll will also be discussed as well as how rock-and-roll has affected the Christian community.

MS 206   Rhythm Studies (3)

This course will investigate the nature of rhythm observed from a rainbow of musical idioms. The idioms used for study will be determined by the students' own prior musical experiences, their main fields of study, and the instructor's recommendations. Topics include clave, hemiola, polyrhythm, north and south Indian rhythm and counting, and time. The topic of time will include timekeeping; metronome and click track techniques, and feel.

MS 209   MAPP Recording Studio Management (3)

Covers the administrative functions unique to the modern commercial recording studio including accounting, marketing, personnel, planning, and facility management.

MS 213   Music Theory III (4)

Music Theory III is a continuation of the study of melodic, harmonic, and formal elements used in the Common Practice Era. Includes an introduction to extended tertian and chromatic harmony; a brief study of each of the standard Classical forms; and early 19th c. Romantic style. Continued development of aural skills includes progressive sight-singing, rhythm, and keyboard exercises; advanced melodic, rhythmic, and harmonic dictation. *(Offered fall semesters, odd years.)*

MS 214   Music Theory IV (4)
Music Theory IV is a continuation of the study of 19th c. compositional techniques, including increased chromaticism and foreign modulation in the Late Romantic and Impressionist periods; and an introduction to the eclecticism and experimental techniques of the early 20th century, including serialism. Continued development of aural skills includes progressive sight-singing, rhythm, and keyboard exercises; advanced melodic, rhythmic, and harmonic dictation. (*Offered spring semesters, even years.*)

MS 221   Introduction to the Recording Studio (3)
Introduction to the equipment of the recording studio and its use, audio session procedures, and guided experiences in recording in the professional commercial recording studio environment. Will include independent work using current multi-track recording and processing equipment at Echo Mountain Recording Studio, a commercial recording facility in Asheville, NC. All classes are conducted off-campus at this location.

MS 223   Advanced Studio Production (3)
This course covers the use of Pro-Tools audio production software and its integration with the commercial recording studio. It will include independent work using current multi-track recording and processing equipment at Echo Mountain Recording Studio, a commercial recording facility in Asheville, NC. All classes are conducted off campus at this location. (*Offered every spring*)

MS 232   MAPP Critical Listening (1)
Ear-training for producers and recording engineers. Class activities involve listening and analysis of master tape and disc formats. Will include a range of music genres as well as specialized technical ear-training.

MS 251   Chamber Choir (1)
A choral ensemble that explores challenging repertoire from the Renaissance to the twenty-first century, the choir performs in concerts with the Concert Choir as well as in chapel and church services, madrigal dinners, and other functions. Above average sight-singing and vocal abilities necessary. Successful audition required.

MS 257   Songwriting Ensemble (1)
The purpose of this course is to develop individual and ensemble creativity and experience in writing, arranging, and performing original music. Students are required to attend rehearsals 3-4 hours per week and to perform live on or off campus. Includes two non-performing opportunities in audio engineering and management. *Prerequisites: Completion of MS-157 or instructor approval, Audition/ Interview required.*

MS 261- 262   Music and Artist Management Seminar I & II (2, 2)
This course integrates theoretical and practical knowledge with experience relevant to the music business through completion of a major live event. Students in this course plan and produce the annual "Battle of the Bands" and are responsible for all aspects of the event from scheduling and marketing, to financial management, to technical aspects to stage design and logistics. Enrollment required for all music business majors. (*Offered every semester.*)

MS 280   Special Topics in Music (Lower-Level) (1-3)
This course will provide students and faculty the opportunity to examine current issues or specialized topics within the discipline at a lower-level of study (appropriate for freshmen or sophomore academic experience). Topics will be determined by the department. Class will meet 15 hours for each hour of credit offered. Repeatable for different topics. (*Offered by department discretion.*)

MS 301　　Midi and Sound Synthesis (3)
An introduction to hardware and software applications for the musician's use. Topics include the use of MIDI for record, playback, sequencing, arranging and preparation of music for publication, composition, and the use of Web and Internet resources for musicians. *Pre- or Co-requisite: MS 113 or permission of professor. (Offered spring semesters, even years.)*

MS 303　　Special Topics Seminar (3)
Emphasis on topics of interest in either keyboard or voice disciplines.

MS 305　　Survey of Musical Styles I (3)
This course is a fast-paced survey of Western music history, antiquity to the 21st century, identifying the defining hallmarks of each period of change and development and citing representative composers and compositions for each. The course seeks to provide the student with a panoramic perspective.

MS 306　　Survey of Musical Styles II (3)
Having completed MS 305, this course moves the student from the panoramic vantage point to a specific locale. This course, with an emphasis on research and writing, allows the student to take up residence with a genre and/or subgenre and discover how it has had an impact on history, society and faith. *Pre-requisite: MS 305.*

MS 307　　History of Congregational Song (3)
This course is an informational and useful survey of the most-incorporated tool in Christian worship: congregational song. Besides the historical survey, the study of song as musical composition is a dimension of the course with students actively involved in creating texts and tunes.

MS 319　　Arranging (3)
Instrumentation, notation, song writing, and other compositional issues related to the creation and adaptation of music for use in worship and other musical environments. Development of skills to provide the student with the musical versatility to flourish within various musical situations. *Pre-requisites: MS 113 and MS 114 or permission of professor.*

MS 322　　Live Sound and Lighting (3)
An exploration of the philosophical foundation and the practical use of current technology employed in worship settings. Students will gain hands-on experience with hardware and software involved with lighting, projection, video editing, and audio recording. Taught by a select team of professionals.

MS 325　　MAPP Digital Sound Processing (3)
An overview of digital audio technology with an emphasis on sound processing related to music production.

MS 326　　MAPP Mastering (3)
An advanced hands-on approach to the principles and practices of mastering. Focuses on the use of digital audio workstations specially designed for audio mastering and related outboard equipment. Additional focus on surround mastering and DVD authoring.

MS 331　　Copyright Law (3)
This course provides an overview of intellectual property law with a focus on copyright law. Special topics covered in the course include communications law, music law and corporate IP issues.

MS 332　　Music Publishing (3)
This course applies the foundation established in MS 331 Copyright Law in a business setting (how those rights are monetized and exploited). The course will cover all aspects of the music publishing industry with a focus on multi-media licensing. Students will learn how to set up a publishing company and be prepared to represent both publishing companies and artists in business matters. *Pre-requisite: MS 331*

MS 341-342, 441-442   Applied Piano (1, 1, 1, 1)
A continuation of MS 141-142, 241-242. Advanced playing techniques are studied. Emphasis on pedagogy, interpretation, mechanics of sound production, and physiological aspects of keyboard playing. Literature includes that from the Baroque through the Modern eras. *Fee. Pre-requisites: Successful completion of 200-level piano instruction and permission of professor.*

MS 343-344, 443-444   Applied Voice (1, 1, 1, 1)
A continuation of MS 143-144, 243-244. Advanced techniques of singing are studied. Emphasis on pedagogical and scientific aspects of the singing art. Literature includes that from classic and Romantic era opera and art song. *Fee. Pre-requisites: Successful completion of 200-level voice instruction and permission of professor.*

MS 345-346, 445-446   Applied Organ (1, 1, 1, 1)
A continuation of MS 145-146, 245-246. Studies include advanced techniques in registration and pedaling. Emphasis on service playing, and artistic and interpretive aspects of the organ. Literature drawn from Renaissance to Modern repertory. *Fee.*

MS 347-348, 447-448   Applied Music (1, 1, 1, 1)
Instrumental: Guitar, Clarinet, Flute, Saxophone, Violin, Viola, Cello, Percussion, Folk Strings. A study of technique and literature open to students of all levels of proficiency. Some studio class and concert attendance requirements included. *Fee.*

MS 357 Advanced Rock Ensemble (1)
This course provides advanced instruction in the technique, musical expressiveness, and stylistic performance practices appropriate for rock, pop, country, R&B, and other modern music styles. Students are required to attend rehearsals 3-4 hours per week and to perform live on or off campus. Includes two non-performing opportunities in audio engineering and management. *Prerequisites: Completion of MS 157 or MS 257 or instructor approval. Audition/ Interview required.*

MS 361- 362   Music Production, Marketing, and Distribution Seminar I & II (3, 3)
This course integrates theoretical and practical knowledge with experience relevant to the music business through completion of a required major project where students produce, market, and distribute a commercially viable music recording. Students are responsible for all aspects of the project from initial research and development of a viable prospectus to production, marketing and distribution. Enrollment required for all upper-division music business majors. *(Offered every semester.)*

MS 401   Choral Conducting (2)
A study of basic conducting patterns, techniques, and rehearsal procedures. Laboratory experiences are concerned with learning about music through the rehearsal and study of choral literature. Emphasis is placed upon gestural technique and score study to effectively communicate characteristics of style and the performance practice of music from various musical periods.

MS 405   Choral Methods (2)
The exploration of resources, methods, and techniques useful for leading a choir in church or school. Of particular emphasis is group vocal techniques, sight-singing techniques, and ensemble diction for choirs using IPA, *Pre-requisite: MS 401.*

MS 451   Practicum in Music Business (2-3)
In-depth experience in selected music industry tailored to the ability and needs of individual students. *Pre-requisites: IS 310, Junior standing.*

MS 461- 462   Music Business Seminar V & VI (2, 2)
This course focuses on the integration of interdisciplinary theoretical and practical knowledge and experience relevant to the music business. Course involves a student independent

project. Course may be included as part of an immersion semester during the senior year. Enrollment required for all upper-division music business majors. *(Offered every semester.)*

MS 480   Special Topics in Music (Upper-Level) (1-3)

This course will provide students and faculty the opportunity to examine current issues or specialized topics within the discipline at an upper-level of study (appropriate for junior or senior academic experience). Topics will be determined by the department. Class will meet 15 hours for each hour of credit offered. Repeatable for different topics. *(Offered by department discretion.)*

MS 481   Directed Study and Research (1-3)

Students may choose to participate in a directed study of their own choice contingent on faculty availability. Credit varies from 1-3 hours. *Pre-requisites: Junior status or above. A cumulative GPA of 2.5 and approval of the department chair is required.*

MS 485   Senior Studies in Music Business (3)

This is a capstone course designed to integrate knowledge and experience established throughout the music business curriculum. Students will develop a unique and practical plan for a viable, music-related venture or develop a solution to a problem or issue related to the industry. Students will be expected to demonstrate the ability to practice innovation, establish a productive team and work schedule and produce a compelling and viable plan that includes an effective marketing strategy.

MS 485L   Senior Studies in Music Business Lab (1)

Lab component of the MS 485 capstone course. This course is a component of the Montreat Audio Production Program (MAPP) immersion semester. In this lab, students address and develop solutions to problems related to the production, distribution or marketing of music.

OUTDOOR EDUCATION (OE)

OE 103   Survey of Outdoor Education I (3)

This course introduces students to foundational topics in outdoor education. Topics include key terms, core competencies of professional outdoor educators and leaders, historical trends, facilitation and processing skills, environmental stewardship, teaching strategies, career options and participation in and development of integrated outdoor experiences. A variety of teaching methods including discussion, field experiences, movies, books, and articles will be used. Students begin development of a portfolio that will continue to develop throughout the program of study. Students are required to attend out-of-class experiences that complement the theoretical content. *Fee*

OE 111   Facilitating Outdoor Education Experiences (3)

This course will cover techniques and principles involved in organizing, presenting and facilitation outdoor education activities and program. Students will develop a repertoire of adventure education and environmental education activities and discuss practices and concepts involved in debriefing activities to maximize participants' growth. This course will also include and integration of the disciplines of adventure education and environmental education.

OE 180   Discovery Wilderness Expedition (4)

An 18-22- day wilderness expedition that may include backpacking, rock climbing, whitewater canoeing, camping, route finding, a solo experience, and a personal challenge event. Through these experiences, students focus on individual and group development in four core areas: stewardship, discipleship, community, and leadership. Emphasis is on spiritual growth and Christian fellowship. A reflective paper will be required. Discovery is a physically challenging course but possible for participants in average physical condition. Challenge and risk are part of the teaching methodologies of the program, and although managed to provide as much safety as possible, all risks cannot be removed. Completion of OE 180 is required in the first year for OE/OM majors. Completion of OE 180 will fulfill one PE credit requirement. *Fee.*

OE 182   Wilderness Journey (2-4)
Students will participate in an expedition to a natural area of the world where they will be involved in experiences that develop their leadership, decision-making, judgment and technical skills using adventure and environmental education. Expeditions will enhance student's training by offering experiences not covered in other OR courses. The expeditions may focus on specific models of travel (ex: sea kayaking, mountaineering, ice climbing, etc.) or a uniquely different environment (ex: international locations, desert southwest, etc.) Trip length will be 12-22 days. A reflective paper will be required. This course is physically challenging but possible for participants in average physical condition. Challenge and risk are part of the teaching methodologies of the program, and although managed to provide as much safety as possible, all risks cannot be removed. Completion of OE 182 will fulfill one PE credit requirement and meets an Outdoor Ministry minor requirement. *Fee.*

OE 191   Outdoor Living Skills I (2)
This course reinforces the skills learned from OE 180 and continues to increase the competency of living safely, comfortably, and respectfully in the outdoors. The primary focus is on honing the skills of shelter set-up, fire building, navigation, and quality backcountry cooking over an open fire. Course includes a required four-day backpacking trip – dates to be announced in class. *Pre-requisite: OE 180 or permission of professor. Transfer OE/OM students can take OE 191 without the OE 180 pre- requisite. (Offered every fall.)*

OE 192   Outdoor Living Skills II (2)
This course will continue to build on the skills learned in OE 191 and will introduce backcountry emergency & risk management, expedition travel techniques, monitoring group safety, cooking using stoves, and leave no trace environmental ethics. It also develops the confidence of those intending to lead others backpacking and camping in a wilderness setting by offering an opportunity for peer teaching. Course includes a required four-day backpacking trip – dates to be announced in class. *Pre-requisite: OE 180, OE 191, or permission of professor. Transfer OE/OM students can take OE 192 without the OE 180 pre- requisite. (Offered every spring.)*

OE 210   Challenge Course Facilitation (3)
This course will focus on the facilitation of challenge course elements including fixed and portable low initiatives, fixed high ropes courses, and climbing towers. The course is intended to provide an overview of the challenge course industry and necessary skills for the facilitation of challenge course programming. Emphasis will be placed on group processing skills, technical equipment and skills, and management/assessment techniques. This course will follow industry standards as set forth by the Association for Challenge Course Technology (ACCT). This course is not an ACCT or Montreat College Team and Leadership Center facilitator certification, training or testing, but should provide students with a foundation to move forward to become certified should they wish to do so on their own.

OE 220   Survey of Environmental Education Curricula (3)
In this course, students will be trained to use curricula, such as Project WET, Project WILD, Project Learning Tree, Aquatic WILD, and/or CATCH so that they can creatively teach others about content included in each curriculum. These curricula can be used in most outdoor education settings with a variety of age groups. Students who participate in this class progress toward fulfilling the instructional workshop requirement for the North Carolina Environmental Education Certification.

OE 225   Conference and Event Planning (1-3)
This course is designed to expose students to the planning and organization of a professional Outdoor Education related conference. The students will gain experience in organization, development and follow through of the details needed to carry out a professional conference including carious levels of the conference planning and evaluation.

OE 241   Field Experience (1-2)
An Outdoor Education/Outdoor Ministry major must fulfill the specified requirements of two different field experiences for 1 credit hour each before doing an OE/OM internship in the junior or senior year. Field experiences consist of hands-on opportunities in various outdoor education/ministry-related events or organizations. Each credit hour earned requires 40 hours of on-site involvement during an agreed upon length of time. *Pre-requisites: Permission of the student's field experience supervisor. (A fee per credit hour is assessed for field experiences during the summer. During the semester the credit counts within the load).*

OE 280   Special Topics in Outdoor Education (Lower-Level) (1-3)
This course will provide students and faculty the opportunity to examine current issues or specialized topics within the discipline at a lower-level of study (appropriate for freshmen or sophomore academic experience). Topics will be determined by the department. Class will meet 15 hours for each hour of credit offered. Repeatable for different topics. *(Offered by department discretion.)*

OE 300   Survey of Adventure-Based Counseling (3)
This course is intended to provide an overview of the theoretical underpinnings, conceptual foundations, and necessary skills related to the field of Adventure-Based Counseling. Topics will include history, theories, ethical issues, populations, faith considerations, and specific skills & techniques related to Experiential Therapy, particularly in an adventure context. Students will be encouraged to participate in personal reflection and processing related to class content. The course will include at least one day-long site visit and one day-long Adventure-Based Counseling experience. *Prerequisite: PY 201 or 202.*

OE 305   Environmental Policy and Law (3)
A course designed to acquaint students with the history of natural resource management, agencies that manage public lands, and laws created to protect natural resources. Students will also explore policies of the United States government, and current agencies and laws that govern use or abuse of the environment. Students travel to Washington, DC as a part of this course. *Fee.*

OE 306   Leadership and Group Dynamics (3)
This interdisciplinary course is for students who want to become more effective as a small group participant and leader. It focuses on different types of small groups and the communication skills essential for effective group participation and facilitation. Theory is coupled with experiential learning to gain an understanding of group development and leadership that enriches individual lives and builds a Christian community

OE 310   Principles of Environmental Interpretation (3)
This course prepares students to communicate clearly in written, spoken and visual forms. The overriding focus of the course is to prepare students to design and present displays, exhibits, brochures and public programs in a professional and understandable manner. The National Park Service (NPS) philosophy of interpretation is used as a model in this course since the NPS has perfected techniques for communicating technical information to lay publics in an informal, relaxed atmosphere.

OE 311   Outdoor Programming and Leadership: Kayaking (4)
A course offering instruction in leading whitewater kayaking programs. Emphasis is on instruction techniques, programming considerations, skill development, and professional leadership. Students gain teaching and leadership experience. Successful completion of this

course may qualify students for certification through the American Canoe Association. *Pre-requisites: OE 340 and PE 240 and/or PE 241 or permission of instructor.*

OE 312   Outdoor Programming and Leadership: Expedition Management (4)
A wilderness leadership course which offers advanced instruction in leadership skills such as judgment and decision-making, group management, route and ration planning, land navigation, teaching and facilitation techniques, and risk management. Emphasis is on professional leadership development. Course includes a required backpacking trip. *Pre-requisites: OE 180, OE 191-192 and OE 340 or permission of instructor.*

OE 313   Outdoor Programming and Leadership: Rock Climbing (4)
A course offering instruction in leading rock climbing programs. Emphasis is on instruction techniques, programming considerations, skill development, and professional leadership. Students gain teaching and leadership experience. *Pre-requisites: OE 340 and PE 220 and/or PE 221 or permission of instructor.*

OE 314   Outdoor Programming and Leadership: Canoeing (4)
A course offering instruction in leading whitewater canoeing programs. Emphasis is on instruction techniques, programming considerations, skill development, and professional leadership. Students gain teaching and leadership experience. Successful completion of this course may qualify students for certification through the American Canoe Association. *Fee for certification. Pre-requisites: OE 340 and PE 230 and/or PE 231 or permission of instructor.*

OE 340   Teaching Methods & Curriculum Development in Outdoor Education (4)
This course focuses on the development of curricula that integrates adventure education and environmental education from a Christian perspective. Students develop a philosophy of teaching and have opportunities to observe teachers and practice teaching techniques in local school and programs. Three hours lecture and three hours lab per week.

OE 341   Practicum (1-3)
A supervised learning experience that provides the student with initial exposure to relevant professional activities. Supervision of the practicum is a shared responsibility between the faculty advisor and on-site supervisor. This course may be repeated; a maximum of three (3) hours may be used to satisfy degree requirements. *Pre-requisites: IS 310, permission of the student's advisor and department chair or designee.*

OE 404   Administration and Management of Outdoor Education (4)
A study of administrative procedures for a broad scope of outdoor education programs. Topics will include personnel and facility management, program development, boards and committees, fiscal planning, staff hiring and training, public relations, insurance, record keeping, marketing and risk management. Students will develop the administrative infrastructure for a new program. Course includes at least three site visits to local Outdoor Education facilities. *Prerequisites: OE 310, OM 300 and senior standing in the major.*

OE 441   Internship (3)
Designed to serve as a culminating field experience for students majoring in outdoor education, this experience provides broad-based exposure to all operational facets of an outdoor education program. The intent is to provide each student with a full-time placement in his or her area of concentration. *Pre-requisites: IS 310 and OE 241(2), junior status.*

OE 462   Current Issues in Outdoor Education (3)
A course designed for graduating seniors preparing to enter the field of outdoor education. Students will be required to read a wide variety of literature and discuss pertinent issues in the field of outdoor education. Students will complete a major literature review and at least two oral presentations on the issues researched. *Pre-requisites: OE 310 and senior standing in the major.*

OE 480   Special Topics in Outdoor Education (Upper-Level) (1-3)
This course will provide students and faculty the opportunity to examine current issues or specialized topics within the discipline at an upper-level of study (appropriate for junior or senior academic experience). Topics will be determined by the department. Class will meet 15 hours for each hour of credit offered. Repeatable for different topics. *(Offered by department discretion.)*

OE 481   Directed Study and Research (1-3)
Students may choose to participate in a directed study of their own choice contingent on faculty availability. Credit varies from 1-3 hours although a student can repeat for up to six hours of credit. *Prerequisite: Junior status or above. A cumulative GPA of 2.5 and approval of the department chair is required.*

OE 491   Senior Seminar (1)
Designed to prepare outdoor education majors to make the transition to professionals in the field, this course includes job search and interview skills and will assist students in gaining a deeper understanding of God's calling and in bringing closure to the student's academic career. Students will complete a résumé, portfolio, and a comprehensive assessment and exit interview. Required of all OE/OM majors in their final semester. *Pre-requisite: Senior standing in major.*

OUTDOOR MINISTRY (OM)

OM 200   Introduction to Christian Camping & Outdoor Ministry (3)
This course will survey the history of organized camping and identify key educational and ministry principles that are foundational to outdoor ministry. It will also explore the application of these principles to different types of camp programs and to a variety of philosophic approaches.

OM 241   Field Experience (1)
An Outdoor Education/Outdoor Ministry major must fulfill the specified requirements of two different field experiences for 1 credit hour each before doing an OE/OM internship in the junior or senior year. Field experiences consist of hands-on opportunities in various outdoor education/ministry-related events or organizations. Each credit hour earned requires 40 hours of on-site involvement during an agreed upon length of time. *Pre-requisites: Permission of the student's field experience supervisor. (A fee per credit hour is assessed for field experiences during the summer. During the semester the credit counts within the load).*

OM 280   Special Topics in Outdoor Ministry (Lower-Level) (1-3)
This course will provide students and faculty the opportunity to examine current issues or specialized topics within the discipline at a lower-level of study (appropriate for freshmen or sophomore academic experience). Topics will be determined by the department. Class will meet 15 hours for each hour of credit offered. Repeatable for different topics. *(Offered by department discretion.)*

OM 300   Outdoor & Camp Programming (3)
This course will focus on the development and implementation of outdoor education and ministry programs. Students will create and propose a new outdoor program for two different organizations. One of the programs will be conducted for a local community agency. *Pre-requisite: OM 200 and Junior standing in major.*

OM 341   Practicum (1-3)
A supervised learning experience that provides the student with initial exposure to relevant professional activities. Supervision of the practicum is a shared responsibility between the faculty advisor and on-site supervisor. This course may be repeated; a maximum of three (3)

hours may be used to satisfy degree requirements. *Pre-requisites: IS 310, permission of the student's advisor and department chair or designee.*

OM 441   Internship (3)
This experience is designed to serve as a culminating field experience for students majoring in outdoor ministry. It provides for full-time involvement an outdoor ministry program with opportunities for the application of classroom theories, leadership development, and career exploration. *Pre-requisite: IS 310 and OM 241(2), junior status.*

OM 480   Special Topics in Outdoor Ministry (Upper-Level) (1-3)
This course will provide students and faculty the opportunity to examine current issues or specialized topics within the discipline at an upper-level of study (appropriate for junior or senior academic experience). Topics will be determined by the department. Class will meet 15 hours for each hour of credit offered. Repeatable for different topics. *(Offered by department discretion.)*

OM 481   Directed Study and Research (1-3)
Students may choose to participate in a directed study of their own choice contingent on faculty availability. Credit varies from 1-3 hours although a student can repeat for up to six hours of credit. *Prerequisite: Junior status or above. A cumulative GPA of 2.5 and approval of the department chair is required.*

PHILOSOPHY (PH)

PH 201   Introduction to Philosophy (3)
An introduction to the major problems and systems of philosophy. This course familiarizes the student with some of the systems of philosophy that have appeared over the centuries and with some of the contemporary systems. *(Offered fall semesters, even years.)*

PH 210   Logic (3)
This course will introduce students to the basic components of sound argumentation. Students will be introduced to the basic categories, language, tools, and concepts of formal logic. This course will teach students to evaluate arguments using these tools of logic. Students will also learn to identify both formal and informal fallacies where they occur in common argumentation. *(Offered spring semesters, odd years.)*

PH 280   Special Topics in Philosophy (Lower-Level) (1-3)
This course will provide students and faculty the opportunity to examine current issues or specialized topics within the discipline at a lower-level of study (appropriate for freshmen or sophomore academic experience). Topics will be determined by the department. Class will meet 15 hours for each hour of credit offered. Repeatable for different topics. *(Offered by department discretion.)*

PH 301   Ethics (3)
This course will introduce students to several major ethical theories, including: virtue, rule, and consequential approaches. Students will read and study several important ethical thinkers, both Christian and secular. These ethical theories will then be applied to case studies in a variety of fields such as: bioethics, political ethics, ecclesial ethics, ethics of counseling, business ethics, environmental ethics, etc. *(Offered fall semesters, even years.)*

PH 321   Contemporary Theologies (3)
This course will survey several contemporary approaches to theology, including: liberation theology, process theology, feminist theology, openness of God theology, Asian theology, Black theology, and other 20th century approaches. Each approach will be understood on its own terms through reading its major proponents. An honest evaluation of each approach will

be undertaken through the use of biblical and doctrinal theology. *Pre-requisite: BB 211. (Offered spring semesters, odd-numbered years.)*

PH 403   Philosophy of Religion and Apologetics (3)
This course will introduce students to the basic questions that concern religious thinkers, including: the problem of evil, miracles, immortality, proofs of God's existence, unity and diversity in religions, the relationship of faith and reason, etc. The works of some of the key thinkers in the philosophy of religion will be read in addition to the general survey of the subject. *(Offered spring semesters, odd-numbered years.)*

PH 480   Special Topics in Philosophy (Upper-Level) (1-3)
This course will provide students and faculty the opportunity to examine current issues or specialized topics within the discipline at an upper-level of study (appropriate for junior or senior academic experience). Topics will be determined by the department. Class will meet 15 hours for each hour of credit offered. Repeatable for different topics. *(Offered by department discretion.)*

PH 481   Directed Study and Research (1-3)
Students may choose to participate in a directed study of their own choice contingent on faculty availability. Credit varies from 1-3 hours although a student can repeat for up to six hours of credit. *Prerequisite: Junior status or above. A cumulative GPA of 2.5 and approval of the department chair is required. (Offered by department discretion.)*

PH 491   Senior Thesis (3)
Students develop an extensive paper under the direction of a faculty member that demonstrates their ability to do senior-level research and writing on a specialized topic in theology, philosophy, or cross-cultural studies. A committee comprised of the course professor, another member of the division, and a member chosen by the student evaluates and grade the thesis. *(Offered every semester as needed.)*

PHYSICAL EDUCATION (PE)

Activity courses that fulfill the physical education requirement in the general education core are those that are 100 and 200-level. Exemptions from activity courses will be considered by the department on a case-by-case basis.

PE 101   Beginning Jogging (1)
An activity course designed for the student to learn about the aerobic aspects of jogging and to develop a personal program of continuous jogging for 30 minutes, three times per week.

PE 102   Fly Fishing (1)
An introduction to fly fishing, its history, equipment selection and maintenance, casting techniques, aquatic entomology, and stream ecology.

PE 111   Introduction to Principles and Philosophy of Physical Education (3)
This course is designed to provide the potential physical education professional with a knowledge of the foundations, principles, and philosophies of physical education from ancient history to the present.

PE 140   Beginning Weight Training (1)
This course is an introduction to weight training with emphasis on principles and techniques. Students develop an individualized weight training program. Related health and safety factors are also considered.

PE 142   Aerobic Dance (1)
This course emphasizes movement to music as an enjoyable means of strengthening muscles, improving flexibility, and developing overall physical fitness.

PE 143   Team Sports I - Soccer and Volleyball (1)
Eight weeks of soccer and eight weeks of volleyball. Instruction in rules, skills, and strategy. Emphasizes physical fitness.

PE 144   Team Sports II - Basketball and Softball (1)
Eight weeks of basketball and eight weeks of softball. Instruction in rules, skills, and strategy. Emphasizes physical fitness.

PE 145   Physical Fitness (1)
This course includes knowledge of cardiovascular endurance, maximal heart rate, and how to work out an individual program to achieve fitness.

PE 146   Racquet Sports (1)
Eight weeks of badminton and eight weeks of tennis. Instruction in basics, such as grip, footwork, strokes, rules, strategy, and tournament play.

PE 147   Yoga (1)
This course is an introduction to the basics of yoga. Focus will be on proper alignment of the body, breath awareness, postures, and meditation. Through yoga, students will strive to honor God with their bodies recognizing that the Holy Spirit dwells within them. In each class, meditations on scripture will be incorporated. All levels of experience are welcome. The student must provide or purchase a yoga mat, block, and strap as well as assigned academic materials.

PE 157   Advanced Yoga (1)
This course is designed for the intermediate to advanced yoga student. The class will build on concepts introduced in PE 147 Yoga such as alignment of the body, breath awareness, postures, and Christian meditation. In addition, students will practice advanced asana (posture), challenging transitions, and arm balancing. Students will explore the concept of full-body prayer through a series of postures and strive to honor God with their bodies recognizing that the Holy Spirit dwells within them. Meditations on scripture will be incorporated in classes. *Prerequisite: PE 147 or permission of the instructor.*

PE 201   Concepts of Fitness (2)
Areas such as cardiovascular endurance, physical fitness, wellness, stress, rest, diet, lifetime sports, and the values of wholesome activities are covered. Each student completes a personal analysis of his/her own fitness based upon testing.

PE 210   Backpacking and Orienteering (1)
This course provides an introduction to backpacking. The content will focus on backpacking and camping skills such as clothing selection, fire building, Leave-No Trace practices, map and compass, and the use of camping gear. At least one backpacking trip is required.

PE 220   Rock Climbing (1)
Designed for the beginning and intermediate climber, students will learn knots, basic climbing skills, and safety.

PE 221   Advanced Rock Climbing (1)
This course is designed for the intermediate and advanced climber. Students will learn technical rope techniques, a variety of options for top-rope setup, proper placement of rock protection, and the basics of lead climbing. Offered spring semesters. *Pre-requisite: PE 220 or OE 313, or permission of professor.*

PE 230   Canoeing (1)
Emphasis on tandem paddling skills, lake and whitewater canoeing, and water safety and rescue. *Pre-requisite: Swimming ability.*

PE 231   Advanced Canoeing (1)
Designed for the novice solo canoeist or intermediate tandem canoeist seeking to move into solo canoeing, the emphasis of the course is on proper solo technique for use in a whitewater

setting. Rolling and C-1 techniques will be also be introduced. Offered fall semesters. *Pre-requisites: PE 230 or OE 314, or permission of professor. Swimming ability.*

PE 240   Kayaking (1)

This course is designed for the beginning and intermediate kayaker. The emphasis will be placed on the self and assisted-rescue techniques, basic paddling strokes, river reading, hydrology, water safety, and rescue. *Pre-requisite: Swimming ability.*

PE 241   Advanced Kayaking (1)

This course is designed for the intermediate and advanced kayaker. Students will learn a variety of rescue procedures, advanced river reading and hydrology, advanced strikes and maneuvers while paddling more difficult rivers/creeks. Offered fall semesters. *Pre-requisites: PE 240, or permission of professor. Swimming ability.*

PE 250   Lifeguard Training (1)

This course covers basic water safety, including swimming strokes, rescues, and escapes. Lifeguard qualifications, pool management and safety will also be studied. Red Cross certification will be awarded to those students who meet the requirements. *Pre-requisite: Swimming ability. Fee.*

PE 260   Winter Outdoor Education (1)

This course, taught in the winter months (typically in the spring semester), has varying content, depending on the weather and location. Emphasis is on how to live comfortably outside in cold environments and winter ecology. Content may include cross-country or Telemark skiing, winter backpacking, and snow shelter construction. At least one backcountry trip is required. No pre-requisite. Previous camping experience preferred.

PE 270   Downhill Skiing (1)

Designed for the beginning and intermediate skier, this course includes two lecture classes and five ski trips to a local slope. Students receive one hour of instruction and three hours of ski time during each trip. *Fee $275.* No refund after first class.

PE 301   Team Sports Officiating (2)

A course designed to teach students the techniques and standards of officiating with emphasis on knowing the rules of various team sports. Course can help lead to certification.

PE 302   Methods and Materials of Coaching (2)

A course designed to introduce students to the rudiments of coaching. Emphasis on administrative and routine tasks plus the techniques and materials used in recruiting and coaching. *(Offered fall semesters, even years.)*

PE 305   Introduction to Athletic Training (3)

The primary objective of the course is to introduce physically active people to the basic concepts of sports injury prevention, recognition, care, and rehabilitation. Course is an essential component for those entering coaching, physical education, or the field of sports medicine. *Pre-requisite: HL 101.*

PE 341   Practicum (1-3)

Supervised field education provides practical on-the-job training in various areas of physical education-related fields. Each experience is administered by the field education advisor and supervising facility. *Pre-requisites: IS 310.*

PE 424   Facility Planning for Physical Education Recreation & Athletics (3)

This course is designed to assist the Sports Management student in acquiring the necessary knowledge and skills needed to manage a sport facility and to plan a complete sporting event. *(Offered spring semesters, even years.)*

PHYSICS (PC)

PC 131-132   College Physics I, II (4, 4)
A series of lecture-demonstration periods in which algebra and trigonometry are used in mathematical analysis. Topics covered in 131 may include classical mechanics, thermodynamics, oscillations and waves. Electricity and magnetism, fluids, optics, and nuclear physics may be included in 132. The lab complements the lecture material. Three hours of lecture and two hours of lab per week. *Pre-requisite: Grade of A or B in high school Algebra II and Trigonometry (or the equivalent) or grade of C or above in MT 122.*

PREACHING (PR)

PR 310   Biblical Preaching and Communication (3)
This course is designed to give a broad overview of the basic tools and techniques necessary for preparing and presenting sermons based on biblical texts. Topics include an introduction to sermon research as well as what it means to preach in a contemporary context, including the use and misuse of technology, film, music, object lessons and a variety of preaching techniques including both narrative and expositional. *Pre-requisite: BB 305. (Offered spring semesters, even-numbered years.)*

PR 410   Preparing for the Gospel Ministry (3)
This course lays the foundation from which effective evangelism will be launched. The class accomplishes this in three stages. The first centers on mastering the very message of the Gospel centered on the cross and resurrection of Jesus and developing skills in sharing the Gospel with others. The second lesson takes seriously the topic of sin: its origins as recounted in the Bible, its consequences in the eternal life of the individual and its systemic effects in the world, and our need of Christ's saving death and resurrection. The third stage focuses on the Great Commission as found in Matthew 28:16-20 as the central evangelical ordinance given to all believers and to become aware of the presence and power of Christ within it.

PR 420   Preaching the Gospel (3)
This course teaches how to effectively communicate the gospel message in preaching. With the Bible as the foundation, students will develop understanding in the essential qualities and preparation of an evangelistic message understanding contextual dynamics which affect an effective presentation of the Gospel, the skills necessary to delivering the Gospel in a winsome and effective way, and appropriate and effective methods for inviting people to respond to the Gospel message. *Prerequisite: PR 410.*

PR 430   Prayer and the Holy Spirit (3)
The power of communicating the Gospel message effectively resides in the operations of the Holy Spirit and the prayer life of the presenter. This course explores in-depth the person and work of the Holy Spirit in evangelism as well as the key elements of effectual prayer. Students will reflect on the movement of the Holy Spirit in their lives as they develop a plan for prayer in their ministries. Some attention will be given to the nature of spiritual warfare and the call to personal holiness. *Prerequisite: PR 420.*

PR 491   Seminar on Ministry (1)
Students will meet in a one week intensive format (3 hours per day for five days) to discuss current issues in ministry and church administration. This course will cover topics of church growth, administration, worship, as well as trends and issues in ministry in a seminar style format. *Prerequisite: PR 430.*

PSYCHOLOGY (PY)

PY 201   Psychology Applied to Modern Life (3)
This course offers majors and non-majors an opportunity to apply knowledge from psychology to practical problems. It provides students with an overview of the theory and research in psychology that is related to the demands and challenges of everyday life. Students examine issues that affect their own adjustment to modern life. The following topics will be addressed: stress, physical health, love relationships, gender, communications, self, personality, work, and development. *Students who earn credit for PY 201 may not earn credit for PY 202.*

PY 202   General Psychology (3)
This course is a basic survey of the discipline of psychology: the science of behavior and mental processes. We will examine the physiological, intellectual, emotional, and social aspects of human behavior and look at the applications of psychological theory and research to daily living. *Students who earn credit for PY 202 may not earn credit for PY 201.*

PY 280   Special Topics in Psychology (Lower-Level) (1-3)
This course will provide students and faculty the opportunity to examine current issues or specialized topics within the discipline at a lower-level of study (appropriate for freshmen or sophomore academic experience). Topics will be determined by the department. Class will meet 15 hours for each hour of credit offered. Repeatable for different topics. *Prerequisite: PY 201 or PY 202 or permission of professor. (Offered by department discretion.)*

PY 300   Child and Adolescent Development (3)
An overview of the physiological, cognitive, psychosocial, and spiritual aspects of development from conception through age 18. *Prerequisite: PY201 or PY 202 and a minimum of sophomore standing.*

PY 305   Adult Development and Aging (3)
An overview of the physical, cognitive, social, spiritual, and emotional aspects of adult development. *Pre-requisites: PY 201 or PY 202 and a minimum of sophomore standing.*

PY 310   Research Methods (3)
This course is designed for upper level undergraduate students majoring in human services and psychological studies. The course will provide an introduction to research methodology and a basic framework to critically evaluate social and behavioral science research. You will be exposed to and tested on the major concepts and methods for generating hypotheses and designing a multi-measure study. This course should enable you to evaluate more critically the claims of "experts" in the popular press as well as in the scientific literature. It will also serve as preparation for graduate-level research. *Pre-requisite: PY 201 or PY 202.*

PY 314   Personality (3)
Basic principles of personality structure, dynamics, development, assessment, and theory are discussed. Consideration is given to both the environmental and biological determinants of personality. *Pre-requisite: PY 201 or PY 202.*

PY 315   Abnormal Psychology (3)
A survey of the current categories of abnormal behavior emphasizing symptoms, major theories of causality, and current treatment methods. *Pre-requisite: PY 201 or PY 202.*

PY 320   Social Psychology (3)
The study of the behaviors and thoughts of individuals as influenced by actual or perceived social factors and other individuals. *Pre-requisites: PY 201 or PY 202*

PY 341   Practicum (1-3)
Supervised field education provides the student with practical on-the-job training in various areas of psychology related fields. Supervision of the practicum is a shared responsibility between the faculty advisor and the on-site supervisor. This course may be repeated; a maximum of three hours may be used to satisfy degree requirements. *Pre-requisites: IS 310.*

PY 412   Theories and Principles of Counseling (3)
An examination of several of the major theories of counseling in working with individuals, families, and small groups. Included are principles and techniques utilized in assessment, crisis intervention, contracts, and development of the therapeutic relationship. A skills component is also included. *Pre-requisite: PY 201 or PY 202.*

PY 416   Learning and Memory (3)
This course provides a basic overview of the principles, theories, and applications of learning and memory. We will cover basic research, theory, and applications in human learning, memory, information processing, verbal learning, conditioning, and social learning. The knowledge you take away from this course will be useful to you in a wide variety of settings— not only psychology but also in your own personal and professional worlds. *Pre-requisite: PY 201 or PY 202.*

PY 420   Physiological Psychology (3)
Explores the physiological, biological, and anatomical mechanisms responsible for behavior. *Pre-requisites: PY 201 or PY 202, sophomore standing or above*

PY 441   Internship (3)
Supervised internship provides the student with the opportunity to integrate classroom instruction with practical on-the-job learning in various areas of psychology related fields. This course is normally taken in the summer after the junior year. *Pre-requisites: 12 hours in the major and IS 310.*

PY 480   Special Topics in Psychology (Upper-Level) (1-3)
This course will provide students and faculty the opportunity to examine current issues or specialized topics within the discipline at an upper-level of study (appropriate for junior or senior academic experience). Topics will be determined by the department. Class will meet 15 hours for each hour of credit offered. Repeatable for different topics. *Prerequisite: PY 201 or PY 202 or permission of professor. (Offered by department discretion.)*

PY 481   Directed Study and Research (1-3)
Students may choose to participate in a directed study of their own choice contingent on faculty availability. Credit varies from 1-3 hours although a student can repeat for up to six hours of credit. *Prerequisite: Junior status or above. A cumulative GPA of 2.5 and approval of the department chair is required.*

PY 490   Senior Seminar (3)
Examines the themes of authenticity, self-actualization, and the application of psychological theory in order to explore major Christian worldview questions (what is success in life, how do I become more Christ like, etc.). *Prerequisites: PY 310 and PY 320, junior standing or above, or permission of the instructor.*

SOCIOLOGY (SC)

SC 204   Introduction to Sociology (3)
This course deals with the general nature and principles of sociology. Special attention is given to the ecological, cultural, and psychosocial forces; and to outstanding social groups; to changing personality under the influences that play upon it through group processes.

SC 205   Marriage and Family (3)
A study of relationships with the opposite sex from first meeting through marriage, having and rearing a family, and divorce and remarriage. Current American norms and Christian principles for marriage and family life are examined.

SC 206   Social Problems (3)
An analysis of the major social problems of contemporary society resulting from technological and social change, population pressure and resources, urbanization, poverty, minority groups with special reference to the black conflicts regarding social values and goals, and social disorganization as related to the family, economic, religious and other institutional relationships. *Pre-requisite: SC 204 or permission of professor.*

SC 311   Social Welfare and Social Services (3)
This course is a survey of the history and philosophy of social welfare and the values and practice of social services as a profession.

SC 414   Counseling Adolescents & Families (3)
This course examines several of the major theories of counseling families. Working with adolescents within the context of their families will be given special consideration. The skills of counseling adolescents and families will also be emphasized. *Pre-requisite: PY 201 or PY 202*

SC 415   Human Sexuality (3)
A study of the historical, physiological, interpersonal, spiritual and health aspects of human sexual behavior within a Christian framework. Consideration is given to contemporary social issues including harassment, abuse, rape, homosexuality, and commercial sex. *Pre-requisites: SC 205 and junior or senior standing in the major.*

SC 480   Special Topics (1-3)
This course will provide students and faculty the opportunity to participate in examining current issues or specialized topics within the discipline. Topics will be determined by the department. Class will meet 15 hours for each hour of credit offered. A student can repeat for up to six hours of credit.

SC 481   Directed Study and Research (1-3)
Students may choose to participate in a directed study of their own choice contingent on faculty availability. Credit varies from 1-3 hours although a student can repeat for up to six hours of credit. *Prerequisite: Junior status or above. A cumulative GPA of 2.5 and approval of the department chair is required.*

SPANISH (SP)

Students with two or more years of high school Spanish must take a placement exam in order to enroll in a language course for credit. Language courses must be taken in sequence since, with the exception of the first course in the sequence, each language course has a pre-requisite. Students may not register for the intermediate level without either placing into it by examination or first completing the elementary sequence successfully.

Students who enroll in the elementary or intermediate language sequences are strongly encouraged to take them in consecutive semesters with no time lapse between the courses in that sequence. In the event that a student's course of study should prevent that continuity, one semester is the maximum time lapse allowed for completing the second part of the sequence. A lapse of more than one semester, in most cases, will necessitate repeating the first part of the sequence unless the student can demonstrate competency in the skills required. Native speakers who wish to take Spanish for credit may not enroll in any course below the 300-level.

SP 101   Elementary Spanish I, (3)
This course will begin developing the four communicative Spanish language skills (listening, speaking, reading, and writing). Emphasis will be placed on fundamentals of grammar,

vocabulary, and pronunciation. Contact with Hispanic cultures will be incorporated. This course includes a lab component. *Grade of C needed to progress to SP 102.*

SP 102   Elementary Spanish II, (3)

This course continues the development of listening, speaking, reading, and writing in Spanish. Emphasis will be placed on fundamentals of grammar, vocabulary, pronunciation and composition. This course will provide increased contact with and appreciation for the diversity of Hispanic cultures. This course includes a lab component. *Grade of C needed to progress to SP 201. Pre-requisite: Spanish 101 or placement test.*

SP 201   Intermediate Spanish I, (3)

This course involves intensive work developing Spanish communicative skills (Listening, Speaking, Reading, and Writing). Students will develop their appreciation for the diversities of the Hispanic cultures and civilization. Emphasis will be placed on grammar, vocabulary, composition and conversation. This course includes a lab component. *Grade of C needed to move to SP 202. Pre-requisite: Spanish 102 or placement test.*

SP 202   Intermediate Spanish II, (3)

This course continues intensive work developing Spanish communicative skills (Listening, Speaking, Reading and Writing) and the study of Hispanic cultures and civilization. Emphasis is placed on grammar, vocabulary, compositions, conversation, and in the presentational mode of communication. This course includes a lab component. *Grade of C needed to move to 300-level Spanish courses. Pre-requisite: Spanish 201 or placement test.*

SP 280   Special Topics in Spanish (Lower-Level) (1-3)

This course will provide students and faculty the opportunity to examine current issues or specialized topics within the discipline at a lower-level of study (appropriate for freshmen or sophomore academic experience). Topics will be determined by the department. Class will meet 15 hours for each hour of credit offered. Repeatable for different topics. (*Offered by department discretion.*)

SP 303   Advanced Conversation and Composition I (3)

This course provides a detailed study of the fundamentals of Spanish usage, oral and written. In training the correct pronunciation, we stress conversation and composition based on practical subject matter of everyday life in Spain, and Spanish-American countries, and the Hispanics in the U.S. *Pre-requisites: SP 201, SP 202 or equivalent. Note: we recommend taking this course first, because in the second semester (SP 304), the vocabulary and grammar continue to a higher level of difficulty. (Offered by department discretion.)*

SP 304   Advanced Conversation and Composition II (3)

In this course, we will continue, to a higher level of difficulty, a detailed study of the fundamentals of Spanish usage, oral and written: Subjunctive, if clauses, passive voice, tenses sequence, etc. Students can expand their vocabulary by reading and discussions of topics on the history and culture of Latin America and Spain. We base conversations and compositions on practical subject matter of everyday life in Spain, and Spanish-American countries, and the Hispanics in the U.S. *Pre-requisites: SP 201, SP 202 or equivalent. (Offered by department discretion.)*

SP 305   Selected Readings in Spanish Literature (3)

Class and readings will be in Spanish using literature from Spain. *Pre-requisites: SP 201, SP 202 or equivalent. (Offered alternate years with SP 303-304.)*

SP 306   Selected Readings in Latin American Literature (3)

Class and readings will be in Spanish using literature from Latin America. *Pre-requisites: SP 201, SP 202 or equivalent. (Offered alternate years with SP 303-304.)*

SP 480 Special Topics in Spanish (Upper-Level) (1-3)
This course will provide students and faculty the opportunity to examine current issues or specialized topics within the discipline at an upper-level of study (appropriate for junior or senior academic experience). Topics will be determined by the department. Class will meet 15 hours for each hour of credit offered. Repeatable for different topics. (*Offered by department discretion.*)

SP 481 Directed Study and Research (1-3)
Students may choose to participate in a directed study of their own choice contingent on faculty availability. Credit varies from 1-3 hours although a student can repeat for up to six hours of credit. *Prerequisite: Junior status or above. A cumulative GPA of 2.5 and approval of the department chair is required.*

SPORTS MANAGEMENT (SM)

SM 210 Principles of Sports Management (3)
An introduction to the sports management industry including event organization, administration, contracting services, and other related functions. Emphasis is placed on written and communication skills for acquiring entry-level positions in sport management. *Pre- or Co-requisite: BS 209 or permission of professor. (Offered fall semesters, odd years.)*

SM 337 Seminar in Sports Marketing (3)
A course designed to examine the unique requirements of planning, designing, developing sponsorship packages, obtaining sponsors, and promoting a sports product or event. Over the course of the semester, students develop and present a plan for production of a sports event. *Pre- or Co-requisite: BS 230. (Offered spring semesters, odd years.)*

THEATRE (TH)

TH 106; 205-206 Theatre Production (1)
These courses allow students the opportunity to earn credit for participating in a main stage production. Students will focus on introductory and intermediate skills needed in aspects of production such as costume, lighting and sound, performance, and business operations. Main stage productions are full-length plays produced by the theatre department and directed by a theatre faculty or invited theatre guest director. Theatre majors must take each course in sequence, but the courses are open to students outside of the major. Student theatre productions outside the theatre department do not count as main stage productions so credit is not given for such participation without approval by the department chair.

TH 110 Theatre History (3)
A survey of the periods, practices and theories of the theatre. A History of Man's spiritual quest through the medium of theatre, its playwrights, structures, and methods of staging and acting from the Greeks to Contemporary Works. Students will demonstrate a thorough understanding of styles & genres, history & development of theatre in order to be informed practitioners.

TH/CM 202 Acting for the Camera (3)
This course aims to inform the student to learn how to present himself on camera in a variety of genres. It will provide instruction and experience in the basics of acting for both television and film. It will also examine informational and news journalism. Cross listed as CM 202. Prerequisite: permission of instructor.

TH 220   Voice/Movement (3)

This course is designed to introduce movement as language while also working with the production of sound, and allows the students to investigate the interconnectedness of thought and feeling issued through the language of the body and the sound of our voice.

TH 230   Acting (3)

Principles of the craft of acting, with emphasis on script analysis from the standpoint of character's objective. Includes the development of voice, movement, rehearsal, and performance process.

TH 232   Stagecraft (3)

A studio course designed to familiarize students with the basic skills of one or more of the following stage technologies: lighting, sound, makeup, costume, set construction, and publicity. *Pre-requisite: Permission of instructor.*

TH 305-306; 405-406 Theatre Production (1)

These courses allow students the opportunity to earn credit for participating in a main stage production. Students will develop advanced skills needed in aspects of production such as costume, lighting and sound, performance, and business operations. Main stage productions are full-length plays produced by the theatre department and directed by a theatre faculty or invited theatre guest director. Theatre majors must take each course in sequence, but the courses are open to students outside of the major. Student theatre productions outside the theatre department do not count as main stage productions so credit is not given for such participation without approval by the department chair. *Pre-requisites: Successful completion of 200-level theatre production and permission of professor.*

TH 317   Directing (4)

This course lays the basic foundation of the techniques of directing a play. Students will analyze a play from a directing standpoint, learn how to assess and honor the playwright's intent and translate that to the stage, understand different approaches to directing, utilize space and movement, and learn how to work with actors from first reading through production. Course will culminate in a public performance of final directed scenes. *Pre-requisite: TH230 and/or permission of instructor.*

TH 330   Advanced Acting (3)

Advanced work in the craft of action, with emphasis on scene work both modern and classical, Shakespearean text and style, stage combat and use of the body, overall focus on personal coaching, and development of students' abilities to act and present themselves in a public forum. Course will culminate in public performance of a showcase of scenes. *Pre-requisite: TH230 and/or permission of instructor.*

TH 333   Theatre Ensemble (4)

Montreat College's touring theatre company, a small acting ensemble that offers the student practical application of basic acting skills and teamwork. The course culminates in performance opportunities within the College community as well as the church and community settings in the Asheville area. The course will introduce the student to theatre as ministry, both in philosophy and application. Course may be repeated. Three rehearsals each week. *Pre-requisites: TH 230 and/or permission of instructor.*

TH/CM 335   Playwriting/Screenwriting (3)

This course covers the foundational elements of stage and/or film script writing: structure, character development, plot development and use of image. It will also develop the use of the imagination and address how to utilize that effectively with the discipline of writing well. Semester will conclude with staged readings of the students' final scenes.

TH 340   Musical Theatre (3)
This course will provide practical training and experience in musical theatre performance. Focus will be given to the particular techniques, skills, and challenges that musical theatre presents as distinct from non-musical theatre.

TH 341   Theatre Practicum (1-3)
Designed for the student who is interested in a time-or-labor intensive study in the field of theatre such as, but not limited to, directing a main stage production or starring in a one-person, full-length play, stage managing a production, technical and/or costume design; and research project or community outreach program. *Pre-requisites: IS 310, EN 102, TH 230, TH 232, TH 317 with a minimum grade of C and/or permission of professor.*

TH 381   Special Topics (1-3)
This course will provide students and faculty the opportunity to participate in examining current issues or specialized topics within the discipline. Topics will be selected by the department head. Class will meet 15 hours for each hour of credit offered. A student can repeat for up to six hours of credit.

TH 441   Internship (3)
An intensive, quality, structured learning opportunity that immerses students in appropriate professional contexts. Supervision of the internship is a shared responsibility between the faculty advisor and on-site supervisor. *Pre-requisite: IS 310.*

TH 481   Directed Study and Research (1-3)
Students may choose to participate in a directed study of their own choice contingent on faculty availability. Credit varies 1-3 hours. Repeatable for up to six hours of credit. *Pre-requisite: Junior status and approval of department chair.*

TH491   Senior Thesis (2)
Students in this course will have the opportunity to apply academic and experiential learning in a production situation. Students will develop an extensive capstone project. A departmental committee will specify the thesis parameters, approve the topic, and grade the final product.

Worship Arts (WA)

WA 101   Worship Arts Survey I (3)
This course establishes the student in the biblical and theological foundations of Christian worship and then provides an overview of the history of Christian worship.

WA 102   Worship Arts Survey II (3)
This course focuses on the role of music and the other non-musical arts (architecture, visual arts, drama, speech, dance, movement, and media) in worship. A thorough discussion of the worship style models that dominate and shape the 21st century American church will be included.

WA 255   Connection (2)
A worship team that builds musical, spiritual, interpersonal and community connections. Practical experience will be gained in vocal and instrumental interactions, sound and projection systems and other technical aspects of worship leading. Successful audition with instructor required.

WA 302   Worship Arts Resources (3)
This upper-level course emphasizes resources and techniques of the worship planner and worship leader. *Pre-requisites: WA 101 and WA 102.*

WA 305   Foundations of Worship (3)
The development of a theological understanding of worship as it relates to Scripture and
Christian practice. Current worship trends and tensions will be considered regarding the
implications for personal and corporate worship.

WA 306   Music in Worship (3)
Students will develop an understanding of music's current role in worship practices, and their
relationship to historical trends. A biblical perspective on music's role in corporate worship
will be developed.

WA 341   Worship Arts Practicum I (2)
This course is the first of two semesters during which the student is taken under wing by a
local professional in the field of worship ministry and volunteers as an intern. The student will
be monitored and observed by faculty on site. *Pre-requisite: IS 310, WA 101, WA 102, WA 301,
WA 302, MS 307, WA 461, WA 462.*

WA 342   Worship Arts Practicum II (2)
This course is the second of two semesters during which the student is taken under wing by a
local professional in the field of worship ministry and volunteers as an intern. The student will
be monitored and observed by faculty on site. *Pre-requisite: IS 310, WA 101, WA 102, WA 301,
WA 302, MS 307, WA 461, WA 462, and WA 341.*

WA 461   Worship Arts Seminar I (1)
Worship Arts Seminar I will provide students with a mentored and monitored laboratory
environment where they will put their knowledge and resources to good work in preparing
worship experiences/events for the Montreat community. *Pre-requisites: WA 101, WA 201,
WA 301, WA 302, MS 307.*

WA 462   Worship Arts Seminar II (1)
Worship Arts Seminar II will provide students with a mentored and monitored laboratory
environment where they will put their knowledge and resources to good work in preparing
worship experiences/events for the Montreat community. *Pre-requisites: WA 101, WA 102,
WA 301, WA 302, MS 307, and WA 461.*

Youth and Family Ministries (YM)

YM 203   Foundations of Youth and Family Ministry (3)
This course will introduce the student to traditional and emerging philosophies of ministering
to youth and their families. It will survey adolescent developmental theories as they apply
specifically to Youth Ministry. Particular attention will be placed on historical and biblical
foundations of Youth Ministry in connection with para-church and camp ministries, the local
church, and the youth leader as an agent of change. *(Offered fall semesters, even years.)*

YM 303   Discipleship and Lifestyle Evangelism (3)
This course focuses on individual experiences in discipleship, personal sanctification, and
evangelism in contemporary society. Special attention will be given to the art of persuasion
and its link to communication theory. The importance of perseverance in the faith of those
who come to know Christ through evangelistic efforts is ultimately highlighted. *(Offered fall
semesters, even years.)*

YM 360   Ministry to Children (3)
A survey of the spiritual, mental, emotional, and social needs of the child and an examination
of the church's and para-church's role in addressing these needs. Issues related to schooling

choices, pedagogical theory, curriculum resources, and administration of programs for children will be examined. *(Offered spring semesters, even years.)*

YM 380   Administrative Ministry and Organization (3)

This course will equip students in both the theory and practice of administrative leadership. Many challenges in ministry exist, and one of the most significant is the discipline required to lead and administer well. This course is designed to serve as an overview of practical administrative and leadership issues in ministry in order to prepare students with the tools necessary to organize and oversee various programs across the age ranges. *(Offered fall semesters, odd years.)*

YM 401   Spiritual Formation and Faith Development (3)

A course to equip students in both the theory and practice of the spiritual disciplines. This course focuses on our personal relationship with God. We will seek to develop an understanding of the necessary aspects of personal spiritual maturation through the evaluation of Scripture and through self-reflection and practice. Second, this course will emphasize theories about the stages of faith and moral development as those theories relate to Christ-centered ministries. *Fee. (Offered spring semesters, odd years.)*

YM 407   Contemporary Youth Culture and Programming (3)

This class offers a perspective on the issues facing elementary, junior high, and senior high students in the 21st Century, while exploring ways to teach and reach them with the gospel. Special attention is given to analyzing and critiquing current understandings of family, media, school, and peer relationships as well as how to design programs to address the unique challenges young people and their families face. We will evaluate various contexts where ministries to youth take place. *Pre-requisite YM 203. (Offered spring semesters, even years.)*

YM 408   Introduction to Pedagogy (3)

This course is designed to guide students in the mastery of teaching. The class will explore the nature of the learner and the role of the instructor in the learning process with special focus on the interpretation and application of scripture. Particular attention will be given to how to best create curriculum and assess learning among various children, pre-adolescents, and teenagers. Special consideration will thus be given to the stages of development from birth through adolescents. The course will reflect elements of lecture, off-sight observations, and student practice. *(Offered fall semesters, odd years.)*

YM 441   Internship (3-6)

Intensive, quality, structured learning opportunities that immerses students in appropriate professional contexts. Supervision of the internship is a shared responsibility between the faculty advisor and on-site supervisor. This course may be repeated in various intervals with six hours needed to satisfy degree requirements. *Prerequisite: Completed contract with signature from the student's advisor and department chair or designee, as well as IS 310. (Offered by department discretion.)*

YM 481   Directed Study and Research (3)

Students may replace a 300 or 400 level course in the concentration by participating in a directed study of their choice. This requires they formulate a research question related to youth and family ministry, conduct appropriate research in line with professional methodology, write a well-developed essay, and defend their research before the primary YM Instructor and another agreed upon faculty member. Contingent on faculty availability. *Prerequisite: Junior status or above. A cumulative GPA of 2.5 and approval of the department chair is required. (Offered by department discretion.)*

Scholarship Opportunities

Special Scholarships

Athletic Scholarships
Board of Visitors Scholarship
Child of Alumnus
Child of Minister
Church Matching Scholarships
Music Scholarships

Returning Student Scholarships

Leadership Excellence Scholarships:
    Campus host
    Campus hostess
    Fellowship of Christian Athletes
    Chapel Band
    Catacombs
    College Choir
    Resident Assistant
    Service & Outreach Council
    SGA Participant
    NAIA Academic All-American

Academic Excellence Scholarships:
Outstanding Achievement/Most Improved (1 each)
    Biblical, Religious, and Interdisciplinary Studies
    Biology
    Business Administration
    Communication
    Cybersecurity
    English
    Environmental Studies
    Exercise Science
    History
    Music Business
    Outdoor Education
    Outdoor Ministry
    Psychology/Human Services
    Theatre
    Worship Arts

Non-endowed Annual Scholarships

These scholarships are funded on an annual basis. Recipients are selected by the Financial Aid Office through information obtained from the Montreat College admissions and FAFSA application.

- Robert C. and Sadie G. Anderson Scholarship
- Glade Valley School Scholarship
- Frank H. and Annie Bell Wilhelm Perry Memorial Scholarship
- Reynolds Missionary Scholarship
- Lettie Pate Whitehead Scholarship Fund
- Friends of Music Scholarship
- Friends of the Library Scholarship
- Golden Leaf
- Ingram Scholarship
- UPS Scholarship
- Wells Fargo Scholarship
- BB&T Scholarship
- Peggy Bradford Long Scholarship
- Joy and Mary Kneedler Scholarship

Endowed Scholarships

- Verda Zoulean Anderson Endowed Scholarship
- Tres Bailes Endowed Scholarship
- Jean Lunsford Breitenhirt Endowed Scholarship
- John R. & Sylvia P. Crawford Leadership Scholarship
- C. Grier Davis Scholarship
- Nancy Boyd Garrison Scholarship
- Lillie Sears Foster Memorial Fund
- Ben Hill Griffin Jr. Endowed Scholarship
- Haynes Endowed Scholarship
- Elizabeth Hoyt Alumni Work Scholarship
- Lucinda Williams Lewis Endowed Scholarship
- Mary & John W. Luke Scholarship
- McCarty Endowed Scholarship
- Foster G. & Mary W. McGraw Scholarship
- Dr. Matthew McGowan Scholarship
- Dr. J. Rupert McGregor Endowed Scholarship
- McMillan-Williams Endowed Scholarship for Christian Education
- J. Alfred & Berenice M. Miller Scholarship
- Arthur N. & Irene Morris Scholarship
- Janet S. & Walter Pharr Scholarship
- Bruce R. Powers Scholarship
- William & Effie Rule Scholarship
- Ralph & Virginia Sanders Scholarship
- Oscar & Sadie Shoenfelt Endowed Scholarship
- W. D. Simpson Memorial Fund
- Patrick A. Thrift Endowed Scholarship
- Silas & Catherine Vaughn Endowed Scholarship
- Elizabeth Wilson Endowed Scholarship

Administration and Faculty Directories

2015-2016 Board of Trustees

2016-2017 Administrative Officers and Cabinet

Paul J. Maurer (2014) ....President
    B.A., University of Cincinnati
    M.Div., Gordon-Conwell Theological Seminary
    Ph.D., Claremont Graduate University
Daniel T. Bennett (2014)..............Vice President for Student Services and Dean of Students
    B.A., Biola University
    M.A., Wheaton College
    Ph.D., Clemson University
Susan DeWoody (2015) ....Vice President and Dean for Adult and Graduate Studies
    B.S., Arkansas Tech University
    M.S., Northeastern State University
    Ed.D. (In progress), Dallas Baptist University
Jack H. Heinen (2014) ....Vice President for Finance and Administration
    B.A., Dordt College
    M.B.A., Harvard Business School
Kristin Janes (2015) ....Vice President for Enrollment Management
    B.A., North Park University
    M.O.L., University of Northwestern
Gregory P. Kerr (2015) ....Vice President for Academic Affairs & Dean of the College
    B.S., Cornell University
    M.S., Colorado State University
    Ph.D., University of Minnesota
Joseph B. Kirkland (2007) ....Counselor to the President
    B.S., University of Southern Mississippi
    M.A., Lancaster Bible College
Alex Miller (2015) ....Vice President for Advancement
    B.A., Mars Hill University
    M.A., Southern Baptist Theological Seminary

Faculty Emeriti

Lloyd Davis..Professor Emeritus of Mathematics and Physics
    B.A., M.A., Miami University, Ohio
Charles A. Lance..Administrator Emeritus
    A.S., Montreat College
    B.S., Florida State University
    M.A.Ed., East Carolina State University
John T. Newton....................................Professor Emeritus of Bible and Philosophy
    B.E.E., Georgia Institute of Technology
    M.Div., Th.M., Columbia Theological Seminary
    Ph.D., Emory University
David L. Parks...Professor Emeritus of Bible
    B.E.E., Georgia Institute of Technology
    M.Div., D.D., Columbia Theological Seminary
James D. Southerland...Professor Emeritus of Art
    B.F.A., East Carolina University
    M.F.A., Pennsylvania State University

Charles Larry Wilson..Academic Dean Emeritus
    B.S., Springfield College
    M.S., State University of New York at Cortland
    Ph.D., Florida State University

2016-2017 Full Time Faculty

Angle, Kimberly G. (2007)............Associate Professor of English, Writing Program Director
    B.A., Mercer University
    M.A., Georgia State University
    Ph.D., University of South Carolina
Armstrong, Noreal (2016)..............................Assistant Professor of Counselor Education
    B.S., Stephen F. Austin State University
    M.S., Texas A&M
    Ph.D., University of Texas – San Antonio
Auman, Kevin C. (2008) ....Associate Professor of Music
    B.A., Montreat College
    M.A., University of North Carolina at Greensboro
Blanton, P. Gregory (1997) ....Professor of Human Services
    B.S., Evangel College
    M.Ed., Converse College
    M.Ed., Clemson University
    Ed.D. East Texas State University
Brandenburg, Benjamin B. (2014) ....Assistant Professor of History
    B.A., Northwestern College
    Ph.D. candidate, Temple University
Burgin, Kelli ....Assistant Professor of Cybersecurity
    B.A., University of Northern Iowa
    M.S. Bellevue University
Daniel, R. Bradley (1984) ....Professor of Biology/ES/OE
    B.A., M.A., Appalachian State University
    M.S., Northern Illinois University
    Ph.D., Antioch University
Dukas, Stephen P. (2009) ....Associate Professor of Accounting/Finance
    B.S., Florida State University
    Ph. D., Florida State University
Faircloth, W. Bradley (2011) ....Associate Professor of Psychology
    B.A., M.A., Ph.D., University of Notre Dame
Forstchen, William R. (1993) ....Professor of History, Faculty Fellow
    B.A., Rider College
    M.A., Ph.D., Purdue University
Gray, Richardson K. (1975) ....Professor of English
    B.A., Malone College
    M.A., Ph.D., Ohio University
Hamblin, Penny (2016)..Assistant Professor of Counselor Education
    B.A., East Carolina University
    M.A., Argosy University
    Ed.D., Argosy University

Howell, Cynthia M. (2005) ....Associate Professor of English
    B.A., Baylor University
    M.A., Vanderbilt University
    Ph.D., University of Kentucky
Joyce, Brian J. (1996) ....Professor of Biology/ES
    B.S., M.S., Ph.D., Pennsylvania State University
Kalisch, Kenneth R. (2008) ....Associate Professor of Outdoor Education
    B.S., University of Nebraska at Omaha
    M.S., Minnesota State University
Kamer, M. Shane (2014) ....Assistant Professor of Exercise Science
    B.S., Shawnee State University
    B.S., D.C., Logan University
King, Don W. (1974) ....Professor of English
    B.A., Virginia Polytechnic Institute
    M.A., Southern Illinois University
    Ph.D., University of North Carolina at Greensboro
King, Nathan (2013) ....Information Technology Services Librarian
    B.A., Montreat College
    M.L.S., North Carolina Central University
Konarski-Fusetti, Monica (2001) ....Instructor of English
    B.A., M.A., East Carolina University
Lassiter, Mark T. (1992) ....Professor of Biology/ES
    B.S., M.A., College of William and Mary
    Ph.D., North Carolina State University
Mullert, Mark B. (2014) ....Assistant Professor of Outdoor Education
    B.S., Houghton College
    M.S., State University of New York at Cortland
Nelson, Lotes (2015)...Assistant Professor of Counselor Education
    B.S., Montreat College
    M.S., Ph.D., Walden University
Neuzil, Linda (2015)............................... Director of Teacher Education/Associate Professor
    B.A., Judson University
    M.Ed., National-Louis University
    Ed.D., Northern Illinois University
Owen, Paul L. (2001) ....Professor of Biblical and Religious Studies
    B.A., Life Pacific College
    M.A., Talbot School of Theology, Biola University
    Ph.D., University of Edinburgh
Owolabi, Isaac B. (1994) ....Professor of Business
    B.S., M.S., University of Wisconsin
    Ph.D., University of Minnesota
Oxenreider, Tom (2008) ....Instructor of Interdisciplinary Studies
    B.A., University of Pittsburgh at Johnstown
    M.B.A., Wheeling Jesuit College
Pearson, Elizabeth R. (1978) .... Professor/Director of the Library
    B.S., University of North Carolina at Greensboro
    M.S.L.S., University of North Carolina at Chapel Hill

Pope, John N. (2016)..........Assistant Professor of Counselor Education, Director of Clinical Mental Health Counseling
    B.A., Stetson University
    M.Div., Columbia Theological Seminary
    Ph.D., Texas A&M University – Corpus Christi
Powell, John N. (2005) ....Associate Professor of Business
Shepson, Donald R. (2005) ....Associate Professor of Bible and Religion
    B.A., Wheaton College
    M.Div., Gordon Conwell Theological Seminary
    Ph.D., Talbot School of Theology, Biola University
Shuman, Dorothea K. (1996)......................................Professor of OE/Environmental Studies
    B.S.Ed., State University College at Cortland
    M.S., Pennsylvania State University
    Ph.D., University of Idaho
Smith, Benjamin S. (2014) ....Assistant Professor of Music Business
    B.A., B.S., Florida State University
    M.M., University of Miami
    J.D., University of Memphis
Taylor, David L. (2013) ....Dean of Spiritual Formation
    B.A., King College
    M.Div., Columbia Theological Seminary/University of Glasgow, Scotland
    M.Th., Princeton Theological Seminary
    D.Min., Talbot School of Theology
Teo, Jeff Y. (2004) ....Professor of Cybersecurity
    B.S., M.S., Western New England College
    Ed.S., Ph.D., Nova Southeastern University
    CISSP, CEH, Security+, Network+ and A+
Toland, Lisa (2016).................... Associate Professor of History, Director of Honors Program
    B.A., Indiana Wesleyan University
    M.A., Miami University of Ohio
    M.St., D.Phil., University of Oxford, Jesus College
Webb, George R. Jr. (2015) ....Instructor of Mathematics
    B.A., University of North Carolina, Asheville
    M.A., Western Carolina University
Wells, Mark A. (2006) ....Professor of Ethics/Philosophy
    B.A., Friends University
    M.A., Fuller Theological Seminary
    Ph.D., Baylor University
White-Hinman, Callan (2007) ....Professor of Theatre Arts
    B.A., DeSales University
    M.F.A., California State University, Long Beach
Wilds, Timothy (2009) ....Assistant Professor of Music
    B.M., Covent College
    M.M., Westminster Choir College
Wilson, Melissa (2015)................................Instructor of Environmental & Natural Science
        B.A., M.S., Montreat College

2016-2017 Part-Time Pro Rata Faculty

Hernandez, Horacio A. (2004)..Associate Professor of Spanish
    B.A., Universito Autonoma de Santo Domingo
    M.A., Ph.D., University of New York at Albany

Southerland, James D. (1987) ....Artist in Residence, Professor Emeritus of Art,
    Faculty Fellow
    B.F.A., East Carolina University
    M.F.A., Pennsylvania State University

Stackhouse, Eunice W. (1996) ....Professor of Music
    B.M.E., Grace College
    M.M., Indiana University School of Music
    D.M.A., University of Kansas

2016-2017 Adjunct Faculty

School of Adult and Graduate Studies

Adams, Nolan (Scott)   Business,
    Computer
  B.A., Montreat College
  M.B.A., Baker College
  Ph.D., Capella University
Ave'Lallemant, Timothy   Mathematics
  B.A., University of Wisconsin
  M.S., Institute of Paper Chemistry
  M.S., University of Akron
Avery, Courtnay   Business
  B.A., North Carolina Wesleyan
  MBA, DeVry University
  M.S., DeVry University
Bailey, Connie   Business
  B.S., Pfeiffer University
  M.S., Pfeiffer University
Bannister, John   Business
  B.S., Strayer University
  M.B.A., University of Phoenix
Barron, Sue   English
  B.A., Mars Hill College
  M.A., Western Carolina University
Bayode, Bola   Business
  B.S., Ogun State University
  M.B.A., Strayer University
  Ph.D., Walden University
Blue, Lucinda   Business
  B.A., Johnson C. Smith University
  MBA, Winthrop University
  Ph.D., The Union Institute
Boer, Robert   Music
  B.C.S., Redeemer College
  M.M., Drake University
  D.M.A., University of Iowa
Boyce, Jeff   Business
  B.S., Michigan Technological
    University
  M.B.A., Ashland University
  Ph.D., Capella University
Brandon, Paul Business
  B.S., California Institute of
    Technology
  M.A., Harvard University
  Ph.D., Harvard University

Busby, Walter (Buzz)   Business Law
  B.S., Louisiana State University
  J.D. Law, Louisiana State University
Canfora, Jennifer   Counseling
  B.S., UNC-Greensboro
  M.A., Webster University
  Ph.D., Capella University
Carlin, Eve   Business Law
  B.A., St. Clairs College
  M.A., Marist College
  J.D. Law, Hofstra University
Cellamare, Alan   Business
  B.A., University of South Florida
  M.B.A., Seattle University
  M.Div., Gordon Conwell
  D.Min., Gordon Conwell
Chabra, Nicolas   Business
  B.A., Farleigh Dickinson University
  J.D., George Mason University
Chuprevich, Robert   Bible, Business
  B.S., Bryant College
  M.S., Western Carolina University
  D.Min., Erskine Theological Seminary
Clark, Matthew   Mathematics
  B.A., Clemson University
  M.S., Columbia University
  Ph.D., North Carolina State
    University
Corbitt, Chris   Science
  B.A., North Carolina State University
  M.S., East Carolina University
Corbitt, Lisa   Science
  B.S., North Carolina State University
  M.S., East Carolina University
Davis, Gary   Business
  B.S., University of North Carolina
  M.A., Western Carolina University
  M.S., Western Carolina University
  Ph.D., North Carolina State
    University
Dollar, Julie   Counseling
  B.S., Lenoir Rhyne University
  M.A., Lenoir Rhyne University

Edwards, Miriam   Spanish
 B.A., Clemson University
 M.A., Winthrop University
Farr, Larry   Music
 B.A., Illinois Wesleyan University
 M.Ed., University of Illinois
Felts, Bennie   Business
 B.A., North Carolina Central
  University
 M.A., Elon College
 Ph.D., Capella University
Fitzpatrick, Troy   Business
 B.S., Troy University
 M.S., Montreat College
Ford, Allison   Counseling
 B.A., Mary Washington College
 M.E., University of Virginia
 Ph.D., University of Virginia
Fox, Joseph   Business
 B.S., Pfeiffer University
 M.B.A., Western Carolina University
 Ed.D., Western Carolina University
Frazier, Bradford   Business
 B.A., Pfeiffer University
 M.B.A., Pfeiffer University
 Ph.D., Lynn University
Gentry, Elizabeth   Accounting
 B.S., Montreat College
 M.A. Gardner Webb University
Gibbs, Mark   Bible and Religion
 B.A., Montreat College
 M.A., Gordon –Conwell University
 Ph.D., University of Wales
Gordon, Michelle   Counseling
 B.S., Appalachian State University
 M.A., Appalachian State University
 Ph.D., Regent University
Gorman, Clint   Business
 B.B.A., Montreat College
 M.B.A., Montreat College
Gorman, Kevin   Business
 B.S., University of Massachusetts
 M.B.A., California State University
 Ph.D., Texas A & M University
Graham, David   Counseling
 B.A., Le Moyne College
 M.S., Syracuse University
 Ph.D., University of North Carolina,
  Charlotte

Gray, Wilma   Social Work
 B.A., Malone College
 M.S.W., University of North Carolina,
  Chapel Hill
 M.A., Western Carolina University
Greenlee, Laura   Psychology
 M.S., Walden University
 M.S., McDaniel College
 Ph.D., Walden University
Griffin, Robert   Business
 B.B.A., Montreat College
 M.B.A., Montreat College
Hall, Robert   History
 B.A., Greenville College
 M.Ed., Florida-Atlantic University
 M.A., University of North Carolina
Harris, Franklin   Communications
 B.A., Eastern Kentucky University
 M.A., Montclair State University
 Ed.D., Rutgers University
Harshaw, Kimberly   Psychology
 B.S., University of North Carolina,
  Greensboro
 M.S., Walden University
Hendrickson, Patricia   Business
 B.B.A., Montreat College
 M.Ed., Francis Marion University
 Ed.D., Fielding Graduate School
Hogsed, Daryle   History
 B.A., Gardner-Webb University
 M.A., Western Carolina University
Hopkins, T. Hampton   Business
 B.S., Winthrop University
 M.S., University of Tennessee,
  Knoxville
 Ed.D., University of North Carolina,
  Charlotte
Howard, Jack   Business, Math, Science
 B.S., Kings College
 M.A., Queens College
Huddleston-Edwards, Sandra   English
 B.A., University of North Carolina,
  Charlotte
 M.A., University of North Carolina,
  Charlotte
Ingrassia, David   Bible and Religion
 B.A., Tufts University
 Th.M., Dallas Theological Seminary
 D.Min., Dallas Theological Seminary

Irwin, Kathleen   Business
B.S., University of North Carolina,
Wilmington
MBA, University of North Carolina,
Charlotte
Ph.D., Capella University
Jordan, Randall   Bible and Religion
B.S., University of South Carolina
M.Div., Southern Baptist Theological
Seminary
D.Min., Southern Baptist Theological
Seminary
Kamer, Shane   Science
B.S., Logan University
M.S., Logan University
D.C., Logan College of Chiropractic
Kehres, Patrick   Business
B.S., University of Phoenix
M.B.A., University of Phoenix
D.M., University of Phoenix
Loelius, William   Business
B.B.A., Montreat College
M.B.A., Montreat College
Lutz, Janet (2013)   Counseling
B.A., Hood College
M.S., Wake Forest University
Ph.D., University of Florida
Mashburn, Michael   Math
B.A., UNC Asheville
M.A., Western Carolina University
Mazzatenta, Ernie   Communication
B.A., Kent State University
M.S., Northwestern University
McLaughlin, Shirley   Business
B.A., University of North Carolina,
Greensboro
M.S., Rollins College
Ph.D., Nova Southeastern University
McMiller, Beniah   Business
B.S., Johnson C. Smith University
M.S., Colorado Technical University
M.S., University of Phoenix
McMiller, Tai   Psychology
B.A., University of South Carolina
M.A., Webster University
Mead, Danielle   Counseling
B.S., Georgia State University
M.A., Webster University

Morgan, Adam   English
B.A., Furman University
M.A., Roosevelt University
Mosely, Jackie   Business
B.S., Winthrop University
M.B.A., Winthrop University
Murray, Peter   Business
B.A., University of Notre Dame
M.B.A., University of Pennsylvania,
Wharton School
Mullins, Melissa   Counseling
B.A., Allen University
M.A., Webster University
Ph.D., Argosy University
Njoku, Matthew   Business
B.S., State University of New York,
Binghamton
M.B.A., State University of New York,
Binghamton
Paul, Eileen   Business
B.A., College of Mt. Saint Vincent
M.B.A., University of Wisconsin,
Milwaukee
Peters, Cindy   Psychology
B.A., Miami University
M.A., Kent State University
Ph.D., Southern Illinois University
Peters, Debra   Psychology
B.S., East Tennessee State University
M.A., East Tennessee State
University
Ph.D., University of Southern
Mississippi
Pouler, Chris   Science
B.S., University of Maryland
M.A., Catholic University
Ph.D., University of Maryland
Priddy, Carroll Sue   Business
B.A., Mars Hill College
M.S., Western Carolina University
Rajagopal, Sanjay   Business
B.A., University of Delhi
MBA, Western Carolina University
M.A., Jawaharlal Nehru University
Ph.D., Mississippi State University
Sams, Jeanette   Business
B.A., Montreat College
M.A., Western Carolina University

Sanders, Laurie   Business
   B.A., California State University
   M.B.A., City University of London
Sheets, Don   Psychology & Science
   B.S., North Carolina State University
   M.S., Central Michigan University
   Ph.D., LaSalle University
Sherrill, Debra   Business
   B.S., University of North Carolina
   M.B.A., Wingate University
   Ph.D., Capella University
Simmons, I-Eesha   Human Resources
   B.A., UNC-Charlotte
   M.S., Pfeiffer University
   J.D., Massachusetts School of Law
Soirez, Rhonda   Counseling
   B.S., Liberty University
   M.A., Liberty University
Spicuzza, Robert   Science, Math
   B.S., Worcester Polytechnic Institute
   M.S., University of Connecticut
   Ph.D., University of Connecticut
Streppa, Michael   Psychology
   B.A., Dickinson College
   M.A., Georgia School of Professional
      Psychology
   Ph.D., Georgia School of Professional
      Psychology
Summers, LaTonya   Counseling
   B.S., Appalachian State University
   M.A., Appalachian State University
Szelwach, Celia   Business
   B.S., United States Military Academy
   M.B.A., Argosy University
   Ph.D., Argosy University

Taylor, Diana   Psychology

   B.A., University of North Carolina,
      Greensboro
   M.S., Winthrop University
   Ph.D., Regent University
Tonini, Edward   Bible and Religion
   B.A., University of Western Ontario
   M.Div., University of Western
      Ontario
Vining, Chip   Psychology
   B.S., University of Florida
   M.A., Reformed Theological
      Seminary
Wallace, Tom   Business
   B.S., Gardner-Webb University
   M.B.A., Montreat College
Walton, Steven   Music
   B.A., University of Houston
   M.M., The Julliard School
Webb, Kirk   Counseling
   B.A., Wake Forest University
   M.A., Colorado Christian University
   M.A., Princeton Theological
      Seminary
   Ph.D., Seattle Pacific University
Wencel, Mark   Business
   B.S., University of Pittsburgh
   M.A., University of Pittsburgh
Whetstone, Kimarie
      Computer Science
   B.S., University of North Carolina,
      Charlotte
   M.Ed., University of North Carolina,
      Charlotte
Whisnant, Jason   Counseling
   B.S., Gardner Webb University
   Ed.S., Gardner Webb University

Administrative and Professional Staff

School of Arts and Sciences

Chris Anderson	Athletic Trainer
Meghan Austin	Head Women's Basketball Coach
Brenton Benware	Head Men's Soccer Coach
Elena Binder	Financial Aid Counselor
Keri Boer	Director of Records & Registration
Michael Bruce	Assistant Men's Soccer Coach
Kristine Buckwalter	Director of Advancement Services
Adam Caress	Assistant Director of Communications
Annie Carlson	Executive Director of Advancement
Martha Chastain	Assistant Director of Auxiliary Services
Jessica Clements	Assistant to the VP for Academic Affairs & Dean of the College
Andrew Cobb	Director of Tennis
Sara Cole	Director of Student Accounts
Hope Deifell	Executive Assistant to the President
Debbie Ferguson	Director of Development
Katharyn Ferguson	Assistant Women's Lacrosse Coach
Adora Fitzpatrick	Help Desk Administrator
Grace Green	Special Events Coordinator
Patti Guffey	Controller
Paul Hawkinson	Director of Technology
Raymond Henderson	Assistant Men's Basketball Coach
Bethany Holder	Admissions Event Coordinator
Eric Hollandsworth	Creative Director
Jeremy Hurse	Associate Director of Financial Aid
Tyler Johnson	Assistant Women's Basketball
Garrett Jones	Head Men's Basketball Coach
Tom Jones	Admissions Counselor
Kristina Kamer	Head Volleyball Coach
Mickie Kelly	Payroll and Benefits Manager
Nathan King	Information Technology Service Librarian
Jessica Langston	Sr. Asst. Dir. of Records & Registration for SAS and Advising
José Larios	Athletic Director
Tim Lewis	Assistant Men's Basketball Coach
Jason Lewkowicz	Director of Track & Field/Cross Country
Heather Maston	Head Softball Coach
MacKenzie May	Financial Aid Counselor
Andrew McAllister	Assistant Volleyball Coach
Heidi McInturf	Admissions Data Coordinator
Will McMinn	Director of Lacrosse, Head Men's Lacrosse Coach
Grace Miller	Campus Nurse
Daniel Mount	Web Communications Specialist
Courtney Nash	Head Women's Soccer Coach
Sandra Owen	Administrative Assistant to the VP of Student Services

Mandi Pike	Associate Director of Admissions
Beth Pocock	Director of Financial Aid
Teresa Price	Director of Auxiliary Services
Jo Reynolds	Accounting & Administrative Assistant
Kirsten Richardson	Admissions Counselor
John Rogers	Director of the Team and Leadership Center
Gloria Sainio	Enrollment Management Office Assistant
Rebecca Shaw	Library Services Manager
Christian Smith	Admissions Counselor
Denise Smith	Special Assistant to the President
Ryan Smith	Assistant Baseball Coach
John Sullivan	Golf Coach
David Taylor	Chaplain
Lyndsey Wall	Assistant Dean for Residence Life & Anderson RD
Robert Walker	Director of Retail & Auxiliary Revenue
Dave Walters	Director of Alumni, Parent, and Church Relations
Ryan Watkins	Director of Service and Davis RD
Audrey Weaver	Accounts Payable Specialist
Joshua Wilcox	Systems Administrator
Jane Woods	Assistant to the VP of Advancement
Holleigh Woodward	Director of Counseling Services
Joshua Yeatman	Information Systems Support Specialist

School of Adult and Graduate Studies

Elena Binder	Financial Aid Counselor
Keri Boer	Director of Records & Registration
Michael Davis	Director of Admission
Susan DeWoody	Vice President and Dean of Adult and Graduate Studies
Elizabeth Hofheins	Records Specialist
Cindy Kirkland	Director of Academic Advising and Student Services
Dr. Eboni Mathis	Director of Online Education
Margót Payne	Associate Director of Records & Registration
Julia Pacilli	Director of Campus and Faculty Services
Jim Paden	Director of AGS Marketing
Beth Pocock	Director of Financial Aid

Asheville Campus

Jesse Boeckermann	Admissions Representative
John Carvajal	Academic Advisor for Online
Jennifer Gardner	Administrative Coordinator for AGS
Marcella Gibson	Campus Services Coordinator
Jonathan McDonald	Academic Advisor
Dr. Isaac Owolabi	Full time Faculty/Business and Marketing
Lyndsey Parham	Admissions Representative

Charlotte Campus

Latwoia Abbott	Academic Advisor
Mary Banks	Admissions Specialist
Nicole Chavis	Campus Services Coordinator
Monica Konarski-Fusetti	Full time Faculty/English
Lotes Nelson	Fulltime Faculty/CMHC
John-Nelson Pope	CMHC Program Director
Laura Ormond	Special Assistant to the President - Charlotte
Rafael Velasquez	Admissions Representative - Charlotte

Extended Campuses

Dr. Penny Hamblin	Full time Faculty/Counseling - Morganton
Ethel Kelly	Campus Advisor – NCWC
Jennifer Strickland	Academic Advisor - Morganton

Index